THE MAKING OF THE UNIV

The Making
OF THE
University of Plymouth

ALSTON KENNERLEY

PLYMOUTH, UNITED KINGDOM

First published 2000

Designed by Media Production Services, Information and Learning Services
Published in the United Kingdom by University of Plymouth
Drake Circus,
Plymouth,
Devon,
PL4 8AA

British Library Cataloguing in Publication Data

A Cataloque record for this book is available from the British Library.

ISBN 1-84102-069-9

Printed by Latimer Trend & Company Ltd, Plymouth
Cover Board 360gsm Novatech Gloss
Text Paper 130gsm Novatech Silk Supplied by Antalis

FOR HELEN,
AND IN MEMORY OF MY FATHER, THOMAS EDWARD KENNERLEY

Contents

Colour illustrations of the University of Plymouth's four campuses are located between pages 270 and 271.

List of Tables

List of Charts

Foreword

Like many organisations, the University of Plymouth decided that the University might best mark its arrival at the new millennium by recalling some of the key events and some of the people who have played a part in our history. Thus some three years of research, of inquiry, of conversations have now been encapsulated in *The Making of the University of Plymouth.*

For a Vice-Chancellor so heavily engaged in future strategies and in today's successes and concerns, this scholarly work by Alston Kennerley, now just retired from the academic staff of the University – is a fascinating and timely reminder of the people, forces and circumstances which have helped shape our destiny over almost 200 years. Alston brings his own perspectives and judgement to the events of history, and his selection of material (from an abundance of archives), his emphasis, his interpretation and analysis all from the standpoint of an historian and an 'ordinary' member of staff provides a valuable and discerning 'bottom up' view of the evolution of the University of Plymouth.

The Making of the University of Plymouth reminds us of a heritage of which we can be proud, blends fact and anecdote with dry humour, providing informative and reflective reading.

Whether you read it from cover to cover or just pick out the parts of which you have personal knowledge or interest, I am sure you will find this brief history fascinating reading.

Professor John Bull
Vice-Chancellor

Acknowledgements

The origins of this study lie in the early 1970s when I found myself teaching the history and organisation of education to the University of London Certificate in Education course. The students, all volunteers attending on a day-release basis, were full-time lecturers from a wide range of disciplines in further and higher education colleges in the region, and nurse tutors from the local schools of nursing. It was one of the earliest examples of regional provision to be offered by Plymouth Polytechnic. With a brief to emphasise post-school education we soon realised that there was no history of local development, and using part of the summer block release period for a class project, we set about filling the gap. The results were published in a booklet by Plymouth Polytechnic in 1976.

A quarter of a century later, after a period so full of educational change, there was a need for a more substantial study, and early in 1997, with the support of my department, I put forward to the Vice-Chancellor, Professor Bull, an outline proposal. Having pondered it for over six months, he called for a properly constructed research proposal, and work started that autumn. A guiding principle from the outset was that the study should be based as far as possible on primary sources and that it should be set properly in the context of education nationally. As sponsor and supervisor of the project Professor Bull has kept in very close but unobtrusive contact with its development. His guidance and advice on the overall design, and particularly on the sections dealing with latter part of the twentieth century, together with his steady support, has been of great assistance and is much appreciated.

Archive collections, record offices and libraries are the laboratories of the historical researcher. Such is the depth of material (accessible to within 30 years of the present) relating to Plymouth, Exeter and Devon, in the national archive, the Public Record Office at Kew, London, that it is almost possible to write the more distant history using that source alone. The PRO's efficient organisation and helpful staff are much appreciated. In Devon much time has been spent delving in the Plymouth and West Devon Record Office, Plymouth Central Library (Local History), Devon Record Office and the West Country Studies Library in Exeter, and the Newton Abbot Public Library. The value of staff who know their collections cannot be underestimated, and I owe a particular debt to Anne Moreton (Plymouth and West Devon Record Office), Fiona Pitt (Plymouth City Museum), Joyce Brown and Ian Criddle (Plymouth Local Studies Library).

Much of the local searching has been undertaken by my part-time, temporary research assistants, successively Jean Hicks and Anna Want, who quickly learned to understand the kinds of information which I needed and where it might be found. They have been a great help. Much of the archival work at Exeter has been undertaken by Helen James, the author of Chapter Five, Exeter School of Art. Her efforts have relieved me of the need to become deeply embroiled in the history of art education, and her contribution is much appreciated.

The list of people who have been of assistance with different sections of this history is extensive. Other commitments (this has not been a full time activity) have prevented undertaking many interviews, but help has been received from numerous past and present members of the establishment (and its predecessors), with information and suggestions, and the reading of early drafts of chapters. In one way or another I am indebted to: Peter Anderson, C.A. Ansell, R.G. Barker, Colin Beardon, Angela Blackman, Rod Blackshaw, John Butler, Jan Chapman, Arthur Clamp, Clare Broom, Paul Brasseley, John Danvers, Francis Cammaerts, Tone Clayden, Eric Cleave, Bob Cope, Barbara Currie, Len Fifield, Derek Fuller, Ken George, Val Harrison, Robert Hole, Penny Holland, Warren Hopwood, David Jeremiah, Mrs Johnson, Rod Lane, Adrian Lee, Alan Lester, Philip Liddicoat, Alan MacFarlane, John Mathews, Stephanie Minhinnick, Brian Mitchell, David Moreby, Monica Mukherji, Donna Nelson, Mike Newby, Audrey Parsons, Gill Payne, Marion Perraton, Doris Potter, Denis Rabley, Alan Richards, Peggy Richter, Chris Robinson, Helen Rowett, Sam Smiles, Stan Starks, Mike Stephenson, Liz Turner, Paul Willerton, Paul Wright

For external evaluations of the text, I have turned to two well-respected historians of education. Bill Stephens, sometime Reader in the History of Education at the University of Leeds, kindly agreed to read and comment on each chapter as it was completed and I have benefited particularly from his advice on the sections dealing with the nineteenth and early twentieth centuries. Harold Silver, currently Visiting Professor of Education in the Faculty of Arts and Education of the University of Plymouth, agreed to look at the completed first draft. His encouragement and suggestions for improvements in many parts of the text are much appreciated. I am also indebted to Evan Davies for his support and interest over the past three years and for textual advice.

One of the early decisions was that the book would be published under the University of Plymouth imprint and that it should be fully illustrated in order to widen its appeal. The University's own Media Production Services would handle production. For my part I failed to appreciate the labour and time involved particularly when dealing with much more than just text. The quality of the end product is here for all to see, but I owe much to the expertise and friendly forbearance of Francis Reis' team in Media Production Services, including John Trewhella, David Griffiths and particularly Gary Batten.

Of the large number of illustrations which have been included, many have come from the collections accumulated by the University and its predecessor establishments. Many are undated, unlabeled and unattributed. Thus it has not been possible to identify the originators of all illustrations, but wherever possible acknowledgements have been included with the captions. Permission to use illustrations has been readily given by Barrie Williams, editor of the *Western Morning News* and Rachael Campey, editor of the *Evening Herald*, the *Express & Echo,* the *Sunday Independent,* Nicola Moyle, Curator of City of Plymouth Museums, Alasdair MacNaughton, Plymouth City Librarian, Paul Brough, Archivist, Plymouth and West Devon Record Office, Ian Maxted, Local Studies Librarian, West Country Studies Library, Nick Price and the Sutton Harbour Company, John Smith and Plymouth Proprietary Library, and Plymouth and Exeter city councils.

It is almost inevitable that, given the scope of this study, a few errors of fact or interpretation will have crept in, for which I must accept responsibility. Needless to say the opinions expressed here are my own, and not necessarily those of the University of Plymouth. One final acknowledgement remains, for the debt of gratitude I owe to my wife, Helen, for comment on the text and for her forbearance at the many hours spent in my study.

Alston Kennerley,
University of Plymouth,
December, 2000.

List of Abbreviations

ACSET	Advisory Council on the Training & Supply of Teachers
AFE	Advanced Further Education
APT	Association of Polytechnic Teachers
ARPA	Automatic Radar Plotting Aid
ASA	Academic Staff Association [Polytechnic]
ASTMS	Association of Technical & Managerial Staff
ATD	Art Teacher's Diploma
ATI	Association of Technical Institutions
ATTI	Association of Teachers in Technical Institutions
BA	Bachelor of Arts [degree]
BAAS	British Association for the Advancement of Science
B.Ed	Bachelor of Education [degree]
B.Eng	Bachelor of Engineering [degree]
BPSA	British Polytechnics Sports Association
BSc	Bachelor of Science [degree]
BTEC	Business & Technician Education Council
BUSA	British Universities Sports Association
CAO	Chief Administrative Officer [Polytechnic]
OND	Ordinary National Diploma
CAPS	Certificate in Advance Professional Studies [education]
CCA	College Certificate in Agriculture [Seale-Hayne]
CCH	College Certificate in Horticulture [Seale-Hayne]
CDA	College Diploma in Agriculture [Seale-Hayne]
CFE	College of Further Education
CGLI	City & Guilds of London Institute
CMJ	College of St. Mark & St John
CNAA	Council for National Academic Awards
DCC	Devon County Council
DES	Department of Education & Science
DipAD	Diploma in Art & Design
DipHE	Diploma in Higher Education
DMS	Diploma in Management Studies
DSA	Department of Science & Art
EDEXEL	Educational Excellence
EHE	Enterprise in Education
FE	Further Education
FT	Full-Time
FTE	Full-Time Equivalent [student numbers]
GTB	General Teaching Block [Polytechnic]
HE	Higher Education
HEFCE	Higher Education Funding Council for England
HEFCS	Higher Education Funding Council for Scotland
HEFCW	Higher Education Funding Council for Wales
HEQC	Higher Education Quality Council
HESC	Higher Education Sub-Committee [of LEA]
HMI	His/Her Majesty's Inspector [of schools]
HMS	His/Her Majesty's Ship
HNC	Higher National Certificate
HND	Higher National Diploma
LEA	Local Education Authority
LRC	Learning Resources Centre [Polytechnic]
MAF	Ministry of Agriculture & Fisheries
MAFF	Ministry of Agriculture, Fisheries & Food
MAR	Mid-Apprenticeship Release [course]

MASN	Maximum Aggregated Student Numbers
MBA	Marine Biological Association
MBA	Master of Business Administration [degree]
M.Eng	Master of Engineering [degree]
MPhil	Master of Philosophy [degree]
MSc	Master of Science [degree]
NAAFI	Navy, Army and Air Forces Institute
NAB	National Advisory Body
NACTST	National Advisory Council for the Training & Supply of Teachers
NALGO	National Association of Local Government Officers
NCDAD	National Council for Diplomas in Art and Design
NDA	National Diploma in Agriculture
NDD	National Diploma in Design
NDD	National Diploma in Dairying
NIAD	National Institute of Agricultural Botany
OFSTED	Office for Standards in Education
ONC	Ordinary National Certificate
PBS	Plymouth Business School
PCFC	Polytechnics & Colleges Funding Council
PCoT	Plymouth College of Technology
PDTC	Plymouth & Devonport Technical College
PEP	Polytechnic Enterprises Plymouth
PERC	Plymouth Environmental Research Centre
Pg.Dip.Ed	Post-Graduate Diploma in Education
PGCE	Post-Graduate Certificate in Education
PhD	Doctor of Philospohy [degree]
PICKUP	Professional, Industrial & Commercial Updating
PSW	Polytechnic South West
PT	Part-time
PYNDA	Plymouth Nautical Degree Association
QAA	Quality Assurance Agency
QEEU	Quality Evaluation & Enhancement Unit [University]
RACFE	Regional Advisory Council for Further Education
RAE	Research Assessment Exercise
RIBA	Royal Institution of British Architects
RNEC	Royal Naval Engineering College
RN	Royal Navy
RSA	Royal Society of Arts
SCL	Student Centred Learning
SCOTVEC	Scottish Vocational Education Council
SEDA	Staff Education & Development Association
SEED	Science Education Enhancement & Development
SES	Seafarers' Education Service
SME	Small & Medium Sized Enterprises
SSR	Staff/Student Ratio
SU	Students' Union
TEC	Training & Enterprise Council
TTA	Teacher Training Agency
UCSWE	University College of the South West of England
UFC	Universities Funding Council
UGC	University Grants Committee
WEA	Workers' Education Association

Education in the National Context [1]

CHAPTER ONE

University Education [2]

In 1992, the polytechnic at Plymouth was one of thirty establishments of higher education elevated by the government to university status in what was the largest single round of university designations in British education history. Overnight the number of British universities was increased to over one hundred. Like many another university, Plymouth had served an apprenticeship which had seen its status as an establishment raised from municipal technical college, to regional college of technology, to polytechnic and finally university, yet throughout this progress it had been involved in degree level work alongside its broad spectrum of other post-school educational activity.

The majority of British universities which came into being in the nineteenth and twentieth centuries have roots in predecessor establishments often serving the educational needs of local society and industry. Many had to fight hard to achieve recognition as universities, and some continued an involvement in what would today be seen as further education rather longer than might be expected. The University of Southampton, for example, still had oversight of sub-degree post-school education at the end of the 1960s.[3] Direct university foundations, that is universities without previous histories as other kinds of college, have been comparatively rare, though a number were founded as university colleges aspiring to full university status. Early direct foundations in the modern period were Durham (1836) and London (1836 as a degree awarding body), and more recently some of those of the 1960s, such as York and Warwick. The University of London turned out to be very important for innumerable colleges in Britain and overseas from the middle of the nineteenth century until the establishment of the Council for National Academic Awards (CNAA) in 1964.[4] As an examining and degree-awarding establishment London's awards were opened to all-comers (subject to academic recognition of staff) in 1858, thus enabling university colleges, university extension colleges, and later technical colleges to offer local courses leading to University of London degrees (London external awards). In Wales the solution was a federal university of Welsh university colleges from 1893. The federal Victoria University in the north of England did not last beyond the series of university creations in the early years of the twentieth century (Birmingham, 1900, Manchester 1903, Liverpool 1903, Leeds 1904, Sheffield 1905, Bristol 1908). University colleges elsewhere had to wait for their charters until after World War II. In 1965 ten colleges of advanced technology with roots in technical education were also advanced to university status, completing that round of university designations. With the creation of the CNAA at that time, to which most of the remaining colleges teaching for London externals transferred for degree awards, the University of London had largely been freed of its external examining role. It was under CNAA oversight that the 30 polytechnics, upgraded from their previous status (mostly colleges of technology) received their tutelage in preparation for 1992 when they achieved university designation.

Diversity in the origins and evolution of British universities also extends to their funding and management. Endowment has been the traditional way in which universities have been financed; it continues to play a part today. But where this was inadequate support might come from, for example, local civic authorities, though student fees paid by parents (or through scholarships), were an essential element. Indeed having a university college, and preferably a chartered university, was a matter of both of civic pride and regional accessibility. In the second half of the nineteenth century it became possible to apply for limited support from the state, but it was not until the establishment of the University Grants Committee in 1919 that a regular system of state finance for universities came into being. Despite the significant levels which state funding reached, they were able to retain their independence to manage their own affairs, whereas the polytechnics (created in 1970), despite in time collectively making more degree awards than the universities, remained under tight government/local authority control until freed from the latter in 1988.

1.1 The Albert Memorial Museum building in Exeter opened in 1868 was one of the earlier multi-use public adult education facilities to be erected in British towns and cities, housing a museum, library, art school and science school. It was the home in succession of Exeter's university extension and technical college (1891) and the University College of the South West of England (1922), which would emerge as the University of Exeter in 1955. Exeter School of Art (1854) now absorbed into the University of Plymouth, occupied the Albert Memorial building for over one hundred years.

[Photo: A. Kennerley]

The debate about the nature and purpose of universities has been continuous over the past two centuries. As already noted, a common differentiation from non-university establishments is supposed to be level of work, with students admitted on the basis of the standard of achievement at the end of their secondary education. Yet universities have often had to teach at lower levels either because the students they were attracting had not reached the entry standard or because the subject lacked a foundation in schools. Although universities might ostensibly have been concerned with 'universal knowledge', the subject scope at particular establishments has never been intended to be all-embracing. But universities are concerned with the intellectual and theoretical bases of subject matter. Areas of knowledge for which such bases had not been developed could often be applied in the world at large but still lie outside the scope of university teaching. Closely associated with industry and employment, their skill and training dimensions were usually prominent. It was well into the nineteenth century, for example, that some of the technologies and business subjects became established a university subjects. Even the oldest of university subjects such as theology, the law and medicine, have both their intellectual and theoretical bases and their training dimensions, though the latter is considered as separate from university study. It has by no means been unusual for subjects to be researched and taught to advanced standards outside the universities. In the latter part of the twentieth century the growing influence of the polytechnics brought an emphasis on the links between higher education study and future employment. Even so, new multi-disciplinary approaches having a close relationship to industry have not always found acceptance.

What does mark out universities today from other educational establishments is the advanced qualifications of their academic staff and their involvement in research. Research has been a growing dimension since the latter part of the nineteenth century. Again research is by no means exclusively a university activity, and there are considerable variations

1.2 Borough support of one or two schools may be identified long before local authorities began the more organised development of forms of secondary education towards the end of the nineteenth century such as this school in Plymouth built in the 1890s. Though many more such schools were built in the early years of the twentieth century it was mid-century before secondary education became available for everyone.

[Photo: A. Kennerley]

between one university and another. The newest universities, including Plymouth, began developing their research portfolios from the time they were designated polytechnics, and much progress has been made, but their core business, as it is with all universities, is the delivery of undergraduate courses of study.

Amongst the patterns of higher education development of recent decades has been the merger of small educational establishments working in a narrow field, with larger adjacent colleges. With state promoted expansion, this has led to many new universities being very much larger in student numbers than some longer established universities, as is the case with the University of Plymouth and its nearest neighbour, the University of Exeter. The history of the evolution of the University of Plymouth, complex enough in the 'Three Towns' (Plymouth, Stonehouse and Devonport) which comprise the modern city, is also about the histories of institutions at Exmouth, Exeter and Newton Abbot. The Plymouth and Exeter campuses have clear links with post-school educational developments in the 1850s, and accepting that it was possible to engage in more advanced post-school learning even earlier, this study will include an overview of educational activity in Plymouth early in the nineteenth century.

The development of higher education in a particular location is not just to do with approaches, attitudes, personalities, courses and facilities: it is interactive with national policy making and coloured by local interpretation. With Whitehall holding the purse strings for much of the period over which this study ranges, and vetting each new local initiative, changes in national policy inevitably provide an important context to local evolution. As developments at Plymouth cannot be appreciated without some understanding of the national context, the remainder of this introductory chapter is devoted to an overview of British post-school education in the past two centuries.

The massive expansion of higher education in the later twentieth century would not have been possible without the national system of secondary education finally put in place under the 1944 Education Act. Likewise, the establishment of a compulsory secondary education system (as it is currently understood), depended on the existence of a national system of primary education which, under the elementary system, only achieved national coverage at the very end of the nineteenth century. Of course there was a widespread availability of schooling at what might be considered secondary levels in the nineteenth century but it was not provided by the state. Mostly fee-paying, this was largely outside the reach of a majority of the population. The lack of a proper secondary education stratum was amongst the factors inhibiting the development of technical education in the nineteenth century and the early part of the twentieth century. Self-help approaches, increasingly facilitated by 'pump-priming' initiatives by state and other central bodies, enabled motivated individuals in most areas of the country to engage in part-time techncial and scientific study related to their chosen careers, from the mid-nineteenth century onwards. This is the background of many of the polytechnics designated in 1970 and granted university status in 1992.

Education, Industry and the Economy[5]

Almost throughout the period from the 1850s to the 1950s, commentators have asserted that Britain was in danger of losing or had lost its economic competitive edge compared with other industrialised countries, and that this could be put down to Britain's repeated failure, despite the warnings, to support a proper national system of scientific and technical education. Repeatedly, examples, notably that of the Germans, of state tertiary educational approaches, were cited with the argument that having a technically trained manpower was an important factor in industrial success. The rapid rise of continental industrial economies from the second half of the nineteenth century and Britain's 'economic decline' were given as evidence. Was it surprising that Britain lagged, the argument continued, when the best that it could offer was a ramshackle system of voluntary part-time study to those who had left school? Britain's secondary education, especially the private and later the state-funded grammar schools, was steeped in the arts and the classics, as were its universities which had been reluctant to embrace higher technological and management education. Further, British industry showed little or no interest in technical education for its employees, and it was common for company managers to have no scientific or technical underpinning knowledge of the industrial processes which they controlled.

In recent years this interpretation of the situation has been challenged by economic historians. Both the economic arguments and those advocating the merits of compulsory systems of scientific and technical education have been shown to be over generalised or based on faulty interpretations of the relative position of the British industrial economy to the situation elsewhere. Further, the denigration of technical education provision in Britain has been a gross disservice to its merits and achievements.

Britain's early lead in industrialisation certainly made it the 'workshop of the world' with all the economic benefits that that offered. However, it was inevitable that other countries would be looking to catch up. The new always grows rapidly before the curve of development levels out. So the growing industrial economies of Germany, France and other countries inevitably loomed large when seen from Britain because they had started later from a low base. Unfortunately the commentators discerning weaknesses in British technical education saw Britain's reducing share in a growing world economy as an absolute decline, whereas modern opinion argues that there was no internal decline, and that British industry continued to be a success story, apart from isolated periods of downturn, well into the twentieth century. It more than maintained its level of activity, but in a much larger world economy. Hence, in the absence of economic decline, it can hardly be maintained that the nature of technical education on offer was at fault.

The debate on the extent, level and nature of technical education has often been clouded by the artificial distinction between education and training. At one extreme the academic world found any hint of application to industry abhorrent, and this carried through to the finance of technical education with the assertion that industry must finance its own training. At the other extreme, refusing to recognise the contribution of his own schooling, the self-made industrialist could see no need for any theoretical preparation. It has, of course, to be accepted that Britain's early world lead in industrialisation was achieved without any state support for any level of education. Privately, however, general education was widely available and there were many establishments operating at secondary levels which provided some scientific and commercial instruction. Then there is the long-standing tradition of in-service training, including apprenticeships, regardless of level, which was to be the mainstay of industrial training at least into the mid-twentieth century. Finally there is the question of to what levels of education and training particular individuals needed to be taken. Here, the negative arguments generally lacked clarity. The numbers of people industry required who might be educated to the highest levels of technological education were relatively small compared with the numbers for whom a less advanced understanding was sufficient. Large numbers of workers in industry probably required no more preparation than normal on-the-job training could provide. Clearly, as time progressed, literacy was increasingly important at all levels and development of the state elementary system provided for this. The varied approaches to adult and technical education catered for the needs of that wide spectrum of industrial craftsmen and managerial staff, while, so long as there was no taint of training and the emphasis was on knowledge of principles of pure science, university level establishments did come to offer the scientific and technological education to the fortunate few in a position to benefit from a university education. Even so, the numbers of scientifically or technically educated graduates working in industry in the first half of the twentieth century matched the levels on the continent. More recently, following the explosion of higher education, Britain's proportion of such graduates has been amongst the best in the world.

1.3 The development of adult education is often traced back to the Sunday school movement in the latter part of the eighteenth century. This sermon by John Bidlake in support of Sunday schools in the Plymouth area, preached in Stonehouse in October 1786, shows that the movement rapidly spread through provincial locations such as the Three Towns.

[Plymouth Central Library-Local Studies]

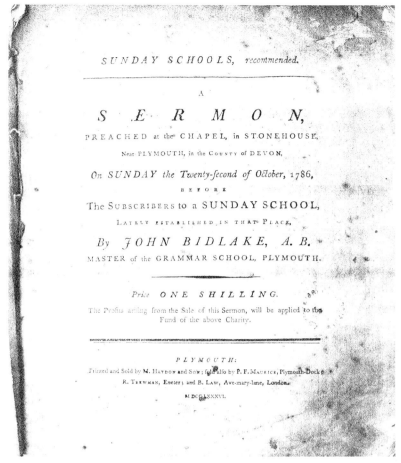

SUNDAY SCHOOLS, recommended.

A

S E R M O N,

PREACHED at the CHAPEL, in STONEHOUSE,

Near PLYMOUTH, in the County of DEVON,

On SUNDAY the Twenty-second of October, 1786,

BEFORE

The SUBSCRIBERS to a SUNDAY SCHOOL,

LATELY ESTABLISHED IN THAT PLACE,

By JOHN BIDLAKE, A.B.

MASTER of the GRAMMAR SCHOOL, PLYMOUTH.

Price ONE SHILLING.

The Profits arising from the Sale of this Sermon, will be applied to the Fund of the above Charity.

PLYMOUTH:

Printed and Sold by M. HAYDON and SON; sold also by P. F. MAURICE, Plymouth-Dock; R. TREWMAN, Exeter; and B. LAW, Ave-mary-lane, London.

M DCC LXXXVI.

The argument that British technical education lacked structure, was often poorly delivered on the cheap, and that it was undertaken part-time after a day's work, is countered by the argument that it was flexible and capable of rapid response to the ever changing needs of industry. Further, because it was voluntary and students had to pay their way, despite the disadvantages of after-hours study, there were high levels of commitment and motivation. Indeed the study undertaken could be seen as directly relevant to employment, and a valid step in climbing the employment ladder. Equally, those who did not wish to progress could step off the ladder. The mushrooming of the numbers studying and sitting the examinations of the Department of Science and Art (DSA), Royal Society of Arts (RSA), the City and Guilds of London Institute (CGLI) and other bodies, is ample evidence of the success of the multifaceted, even *ad hoc*, approach. The systems on the continent may have been in some cases in place at the end of the eighteenth century, but they were rigid, sometimes idiosyncratic, and could produce too many over or wrongly qualified people than industry currently needed. The achievement of the DSA, which may have been based on payment-by-results and the teaching often over-theoretical (only costing the country £200,000 in 1900), was viewed with envy by continental observers who could see the limitations of their own systems. There was no equivalent elsewhere. It demanded local initiatives and was relevant to local industrial needs, and there was certainly no waste of resources.

Well into the twentieth century, industry in Britain has been accused of not showing any interest in technical education. Given the tradition of in-house training and industry's survival from the beginning of industrialisation without the benefit of any compulsory system of technical education, though overstated, this is hardly surprising. But there was ample concern for a continued supply of appropriately trained manpower capable of the jobs at the levels which industry required. Certainly the larger industrial companies ran apprenticeship schemes, sometimes with their own teaching, though more often relying on evening classes locally for the educational dimension. Those criticising industry did not perhaps take sufficient account of the employer perspective, which looked for fitness-for-purpose and in providing training, though not necessarily stated, may well have been as much concerned with industrial socialisation as technical knowledge and skills.

Continuing the theme of attitude, the negative viewpoint of those brought up with a classical education, towards industry and trade, and by association any occupation which was thought, often incorrectly, to require people to get their hands dirty, has often been seen as a key factor inhibiting the provision of technical education. The loose generalisation embraced teachers in

1.4 The distribution of adult educational organisations in the south west peninsula in 1850
[UPPLY, Media Services]

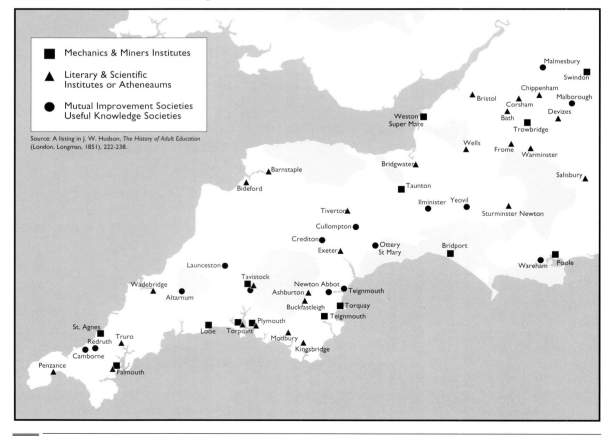

THE PLYMOUTH PROPRIETARY LIBRARY.
(From an old Engraving).

1.5 Most adult education organisations offered small libraries for members' use, but only the better off could afford membership or subscription libraries such as Plymouth Proprietary Library (1810).

[PCL-LS]

'public' and state grammar schools, the professions narrowly defined, the gentry and many of those in government. Though present, this is now thought to have been overstated. Despite their place in society, the proportion of society involved was comparatively small.

In summary, then, there was no lag in the British industrial economy compared with other countries, though it might have grown at a slower rate. The British flexible approach to post-school education was singularly successful and its achievements, including the ability to tease out latent talent, at least the equal of the different approaches on the continent, and right for its time. Developments at all levels of technical education in the second half of the twentieth century have supplied the technically more advanced industries with the technically educated manpower upon which to build their own training. It is now appropriate to look in general at what was provided in Britain.

Adult Education[6]

Adult education is a term used to encompass both formal instruction and other means by which people beyond normal school age improve their educational skills and knowledge. The alternative sources include the press, the pulpit, libraries, public lectures, the cinema, radio, television, the internet, and so on. Further, adult education includes catching up on missed schooling and indulging in educational activity as a hobby or relaxation. Thus it may range from learning to read and write to spare time research for a higher degree. Perhaps there has always been a measure of adult education taking place, but it was the development of a variety of movements from the late eighteenth century which made it more identifiable, and of course it is very much part of today's learning environment. At the level of basic literacy the participation of adults in the Sunday school movement was important. But as well as church based organisations, many of the later movements also made provision for adult literacy including, for example, the mechanics institutes, the co-operative education movement and trades unions, a tradition continued to the present in, for example, local authority evening institute provision.

But much of the demand for and interest in adult education has come from people who, having passed through their schooling, were looking for education with other personal educational agendas, including intellectual stimulation, simple entertainment and career advancement. From the late eighteenth century literary, philosophical and scientific societies were formed in most provincial towns and cities, exemplifying the long standing principle in adult education of self-help. The scientific dimension, of course, reflected the inadequacy of the scientific provision in the grammar schools and universities well into the nineteenth century, in a period when interest in scientific principles associated with advancing technology, was very strong. The Royal Cornwall Polytechnic Society (1833) was a significant example of this kind of organisation. The local example, the Plymouth Institution (1812) will be discussed in Chapter Two. Their parallels exist today. Plymouth is also noteworthy in having one of the oldest medical societies in the country. Not far removed are the learned institutions (chemistry, geology, civil engineers, electrical engineers, etc.), usually based in London, with their branch programmes of lectures and other activities. Active today, they often have close links with the local university.

In comparison with these middle class educational interests those who thought of themselves as working class had different adult educational agendas, often political, but also social, economic and vocational. The number of movements which came and went was extensive, but what they often had in common were educational programmes which related to their aims. The co-operative movement, for example, as a trading movement, provided reading rooms, libraries and classes in book-keeping and accounts. The Plymouth Co-operative movement (1860) today continues this tradition. The working men's associations, which spread rapidly in the 1830s, met to discuss newspapers and radical writers. The Chartists had a strong political and social agenda promoted through classes and literature in reading rooms. Where some movements arose from the ranks of working class people, other movements were started by middle class people for the benefit of the working classes, such as the people's and working men's colleges (Sheffield, 1842, London, 1854), which were emulated in other centres. The quaker Swarthmore Settlement movement, dating from 1840, was concerned with offering education and with providing opportunities for fellowship. A quaker adult school opened in Plymouth in 1912, but the more widely based settlement in Mutley Plain dates from 1922, and now provides its classes in collaboration with the local authority.

Perhaps the best known and the most widespread of the self-help educational movements was that of the mechanics' institutes, drawing support, variously, from the working classes and the middle classes, though increasingly dominated by the latter. In Britian by the 1850s they numbered over 600. In many places mechanics' institutes were sufficiently successful that they could afford to build their own premises. Their roots lay in the provision of lecture series in scientific principles for artizans by George Birkbeck in Glasgow, but the real expansion of the movement took place in the 1820s. Those in Plymouth and Devonport were founded in 1826 and 1825. Although the lecture programme was the hall-mark of mechanics' institutes' activities, they often developed into local centres for adult educational activity, and might include libraries and reading rooms, museum collections, and elementary classes in a wide range of subjects. Sometimes they functioned as examination centres, and often other local adult educational groups hired rooms in the institutes for their functions. In time the early strong scientific emphasis to the lecture programmes, which represented a rather specialised educational interest, gave way to more varied programmes which included lectures on a wide range of subjects, and musical and other kinds of entertainment. By the end of the nineteenth century, growing local authority provision of libraries, museums, evening classes, and technical college buildings superseded the offerings of the mechanics' institutes. In many instances local institutes were simply taken over by the local authorities, so that many 1992 universities have their roots in the mechanics' institutes movement.

With such a variety of adult education, it is perhaps not surprising that thoughts turned to finding ways of bringing university level education within the reach of working people. Although there were earlier examples, the delivery of a course of lectures by a university lecturer, open to any one, at a location away from the university buildings is considered to date from 1867 when a Cambridge university fellow gave courses in Leeds, Liverpool, Sheffield and Manchester. The number of such courses grew rapidly and the next step was the formation of university extension colleges, such as that at Exeter drawing on links with Cambridge University. University people were also brought into contact with working people through the university settlements, of which the residential Toynbee Hall in the east end of London is the most notable example. Several extension colleges, such as Exeter, were to develop into full universities. Extension work has from the 1920s been organised by extra-mural or continuing education departments of universities.

The development of local authority adult education provision, present today in the evening institute programmes announced each autumn, did not halt the development of new adult educational initiatives. Most notable was the Workers' Education Association (WEA, 1903) promoted by Albert

1.6 The distribution of schools and classes under the Department of Science and Art in 1890.

[UPPLY, Media Services]

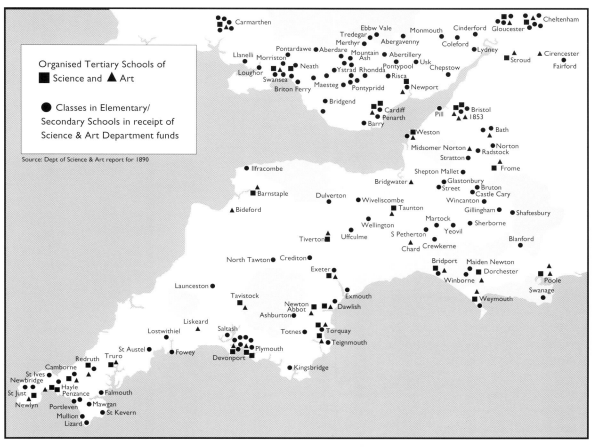

CHARLES' PARISH MAGAZINE.   1

Plymouth Corporation Grammar School,

42, PARK STREET, PLYMOUTH.

BOARDING HOUSE AND MASTER'S RESIDENCE : 13, THE CRESCENT.

HEAD MASTER :—

J. KINTON BOND, B.A., B.Sc., LONDON.

Assisted by ENGLISH AND FOREIGN GRADUATES IN HONOURS.

A Public School, with all the advantages of Special and Private Tuition.
Special Classes for Bookkeeping, Indexing, Precis, Shorthand, and Commercial French

During the Years 1884, 1885, 1886, 1887, 1888 Successes were obtained by the Pupils at the following Examinations:— Oxford and Cambridge Locals, The Oxford and Cambridge Schools Examination (Higher Division), London Matriculation, Naval Engineer Studentships, Assistant Clerkships, and Cadetships, The Civil Service, Phonetic Institute, School Ship Conway Gold Medal (third time), College of Preceptors, and Pharmaceutical, Medical, Veterinary, and Legal Preliminary. The total number of Successful Students for the five years amounted to TWO HUNDRED AND FORTY-SIX.

THE HOLMES PRIZE, given annually to the BEST CAMBRIDGE JUNIOR at the Plymouth Centre, fell to this School TWICE during the above period.

1889-1890.

CAMBRIDGE LOCAL.

Thirty-four Successes.—Three Seniors and Thirty-one Juniors.
Seventeen in Honours.

Two Seniors.—One First Class Honours.—The only First Class Senior in Devon and Cornwall—Winner of the Committee Prize.
One Third Class Honours.

Fifteen Juniors.—Five First Class Honours, Four Second Class, Six Third Class.

ARMY PRELIMINARY—March, 1890.

One Candidate entered from the School and was successful.

ENGINEER STUDENTSHIPS—April, 1889.

Two were successful in the Open Competition, and another passed as a Service Candidate.

April, 1890—Five were successful. The record for the School now amounts to Fifty-five.

NAVAL ASSISTANT CLERKSHIPS.—June, 1889.

The First and the Third on the list of successful candidates. The 4th time in five years that a pupil from this School has headed the list, November, 1889.—Third, Fourth, and Eighth. One fourth of the successful candidates.

June, 1890.—Fifty-ninth in the competition for 103 places.

BOY CLERKSHIPS IN THE CIVIL SERVICE.—July, 1889.

Twelfth out of nearly 600 Competitors.

January 1890.—Fifty-ninth in the competition for one hundred and three places.

THE JOAN BENNETT EXHIBITION OF £50 a year, for three years at the University of Oxford, was awarded to a pupil of this School as the result of an open competition. The subjects of examination were the Latin and Greek classics, pure and applied mathematics. The same pupil passed his Responsions direct from the School.

Another obtained an Open Scholarship in Ancient and Modern History, at King's College, Cambridge, of the value of £80 per annum.

The work of every boy in the School, from the youngest to the oldest, receives the careful supervision of the Head Master. Great attention is paid to the training of young boys, who are received from the age of 8 years. Delicate Boys receive every consideration.

THE BOARDING HOUSE is situated near the Hoe, in the most beautiful part of Plymouth, and is replete with everything that can conduce to the health, happiness, and comfort of the resident Pupils. The domestic arrangements are under the personal superintendence of Mrs. Kinton Bond.

A LARGE FIELD FOR CRICKET AND FOOTBALL.

Next Term, Thursday, September 11th, 1890.   Apply—13, THE CRESCENT, PLYMOUTH.

1.7 In the latter part of the nineteenth century, public examinations taken by school leavers became wide spread. Often they were part of the admission process for future employment, and schools such as this one Plymouth specialised in preparing youngsters for the examinatiions.

[PCL-LS]

Mansbridge. The idea was an association to link working class people to the university world to prepare people for participation in university extension work. Both the universities and working class organisations responded, with co-operative societies and trade unions affiliating to the WEA. The spread of WEA branches was very rapid, and its ideal was in due course adopted overseas. The timing was perfect, as the 1902 Education Act had just come into force which allowed local authorities to assist evening classes regardless of subject. Plymouth was amongst the early branches and is still active. A by-product was the Tutorial Class movement in which groups of students committed themselves to classes taken by a university lecturer and to regular attendance and essay writing. These were mostly arranged in association with the WEA, and with stable memberships, some classes, including one at Plymouth, ran for many years.

In recent years there has been a series of initiatives concerned with youth and adult continuing education and training. The youth schemes have been closely related to vocational education, while for more academic studies there has been a strong emphasis on improving access, through pre-degree access courses, Open Colleges, and another form of university extension in the Open University approach. At the other end of the spectrum, for people beyond retirement age, largely neglected in earlier movements, has come the University of the Third Age, an idea imported from France, with the same self-help, self-governing objective as in the nineteenth century, but looking to local universities for support, as is happening in Plymouth.

Technical education[7]

Despite the rapid pace of industrialisation and the interest in scientific and technical subjects demonstrated by the various adult education movements, it was not until the middle of the nineteenth century that the need to develop technical education began to be addressed. However, although progress became noticeable at the end of the 1860s there remained a reliance on *ad hoc* local committees for management and delivery as there were no suitable local government structures. Following the creation of county councils in 1888, provision came increasingly under the oversight of councils' technical instruction committees. It should be noted that 'science' was in this period used more loosely than at present, and that it often embraced technical subjects.

State provision was not totally lacking before the 1850s. The underlying importance of design to industrial production was recognised in the founding of a school of design in London in 1837 (now the Royal College of Art) under the Board of Trade, and from 1841 finance for maintaining and founding design schools in the provinces was offered (seventeen up to 1852). Separately, the Board of Trade promoted schools of navigation from 1851.

1.8, 1.9 Like many other towns across the country Plymouth above and Devonport righttrected technical college buildings in the 1890s.

[PCL-LS, PDTC Prospectus, 1939, Plymouth, A handbook, 1910]

Technical School and Art College.

[Heath, P

Through the Admiralty, which had founded the Naval Academy at Portsmouth (1729) and the Royal Naval Schools at Greenwich (emulated by the army from 1857), had come the establishment of the Royal Dockyard Schools from 1843 The central administration of state support for design was *ad hoc* and increasingly chaotic, so as a remedy, a new section within the Board of Trade, the Department of Practical Art was created in 1852 to promote elementary instruction in drawing as part of national education, to provide advanced instruction in art, to promote technical art principles to improve manufactures, and to be self supporting. Meanwhile the Great Exhibition of 1851 had demonstrated the need to develop science education in support of industry, and in 1853 the Department of Practical Art became the Department of Science and Art with much the same brief extended of course to the sciences. It was to generate interest in science and art and provide facilities for study by developing a network of schools of art and of science, and creating central institutions (in London) for more advanced instruction and teacher training.

In the 1850s, most of the effort of the DSA went into the art side, with the number of art schools being increased to nearly sixty. They included those at Exeter (1854), Plymouth (1856) and Devonport (1858). The science side took much longer to make its mark, though this had started by being given oversight of the navigation schools and a few trade schools. The main

1.10 The distribution of institutions of further and higher education in the south west in 1955.

[UPPLY, Media Services]

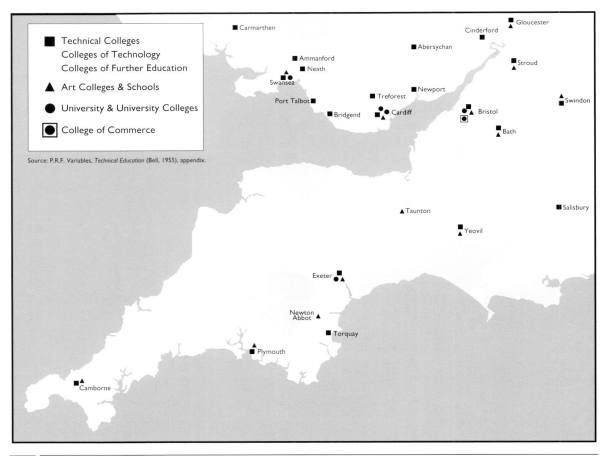

achievement in the first decade was perhaps the network of seventeen navigation schools, including that at Plymouth (1862). Of the few Science schools that had opened, only four were functioning in 1859. Better progress came in the 1860s, including the start of science classes at Exeter (1863), Plymouth (1866) and Devonport (1868), though significant expansion really came in the 1870s.

Partly because the Department of Science and Art (DSA) brief included elementary education, local science and art teaching could take place in existing schools or as separate classes wherever accommodation could be found. Such classes might exist one year but not the next. Dedicated buildings were rare. The DSA intended method of encouraging local science and art education was a pump-priming approach, through which it was hoped that the classes would become financially self-supporting. Local management committees had to be formed, which had to provide the accommodation, books and apparatus. Provision was made for inspection by DSA inspectors. Student fees were graduated, with students at the lowest levels attending free or at much reduced fees. Fees went towards operating costs of the premises and to teachers' remuneration. In 1859, the payment-by-results approach was applied to science classes (it already applied to art classes). The teachers had to hold the separate subject teachers' certificates of the DSA, and they received payments related to the grade of their certificates on their students' results in the annual DSA students' examinations introduced in 1860. The early subjects included geometry, mechanical drawing, building construction, physics, chemistry and natural history. Eventually there were examinations in about twenty five subjects, the list being augmented to include for example mineralogy, animal physiology, navigation, steam and metallurgy. Although by the end of the century, the DSA was spending £200,000 per year on science classes, when it could count 170,000 students, the whole regulatory framework had been designed to minimise the cost to the state. By placing examinations at the heart of its method of support, with rigid, theoretical syllabuses, the DSA negated the wider purpose of technical education, to teach a trade or art while involving scientific principles. The trade dimension taught in workshops or in collaboration with industry was ignored.

Through this essentially a low-cost approach the DSA could avoid any accusation of being profligate with government money, and by promoting theoretical learning, it could avoid financing industrial training, a cost which many thought should be borne by industry. In a way it reflected the prevailing low status of applied occupations, particularly engineering, but extending also, for example, to chemistry. Apart from the DSA, however, there were other some central foundations concerned with technical subjects. The Royal College of Chemistry was established in 1845, and the Royal School of Mines in 1851. The Royal School of Naval Architecture was formed in 1867, only to be subsumed by the Royal Naval College established at Greenwich in 1873.

The DSA was not to be the only body offering examinations in technical subjects. The Royal Society of Art (RSA) offered examinations intended for artisan classes from 1856 and started technical examinations related to particular industries from 1873, transferring them to the CGLI in 1881. It was the City and Guilds of London Institute (CGLI) which founded the first technical college at Finsbury that year with departments for mechanical engineering, electrical engineering, technical chemistry, applied art, and provided vocational trade classes. The RSA subsequently concentrated on examinations for commercial subjects, a role it still performs, as did the CGLI for a wide range of trade and technical subjects. CGLI also founded a Central Institution (now merged with Imperial College of Science and Technology), for high level study by technical teachers, engineers, architects and works managers, and made grants to provincial educational establishments, promoting local classes for its examinations.

The expansion of the sector was made possible through a series of acts of parliament which facilitated the local development of technical education. A more suitable local administrative structure was created by the Local Government Act, of 1888, which designated 62 county councils and county borough councils for towns having populations of more than 50,000. Then the Technical Instruction Act, 1889, allowed the new councils to levy up to a penny rate for technical education. Touching local pockets, this permissive legislation was taken up slowly, only eleven councils having taken advantage by 1892, though by the end of the century all councils were raising rates for technical education. However real progress followed in the wake of the Local Taxation (Customs and Excise) Act of 1890: some monies (soon to be known as 'whisky money') raised from duties could be applied to relieve the rates or to develop technical education. Many councils opted for the latter, one outcome being the widespread erection or extension of central buildings for science, art and technical education. Some towns like Exeter (1868) had already opened such buildings with the aid of local donations. Plymouth's building opened in 1892, Devonport in 1898 and Newton Abbot in 1904. Though these buildings were to become technical colleges in the modern sense, well into the twentieth century they remained simply multi-purpose educational buildings managed by local authorities which might be used alike (and often simultaneously) for elementary or secondary classes, and any form and level of post school education up to university extension. Some councils set up technical education committees to focus the development of this new branch of state educational provision; others, like Exeter from 1902, had a higher education committee (*ie* everything apart from elementary education), so that technical education was seen as little different from secondary education. Indeed the upsurge in local authority interest in secondary education following the Education Act of 1902 sidelined technical education in many areas.

One outcome of other measures in the 1890s had been the re-invigoration of evening classes in evening continuation schools. More enlightened employers were increasingly releasing apprentices early to attend such classes. Indeed until after World War II, technical education was to remain essentially part-time evening work. Numbers of full-time staff remained small, with the bulk of the teaching was undertaken by part-time staff, as was mainly the case under the DSA regime. The term now in use for the buildings and their classes, technical college, still encompassed a wide range of levels of education, which was not helped by the Board of Education practice of designating and inspecting different 'schools' for what would later be considered the work of technical colleges. Had the proposals for compulsory day continuation in the 1918 Education Act been put into effect, the colleges would have had a much enhanced role. However a new important qualification, a joint award of the Board of Education and industry, was introduced after World War I. The National Certificate scheme offered certificates for part-time study and diplomas for full-time study at ordinary and higher levels, in subjects such as mechanical and electrical engineering, chemistry and naval architecture, with related attendance at classes and internal examinations with external moderation. This was a departure from the discontinued, centralised DSA approach. The number of subjects was greatly expanded after 1945. These qualifications were highly respected in industry, the most advanced courses being considered to be near degree level, but they must not be confused with the Technical Education Council and the Business Education Council (since merged as BTEC and now EDEXEL) national diplomas which replaced them in the 1970s.

1.11 University of Plymouth partner colleges in 2000.

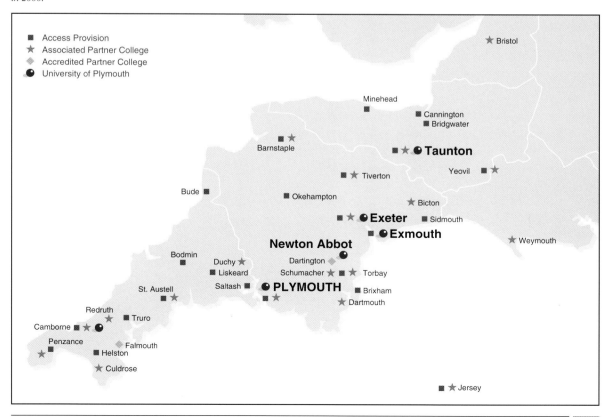

While the 1944 Education Act clearly distinguished further education from primary and secondary, and by recognising it as a distinct sector provided a basis for the great expansion from the 1950s, further and local authority higher education has been shaped and reformed during the second half of the twentieth century through a whole series of reports, policy statements and enactments. The Percy Report (1945) on higher technological education recommended the development of university standard courses at a number of technical colleges, new technological awards, a national council and regional advisory councils to co-ordinate provision. The Barlow Report (1946), identifying the need to increase the output of scientists, endorsed the Percy proposals, and in due course they were put into effect. Meanwhile, the need to retrain ex-service personnel was stretching post-school educational facilities to the limits, with full-time courses becoming a much more significant part of the work. Then in 1956 came the white paper on technical education with its five year development plan and definition of the levels of technologist, technician and craftsman. It also identified over twenty colleges which might be eligible for additional grants for advanced work. As a result ten colleges of advanced technology were designated to form the highest level of a four tier classification of colleges, the others being local, area or regional colleges. The college at Plymouth would fall into the regional category, with substantial full-time and sandwich advanced courses. The 1960s saw new qualifications for art colleges, notably the National Diploma in Design and the full transfer of agricultural education to the Ministry of Education. At the same time the ministry was engaged in a massive programme of new building in all sectors of education (which continued through the 1970s), of particular interest here as it created a new range of buildings on all the campuses which now comprise the University of Plymouth.

Behind the debates of the 1960s was the question whether non-university higher education should remain within local authority control. Tied up with this was the future of teacher training colleges, an area of professional training in which local authorities had a major stake (including of course Rolle College). As well as university expansion and the creation of the Council for National Academic Awards (CNAA) (already noted), the Robbins Report on Higher Education had recommended that a selection of regional colleges and colleges of education be granted university status by 1980. The Labour Government, with opposition support, settled on its binary policy for higher education, that is a sector under local authority control delivering CNAA degrees and other advanced courses in parallel with the much more independent university sector, setting it out in its white paper of 1966. The new sector, which came into being in 1969/70, was not, however, to be managed by the local authorities in the way which they had previously controlled their technical colleges. Through the creation of new governing bodies and provision for colleges to have their own administrations, a degree of self management was transferred to the new polytechnics, approval of the instruments and articles of government by the Department of Education and

Science (DES) being a requirement. With the designation of the polytechnics came the division of work according to level, advanced work such as degrees and higher national diplomas being the work of the polytechnics and lower level work for craftsmen and operatives passing to the colleges of further education. In many conurbations polytechnics were created through the merger of as many as five colleges. Exceptionally, at Plymouth, the College of Technology was divided and a new College of Further Education built for the non-advanced work. Plymouth College of Art remained separate, though its architecture department was transferred to the Polytechnic. Only much later, in 1988/89, did the mergers take place of Rolle College, Exeter College of Art and Design and Seale Hayne Agricultural College with Plymouth Polytechnic to create Polytechnic South West.

During the final quarter of the twentieth century non-university higher and further education has had to adapt to an almost continuous series of government initiatives, both structural and financial, which has seen a massive expansion of the numbers of students and sudden changes designed to control and reduce state expenditure on post-school education. Following the James report on teacher education in 1972, the training colleges were forced to expand and diversify, to close or to merge (usually with the nearby polytechnic). In 1974 local government reorganisation put many establishments under different local authorities. Plymouth Polytechnic, for example, was transferred from Plymouth City to Devon County Council, a change which was to impact on its composition after 1988. In 1982 came the National Advisory Body which assumed much of the oversight role previously undertaken by the DES. But the major change came in the wake of the Education Reform Act of 1988 with provisions concerning quality and efficiency, encouragement of wider access to higher education, the creation of the Polytechnics and Colleges Funding Council and the parallel Universities Funding Council, and, most importantly, the elevation of the polytechnics to university status, free of local authority control and with degree conferring status. This last meant the demise of the CNAA.[8] The Further and Higher Education Act of 1992 provided a similar independence for further education colleges. But that was also the year the government decided to halt the growth in student numbers by means of penalties for over recruitment. In recent years, access to higher education has been enhanced through partnership arrangements, particularly between the new universities and their neighbouring further education colleges. The partnership network of the University of Plymouth is substantial and involves most non-university colleges in the southwestern counties.

The coats of arms of the 'Three Towns' of Plymouth, Stonehouse and Devonport [1]

Education in the
Three Towns, 1815-1914

CHAPTER TWO

By the third quarter of the twentieth century the involvement of the local education authority in the oversight and provision of the great bulk of most kinds of education in Britain, was a commonplace. It ranged across the primary, secondary, technical, vocational and recreational spheres and included some degree level work. Universities were clearly outside the local education authority (LEA) remit, and nursery schooling was largely in the hands of other organisations. A minor proportion of primary and secondary schooling, influential beyond its scale, was delivered by direct government grant, endowed and private schools, and there were a number of industry or vocationally oriented colleges directly supported by the state. Several voluntary bodies were involved in promoting adult education, but the majority of the population in a local area, such as modern Plymouth, thought of the LEA as the dominant provider. People had become aware that the oversight and provision of educational qualifications lay with various national bodies. However, the changes made in the later years of the twentieth century have shown that, as well as some compulsory schooling, the bulk of further education and higher education need not necessarily be

2.1 This chart of Plymouth Sound shows the physical extent of each of the Three Towns of Plymouth, Stonehouse and Devonport in the 1840s.

[University of Plymouth, Plymouth Campus, Marine Studies collection (UPPLY-MS), An Improved Chart of the English Channel (London, Charles Wilson, 1851), insert.]

managed by the LEA. That indeed was the situation throughout most of the nineteenth century as far as such post-school local educational provision as existed, was concerned, until the county and county borough councils came into being. From the 1890s, the government placed an increasing range of responsibilities on local government.

Understanding who managed what in local educational provision in the nineteenth century is complicated not only by the range of local voluntary effort and the creation of *ad hoc* committees to manage particular approaches to education, but also by the existence (until 1914) of three separate 'towns' in the, to modern eyes, small area between the mouths of the rivers Plym and Tamar. Sometimes there was co-operation in educational provision, but mostly there was duplicate provision in Plymouth and Devonport, a situation which has left its mark today in the locations of the University of Plymouth and the Plymouth College of Further Education. Although there was potential for additional complication in East Stonehouse, its small size often meant that it did not seriously compete in post-school educational initiatives. Whatever the period, the existence of institutions concerned with education, did not mean that they necessarily owned the buildings in which their lectures or classes took place. The hiring of rooms for educational purposes was and remains very common. For small voluntary societies buying or building their own premises of course offered the advantages of fitness for purpose, accessibility and control, together with the opportunity to hire to others, but carried the penalties of high capital costs and on-going management and maintenance expenses. Capital for building might be raised on a wave of enthusiasm, but could leave the organisation with a residual debt not easily discharged from operational income.

With its medieval origins, a charter of incorporation as a borough in 1440, and its national and international fame, especially in the Tudor period, Plymouth was well established as a significant local government unit with a mayor and corporation long before Devonport and Stonehouse.[2] Devonport, Dock or Plymouth Dock until 1824, was a single industry factory town, which grew up around the Royal Dockyard. Authorised in 1691 this incorporated the latest technical thinking and is considered by some to be the first factory in Britain. The importation of dockyard workers from other dockyards and the progressive expansion and modernisation of the dockyard meant that by 1821, with a population of 33,578, Plymouth Dock was significantly larger than Plymouth whose population then numbered 21,591.[3] The local goverment of Plymouth Dock until 1780, when poor law commissioners were appointed, depended on the parish system. In 1837 it became a municipality of six wards and appointed its first mayor, though some functions remained with the commissioners and the surveyors of highways.[4] Following the Local Government Act of 1888, Plymouth and Devonport emerged as county boroughs and Stonehouse soon after as an urban district, but elementary education remained with the school boards (created in 1870), and science and art educational support continued under local committees. Following the Technical Instruction Act (1889), Plymouth and Devonport gained technical instruction committees to manage science, art and technical educational provision. It was only following the Education Act of 1902 that the control of local state-aided educational provision passed fully to the respective county borough councils. The merger in 1914 of the Three Towns into a single county borough with the name of Plymouth produced at last a single local education authority for the area. The designation of Plymouth as a city did not come until 1928.

At the heart of this overview of educational developments in the Three Towns of Plymouth, Stonehouse and Devonport, is the progression of developments in post-school educational provision which would culminate in the erection of central 'science, art and technical' school buildings in Plymouth and Devonport in the last decade of the nineteenth century. While the schools of art and of science in those towns operating under the Department of Science and Art regime, were the main elements, the three towns also supported those other features of Victorian post-school self-help educational enterprise, middle class educational societies, mechanics institutes, libraries and museums. In addition instruction in basic literacy could be found in adult schools. Elementary vocational instruction could be found in trade schools, while some more advanced vocational education in specific fields was offered in schools run as businesses. However, before exploring these approaches to more advanced educational provision, some note must be taken of the changes school provision for the children of the three towns during the century. In the nineteenth century as today, the word 'school' was used to cover a wide range of educational levels and establishments. It could often refer to a single free-standing class or to a class within an establishment.

Schools

At the start of the nineteenth century the bulk of elementary/secondary schooling in the area, such as it was, was to be found with private establishments charging fees. Usually very small when compared with schools today, often with only one or two teachers, they covered the spectrum from little more than child minding to advanced secondary education which could, very rarely, enable a pupil to go up to university. In Plymouth, private schools numbering 56 in 1840, were to remain a feature of provision throughout the century.[5] In 1904, there were 61 such establishments in Plymouth with an enrolment of 2,194 pupils.[6] Perhaps their continued existence partly reflects the great increase in the population of the three towns during the century, which rose from 43,194 in 1801 to 193,184 in 1901,[7] the spread of elementary education being pressed to catch up, as much as the lack of a secondary system and middle class preference for private or endowed schooling. In Plymouth, at the start of the century, there was only a handful of endowed or charitable schools, though one had roots in Elizabethan times. However, in 1809 Plymouth Public Free School was established on the monitorial system, which moved into purpose-built premises in Coburg Street. Nearby, another school building, now the University of Plymouth's Scott Building, was erected in the 1920s. Under the auspices of the National and British Societies and backed by Education Department grants, ten elementary schools were opened between 1838 and 1870. Following the Education Act of 1870, Plymouth School Board was elected in January 1871. It absorbed or replaced some existing schools and continued expanding provision until its abolition in 1903, when eighteen groups of buildings were transferred to the local education authority of Plymouth County Council. Plymouth Dock, could not, of course look to Tudor free school foundations, but it had a free school at the end of the eighteenth century and, following the same pattern as at Plymouth, it founded monitorial schools from 1809 and progressively expanded its elementary school provision to 22 schools in 1910.[8] Similarly Stonehouse had two monitorial schools in the 1820s, while in all three towns the churches were active in establishing elementary schools in mid-century. Special school provision was also made for disabled children, and at the end of the century higher grade elementary schools came into existence offering education beyond the levels normal in elementary schools. After 1902 both Plymouth and Devonport LEAs were active in developing secondary schools where fees remained payable though offset or reduced by scholarship awards. That a substantial proportion of what were then considered school age children were in receipt of some form of education twenty years before elementary education was freed of fees in 1891, was shown by a survey undertaken by the new Plymouth School Board in 1871. In the Borough of Plymouth the survey report found 3,114 children aged between three and five and 10,966 between five and thirteen; of the total 82 per cent were attending a school.[9]

THE OLD SCHOOL.
(Coburg Street frontage).

2.2 The sign over the doorway at the left of the drawing reads Plymouth Public Free School. The illustration records the scene in the 1860s. Established in 1809, it was soon relocated in 1810 to the north side of Coburg Street. The present building, now used as teaching accommodation by the University of Plymouth, dates from the 1920s.

[Plymouth Central Library, Local Studies (PCL-LS), C.W. Bracken, A History of the Plymouth Public School (Plymouth, Underhill, 1927), 18]

2.3 2.4 These wall plaques record the earlier changes.

[photos: A. Kennerley]

2.5 For many years in the nineteenth century, this building in Princess Square, was the home of the Classical and Mathematical School. Later it accommodated the Plymouth School of Art.

[PCL-LS, illustrations collection]

2.6 This advertisement of 1914 for the Hoe Grammar School, emphasises a well qualified staff, modern facilities (especially a science laboratory) and preparation for external examinations.

[PCL-LS]

By the beginning of the twentieth century, owing to the multifarious origins from which educational provision had evolved, the system in Plymouth and Devonport, as in other parts of the country, was quite complex. Particularly at secondary and tertiary levels there was considerable overlapping of age bands. Figure 2.53, from the Plymouth Education Directory (1907-8), illustrates this clearly. In particular, the emergent technical college, taking pupils into some of its classes at the age of 15 years, was by no means a separate entity from the school system, even though significant proportions of the students enrolled in advanced science technical and art classes were over 21 years of age, 363 out of 630 (58%).[10] The progression beyond the age of 18 indicated on the diagram was for the small proportion of students who were able to go on to teachers' training colleges or universities outside the Plymouth authority's control. Apart from H.M. Dockyard School, the diagram omits progression to establishments entirely concerned with adult technical education, most notably the Plymouth School of Navigation.

Libraries and Museums in the Three Towns

An exhaustive study by Margaret Lattimore, formerly librarian at Plymouth Polytechnic, has demonstrated the scale and importance of the early efforts to make reading material accessible to a wider range of the population through the provision of libraries and reading rooms in association with educational societies, professional bodies and schools and as commercial ventures, often pre-dating the formation of adult educational classes.[11] Indeed development of new libraries having wider access was already taking place in the eighteenth century. Of course only those people who could read, had the time, and had sufficient income to afford the subscription to an organisation offering library and reading room facilities, could benefit, but throughout the nineteenth century this was a widening

circle. While acknowledging that many libraries were associated with middle class educational organisations, during the nineteenth century, increasing literacy and the growing number of working class organisations having educational dimensions, which almost without exception meant providing at least a small library, ensured that more and more working class people had access to reading material for self improvement. The movement for free access to libraries was already in evidence at the start of the century, and the passing of the Museums Act in 1845 and the Public Libraries Act in 1850, enabled local authorities to provide rate-supported public libraries.[12]

2.7 This 1825 view shows some of Devonport's most important buildings. The Civil and Military Library (a proprietary library) occupied the building on the right with the Egyptian façade. This library later merged with that of Devonport Mechanics' Institute. The other buildings are the Town Hall, the Devonport Column and the Ker Street Methodist Chapel.

[PCL-LS, F.W. Hunt, Libraries of Devonport, Naval, Military and Civil (Devonport, 1902) frontispiece]

Certainly in the Three Towns most of the main categories of library existed including commercial and private subscription libraries, literary and philosophical society, mechanics institutes, co-operative, school, scientific, medical, law, naval and rate-supported. Compared with the stock of the University of Plymouth Library, many of these nineteenth century libraries were tiny with numbers of volumes in the hundreds, perhaps increasing to a few thousands as the century progressed. Further, many societies lacked the finance to operate proper book acquisition policies, resulting in imbalances in subject coverage, slow or stagnant expansion, and out-of-date holdings. Only the better-off societies could afford a paid librarian, though when such an investment was made it paid dividends in the form of improved organisation, control and cataloguing.

2.8 In 1881, Devonport Mechanics Institute became the Free Public Library allowing the general public access to its 8,000 volumes.

[PCL-LS, Hunt, op.cit., 9]

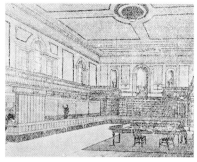

2.9 The interior of Devonport Public Library allowed ample reading room space for the general public.

[PCL-LS, Hunt, op.cit., 9]

2.10 This interior view of Plymouth Proprietary Library, in its original Foulston designed building, demonstrates the quality of the facilities which subscribers were able to enjoy from early in the nineteenth century. The Library now occupies a house on North Hill.

[PCL-LS, Ernest Benn, 1935]

2.11 This Plymouth Proprietary Library regulation of 1843 illustrates the measures its management committee had to take to ensure equitable access for subscribers, to the current newspapers. The title Plymouth Public Library, then in use, is misleading, as the Library was not freely open to the general public.

[Plymouth Proprietary Library]

Devonport Mechanics' Institute appointed a part-time paid librarian in 1847 at the time it was rebuilding, a move which no doubt contributed to the Institute's regeneration. However members' interests influence stock, and in 1852 only 10 per cent of the Institute's holdings comprised scientific and technical works, compared with fiction 16 per cent and history 19 per cent. The librarian's post became a full time appointment in 1863 when the Institute absorbed the Devonport Civil and Military Library (a proprietary library), increasing the stock to 8,000 volumes.[13] The building with its library were transferred to Devonport Town Council in 1881 to become the Devonport Free Public Library. In 1851 Plymouth Mechanics' Institute was also regenerated through rebuilding, including a new library and reading room. By 1885 its stock numbered about 8,000 volumes, but this was predominantly fiction and it was feeling the impact of the Plymouth Free Public Library which had opened in 1876. When that Institute was absorbed by the Plymouth Institution in 1899, its residued fund allowed the building of a new library on the rear of the Athenaeum building.[14]

Important though the libraries of the mechanics' institutes were in their time, they were pre-dated by several other libraries. Subscription libraries, were an eighteenth century development, and might be commercial ventures or financed on a joint stock basis. Their very nature meant that some were not long-lived. Nevertheless, despite the development of free public libraries, the type has lasted to the end of the twentieth century, with the Plymouth Proprietary Library still operating today. Some subscription libraries were also known as circulating libraries and Lattimore has identified nine functioning in the 1840s. Often they were associated with booksellers. That of W.H. Smith, which opened in Plymouth in 1860, must be amongst the better known. Plymouth Proprietary Library, which was known as Plymouth Public Library for much of the nineteenth century, was formed in 1810 with shares of £30, making it a private library for the well off. Its new building was opened in 1813 and the building debt was liquidated by a further call on members of £10. It was a successful venture and was extended at mid-century, and by the end of the century it held 25,000 volumes.[15] Libraries were also key features of literary and philosophical societies, such as those of the short-lived Dock Literary and Philosophical Society and the Plymouth Institution.[16]

Probably the earliest special library was that of the Plymouth Medical Society, founded in 1794, whose permanent collection was to become the library for the Plymouth hospitals. The most significant special library would, in the twentieth century, be the scientific library of the Marine Biological Association (1885). Stocked originally through donations from around the country, its library was started with 300 volumes and fourteen scientific journals. The decision to publish its own journal was taken in 1887, and through exchange with scientific research institutions around the world, the Association built up a world class holding of scientific serials as well as a specialist book stock. The library at Western College, with its emphasis on theology, was a third special subject library, with 8,000 volumes in 1900 at the time it was about to move to Bristol.[17]

A quarter of a century after the Public Libraries Act, Plymouth at last took steps to open a free public library. A penny rate was agreed for operational funding, but to make a start with the book stock it relied on donations. Plymouth Free Public Library was accommodated in the former police court opening a news room immediately, with lending and reference departments following soon after. By 1877 the stock numbered 8,000 volumes, with 125,000 annual issues and 210,000 visitors. By 1910 the stock had quadrupled. In the 1890s came the first branch libraries and reading rooms, and loans were being made to the Police Library and the Workhouse. As already noted, Devonport had acquired its public library in 1881. This grew rapidly towards the end of the century and also established branches. Certainly at the end of the century the familiar pattern of public library provision was well established in the area, reducing the need for some of the smaller subscription libraries, though many organisations, such as the Co-operative movement, working men's associations, schools and the forces, continued to maintain their own libraries.[18] Despite the limitations of the numerous non-rate-supported libraries and museums in the area, their numbers and scale made an early and valuable contribution to the adult education facilities in the area of the Three Towns.

Having a collection of artefacts, usually referred to as a museum, no matter how small the collection, was also an aspiration of many of these educational societies. But in the Three Towns it was the Plymouth Institution

2.12 These buildings for Plymouth's Free Library, Museum and Art Gallery, had only just been completed on the east side of Tavistock Road when this photograph was taken in in 1910. Although bombed in World War II, they were renovated and remain in use at the heart of Plymouth's educational zone.

[PCL-LH, Plymouth: a Handbook for the Forty-Second Annual Co-operative Congress, Whitsuntide 1910 (Manchester, 1910), 76, photo Heath]

New Free Library, Museum, and Art Gallery.

[Heath,

2.13 An early bookplate used at Plymouth Free Public Library. The use of the then Plymouth armourial device emphasises the support the library received from the local rates.

[PCL-LS]

2.14 An early technical college bookplate.

[PCL-LH]

with which a museum of greater magnitude was identified in the area for much of the nineteenth century. It provided accommodation from 1828 and in 1883, claiming to be the oldest in the west of England, it built a new museum and art gallery on its site.[19] This was intended to serve the Borough, previous efforts to establish a council museum having failed. Evenually, however, in 1897, the Borough of Plymouth founded its Museum and Art Gallery, in Beaumont House, Beaumont Park, as a memorial to the Queen's Jubilee. This could only be an interim solution, and in 1907 work started on the building it now occupies in Tavistock Road, which opened in 1910. In 1916 the Cottonian Collection, donated to Plymouth in 1852 and housed in the premises of the Plymouth Proprietary Library, was transferred. With other donations and aquisitions, this has become a significant provincial museum. The 1910 building was a joint development designed also to provide a new home for Plymouth Free Public Library, which occupied its section at the same time at the Museum. The book stock was lost in the bombing of 1941. Rebuilt in 1954, it remains the central library for the City of Plymouth.

Adult education for working people

The movements for the teaching of basic literacy and elementary education to adults manifested themselves in the Three Towns as in other parts of the country. There can be no doubt that the Sunday school movement, through which adults as well as children attended schools run by churches and chapels, was a force in the area. Hudson, writing in 1850 reported an adult school in Plymouth in 1815, and gave details of a Working Men's Association meeting in the 1840s under the auspices of the Plymouth Mechanics' Institute.[20] There were 150 members in 1847 and 1848. Classes 'on the mutual improvement principle' in reading, writing, arithmetic, and composition, were apparently a success, and the members wrote and published a monthly magazine. Other activities included occasional miniature exhibitions of 'natural history and manufactures'. The fees, six pence for entrance and one penny per week, were, appropriately, significantly lower than those of the more sophisticated educational societies. The association was still functioning in 1859.[21] Hudson also noted an adult school in the dockyard, teaching arithmetic, geography, history and mathematics. Whether this is a reference to the Royal Dockyard School (1844) is uncertain.

That societies concerned with improving the education of working men were a common feature, particularly from the middle of the nineteenth century, has been demonstrated in the detailed analysis undertaken by Lewis.[22] Between 1813 and 1897 he lists the formation of some eighty adult schools, classes, institutes, societies or associations. Though one or two lasted over 25 years, most were relatively short-lived. About half the organisations had been formed in association with churches and chapels and tended to have a religious dimension to their programmes of lectures and classes. A number of societies were aimed at young men (including the YMCA branches) and societies in Devonport and Stonehouse were promoted by Sunday school teachers. Given the very large Sunday schools of the

2.15 Emulating the co-operative pioneers in Rochdale, the Plymouth Co-operative Society had a library and reading room above its first shop in Treville Street at its beginning in 1860.

[PCL-LS, Co-op Handbook, op.cit, 141]

First Property.

THE PLYMOUTH CO-OPERATIVE RECORD.

EDUCATION DEPARTMENT,

CENTRAL BUILDINGS, PLYMOUTH.

Attention is directed to the

Classes for Adults

In connection with the Department.

HISTORY AND PRINCIPLES OF CO-OPERATION

(PRELIMINARY, ELEMENTARY AND ADVANCED),

Held on Tuesdays · · · · · 7.30 to 9.30 p.m.

CITIZENSHIP	INDUSTRIAL HISTORY
(ELEMENTARY AND ADVANCED),	(ELEMENTARY AND ADVANCED),
Held on Thursdays, ·	Held on Mondays,
7.30 to 9.30 p.m.	7.30 to 9.30 p.m.

CO-OPERATIVE BOOK-KEEPING

(PRELIMINARY, ELEMENTARY AND ADVANCED),

Held on Tuesdays · · · · · 8 to 9 p.m.

The above Classes are free to Members, and families above 16 years.

Substantial Prizes, and Certificates, are awarded on the results of the Examinations, by the local Committee, and Scholarships and Grants are awarded by the Co-operative Union.

Application to join can be made to the Teachers on Class nights.

2.16 The Co-operative classes for adults early in the twentieth century typified the educational work of adult social movements in the second half of the previous century.

[PCL-LS, Monthly Record (October, 1909), 260]

period, usually with a 'head', the Sunday school superintendent, in charge, Sunday school teachers must have been quite numerous. The Stonehouse Wesleyan Sunday School Teachers' Association (1847) met once a fortnight and in 1850 had 116 members. The Batter Street Christian Improvement Association (*ca* 1860) had a fortnightly lecture programme and offered a choice of three or four classes in subjects such as essay, bible, devotional, discussion, elocution, English language and singing. Fees were about half those prevailing in the mechanics' institutes. Its membership peaked at 270 in 1865. In contrast, the Plymouth Mutual Improvement Society (1843) (there were several societies having similar titles) for young men, held weekly meetings in a school room close to Gibbon Street (where some of the University's student accommodation is now located). Amongst its lecture subjects were legislation, drama, physical and mental diseases, atmospheric currents, and moral causation.[23]

Adult education was also promoted by the Co-operative movement which came to the area in 1859. By 1860 the Plymouth Society had a reading room and library for use by its staff and members and from 1872 regularly offered lectures and entertainments in addition to classes. In 1910 it was offering classes in co-operation, citizenship, industrial history, managers' training, book keeping and dressmaking, and it was paying the half the fees of some members at the technical college.[24] By then the library contained 12,200 volumes. The Plymouth and South Devon Co-operative Society continues this educational tradition to the present. For many years the work was based in the former Western College building, but it was recently moved into the Society's department store at Derry's Cross reverting to the mid-nineteenth century relationship where educational activities took place above the shop.

NOTICE TO LIBRARY BORROWERS.

It is deemed necessary by the Education Committee to have

The Library Books called in

for overhauling and stockchecking—a process that was performed annually for many years, but dropped on account of insufficiency of shelf accommodation. The issue of books will therefore be **stopped after Saturday, July 31st,** and those who borrow books up to that date are asked to be sure and

Return them by August 14th

in order that the work, which will be of a laborious nature ——— ——— being expeditiously done and ———

The Library RE-OPENED on Monday, August 30th.

2.17 A century ago, the library of the Plymouth Mutual Co-operative & Industrial Society was clearly heavily used by its members

[PCL-LH, Monthly Record (July, 1909), 226.]

DEVONPORT AND STONEHOUSE
MECHANICS' INSTITUTE

2.18 This entrance card to the Devonport and Stonehouse Mechanics' Institute was explained in 1826: "In front a shield...being the arms of Sir John St Aubyn, patron and Lord of the Manor...the frame of a ship...illustrative of our grand naval arsenal...Supporter - The Devonport Column; thus showing the power of mechanics in the erection of a monument to perpetuate the condescension of his Majesty, who lately conferred the name of Devonport on our town. A portion of the Hamoaze is exhibited on which is reposing a ship ready for sea, and the steam packet entering the port. Distance- the seat of the Earl of Mount Edgcumbe, Patron, and Lord of Stonehouse."

[PCL-LH, R. Burnet, A Word to the Members of the Mechanics' Institutes (Devonport, 1826), 17, 121; Banks, del. & sculp.]

Mechanics Institutes in the Three Towns

The formation of a single mechanics' institute committee for Plymouth, Devonport and Stonehouse in 1825, with plans for the joint management of institutes in Plymouth and Devonport, was an early attempt at a joint adult education venture between the towns. But almost immediately Plymouth seceded, possibly owing to the desire for a more sophisticated tone than seemed possible in a link with Devonport.[25] So two separate societies emerged that year. Initially the Plymouth Institute met in the Guildhall or the London Inn Assembly Rooms, but in 1827 it acquired its own building in Princess Square, erecting a replacement building in 1849. The Devonport Institute met in the Town Hall. In 1844 it erected its own building, and completed an adjacent extension 1849. Now its lecture theatre could accommodate over 1000 persons, and the building contained a library (3,000 volumes in 1850) and reading room, smaller rooms for evening classes, attended in the late 1840s by up to 150 students. In 1825 the subscription was set at eight shillings per annum for persons under twenty and ten shillings for

Plymouth Mechanics' Institute.

⚹ TERMS OF MEMBERSHIP. ⚹

Winter Quarters.

Senior Members	3/-
Ladies and Junior Members	2/-

Summer Quarters.

Senior Members	2/-
Ladies and Junior Members	1/6

ANNUAL SUBSCRIBERS 10/-
LADIES & JUNIOR MEMBERS ... 7/-

ENTRANCE FEE, ONE SHILLING.

⚹ CHESS ÷ CLUB. ⚹

Science and Art Classes

Are held in connection with the Science and Art Department,
South Kensington.

Building Construction & Applied Mechanics	Mr. F. S. Warren
Magnetism and Electricity	Mr. S. Andrews
Practical, Plane, and Solid Geometry	Mr. J. Pearce
Art Classes	Mr. F. Babb

Orchestral Society for Members only, conducted by Mr. Holloway

Members will be required to show their Cards on Admission.

THE LECTURES, &c., COMMENCE AT EIGHT O'CLOCK.

2.19 A page from the Plymouth Mechanic's Institute prospectus for 1892. With the opening of the Science, Art and Technical School building that year, this must have been one of the last occasions that some of the Science and Art classes were held at the Mechanics' Institute.

[PCL-LS, Plymouth libraries collection]

older subscribers. Membership did not exceed 70 until the 1840s, when with a new building numbers rose to over 800. Hudson notes that in 1850 about 200 working men and 120 females were members. As well as the lecture/entertainment programme, a strong feature of the Devonport Mechanics' Institute were the annual 'polytechnic exhibitions' with prizes for mechanical inventions, drawings and essays. The Plymouth Institute was more expensive charging thirteen shillings per annum for adults and eight shillings and eight pence for juniors. In the 1840s its library contained two thousand volumes, and membership was about four hundred. The fare offered was similar to that at Devonport, though towards the end of the century the main usage was for entertainments. Stonehouse Mechanics' Institute was formed about 1845, and held classes in French, drawing and mutual improvement. When the local government complex, St George's Hall, was completed in 1850, which also included new law courts, police station, prison, and a ball room, it was allocated accommodation.[26] Its library had 550 volumes and the subscription was ten shillings annually. The Stonehouse Institute was not a success and had closed by 1854.

The original scientific/technical dimension of mechanics' institutes was stronger in Devonport than in Plymouth, but there was never any enduring support from the leading figures in the Dockyard or the mechanics working in the yard where the main concentration in the area was located. So it is not surprising that by the mid-1850s this element had disappeared from the reports on Institute activities. In 1849 tradesmen were the main participants, though a small core of working class men continued in membership to 1869 despite the middle class trends.[27] The broadening of the appeal of the lecture series of the Plymouth and Devonport Institutes, after mid-century is clearly illustrated by the programmes published by the societies in January 1859:[28]

Plymouth Mechanics' Institute Lecture Series

10 January	The National Flags of England
12 January	Monumental Memorialists
19 January	Literary, Pictorial and Musical Entertainment
26 January	Two Great Cardinals
2 February	Two Great Cardinals
9 February	Musical Entertainment
16 February	Abuses of Civilisation
23 February	Pompeii (illustrated)
2 March	The Poets Workshop
9 March	An Evening with Great Statesmen
16 March	The Language of the Skies
23 March	The Advantages of Biographical Studies
30 March	Dramatic reading (Shakespeare)
6 April	The Last Fifty years of British History
13 April	Literary and Musical Entertainment
20 April	The Influence of Women in Society
27 April	Concluding Lecture: Retrospective

Devonport Mechanics' Institute Lecture Series

4 January	The Atlantic Cable and the Life of a Gust
11 January	The Poetry of Mathematics
18 January	Musical Entertainment
25 January	Two Great Cardinals
1 February	Two Great Cardinals
8 February	English Customs - an Entertainment
15 February	Recent Discoveries in Electrical Science
22 February	Musical Entertainment: Life at the Diggings
1 March	Exposition of British Arts and Manufactures
8 March	Lord Macauley
15 March	Life With and Without Method
29 March	Magic, No Mystery
5 April	Washington
12 April	Barbarism and Civilisation Contrasted.

In addition to the lecture programme, classes (not to be confused with those operated by other groups using Institute premises) were operated by all three institutes, but were not over successful. Except for the mechanical science class at Devonport, the few subjects offered reflected middle class interests, with French, drawing and mutual improvement seemingly most successful. The efforts to offer elementary classes appear spasmodic.[29]

Towards the end of the century, with the new technical college buildings providing teaching accommodation and new forms of entertainment gaining ascendancy, the mechanics' institute movement had run its course. The Plymouth Mechanics' Institute Society merged with the Plymouth Institution in 1899, and its building was subsequently used as repertory theatre.[30] The Devonport Mechanics' Institute building was subsequently used as the public library, and later as a motor taxation office.

Literary and Philosophical Societies

Offering education at the more academic end of the spectrum were the literary and philosophical societies of which the Plymouth Institution was the main local example. However, it was predated by the short-lived Dock

Royal Hotel and Athenæum, Plymouth.   (After Foulston.)

2.20 The Athenaeum (1818) (on the right of this picture), the home of the Plymouth Institution, was one of several major buildings by the architect John Foulston which were erected in Plymouth and Devonport in the first half of the nineteenth century.

[PCL-LS, illustrations collection, Western Morning News]

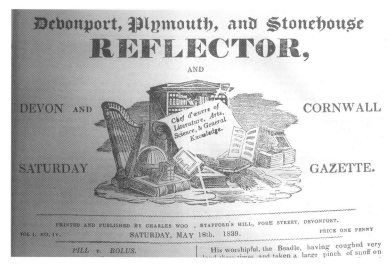

2.21, 2.22 Magazines, with a literary and scientific bent, such as these two examples from 1814 and 1839, would have found been taken by societies such as the Plymouth Institution, but would also have found a wider readership in the locality.

[PCL-LS]

2.23 Mechanics' Institute members and those of literary and philosophical societies would have been attracted to public lectures series such as these on astronomy offered in 1883.

[PCL-LS, The Western Figaro, 28 September 1883, 10]

Literary and Philosophical Society, formed in 1808, though both were amongst the earliest of the type nationally. The rules and regulations for members of the Dock Society were quite stringent. Full members (40 in 1816) subscribed twelve shillings each quarter, while subscribers (91 in 1816) paid six shillings and six pence, fees well beyond the capabilities of working people.[31] However it was unusual in admitting ladies. But full members were also subject to a system of fines for non-attendance. The rules provided for the purchase of apparatus to illustrate lectures and funds for building up the library. Its main activity seems to have been the lecture programme which certainly seems to have had a scientific bent. Perhaps the approach was too rigid and the fees too high, as the Society collapsed in about 1821. Lewis, however, sees it as the forebear of the Devonport Mechanics' Institute, which may have used the rooms it once occupied.[32] The Plymouth Institution (1812) survives to the present, though since 1961 under the name The Plymouth Athenaeum. Athenaeum was the name the Society gave to its new building erected in 1818 to the design of the famous Plymouth architect, John Foulston.[33] Foulston was one of a small community of scholars living or associated with Plymouth in the latter part of the eighteenth century and the early part of the nineteenth, which included Mudge, Cookworthy, Smeaton, Brunel and Rennie .

The purpose was the delivering of lectures on scientific and other subjects, and initially its membership was limited to thirty. Before the Plymouth Institution moved to its new building, it met in the houses of members and at the Plymouth Dispensary (built in 1807). The first lecture programme for 1812-13, reflects the desire for scientific and technical knowledge amongst the prosperous citizens of Plymouth who had not had the advantage of a university education (in those days at Oxford or Cambridge) and those having a university education who wished to continue their further education.[34] The twelve lectures for the first season covered pneumatics, hydrostatics, river bar formation, architecture, animal and plant physiology, history of chemistry, calorie, electricity, galvanism, and the characteristics of poetry. Members also had access to a library and museum. An early crisis in the management of the society was over the issue of membership for persons of ability but of 'a humble situation in life'. Snobbery prevailed and the Plymouth Institution remained essentially a middle class organisation. It sustained its annual lecture cycle and in the 1860s also had a herbarium. But a key feature differentiating it from the mechanics' institutes, in addition to research, was, by the 1860s, the publication of its formal proceedings. These included at least synopses of lectures and often the full text, and reports on projects. For example Dr Merrifield, head of the Plymouth School of Navigation, a regular lecturer, also for many years reported on the weather in Plymouth. Lewis comments that in the 1870s and 1880s Merrifield and R.N. Worth, the historian of Plymouth, were the only members sustaining the research objective, which thereafter depended on staff of the Marine Biological Association who joined the society.[35] By the 1870s a wider programme of lectures was offered which included: female education, the condition of our national universities, and iron. In the 1890s topics included the paraffin industry, Goethe as an educator, and cremation. The Society did make provision for working people in the 1880s, in connection with the Museum, classes which were apparently well attended, on physiology, locomotion (Dr Square, the President, who resided at 22 Portland Square, now owned by the University), the motions of the earth (Dr Merrifield), entomology, and the philosophy of an old bone. This attempt at serving others and that of opening its museum on Saturdays, seem not to have been particularly successful. Allowing local clubs to use its premises also became a feature towards the end of the century, though in most cases it was a passing phase.[36] Lady members were admitted from 1876, though numbers were not large. Other activities of the Plymouth Institution included archaeological digs, demonstrations (such as that of the telephone in 1878), painting exhibitions and cultural *conversaziones* and readings. Significant contributions were a number of catalogues, such as that of the flora and fauna of Devon and Cornwall.[37] The sometimes extensive newspaper reports of its proceedings served also to make them accessible to a wider audience. As the Athenaeum, the society continues along much the same lines to the present day.

2.24 The seal of the Devon and Cornwall Natural History Society which merged with the Plymouth Institution in 1851. The group produced a number of significant catalogues of Devon and Cornwall flora and fauna.

[PCL-LS, Western Antiquary, 3 (1883-4), 16]

Western College

An institution which was clearly delivering a programme of higher education with a vocational slant in the second half of the nineteenth century, was Western College. It was a theological college training ministers for the free churches, particularly the Congregational Churches.[38] Dating from 1752, it had migrated from Exeter to Plymouth in 1845 because the town was seen as centred for the western counties. Prior to coming to Plymouth, as Western Academy it had moved with the domicile of the tutor in charge: Ottery St Mary, Bridport, Taunton, Axminster and Exeter. At Plymouth it achieved the permanency of a specially designed building. Entirely financed by subscription and donation, no doubt mainly given by the chapels and their members, amongst which some of its graduates would commence their ministries, it was independent and self governing. Student

2.25 Taken, perhaps, in the 1880s this picture of Western College, may well show the whole student body with the few full-time staff. After the college left Plymouth in 1901, the building was for many years used by the Co-operative educational services. It is now private housing.

[Plymouth City Museum].

numbers were very small; between 1848 and 1860 41 students attended, and in 1860 there were sixteen students on the register. There appear to have been only two or three full-time resident staff, university men of high academic attainment, but these were augmented by visiting lecturers. The external examiners were drawn from across the country, and their reports were printed in the College's annual reports. The five year course clearly demanded a thorough secondary education, and though vocational, appears to have been highly academic. Thus it is hardly surprising that from 1847, it was affiliated to the examining university of London, though this recognition only allowed Western College students to sit the University's arts examinations as external candidates, there being as yet no theological examinations. The curriculum makes impressive reading:

Year One   Logic. Rhetoric, Elocution, Homiletics (preaching), Elements of Universal Grammar, English Language, Classics, Mathematics, Natural Philosophy (science)

Year Two   Mental and Moral Philosophy, Hebrew, Homiletics, Classics, Mathematics and Natural Philosophy

Year Three   Natural Theology, Textual Criticism, Hermeneutics (scriptural interpretation), Evidence of Christianity, Hebrew, New Testament Exegesis (interpretation), Homiletics, Classics, Mathematics and Natural Philosophy

Year Four   Inspiration (divine utterances), Sacred Hermeneutics, Doctrinal Theology, Old Testament Exegesis, New Testament Exegesis, Homiletics, Classics

Year Five   Doctrinal Theology, Ecclesiastical History, Old Testament Exegesis, New Testament Exegesis, Chaldee and Syriac (Aramaic language and culture), Homiletics, Early Christian Fathers.

This formidable programme contained the elements of medieval university courses and classical studies, tempered with mathematics and science, as well as the vocational studies of the scriptures and the church, and the skills of religious ministry. In 1860 the College raised the money to erect its own building at a cost of £6,521, just north of Mutley Plain, moving in, in 1861, with 23 students.[39] A conference in Plymouth that year saw Western College maintaining links with similar institutions in other parts of the country.

But it was in 1891 that the seeds were sown for the final migration of Western College to Bristol, when the Bristol Congregational Institute merged.[40] The same year the standard course of study was extended to six years. Much of the syllabus noted above was retained, but the course now included the very modern subject of Psychology and also Philosophy. No doubt this change was related to the establishment by the University of London of a Faculty of Divinity, which allowed Western College students, in addition to the arts examinations, to sit as external candidates the intermediate and final examinations for the Bachelor of Divinity degree. This was an award normally considered a second degree. From 1897 higher academic study for the award of Associate of Senatus Academicus, something like a taught masters' degree, became possible.

2.26 Sherwell Congregational Chapel was closely associated with Western College which trained Congregational ministers. The Chapel, converted to lecture theatres, now belongs to the University of Plymouth.

[PCL-LS, Ancient Order of Foresters, High Court, Guide to Plymouth (1900), 118]

The move to Bristol finally took place in 1901. Bristol was now seen as more central than Plymouth (communications were much easier by then); there was a much stronger Congregational community there as well as the fact that Bristol had previously had its own college; there were links with the Baptist college there. But perhaps a more telling reason was the existence of an established university college (opened in 1876) running arts courses, with which links were rapidly developed. Prior to the move Western College was no larger than previously, numbering nineteen students in 1899.[41] Although it had been in its own buildings since 1861, there was a strong link with the Sherwell Congregational chapel in North Hill. For the last annual meeting in Plymouth, 25 June 1901, lunch was taken in the Sherwell school room and the anniversary sermon was preached at a service in Sherwell Chapel. Co-incidentally, this is now part of the University of Plymouth, having been converted into a lecture theatre facility now called the Sherwell Centre. Western College had moved into new buildings in Bristol by 1906, and survived for a further sixty years until closure came in the mid-1960s.

The Marine Biological Association

Another specialised institution, concerned with advanced scientific research, came to Plymouth in 1885, the Marine Biological Association of the United Kingdom (MBA), which soon developed a world class reputation for its work and publications. As the Plymouth Marine Laboratory, it still

2.27 The laboratories of the Marine Biological Association of the United Kingdom on Plymouth Hoe, with the wall of the Citadel behind. The building opened in 1888.

[PCL-LS, Co-operative Handbook, op.cit., 28, Mercantile Assn.]

occupies premises erected under the walls of Plymouth Citadel, on the Hoe. The background to the formation of the MBA lay in fears about the over-exploitation the fish stock reported by the Select Committee on Sea Fisheries in 1866, and the growing interest in the sea and sea products, stimulated in particular by the Challenger Expedition, 1872-1876. However the formation of the MBA was a direct outcome of the World Fisheries Exhibition in 1883. The event, which included a conference, was attended by many of the leading scientists of the day, who reiterated the concern about declining fish stocks and over fishing. In particular, Professor E. Ray Lankester pressed for a society to study marine life.[42] This was not the only marine biological initiative in that period; for example, it was introduced as a subject in the university college at Liverpool.

The group of leading scientists came together again in March 1884 at the Royal Society in London and formed the MBA which would set about the task of rectifying the dearth of knowledge about fish and their behaviour. Lankester undoubtedly played a leading role in the foundation and early years during which the Association was developing. From the start the members envisaged a laboratory at a suitable coastal location with tank rooms for live fish, the associated apparatus, laboratory accommodation, a resident director and assistants, the publication of a scientific journal and a research library. A key feature was to be the provision of facilities for

2.28, 2.29 A fish tank room and one of the laboratories of the MBA in 1900.

[PCL-LS, Doidge's Annual, 1900]

members making research visits. At a meeting in May, which considered the merits of locations including Plymouth, Weymouth and Bangor, the offer of a site on Plymouth Hoe by the Borough Council of Plymouth appears to have enabled a speedy decision to be reached. It is likely that the leading Plymouth marine scientist, C. Spence Bate, played an important role in achieving the selection of Plymouth for the site of the marine laboratory. However, a substantial donation towards building costs, by the Plymouth merchants John and Robert Bayly, who were involved in operating Sutton Harbour, must also have weighed heavily.

Building, equipping and staffing the laboratory required significant financial investment which could hardly be met through membership subscriptions. The more affluent scientists made donations and substantial sums were raised from organisations such as the Fishmongers Company (a City of London livery company) and the universities. But no doubt what determined speedy progress was a major grant by the Government, increasingly concerned with international fisheries management, of £5,000 supported by an annual operational grant of £500 for the first five years. By April 1885, Spence Bate was writing to the *Western Daily Mercury* reporting that problems with the War Office, who controlled Plymouth Citadel, had been overcome, that the general public would benefit from the building of new roads which would enable people to drive round the Citadel from the Barbican, and that they would in due course be able to visit the marine aquarium at the new Laboratory.[43]

By 1887 a temporary Laboratory had been opened and building work had started. The permanent Laboratory opened in 1888.[44] An appeal for books and periodicals, often repeated in the years to 1914, had led to some generous donations and a start had been made in creating the library. The first issue of

2.30 A lecture programme organised by the local university extension Students' Association which played an important role in sustaining advanced educational activity in the Three Towns in the 1880s and 1890s. Merrifield was a leading local academic scientist.

[PCL-LS, Merrifield file]

what was to become a most prestigious scientific journal, the *Journal of the Marine Biological Association of the United Kingdom*, appeared in August 1887. One of the disadvantages of the estuarine site, the variable quality of the sea water which had to be circulated to the fish tanks, was to cause problems for a good many years, but this was outweighed by the other aspects of the general location which included the large harbour of Plymouth Sound, the resident fishing industry, easy access to the waters of the English Channel and safe inner harbours for the laboratory research ships. The first of these, the *Busy Bee*, a 60 ft. steam boat was acquired in 1896. This was replaced by a large yacht in 1901 to be used for deep water operation. Since then there has been a succession of research vessels.

Established from the start with government money, the MBA laboratory may be seen as part of a network of state scientific research laboratories, which worked on state funded projects as well as facilitating the marine research of MBA members and visiting scientists. For example, in 1899 it was contracted by the Government to undertake the English share of an international investigation of the fisheries of the English Channel and North Sea. A local educational contribution was made by the resident staff through the delivery of lectures on marine life at numerous locations in the South West, and participation in the programmes of the Plymouth Institution and Devonshire Association. With the development of scientific research at Plymouth Polytechnic from the 1970s, the MBA has collaborated in both joint research programmes and marine science teaching in Plymouth, more than justifying the local initiative of the 1880s in securing the laboratory for Plymouth.

University Extension

Lewis identifies three phases of university extension activity in the Three Towns, noting the difficulty encountered in trying to sustain separate university extension centres for Pymouth and Devonport, and the debate on whether any centre should have a presence also in Devon and Cornwall or just in the Three Towns.[45] The response in 1875/76 was essentially middle class, with a significant proportion of teachers following the lecture courses offered. The lecture series in Plymouth on English History attracted 150 for the lecture course, 70 for the follow-up class and 44 who submitted written work. The same course in Devonport attracted 42 for the lectures, with 20 for the class and 14 scripts. The Course in Political Economy, supposedly of interest to working men, attracted 100 at the lectures in Plymouth, but only 30 in Devonport. After the initial interest support for a further series fell to 36 and the experiment was discontinued. A further attempt in 1886 started slowly, but stabilised with the formation of a University Extension Students Association designed to encourage interest in the movement and provide mutual support between lectures and classes. This complemented the Three Towns University Extension Society (1887) which undertook the organisation. From 1888 it entered a four year affiliation with the University of Cambridge for University Extension provision. The lectures in 1888/9 attracted 350 people, the classes 150 and 49 candidates attempted the examination. The subjects offered included History, Literature and General Science. Again numbers were not sustained and failing to become self sufficient, the Society was in financial difficulties by 1894. However there was some revival in subsequent years, and by 1904 Plymouth Council was subsidising the attendance of teachers. Finally in 1911 Plymouth Education Committee assumed financial responsibility, when numbers at lectures averaged 204.

Royal Naval Educational Establishments

Naval dockyard ports such as Devonport, had long served as base ports for sections of the fleet offering supply and manning services as well as building and re-fitting naval vessels. They were also natural locations for the education and training of both naval and dockyard manpower once it had been accepted that something more structured than on-the-job training was needed for all levels of manning, in the 1840s and 1850s. So the Three Towns became an important centre, with a number of naval training ships and shore establishments, some of which survive to the present day. Redundant naval ships were widely used as static training ships, and were a familiar sight in the Hamoaze well into the twentieth century. The names allocated to the ships, once assigned to their training role were familiar to generations of local people: *Implacable* (boys from 1855), *Fisgard* (artificers from 1870), *Indus* (stokers from 1890), *Cambridge* and *Lion* (gunnery from 1907), *Defiance* (training from 1920), *Raleigh* and *Drake*.[46] Except in minor ways these did not interact with the local tertiary educational scene and will not be discussed here. The Royal Dockyard School and later the Royal Naval Engineering College impinged on or interacted with local provision, and so will be explored in more detail.

Apart from one or two small private schools offering preparation for the lieutenant's examination in the Royal Navy, the earliest establishment in the Three Towns founded with technical education as its core activity was the school for apprentices, opened in Devonport Dockyard in 1844. Its existence, of course, had nothing to do with any local thinking on the need for an educational stratum concerned with technical or vocational education, but rather with the needs of the Royal Navy for suitably educated and trained personnel in its various dockyards. These were undergoing rapid expansion and re-development with the coming of steam propulsion and iron hulls, and the number of naval dockyards was increasing around the world as British domination of the world's seas approached their maximum extent. Dockyard apprenticeships were the established means by which the bulk of the technically skilled workforce was kept up to strength and in earlier periods these had been restricted to relations of existing dockyard or naval personnel. The introduction of a system of promotion by merit demanded a means of evaluation and this needed to start with the selection of prospective apprentices. A school master in each of the main naval yards was now required to examine and rank apprentices, and the provision of classes to be undertaken by apprentices on a release basis was made part of the process.[47]

Photo by R. Murray White

2.31 From the 1850s the Royal Navy provided training for officers and ratings aboard the hulks of ships no longer required for active service. By the early twentieth century when this picture was taken, some of the technical teaching was of quite an advanced standard.

[PCL-LS, The Book of Plymouth; photo: R. Murray White]

The involvement of the Navy in education was not new. Its larger ships had long carried school masters and as early as 1729 it had established the Royal Naval Academy at Portsmouth. The Navy was also responsible for the Royal Naval Schools at Greenwich (for the children of naval personnel). The 1840s was a period of educational remodelling and experimentation, during which the reorganisation of elementary education and teacher training was taking place and in which schools at Greenwich were reformed and the education of naval officers was in a state of flux. With two important early schools inspectors, Revd. H. Moseley and Revd. Dr. J Woolley, who were actively involved in those reforms, appointed to inspect the dockyard schools, this new development was in line with national educational thinking. An Order in Council of 1 February 1843 authorised the creation of the schools, though that at Chatham had been formed in 1842, and was followed by that at Portsmouth in 1843. The dockyard school at Deptford came in 1847.[48] The training scheme not only provided instruction and assessment during the apprenticeship, but also provided a ladder for the most able students to progress to the Central School of Mathematics and Naval Construction at Portsmouth (1847), the Royal School of Naval Architecture (1864) (South Kensington), of which C.W. Merrifield from Tavistock became head, and to the Royal Naval College (RNC) at Greenwich (1873), with which the Royal School of Naval Architecture was integrated. One Devonport apprentice, subsequently Sir William White, climbed the ladder to become Professor of Naval Architecture at RNC Greenwich, and later Director of Naval Construction.[49]

The Dockyard School at Plymouth of course operated under the standard regulatory framework laid down centrally for all the schools. In the early years these changed frequently as both the outside world and those working in the dockyards adjusted to the new system. Several schools in the Three Towns recognised that the attractiveness of Dockyard careers and the standard of the entrance examination provided opportunities for the provision of special classes for their older pupils in preparation for attempting the entrance examination. That was to become the standard route into technical employment for generations of young men from the area. Under new regulations promulgated in 1860 the Dockyard entrance examination covered handwriting, orthography, reading arithmetic, grammar, English composition, geography and mathematics (geometry and algebra).[50] The main focus of the studies apprentices undertook was the work of the shipwright, but once enrolled they faced quite a broadly based syllabus which included religious instruction, reading, spelling, history, geography, arithmetic, algebra, geometry, mensuration, mechanics, hydrostatics, and chemistry. This early programme no doubt reflects the culture of the period and certainly appears to start where elementary education left off.

2.32 The industrial training ship 'Mount Edgcumbe', 1877-1921, formerly H.M.S. 'Winchester', provided a sealife training for youths, most of whom had been sent under court orders. The educational standard was elementary except for a few boys capable of learning navigation.

[Author's collection; photo Mrs F. Parcelle]

Teachers were typically drawn from and augmented by dockyard staff, and for many years only two were full-time. However, by 1875 the head's salary was in the range £300 to £400 which compared very well with the salaries enjoyed by the captain-superintendents of the civilian static training ships, such as the industrial TS *Mount Edgcumbe*, moored off Saltash from 1877.[51] Depending on the stage reached in their apprenticeship, students attended the school for up to three evenings each week, averaging about thirteen hours of study, though pressure of work in the yard made this very variable.[52] Of course throughout they were getting the practical training in the yard and keeping dockyard hours of work. This typifies the level of investment in combined education and practice which anyone wishing to make progress in technical and technological careers had to make well into the twentieth century.

Another scheme, for engineering students, was offered at the Royal Dockyards from 1863, related to the creation of the Engineering Branch of the Navy (1836). A more testing entrance examination than for the apprentices involved, arithmetic, orthography, handwriting, reading grammar, English composition, geography, French to English translation and Euclid. Then came six years in the dockyard experiencing the main departments and attending the school two afternoons and two evenings per week, studying naval architecture, marine engineering, plane trigonometry, hydrostatics, mechanics and properties of steam, again with the opportunity of progression to college in London. A special new college building was opened at Keyham in 1880, catering for 100 students.[53] Naval engineering students were also being taught at Portsmouth, but from 1888 all the Navy's future engineering officers received their technical education and training at Keyham, for which the new laboratories were built and the existing building modified. Such was the genesis of the Royal Naval Engineering College

Royal Naval Engineering College.

[Heath, Photo.

2.33 This building for the Royal Naval Engineering College, sometimes thought of as the Navy's engineering university, was completed in 1880. It was closed in 1958 when the College completed its relocation to the Manadon campus.

[PCL-LS, Co- operative Handbook, op.cit, 113]

(RNEC), a title in use by 1903. Some of the work was of university standard and the establishment was sometimes referred to as the Navy's university. In 1880 the dockyard school had been divided with the lower section handling less advanced work in its original rooms where it was to remain, the higher section being concerned with the engineering students and the best apprentices. Reforms in 1905 advanced the syllabus at Keyham to include mechanics, strength of materials, and electricity, and it began to be thought of as achieving university standards. However the reforms in naval training under the Selborne scheme led to closure in 1910, though the Keyham building was used from 1914 for training cadets for seagoing ships.[54] The RNEC would be resurrected in the inter-war years, from 1938 with additional facilities at Manadon, Keyham finally being closed in 1958. Later in the century RNEC Manadon would interact with the Polytechnic and University at Plymouth.

Classes Under the Department of Science and Art

Because of the methods by which the Department of Science and Art (DSA) aided local classes, including a willingness to recognise more than one organising committee in the same locality, because it funded individual teaching rather than whole schools, and because individual classes could lead unstable existences, it is not easy to identify reliable starting dates or clear continuity for this sector of education, which in the Three Towns was eventually to come together in the municipal technical colleges. The sub-division of the DSA into separate sections dealing with Art and Science, having somewhat differing approaches, also plays a part in complicating the local scene, though perhaps its most lasting effect may be the existence in some towns at the end of the twentieth century, notably in Plymouth, of art colleges, separate from the multi-disciplinary local colleges of further and higher education.

2.34 When Devonport's Science, Art and Technical School was erected in 1898, its School of Art was provided with its own entrance

[photo: A. Kennerley]

The tenuous nature of the links in the 1850s is acknowledged in the DSA annual reports, which go into great detail, through the use of phrases such as "Local Schools of Art in Action on 30 June 1856". Lewis notes some aid for art equipment being granted by the DSA to the Royal Naval and Military School in Devonport in 1852, and expressions of interest in Plymouth in 1853.[55] But from the 1856 list of art schools we learn that the Plymouth School of Art was established in 1856, and had enrolled 297 students who paid fees of £135 3s. 9d. The 1856 report also says there were three schools giving two lessons per week in addition naming the Charles National School, St. James National School and the Royal Naval and Military School, illustrating the practice of supporting classes in elementary and secondary schools as well as in a dedicated "school", but failing to give any indication of the level of work. That adults attended and that some teacher education was involved, is clear from the report that 21 school masters, school mistresses and pupil teachers had been in attendance. Science and Art teachers, with their qualifications, are also named, together with the chairman and secretary of the local management committee.[56] The local art management committee had been formed by the spring of 1855 for Plymouth, which appears reasonably representative of local commercial, professional and artistic interest. The 23 members included three artists, a lithographer, two architects, two clergy, two solicitors, an admiral, a colonel, two gentlemen, a stockbroker, a draper, a coal merchant. The president was the member of parliament for Plymouth, R.P. Collier; vice president W. Eastlake, an artist, the secretary G. Jago, master of the free school.[57] The latter would have done the real work and must have functioned effectively as unpaid principal. The art subjects offered at that time included freehand drawing, practical geometry, model drawing, elementary colouring and shading, drawing and painting landscapes, figures, artistic anatomy, modelling, architect and mechanical drawing.

2.35 For a time at the end of the nineteenth century Plymouth School of Art was using the former Mathematical and Classical School building in Princess Square.

[PCL-LS, Foresters' Guide, op.cit.,79]

The Devonport School of Art was a new school with 53 students in 1858, offering simply drawing and painting. Held in the Mechanics' Institute, numbers in 1859 were 857, of whom 788 were children and 57 school and pupil teachers. In 1862 the 1278 pupils included 55 teachers. However, although art classes at two Plymouth schools continued, the Plymouth School of Art of 1856 seems to have failed as it was not listed after 1857. However, a Devonport and Plymouth School of Art under a unified management apparently existed from 1859 for a number of years. In 1867 Plymouth and Devonport Schools of Art were separated, with Plymouth dropping out of the listing the following year, and Devonport disappearing from 1871, though apparently art classes continued in a few schools. Fresh starts with schools of art were made in Plymouth in 1875 and Devonport in

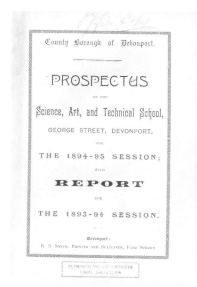

County Borough of Debonport.

PROSPECTUS

OF THE

Science, Art, and Technical School,

GEORGE STREET, DEVONPORT,

FOR

THE 1894-95 SESSION;

WITH

REPORT

FOR

THE 1893-94 SESSION.

Devonport:
R. S. SMITH, PRINTER AND STATIONER, FORE STREET.

2.36 This prospectus shows the unification of Science and Art teaching in Devonport under the local authority following the County Councils Act, 1888, with classes based temporarily in George Street, while planning the new building was taking place

[PCL-LS]

CHARLES S. JAGO.
Headmaster 1885   1908;   Died 1915.

2.37 Charles Jago, Headmaster of the Plymouth Public School, played an important role in managing Science and Art classes and in planning Plymouth technical schools building.

[PCL-LS, C.W. Bracken, A History of the Plymouth Public School (Plymouth, Underhill, 1927) 46]

1876 under the leadership of H.R. Babb at both locations. From 1887 a School of Science and Art appears in the DSA directories, perhaps anticipating the plans to erect a central building in Plymouth. This was still in existence in 1898 despite the opening of Plymouth's technical college building in 1892. Devonport's School of Art finally came to rest in the new technical college building opened in 1898.[58] What seems clear is that art teaching supported by the DSA existed in the area by 1856, but that schools of art for adults were of a transient nature until the mid 1870s from which time there was continuity and that they came to occupy rooms in the technical college buildings in the 1890s.

Apart from the Plymouth School of Navigation (chapter 4), which has an acknowledged continuity from 1862, science classes under the DSA did not become properly established until the early 1870s, when the term Science and Art School first appears in the DSA directories. However, the DSA provided the necessary encouragement through its travelling 'Organizing Teacher' , who held meetings in Plymouth in October 1864, Devonport in April 1865 and again at Plymouth in September 1865. Plymouth formed a provisional committee following the first meeting, but the Devonport meeting in the Mechanics' Institute was "...most meagerly attended, those present being chiefly youths... no one of position expressed himself at all favourable to the scheme."[59] It was only following the third visit to the area, that real action resulted. With a local committee presided over by the Mayor of Plymouth and C. Spence Bate as Chairman, accommodation was rented at the Working Men's Institute (Catherine Street). The subjects offered were practical geometry, mechanical and machine drawing, building construction, elementary mathematics, magnetism and electricity, inorganic chemistry, geology, mineralogy, steam and physical geography. Science and Art examinations were held in May and 46 passes out of 81 candidates in science subjects were achieved at Plymouth. In 1866 acoustics, light and heat, animal physiology and zoology were added to the list of subjects, and there were 142 passes from 162 candidates in the May examinations. The following session the classes moved to a building in Courtney Street, using the name 'Plymouth Science School', and the list of subjects extended by the addition of naval architecture, higher mathematics, theoretical and applied mechanics, systematic botany, navigation and nautical astronomy. Science schools under separate committees were set up by Dr Hearder in 1867 and Mr Evers in 1870. The concentration of the role of secretary of all the science school committees in 1875 in the hands of J.M.H. Cawse brought some sense to the organisational side. Hearder adopted the title Polytechnic School of Science, which appeared in the DSA directory for 1867/8 as Plymouth Polytechnic Institute of Science, a form which was to reappear one hundred years later.

By 1871, science classes had spread to a number of other locations in Plymouth, and Devonport, in 1870, had also introduced classes in science subjects. The author of the articles in *The Western Critic* in 1871 (almost certainly Dr. Merrifield) was enthusiastic about the progress made and looked to a central science and art college:[60]

2.38 The account sent to the Department of Science and Art in 1892, for the costs of building Plymouth's. Jago was secretary to the organising committee.

[Public Record Office, ED 29/31]

"We look upon these (developments) not only as a means of vastly extending technical education, but also of what we consider of more value - viz., the fostering of a love for scientific pursuits. The appreciation of the different science schools in Plymouth is shewn by the number attending the classes...at the last examination, May 1871, no fewer than 586 (papers) were answered, and 426 were passed; and it must be remembered that the pupils examined form but a proportion of those who attend for instruction....We feel certain that the young men of the Three Towns cannot employ their winter evenings more pleasantly or more usefully than by attending classes in the Science Schools; and that they would thus materially benefit themselves and the towns at large by becoming more useful members of society, and more intelligent workmen. The masters [of industry] also would reap the benefits of increased intelligence, because improvements in machinery and methods of manufacture would be more likely to force themselves on the attention of that artizan who could trace the principals employed from their sources, than on the attention of the ignorant workmen; thus a saving of time and material would probably accrue. From the very first the Schools have taken that position in the examinations of which every Plymothian may be proud: still there are objects in which we lag behind. Other towns with not nearly the population or the wealth have buildings appropriated to science teaching; and we think a scheme of such importance to masters and workmen should have a full and fair consideration from the public. Such a building should contain room enough to accommodate a trade school by day, in which every youth should be taught the rudiments of those sciences which bear nearly on his future work. There should be a laboratory and apparatus to elucidate and explain as far as possible all natural phenomena; and teachers from the two counties [Devon and Cornwall] should be allowed to spend their holidays (on a given payment) at this Institution, in order that they may carry back to their own Schools such new ideas as may be obtained from a central establishment. We also have an art school; here again we are behind towns of less importance than our own, and we would suggest that whether on the formation of a free reading Room and Library, the establishment of a Science and Art College worthy of the town in which we live, should not also be taken into consideration by the inhabitants."

This article has been quoted at length as it represents the thinking of those promoting technical education at the time, and because it contains ideas about continuing education which, provisions in the Education Acts of 1918 and 1944 having been still born, only became widespread in the latter part of the twentieth century. No doubt in calling for a municipal technical college in a new building, the author had in mind what had been achieved in Exeter, which had opened its multi-use building in 1868. Science classes became increasingly widespread during the 1870s, with twice the number of locations where art classes were offered. In Devonport classes in science subjects were offered at fifteen locations, while classes in art subjects were

2.39 This view, with the Victoria Science, Art and Technical Schools building in the background, was taken on the occasion of the return of the Devon Volunteers in 1901. It conveys something of the bustle in the streets which students going in and out of the building one hundred years ago would have experienced.

[PCL-LS, illustrations collection, photo: Rugg Monk]

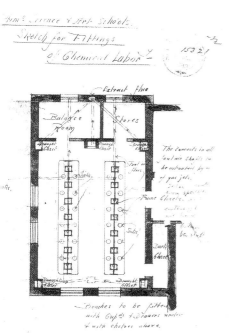

CHEMICAL LABORATORY.

2.40, 2.41 The chemical laboratory on the first floor of the south wing of the Plymouth building made provision for the extraction of the fumes generated during experiments.

[PRO, ED 29/31; PCL-LS, Plymouth Education Directory, 1907/8]

available at six locations. The pattern was similar in Plymouth: sixteen science locations, seven art locations. With the opening of central buildings in the 1890s the numbers of locations for classes declined, the new centres becoming the focus for science and art classes.

Through the detail in the DSA directories Lewis has identified no less than 95 teachers involved in delivering science classes in the Three Towns over the period between 1863 and 1882 when recording that data was discontinued. The numbers of students who enrolled in classes receiving DSA aid are shown in Table 2.1, set against numbers enrolled in art classes.

The science class enrolments for 1863 and 1864 are the enrolments at the Plymouth School of Navigation alone, and are probably for full time attendance for periods of no more than about four weeks, suggesting average

Table 2.1

Students Enrolled in Science and Art Classes in the Three Towns, 1858-1900.

Year	Science	Art	Year	Science	Art	Year	Science	Art
1858		53	1873	1751	706	1887	1435	1305
1859		110	1874	1349	756	1888	1402	1023
1860		104	1875	1754	801	1889	1546	1012
1861			1876	1135	1039	1890	1687	763
1862		188	1877	1207	781	1891	1712	520
1863	240	172	1878	895	688	1892	1695	738
1864	343	118	1879	885	652	1893	1622	1055
1865		194	1880	902	810	1894	1538	1023
1866	520	192	1881	1008	667	1895	1577	837
1867	175	150	1882	964	809	1896	1544	974
1868	538	208	1883	1030	952	1897	1774	967
1869	473	247	1884	1013	855	1898	1536	967
1870	420	289	1885	1080	1052	1899	1925	992
1871	919	367	1886	1147	953	1900	2078	1027
1872	859	404						

Source: Lewis, 217-220, abstracted from DSA reports, 1858-1900.

class sizes of under 20 students. All the other enrolments, which include children as well as adults, are the sums for the year of all the individual classes most of which will only have met for one or two hours per week (day or evening), and thus may by no means be read as full time equivalent data. The totals conceal occasional missing data, and should be taken as indicative rather than absolute. Further, in the case of the Navigation School at least, later returns indicated only students qualifying for DSA payments, and do not include other students studying privately in the same class, or other classes in technical subjects. Thus, excluding classes in the Dockyard School, Table 2.1 certainly understates the numbers studying scientific and technical subjects in the Three Towns in that period.

2.42 Plymouth: the physics laboratory.

[PCL-LS, Plymouth Education Directory, 1907/8]

Central Science, Art and Technical School Buildings

The need for substantial buildings dedicated to local post-school educational provision had long been recognised, but they were not to appear in the Three Towns until the 1890s, by which time a source of central funding had been found in addition to the permissive legislation which allowed the raising of a penny rate in aid of technical education. Both county boroughs formed technical education committees which took over from the *ad hoc* science and art committees, though of course funding could still be obtained through the DSA until it ceased to exist at the end of the century. Its examinations continued for some years in the new century but had been discontinued by the end of the 1914-18 war. Having a central building (Plymouth from 1892, Devonport from 1898), by no means meant that it would be reserved for post school education in science, art and technology. Well into the twentieth

2.43, 2.44 The north wing of the Plymouth building was occupied by the Plymouth School of Art

[PRO, ED 29/31]

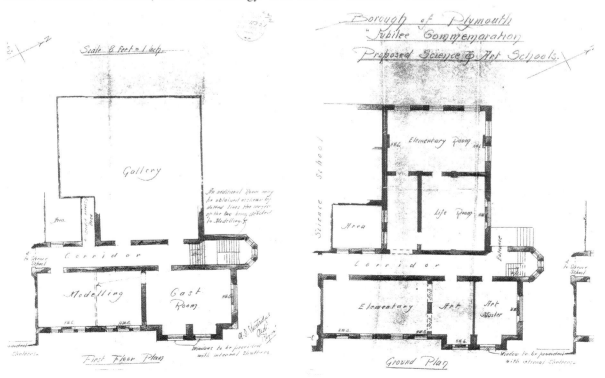

century, there would be relatively little full-time day teaching in technical college buildings. Most of the work took place in the evenings leaving the buildings relatively empty during the day, so it was very tempting for local authorities to usurp accommodation during the day for elementary or secondary schooling, of which they seemed permanently short owing to the expansion of secondary education as well as an increasing population. Multiple use of the buildings was to continue until after the 1939-45 war, by which time it had long been a bone of contention, and possibly a factor in the retarded development of technical education in post 1918 Plymouth.

The Plymouth building was a product of efforts to mark Queen Victoria's 1887 jubilee, and, although not opened until 1892, was the principal local memorial. A Jubilee Memorial Committee had been formed to seek local donations from the public at large and to assess opinion on the most suitable ways of using the money raised. Only small sums were allocated to celebrations on Jubilee Day (feasting and fireworks, children's demonstration), and a donation was made to the Imperial Institute in London. A tender from A.R. Debnam of £4,972 was accepted for building work, but the final bill for the finished building was a little over £6,000. The site, at the old cattle market, had been provided by Plymouth Borough Council which also contributed £500, and a building grant of £1,000 was made by the DSA. The memorial fund contributed £4,306.[61] The building was designed by the Plymouth architect, A.D. Shortridge, and its foundation stone was laid on 30 September 1889. The contemporary description which follows, demonstrates the multiple uses which had to be taken into account (trade, science school, art school and university extension), and the adoption of the latest in educational technology.[62]

The main building is 140 feet long by 80 feet broad and consists of three storeys....The sub-ground floor is devoted entirely to workshops, for plumbers, engineers, carpenters, etc., and the somewhat rough work performed here in no way interferes with the students of science and art in their gentler occupations above...the concrete floors. The lower regions also contain the boiler house, the source of an elaborate scheme of water heating....Students and visitors enter from Tavistock-road by a flight of steps leading to a fine hall, floored with geometrical tiles. Passing the glass doors one faces a staircase of generous proportions and hansom design. It is built entirely of Portland stone, balustrading, handrail, steps, and all. Above is a stained glass window, with the borough arms. Close to the entrance are a waiting-room and the secretary's office....Next comes the Committee-room...which is used as a students' room, museum, and general library...A class room and master's room are close by. On the other side of the corridor are the machine and building construction and machine drawing rooms...The lecture theatre is a room measuring 32 feet by 30. Near it is the physics and chemistry lecture preparation room, 30 feet by 11. There is a second staircase at the north end of the building. Returning along the corridor, and passing the hall, one arrives at the physics class room, 24 feet by 17, completing the apartments on the first floor. The chemical laboratory is reached by ascending the main staircase. With its spurs, the laboratory measures 48 feet by 24. These spurs are being used as master's room, balance room, etc. Next on the east front is the chemistry classroom, 31 feet by 30. Passing it we come to the first of the art rooms proper. It is 32 feet by 18, and is being used for modelling, while next door is a room for the study of life subjects and the antique. This is 26 feet by 21. The best room in the house is that which was to be called the Art Gallery, but is being used as an elementary art room and a room for general assembly purposes. It is lofty and light, and there is an arched appanage, where the students store their models, drawing boards and so forth. The room is used for meetings, one of the most interesting gatherings that regularly take place, being the weekly assembly of the Cambridge University Extension Society, to hear Mr Callendar's and other people's lectures on

ANTIQUE ROOM.

MODELLING ROOM.

2.45, 2.46 Students in class at the Plymouth School of Art.

[PCL-LS, Plymouth Education Directory, 1911/12]

science. The building was first occupied by a public audience on the occasion of the opening lecture of the Society's Autumnal Session of 1892 on September 26th.

...Every classroom is fitted with sliding blackboards, but the perfection of this form of appliance is to be found in the lecture theatre. There the boards are very large...they are constructed with traps in the floor, so that they will slide down until the tops are level with his [the lecturer's] arm. In this theatre there is a sloping gallery for the students, and two sets of hot water pipes are provided. Underneath is the diagram room, and another trap door, with a winding arrangement, permits of any diagram or plan the professor may require for the purpose of demonstration being lifted into the room and exhibited on a frame...the lime-light lantern has come into vogue as an aid to education...it is very popular, and a good deal of the illustrations of lessons at the new School will be accomplished by its aid. For a lantern lesson, and for some chemical experiments, absolute darkness is required. This can be obtained in the lecture theatre, by an arrangement of black American cloth screens on frames, which by rope and pulley can be drawn over the skylight, and the result is night. In the wall, facing the students, and communicating with the laboratory, is a fume closet with a shaft to carry off the noxious gasses engendered...Gas and water jets are provided at the lecturer's table... At intervals, on the wall, there are small patches of a substance known as black graphikos...quite ready to receive the mark of chalk or pencil. By means of these a lecturer or teacher can move about among his pupils and impart lessons, or make demonstrations to them in little groups. In the plumbers' shop...the Worshipful Company of Plumbers, have placed some coloured windows, representing their insignia... the progress made in sanitary science...has been so great that the committee of the Schools have done well to give it a good place. There are many of the appliances necessary to its study to be found here. The carpenters' shop is spacious, with several rows of well furnished benches, fitted all with patent vices." Growing pressure on accommodation, owing to additions to the range of subjects, led to an extension of the building in 1903 at a cost of £10,000.

Devonport had to wait until 1899 for its permanent central technical college building to be completed. From the time its Technical Instruction

2.47 An architect's impression of the Devonport Science, Art and Technical Schools building; it foundation stone was laid on Jubilee Day 1897, being the 60th anniversary of Queen Victoria's accession to the throne.

[PCL-LS, illustrations collection, Henry J.Snell]

2.48 The noise from this engineering workshop in the basement of the Plymouth building, must have interfered with the classes above. The unguarded belt drives to the lathes were typical of factories well into the twentieth century.

[PCL-LS, Plymouth Education Directory, 1911/12]

METAL-WORK SHOP

Committee was constituted in 1892, to take advantage of the provisions of acts impinging on technical education (1889-91), Devonport was searching for a suitable site.[63] Classes were brought together in temporary accommodation at 38 George Street, Devonport, where the sixteen teachers taught in eight classrooms. Eventually land was purchased from the War Department near the King's Road station. An authorised loan of £14,000 enabled work to start 1897 on the building which was to be a commemoration of Queen Victoria's sixty years on the throne. Meanwhile, by 1894, the Technical Education Committee had grouped post-school classes into four divisions, science, art, commercial, and technical. Most classes were offered by the science division: geometry, machine construction and drawing, building construction, naval architecture, mathematics, steam, theoretical mechanics (solids and fluids) applied mechanics, sound, light and heat, magnetism and electricity, inorganic chemistry, metallurgy, navigation and nautical astronomy. Most subjects were offered at elementary and advanced levels, and were delivered in the evenings by a team of eleven lecturers. Mr Babb was the sole art lecturer offering the range of art subjects noted earlier. The commercial division, with two teachers, covered commercial correspondence and book keeping, arithmetic and mensuration, shorthand and typewriting. The technical devision, offering trade instruction, had classes in theoretical and practical plumbing, sanitary science, mechanical engineering, theoretical and practical dressmaking. All except one of the art classes were held in the evening starting no earlier than 7 pm, no doubt to allow time for working men to change and eat before taking a class. This pattern, with one or two extra subjects was maintained until 1914, but the Technical Instruction Commitee was absorbed into the Borough's Higher Education Committee following the 1902 Education Act, and technical education became submerged in the Committee's responsibilities for secondary education.

A snapshot of early technical college work was provided by two reports of H.M inspectors of schools on work in the Plymouth building, one for evening work, the other for day work. The separate reports emphasise the multiple usage, as the Board of Education treated the educational activity as separate entities, school No. 21233 being the evening school and school No.80800 being the day. Of the evening school the report comments that there was no commercial work, which was provided elsewhere, and that it was mainly devoted to technological work connected with engineering and constructive work.[64] There were science courses for the examinations of London University, useful for science teachers in secondary schools, and for the Board of Education examinations for the Elementary Teachers' certificate. There was also teacher training for the City and Guilds of London Institute Teachers' diplomas in woodwork and metal work. In addition there was a group of students for domestic work. The inspectors were complementary about provision for grouped courses in engineering and shipbuilding, though the classes were small (Table 2.2).

2.49 *This view was taken looking down Tavistock Road towards the town centre on 20 May 1918, but the scene was little different from that 25 years earlier. The Plymouth technical schools building is on the right of the street in the distance.*

[*Plymouth City Museum, photo: Rugg Monk*]

Table 2.2

Enrolments in Evening Engineering and Building Trades Courses Examinations of the University of London and Teachers Courses at Plymouth Municipal Technical College, 1911.

Class	First year	Second Year	Third year	Fourth year
Engine Fitters	9	1	4	4
Metalworkers		32	10	1
Civil engineers	1		3	
Electric fitters	2	2	6	1
Electric wiremen	10	3		
Shipwrights	3	4	3	5
Architects	5	4	5	5
Plumbers		4	4	3
Carpenters		10	5	4
Masons and Bricklayers	1			1
London U. Exam Courses	9	5	4	5
Teachers' Cert. Course	15	13		
Woodwork diploma	2	6		
Metalwork diploma		1		

Source: PRO, ED 114/113, HMI report, 1911

There were additional students taking isolated subjects. Naval architecture and mechanical engineering subjects were taught by dockyard employees, but there was a full time teacher of electrical engineering subjects. The electrical engineering laboratory was well used but the mechanical engineering laboratory ought to be used more. Weaknesses were noted in machine drawing teaching and equipment, but there was a keen teacher of naval architecture for which there were only 22 students across four stages. A fair amount of home work was set to all classes, and with terminal examinations, the work was judged generally efficient. Grouped courses for architects and building trades were also found satisfactory, though the third and fourth year of the architects course was in the art school; nevertheless the students were in a good position to specialise for the Royal

2.50 A little higher up Tavistock Road, this view, dating from the 1890s, shows several properties now used by the University of Plymouth: Sherwell Chapel on the left with Drake's Place gardens just above, and Queen Anne's terrace on the right.

[PCL-LS, illustrations collection]

Institution of British Architects (RIBA) diploma. There were nine students in the University of London matriculation class, nine working for the intermediate examination and five for the final examination. But the HMIs were worried about the long three and half hour Saturday morning session, where they thought a break was needed. Separating course from non-course students, there were 221 taking courses (155 on technological courses, 60 on university or teachers courses, and 6 on a course for pharmacists); non-course students totalled 218, of whom 73 were enrolled for domestic work. Clearly in that period, the idea that one should study a group of subjects forming a course rather than individual subjects, was gaining momentum.

The day school provided three courses of instruction in engineering, general science and biology, the last associated with preparation for medical, dental studies and pharmaceutical studies.[65] There were 33 students in attendance, 29 male and 4 female, who had the use of the laboratories already mentioned, and special rooms for physiology and biology and a greenhouse with experimental plots in one of the public parks. However it seems that students were drawn from various secondary schools and that the studies undertaken were mainly in preparation for university matriculation examinations and other qualifying examinations. The Engineering Course, ranging over subjects already noted, with twelve boys, did not impress the inspectors, but they concluded that demand for those studies was negligible. The General Science Course extending over four years (seventeen students in total), was most useful for those planning to become science teachers. The subjects included mathematics, physics, chemistry and botany, with some English and French. There were only three students taking the two-year Biological Course which offered preliminary preparation for medical and dental studies. The various courses were clearly full-time, but it is difficult to judge the level in modern terms.

2.51 Taken looking up Tavistock Road from the north corner of the Plymouth technical school building (at the junction with Glanville Street), this view shows the housing which was demolished in 1908 to make way for Plymouth's museum. art gallery and public library (completed in 1910) .

[Plymouth City Museum, photo: Rugg Monk]

Drake's Reservoir, Tavistock Road.

[Heath, Photo.

Conclusion

In many respects the manner in which post-school education developed in the Three Towns reflects developments across the country. As elsewhere, apart from the better-off sections of the population who could afford private schooling to university entrance standards, educational attainment was variable. Certainly a small proportion of the local population did get to university, relying of course on parental support. Only at the end of the century would compulsory elementary education provide a ladder of opportunity for more able young people to progress to higher studies.

Throughout the century there were growing opportunities for adults to progress their education at various levels from basic literacy to university level studies. Provision for working people was widespread and vibrant after mid-century, if fragmented and ephemeral. Access to reading material through reading rooms and libraries was well abreast of developments elsewhere, and the Three Towns had examples of literary and philosophical societies and mechanics' institutes relatively early. However, it seems that duplication of these societies within a small geographical area, may not always have been the best solution. Support for new initiatives was often ample at the beginning but soon waned so that weaker organisations passed away after a few years. While the mechanics' institutes in the area did run educational classes they seemed not to have achieved the levels of success reached in other towns. Though part of the evolution of scientific and

2.52 Drake's Place Gardens and Reservoir in 1910 when the reservoir was open to the general public.

[PCL-LS, Co-operative Handbook, op.cit., photo: Heath]

technical education, they did not in the Three Towns lead directly into the technical colleges at the end of the century.

It was the Science and Art classes promoted by the Department of Science and Art at South Kensington which were really ancestors of the municipal technical colleges in Plymouth and Devonport, and progress here came later than in other towns. Only in the 1870s may it be said to have taken a hold. University Extension likewise had a difficult beginning, though eventually it came together with the Science and Art work in the technical colleges under the local education authorities. The areas of advanced education and academic research which came to Plymouth, Western College and the Marine Biological Association laboratory, did so for reasons disassociated from national trends. One proved small and ephemeral, but the other has lived on to become an international force working in collaboration with the modern University of Plymouth.

2.53 "Plymouth Education Authority: diagram showing an arrangement of the Local Co-ordination of Schools (Day Instruction)"

[PCL-LS, Plymouth Education Directory, 1907/8]

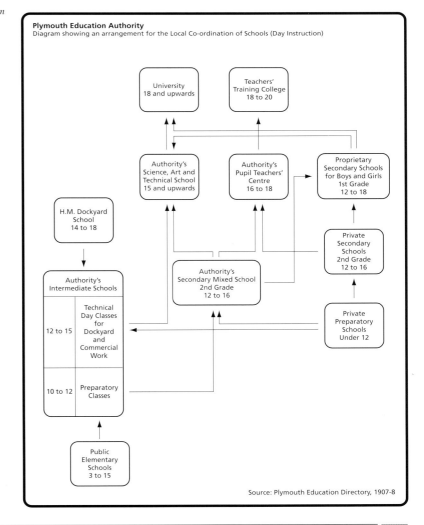

Plymouth Education Authority
Diagram showing an arrangement for the Local Co-ordination of Schools (Day Instruction)

Source: Plymouth Education Directory, 1907-8

3.1 Plymouth Borough/City Council was the responsible authority for tertiary education in Plymouth until 1974. The motto translates 'The strongest tower is the name God'.[1]

[Plymouth City Council]

Technical Education in Plymouth, 1914-1970

CHAPTER THREE

Although Plymouth had yet to be elevated to the status of a city, from 1914, with the unification of the Three Towns into a single county borough, there was now one local education authority for public education in the area. Undoubtedly the rationalisation was necessary as far as tertiary education provision was concerned, and perhaps it was necessary with respect to relations with the military authorities in time of war, but the timing could hardly have been ideal given the disruption which being at war caused to all walks of life, not least to the management and delivery of an education service. Indeed, although slow progress was to be made with the development of technical education and Plymouth's involvement with university level studies was on the agenda for much of the time, the period embracing two world wars and a lengthy and deep depression was not conducive to the evolution of a clear and well organised tertiary sector in the new Plymouth. The two centres for science, art and technical education, though nominally unified, appear to have functioned almost as separate entities for far too long. Very little redevelopment took place, and expansion was handled through the use of inadequate, temporary premises scattered

3.2 This aerial view of the area between Coburg Street, North Road and Tavistock Road in the 1930s clearly illustrates the density of housing in what in the future would be designated as Plymouth's educational and cultural zone. Prominent in the centre is the Public Secondary School's then new building (1925). To its right is the Plymouth building of the Technical College whose roof reveals scale of the extensions added in 1897. In the top right hand corner of the picture is Portland Square, where the residential nautical college would be built in the 1960s.

[Sutton Harbour Company]

across the Borough. Where development plans were made, they were interactive with other changes in school provision; results were invariably delayed and were often overtaken by changing circumstances.

Effectively, the buildings of the 1890s had to serve the needs of Plymouth past mid-century, and the lack of clarity in the structure of tertiary education provision persisted. Perhaps this was inevitable given the central role of the Education Committee of Plymouth Borough Council in finance and management. In a sense the unification of the various independent committees of the previous century in the single authority was a swing of the pendulum from one extreme to the other. In management terms the authority's various educational establishments were not separate entities. Tertiary education was administered almost in the same breath as elementary and secondary levels. The 'schools' had no separate existence, they had no separate constitution and indeed were devoid of any separate administrative provision. As late as 1965 when the author was appointed to Plymouth College of Technology, candidates were interviewed by the Education Committee with the College Principal and Head of Department in attendance as advisers. Tertiary provision was no more than a sub-set of a large, amorphous educational organisation controlled by the Education Committee and managed by the officials in the Council's Education Department. As a single organisation the resources available could be moved relatively easily from one area to another as current pressures might demand. So the sharing of technical college buildings with secondary schooling could persist, and what might in some contexts be seen as separate elements of tertiary education might be treated as one when it suited the authority, as happened in the 1930s when a single principal was appointed to the technical and art schools.

So it is inevitable in examining post-school educational provision in Plymouth in the first half of the twentieth century that the discussion ranges across areas of activity in the local area beyond what would eventually be absorbed into the University of Plymouth. With some understanding of the state of technical education provision in Plymouth over this period, it will then be appropriate to address the long drawn out, and eventually unsuccessful interaction of Plymouth with the University College of the South West of England (UCSWE) at Exeter, involving Plymouth's aspiration for technology and commercial faculties as precursors to having its own university.

Plymouth and Devonport Technical Schools between the wars

While the logic of bringing public educational provision in the Three Towns under one authority may have been irrefutable and anticipated, the merger would inevitably have led to considerable anxieties amongst those most directly concerned, the employees of the previous authorities in Plymouth, Stonehouse and Devonport. In the education service the main groupings affected would have been the teachers in the various levels of schooling and the educational administrative and management staff in the council offices. There has been ample experience of such critical changes affecting modern further and higher education in the latter part of the twentieth century with the designation of Plymouth Polytechnic in 1970, the transfer of education management from Plymouth to Devon in 1974, and the creation of the multi-site Polytechnic in 1988/89. In 1914 education employees would have had to wait for the election of the Council for the new Borough of Plymouth and the nomination of the Borough's new Education Committee. No doubt a fair amount of preparation was undertaken in advance, but only when the new authority was in being could the work of

3.3 This picture covers the eastern section of Plymouth's future educational and cultural zone. At centre bottom is the Technical College building and opposite it the Museum, Art Gallery and Public Library. In the 1990s the area behind the Museum would be developed as the student village. On the left of the picture Drake's Place reservoir is conspicuous, and below it Sherwell Chapel which 60 years on would be converted into lecture theatres for the University of Plymouth.

[Sutton Harbour Company]

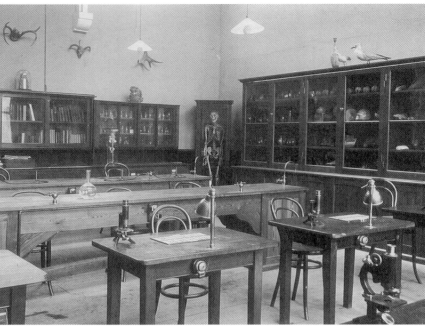

3.4 The Biology Laboratory of the Plymouth and Devonport Technical College in the mid-1920s set out ready for class use.

[PWDRO]

unifying educational provision be put into effect. All staff would need to be re-employed. No doubt for many teachers in elementary and secondary schooling the merger amounted to no more than a substitution of similar employers, but in more specialist areas such as in administration and technical education, where, in simple terms one could replace two, jobs must have been affected.

Table 3.1
Borough of Plymouth, Higher School Departments, 1915.

School Departments		*Teachers*	
Technical schools	3	Head teachers	42
Junior technical school	1	Assistant teachers	250
Technical day classes	1	Visiting/part-time teachers	48
Art schools	2	Total	340
Commercial departments	2		
Preparatory evening schools	29	*Students*	
Secondary schools	3	Men and boys	2812
Navigation schools (D & E)	2	Women and girls	1964
Total	43	Total	4776

Source: Plymouth and West Devon Record Office (PWDRO), Acc 1644/6/4/1:
Higher Education Sub-Committee Minutes (HESC), 16 April 1915, Minute 2315.

In 1915 the new Higher Education Sub-Committee (HESC) for Plymouth was responsible for 43 school "departments", 340 teachers and 4,776 students spanning the secondary and adult age groups (Table 3.1). The use of the term 'departments' by the Committee emphasises its role in managing a single, multifaceted, educational entity. Certainly, the joint development of secondary/tertiary education provision in Plymouth was in the minds of Committee members as they set about unifying the resources they had inherited:[2]

Resolved...that a report be made, first, upon the present condition of Technical and Secondary Education in the new Borough of Plymouth, and upon the best means of extending and improving it, and, second upon the relation of Technical and Secondary Education to Elementary Education on the one hand and to University Education on the other; and that under the heading of Secondary Education, the question of establishing a Training College for Teachers be discussed.

The Committee would have been aware that local authorities in other parts of the country had established teacher training colleges under the Education Act, 1902. But with church colleges in Exeter and Truro and provision at the Royal Albert Memorial College at Exeter, it is not surprising that this idea was not pursued. The Committee would also have been aware that the movement for a university college in the south west was gathering momentum.[3] A key decision was that to unify technical education provision under a single principal, and in 1916 Mr W.S. Templeton accepted the position of 'Principal of the Technical Schools East and West and Superintendent of Trade Instruction in Preparatory Evening Schools' (PDTC). He had been Principal of the Devonport Technical School since 1910, and the new appointment was made in 1916 at the time of the retirement of the Headmaster of the former Plymouth Technical School, J. Burns Brown.[4] Changing attitudes towards female education were amongst the effects of the war, and were reflected in the desire of the HESC for a Commercial Day School for girls and women, and for improved access to 'higher education', that is secondary education.[5] New courses developed as part of the war effort included accommodation at the Devonport site for a training centre for the Ministry of Munitions and a 'Centre of Instruction for

3.5 The Chemistry was one of the principal subjects at the Technical College but the Laboratory would have been little changed in the 1920s from the 1890s.

[PWDRO]

Table 3.2

Plymouth & Devonport Technical Schools in 1916/17: Courses & Subjects.

Day Courses at the Plymouth building

Preparatory General	1 Year	Mathematics, Chemistry, Physics, Mechanics, Machinery, Metalwork, Drawing, Woodwork, English, French
Engineering	2 Years	Mathematics, Physics, Geometrical Drawing, Mechanics, Heat Engines, Machine Drawing, Woodwork, Electrical Engineering, English.
Advanced Science	2 Years	Mathematics, Chemistry, Physics, Mechanics, English, French, German, Drawing
Medical	2 Years	Chemistry, Physics, Mechanics, Botany, Zoology, Materia Medica, Anatomy, Physiology, Bacteriology
Dental	2 Years	Chemistry, Physics

Evening Courses at the Plymouth building

Shipwrights	5 Years	Naval Architecture, Mechanics, Mathematics, Structures, Geometry
Fitters	5 Years	Heat, Physics, Mathematics, Machine Drawing, Heat Engines, Machinery, Materials, Structures, Mechanics, Solid Geometry
Architects	5 Years	Mathematics, Geometry, Mechanics, Building Construction, Structures, Brickwork/Masonry, Surveying, Architecture, Quantity Surveying
Civil Engineers	5 Years	Heat, Physics, Mechanics, Mathematics, Structures, Building Construction, Machinery, Surveying, Brickwork/Masonry
Electrical Engineering.	5 Years	Heat, Physics, Mechanics, Mathematics, Chemistry, Electricity, Machinery, Drawing, Electrical Engineering, Distribution
Wiremen	5 Years	Preparatory Technical Course; Wiring, Building Construction, Mathematics, Geometry, Machine Drawing
Sanitary Engineering		Special Course to suit students
Plumbers	5 Years	Preparatory Technical Course; Plumbing, Physics, Geometry, Sanitary Science, Building Construction, Wiring
Carpenters	5 Years	Preparatory Technical Course; Mathematics, Carpentry, Geometry, Building Construction, Architecture
Metal Workers	5 Years	Preparatory Technical Course, Metalwork, Mechanics, Mathematics, Geometry, Machine Drawing, Materials, Heat Engines
Manual Woodwork	2 Years	English, Geometry, Timber Biology, Manual Training
Manual Metalwork	2 Years	English, Machine Drawing, Metalwork, Geometry, Manual Training
Pharmacists	4 Years	Inorganic Chemistry, Botany, Heat, Physics, Organic Chemistry, Electricity, Practical Chemistry
University Matriculation	2 Years	Chemistry, Physics, French, English, Mathematics, Botany, Mechanics
University Intermediate Science	2 Years	Chemistry, Electricity, Heat, Physics, Mathematics, Mechanics
University Final Science	2 Years	Mathematics, Mechanics, Heat, Physics, Electricity, Chemistry
Teachers Certificate	1 Year	English Literature, Method, Music, Mathematics, Geography, History, Needlework, Physics, Drawing
Preparatory Technical	1 year	Mensuration, Physics, Metalwork, Woodwork, Plumbers work
Preparatory Professional	1 year	Latin, English, French, Mathematics, Mechanics
Scholarship	1 year	Special course to suit students (Whitworth and Royal Scholarships)

Evening courses at the Devonport building

Mechanical Engineering	5 Years	Machine Drawing, Mathematics, Mechanics, Physics, Heat Engines, Structures, Materials, Mechanical Engineering, Hydraulics
Shipbuilding	5 Years	Geometry, Naval Architecture, Mechanics, Physics, Mathematics
Electrical Engineering	5 Years	Mathematics, Mechanics, Physics, Machine Drawing, Electricity, Heat Engines, Electrical Engineering, Machines, Hydraulics, Design
Shipwrights	3 Years	Shipwrights Work, Geometry, Mathematics, Naval Architecture, Mechanics
Marine Engineering	3 Years	Boilermaking, Fitting, Geometry, Mechanics, Physics, Machine Drawing, Heat Engines, Materials, Structures, Machinery, Hydraulics
Sanitary Engineering	3 Years	Chemistry, Mathematics, Sanitary Science, Plumbing, Geometry, Mechanics, Physics, Electrical Engineering, Metals
Carpenters/Joiners	5 Years	Chemistry, Mathematics, Carpentry, Joinery, Building Construction, Architecture, Quantities, Paint, Materials
for Mason/Bricklayers	5 Years	Chemistry, Mathematics, Masonry, Brickwork, Building Construction, Architecture, Carpentry/Joinery, Quantities, Cements/Lime
Civil Engineering	5 Years	Physics, Mechanics, Mathematics, Building Construction, Machinery, Surveying, Architecture, Quantities, Materials, Structures
Naval Courses	1 Year	Mathematics, Mechanics, Electricians Work, Navigation, Nautical Astronomy.
Excise Course	1 Year	Chemistry, Mechanics, Physics, English
Domestic	1 Year	Cookery, Dressmaking, Millinery, Home Nursing, Laundry
Red Cross	1 Year	First Aid, Home Nursing, Hygiene, Sanitation, Cookery

Source: Plymouth Education Directory, 1916-17.

3.6 The Materia Medica Laboratory, shown here with illustrations of plants set out ready for study, was used by pharmacy students engaged in the study of drugs.

[PCL-LS]

3.7 The local authority's annual calendar publicised the wide range of courses on offer, but in the early 1920s it persisted in referring to the establishment as schools, which obscured the advanced courses which some students, were taking. The title 'college' was not conceded until 1925.

[PCL-LS]

Wireless Operators' at the Plymouth site, in association with the Marconi International Marine Communication Company.[6] At the end of 1917 in a meeting with Dr. A.E.H. Tutton (His Majesty's Inspector (HMI) for Technical Education), the Committee listed its concerns and aspirations, no doubt in the hope of favourable treatment at the Board of Education:[7]

> Extension of the Devonport building
> Over crowding at the Plymouth building
> Separate building for the School of Arts and Crafts
> Improvement and enlargement of the Plymouth building
> Two new junior technical schools
> Dressmaking courses for teachers
> Additional teachers for the North Hill Commercial School

Progress on these and other deficiencies was not to prove easy or rapid. Despite the Committee's awareness of trends in technical education and apparent support for improvements locally, over the next two decades provision in Plymouth was repeatedly to be found seriously wanting.

Nationally, technical education was growing in coherence and recognition. The Board of Education had a section handling its administration and a set of specialist technical education inspectors. Technical colleges were collaborating with enlightened local employers. Teachers working in the evolving sector were beginning to emerge as an identifiable group in the teaching profession, the Association of Teachers in Technical Institutions (ATTI) having been formed in 1904.[8] Even earlier in 1894, leading establishments had formed the Association of Technical Institutions (ATI), and early in 1917, the Plymouth HESC had lent its support to an ATI agenda for the development of technical education:[9]

1. no child to leave school before the end of the term in which it reaches its 14th birthday.
2. compulsory day attendance up to the age of 17 (alternative 18) for at least six (alternative eight) hours per week at continuation classes.
3. each large centre of population to have at least one school preparing for commercial careers.
4. uniform university admission criteria; university entrance tests for mature students to be distinct from secondary school examinations.
5. large increase in scholarships giving access to technical colleges.
6. teachers in technical colleges be encouraged to undertake research.
7. state to assume higher proportion of education costs.
8. government grants in aid for technical research to be greatly increased.
9. chief officials in technological branch of Board of Education to have scientific training.
10. general civil service examination to include science subjects as well as literary subjects.
11. state to make grants for free scholars proceeding from primary to secondary and junior technical schools.

The only item which the Committee did not support (4) anticipates modern mature student access to university provisions. Provision for compulsory continuation education (2) was made in the 1918 Education Act but eventually abandoned, so Plymouth's ability to extend that form of provision was not tested. However, Plymouth was already developing something of a reputation at the Board of Education for dragging its heels in educational matters. In 1919 Board of Education officials reproved Plymouth for its failure to develop a local scheme providing for the education of 12 to 15 year olds (school leaving age had been raised in 1918 to 14 years). They noted that Plymouth had been frank about its inability to

3.8 In 1924 as a result of Plymouth's collaboration with the University College of the South West of England, courses in pharmacy were transferred from Exeter to Plymouth. The School of Pharmacy, which trained most of the pharmaceutical chemists in the area from the 1920s to the 1960s, had its own Pharmacy Laboratory, at the technical College in Plymouth, until 1963 when the School was closed down.

[PWDRO]

get on with scheme formation owing to weakness of staff, but this was not acceptable to the Board: "Plymouth must be told plainly to get on with it".[10] A similar story was to emerge with respect to rectifying accommodation problems in the technical college buildings. In 1914 the Board of Education had approved an extension to the Devonport building put forward by the old Devonport authority, but owing to the war no action was taken. The plans were re-approved by the Board in 1920, but were again allowed to lapse owing to the economic climate.[11] The failure to upgrade facilities would be a factor in the debate on Plymouth's involvement in the University College of the South West. However, for technical education at secondary level, Plymouth had established its Junior Technical School in 1914, conducted initially in the Science, Art and Technical schools building, and would in the 1920s add one or two similar schools. This first school offered a two to three year pre-apprenticeship course for 13 to 15 year olds who transferred from other local schools on head teachers' recommendation. It was moved out to Durnford Street, Stonehouse, in 1921. The curriculum of this valuable, but forgotten stratum of education, included English, mathematics, science, technical drawing, workshop practice and physical training, and its students readily found places in Plymouth's local industries.[12]

When Principal Templeton was appointed in 1916, he took charge of a full-time staff of nine, six of whom were graduates and one who also acted as headmaster of the Advanced Commercial Evening School in Regent Street. In addition there were 48 part-time staff who assisted the delivery of the extensive range of evening classes listed in Table 3.2. Templeton was also responsible for Preparatory Evening Schools held at seventeen other locations across the Borough. Serving as feeder classes for the technical schools, these were:

"...for the purpose of giving instruction to young persons and adults who desire to improve their knowledge and make them better fitted for the duties of life, or... to be thoroughly prepared for the higher branches of study at the Advanced Evening Schools."[13]

Effectively the preparatory school provided a bridge between elementary schooling and technical education. As ever in further education, this was only one of several routes of admission to courses at the Technical Schools. The minimum age for engineering and building trades courses was 15 years, and for other courses 16 years, but always evidence of previous study, full-time or part-time was expected. Admission was at the discretion of the Principal and a key factor was ability to benefit from the proposed course. Though it remained possible to take individual subjects, the grouping of subjects into courses leading to internal certificates or external awards had become well established. Small numbers of students took day courses in the modern manner, of up to three years, the most advanced being degree level studies for London external degrees. But with most young people entering employment in their early 'teens, vocational study on courses which would assist progression in their chosen occupation was through evening classes. Evening courses were typically spread over five years, often with provision for intermediate certification. Those students who completed the full duration of study reached quite advanced standards enabling them to attempt, for example, professional examinations. Students taking subjects under Architecture could aim at the examinations, for example, of the Royal Institute of British Architects (RIBA), Royal Sanitary Institute, the Surveyors' Institute or the Institution of Naval Architects. Others took City and Guilds of London Institute (CGLI) examinations or those of the Board of Education. In 1922, Plymouth's first National Certificate course, in Mechanical Engineering, was approved.[14]

Managing such a diverse and under-resourced further education organisation could have been no sinecure, and it seems likely that the HESC was not as understanding or as helpful as it might have been. In 1920 Templeton tried to have the name changed from Plymouth and Devonport Technical Schools to Plymouth and Devonport Technical College in a reasonable attempt to enhance the image of his establishment as a centre for tertiary education involved in advanced work and to distance it from the secondary schools and junior technical schools which occupied much of the Committee's attention. The Committee turned him down, noting only that it hoped the Technical School would one day be part of a university college (it agreed to the change in 1926).[15] In 1921/22 difficulties such as a decline in student numbers and the loss of the Marconi course for radio operators, together with unspecified problems, appear to have been blamed by the Committee on the Principal. Probably the heart of the problem lay in the Committee's unwillingness to delegate management sufficiently to the Principal, who had to refer to it for quite minor decisions. Matters needing the Committee's attention would normally pass though the Secretary to the Education Committee or its Chairman, circumscribing access of Council employees' to the Committee and leaving room for mis-representation especially where there was a clash of personalities. The detail has not survived but circumstances were serious enough for Templeton to seek the support of the ATTI. The letter to the Council from the president of ATTI set out the flexibility which needed to be vested in the Principal:

3.9 As the PDTC two sites had separate origins, facilities such as laboratories and workshops were duplicated. The illustrations in prospectuses are no labelled with the location, so today it is not always clear to which building a facility belonged. This Physics Laboratory picture appeared in 1914.

[PCL-LS, college Prospectus, 1914/15]

"The problems which arise in Secondary or Elementary schools are rarely urgent; the classes remain uniform; the staff is nearly all full-time; changes are infrequent; and the general policy of the school is seldom changed. In Technical Schools the circumstances are altogether different: industrial conditions frequently cause a sudden demand for instruction to arise or to cease (as, for instance, has recently happened with your Wireless Classes); classes which are large one year may, without apparent cause, be very much smaller in the succeeding year; a class which begins with a small number of pupils may so increase as to demand additional staff; the staff contains a large proportion of part-time members of a great variety of qualifications, attainments, and teaching ability, and is more or less constantly changing. These conditions involve the appointment and dismissal of staff, the reorganisation of rooms, changes in the purchase of material, and, in fact, constant supervision and frequently immediate action. Thus if the varying demands of industry are adequately to be met, if advantage is to be taken of all possible savings in expenditure, and, indeed if the Institute is to be run with a maximum efficiency, the Principal must in some way be given much wider powers than are required by the Headmaster of a Secondary or Elementary School. With the consent of the Chairman [of the Education Committee] only he [the Principal] should be allowed to take such action in the circumstances described as may become necessary - with the proviso, of course, that he should report his action to the Committee for its approval at the next meeting. It is obvious that if there be an intermediate link, and if he do not feel he will be able personally to justify his action to the Committee, there will be want of confidence on both sides which cannot but result in misunderstandings and failure. For these reasons we feel that Mr Templeton, has not, in the past, been given a fair opportunity of proving his ability, and we should like to urge that before the serious step which the Committee has contemplated to be taken, he should be given a further period of - say - twelve months under conditions such as we have outlined, when we hope and believe that Mr. Templeton would show that his apparent failure has been due mainly, if not entirely, to the conditions under which his task has hitherto been attempted."[16]

Templeton retained his position until his death just before his retirement in 1933, though he was in indifferent health in the later years.[17] However, following his clash with the Higher Education Sub-Committee, he was soon endorsed by a full Board of Education inspection of the Technical Schools which also took in the four junior technical schools which existed in 1923.[18] The HMIs commented:

"The Principal...is well qualified for his duties by his knowledge, teaching experience and organising ability; during a very difficult period he has succeeded in effecting noteworthy improvements in the equipment and general organisation. He has been handicapped in two ways, first, by the fact that the two school buildings are a mile and a half apart, and secondly by the rival claims on the accommodation put forward by schools and departments over which he has no control. Notwithstanding these circumstances he has constantly kept in view any possible development of the work of the school, and has made commendable efforts to enlist the co-operation of employers".

The Plymouth building was used for: (a) day and evening classes in science and technology, plus a few language classes; (b) School of Art with a junior department; (c) a Trade School for Girls; (d) a Domestic Economy School for Girls; (e) Day and Evening Classes in Domestic Subjects. At the Devonport Building there were: (f) a Secondary School for Girls; (g) Evening Classes in Art; (h) Day and Evening Classes in Science and Technology. Yet only (a) and (h) in this list came under Principal Templeton. Given the context it is hardly surprising that at the Devonport Building neither the Principal nor the Heads of Departments of Mechanical and Electrical Engineering had personal rooms, that there was no common room or library for students and no staff room. Indeed during the day the Technical School had access only to the laboratories in the basement. Devonport was 'unique' among engineering schools in not having a room fitted as a Drawing

3.10 This Physics Laboratory illustration is from the 1920s.

[PCL-LS]

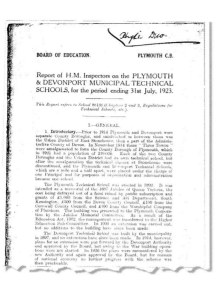

3.11 As with all Government assisted educational establishments, Plymouth & Devonport Technical Schools (College) was inspected by His Majesty's Inspectors of schools at intervals of about ten years. Their reports provided a detailed review of local provision and did not hesitate to pinpoint circumstances and conditions which lagged behind prevailing national standards.

[PWDRO, acc. 1644; PRO, ED 114/122]

Office and there was still no heat engines laboratory. The lack of this last facility throughout the 1930s meant that Plymouth was refused permission to offer the heat engines option in the HND in Mechanical Engineering, and weakened its drive for an engineering faculty under the University College of the South West of England (UCSWE). The HMIs description of the shared use of the largest room in the building has a touch of humour:

... the work at Devonport... is carried on under conditions unworthy of an important engineering school. The largest room in the building is used for the Drawing Office and also as the Assembly Hall for the Girl's Secondary School. But the requirements for these two purposes have nothing in common except the floor, walls and ceiling. For an Assembly Hall a polished floor free from furniture, works of art on the walls and a piano are the main requisites. The main essential of a drawing office are rigid drawing benches and stools; shelves for the smaller and lighter machine parts, benches and floor space for heavier machines or other apparatus; cupboards for articles properly kept under lock and key; walls covered with interesting working drawings and a variety of illustrations of engineering working products....It was decided that the room must be arranged for the secondary school. This meant that only flimsy drawing benches, capable of being removed after each drawing lesson, could be used, and no equipment must be left visible; the cupboard was allowed to remain, as was also the piano, an object rarely seen in a drawing office. Further, machinery which had been purchased at considerable cost and suitable for the purposes of machine drawing, remains stored away unused.... It is hoped that the Managers [the HESC] realise that from the point of view of the Technical School, the position is one which creates impossible conditions of working."

At the Plymouth building the Technical School lacked a room fitted for practical work in electrical wiring. The facilities for teaching Physics and Chemistry were 'very limited' and there was only one room for lectures and practical work in biological subjects. An earlier report on Art provision (1919), had commented on the lack of cleanliness throughout the building and that the 'offices for men students' were so inaccessible that art students preferred to use the public lavatory in an adjoining street.[19] Of the building generally, in 1923 the HMIs commented that the site was unsuitable, the building was unattractive externally, and the interior ill-planned, gloomy and uninspiring (yet it was to last until 1966). The lack of investment, then, extended across the strata of education and appears to have extended to cleaning and low level maintenance.

But the situation in Plymouth was by no means unique. Similar conditions prevailed in many another local authority area, and it would need a culture change nationally as well as locally to effect a real improvement. Of course the Board of Education was well aware of the situation and indeed spelt it out in a pamphlet issued in 1926, emphasising the need both to improve technical education premises and to free college management from much of the petty bureaucracy of local government. It quoted many similar examples to those noted here.[20] The influential former President of the Board of Education, Lord Eustace Percy, writing in 1930, noted the waste of facilities in technical colleges and advocated technical colleges as advanced learning establishments linking education and industry, and involved in management training as well as technical subjects.[21] In addition to local causes, there was also the restraining hand of the Treasury on initiatives involving expenditure and the reluctance of industry to release employees for in-service education. The attitude of industry was still influenced by the

Science and Art regime with its emphasis on theoretical aspects of scientific and technical subjects. This problem was highlighted by the Malcolm Committee (1926-8), one of several investigations commenting on aspects of technical education. But it was not to be until later in the 1930s that the Board of Education was able to initiate a drive to improve matters. HMI surveys in 1935, designed to assess the investment needed, found much the same conditions as in the 1920s. New policies were set out amongst other things emphasising the value of area committees for facilitating collaborative further education provision between adjacent education authorities, involving financial compensation and agreed syllabuses.[22] Extra central funds were made available, but local authority matching finance was required and the Board could not force compliance. The initiative failed, as did a further attempt in 1938, by which time World War II was looming.[23]

3.12 A view of the Electrical Engineering Laboratory published in 1914.

[PCL-LS, college Prospectus, 1914/15]

Table 3.3

Plymouth and Devonport Technical College, Student Numbers 1923/4 - 1937/8.

Students	1923/4	1934/5	1935/6	1936/7	1937/8
Full-time day	44	159	189	237	239
Part-time day	74	131	139	113	101
Part-time evening	540	567	696	798	884
Total	663	857	1024	1148	1224
Teacher hrs day	8715				
Teacher hrs eveing	6975				
Total	15689				
Student hours					
Possible, day	69596				
Actual, day	44672	128556	160196		
Attendance rate, day	64%				
Possible, evening	100444	81730	86651		
Actual, evening	60250				
Attendance rate, evening	60%				
Actual total student hours	104922	210286	246847	262299	276836

Sources: HMI Report 1923; UPPLY, Principal's Annual Reports, 1934 - 1938

Nevertheless at Plymouth the inter-war period did see some increase in evening student numbers and in full-time day activity (Table 3). By 1923 full-time staff numbers had risen to twelve, of whom four were now designated heads of department, for mechanical engineering, electrical engineering, chemistry and mathematics, with the Principal acting as head of physics. The HMIs did not consider the staff a particularly strong team, despite some well qualified members. The 33 part-time staff were adequately qualified and enthusiastic, but were thin on teaching experience, probably owing to the low levels of remuneration. In the 1922/3 session full-time staff attended on average for 39 hours per week, though it is not clear what proportion was class contact; their salaries averaged £315. Part-time teacher attendance was just over four hours per week, almost certainly all class contact, at five shillings per hour.[24] The attendance of part-time and evening students has always been notoriously variable. The rate of about two-thirds of possible student attendances for 1923/4 was typical of technical education in other areas. Very much higher rates were reported for Plymouth in 1926/7 and no doubt reflect a concerted drive of staff and employers who released

3.13 This picture of the Electrical Engineering Laboratory appeared in the 1920s.

[PCL-LS]

apprentices to attend classes. Keeping attendance records had long been a part of education, especially where national and local authority funding was involved. It was part of the reporting process justifying the existence of classes. In technical education it was normal practice to discontinue classes where recruitment was low or attendance had fallen significantly. Further, in addition to passing the academic assessments, students had to attend a significant proportion of classes (50 to 80 per cent depending a course) to be awarded their qualifications. This applied to local awards as well as national certificates and diplomas.[25] As the numbers of names on the registers was particularly variable in technical education, often giving rise to differences in reported data for the same year, total hours taught by the staff and total student attendance hours provided a more satisfactory means of comparing one year with the next. These remained standard data in returns until superseded by the full-time equivalent (FTE) student methodology in the 1970s. Student hours at the PDTC increased by 164 per cent between 1923/4 and 1937/8, whereas numbers enrolled increased 185 per cent. Despite this progress, the proportion of the local population engaged in technical education in Plymouth still lagged behind the national average.[26]

Running through the Principal's reports in the 1920s is his concern that only a small proportion of youngsters leaving Plymouth secondary schools were being directed on to further study at the technical schools. Indeed he argued that through fees, scholarships and maintenance grants Plymouth was exporting students who could easily study locally. In 1921-22 these had cost the authority £6455 compared to the £1125 spent at Portsmouth. The technical college there had 553 day students and 1659 evening students, compared with 88 and 547 at Plymouth. Portsmouth was much more effective at feeding its College, and Principal Templeton felt that the Education Committee should devote more of its spending to scholarships tenable at its technical schools. Shortage of money was undoubtedly a key factor in the list of problems noted earlier, but an increase in fees for the 1922/23 session of 25 per cent could hardly have increased the numbers of students at the Technical Schools. In order to demonstrate the cost-effectiveness of technical education in Plymouth, the Principal compared costs per technical student (£13 8s 8d per annum) with pupils at elementary schools (£12 per annum) and secondary schools (£14 to £15 per annum). With the exchequer paying half the costs of technical education, the cost to the rates worked out at only £4265, that is about one penny in the pound.[27]

With a high proportion of students studying part-time, little in the way of recreational facilities and a student body split between two sites, there was little opportunity for student life to function in the manner of universities and colleges where students were mostly full-time and residential. At best student activity was sporadic, though some encouragement seems to have been given by staff. In 1923 the HMIs noted a decline in the number of 'socials' to a single event at Christmas. No playing field was provided for student use, and there was no gymnasium. Beacon Park had to be hired for the annual sports where the Principal's Challenge Shield was awarded. There was however a

3.14 The Mechanical Engineering Workshop in the 1920s still simulated factory conditions.
[PCL-LS]

very active Wireless Society.[28] In 1923/4 "...a pianoforte was purchased for the benefit of the Technical and Art Departments, both educationally and socially...", and the Plymouth and Devonport Technical Students' National Savings Association was formed. But the Annual Athletic Sports had to be cancelled owing to lack of support.[29] However by 1935/6 the Students' Union led by a President, Secretary and Treasurer was functioning and there were clubs and societies for Association Football, Rugby Football, Hockey, Cricket, Hiking, Commerce, Engineers, Pharmacy and Student Christian Movement.[30] By 1939 there was also a student magazine, The Collegian. No doubt the opening in 1929 of the Astor Hall of Residence for university course students, was a factor in improving student life. One annual event which was sustained throughout the inter-war period was the Annual Prize-Giving, The list of prizes was already extensive by the late 1920s, and in 1938 numbered 49 awards, with many prizes donated by local industry, professional bodies and dignitaries.[31]

At the depth of the depression in the early 1930s, something of a hiatus in the leadership of both the Technical College and the Art Schools emerged. Principal Templeton was not in the best of health and by 1930 Board of Education officials were expecting his forced retirement at the age of 60 in 1931.[32] However, Templeton lingered on as already noted. The Head of the Schools of Art, R.H. Parker had died in January 1930, and the head of the small Art School at Devonport, Mr D.H. Hodge had been upgraded to be head also of the Central School of Arts and Crafts (*ie* Plymouth), effectively merging the two art schools. There is some doubt about the nature of this appointment in view of events in 1934. The weakness at the top of both institutions left the Secretary to the Education Committee in Plymouth, E. Chandler Cook, in a controlling position. In March 1934 Plymouth advertised for a new Principal, who was to be in charge of both the Technical

College and the Art Schools, which effectively demoted the Art School Principal to the position of a deputy.[33] From the perspective of the officials in the Board of Education such an arrangement was irregular. They were not at all pleased that the Plymouth LEA had advertised the joint position (and apparently appointed the new principal) without consulting the Board or even the local HMIs. Worse, Plymouth appeared to have paid no attention to the Board's recent Circular 1432 on the future structure of art education which provided for the creation of a regional system of colleges of art.[34] Yet Chandler Cook must have realised that Plymouth was seen as an obvious centre for such a college for the extreme south west, but perhaps did not appreciate that no such designation would be forthcoming while the joint appointment existed. Unfortunately for the Board there was a precedent as it had allowed such an arrangement at Halifax, where there were special circumstances. The Board was mollified to some extent because the Principal appointed in 1934, Mr A.R. Boeree, had previous experience of managing art as well as technical education. However, the joint appointment was to last only two years. In 1936 Mr. Hodge died following a traffic accident. Plymouth Council broke its contract with Mr Boeree, removing his responsibility for the Art School and appointing a new head of the Plymouth Central School of Arts and Crafts, Mr L. Duckett, from April, 1937.[35]

The difficulties of separate establishments sharing buildings have already been explored. Principals must have been all too familiar with the demarcation conflicts implicit in such situations. Another area of potential overlap concerned the ownership of subjects and courses. This could operate vertically between establishments dealing with different levels of a subject, for example between junior technical schools and the technical college or between a technical college and a university college, or horizontally between establishments involved in similar levels of work. But for Government policy, having art and technical colleges under the same principal made some sense for subjects at the technical end of the art spectrum, such as architecture and printing. It also applied with commercial or business subjects, where a separate commercial college might exist, but where the technical college would have an interest associated with the business dimension of technical subjects. In Plymouth, architecture in particular seems to have had a long history of straddling the interests of the two establishments. As a design subject and as a subject for historical study, classes in architecture were offered by the Schools of Art in the Three Towns from the late 1850s. The subjects of the building industry, originally offered in trade schools, were clearly part of the work of the technical schools by the early years of the twentieth century. The syllabuses for building and architecture in Table 3.2, show a considerable overlap of content, and in 1916/17, architecture was advertised with the subjects of the Plymouth and Devonport Technical Schools. In 1928, architecture was established as a department of the Plymouth School of Arts and Crafts but there was considerable discussion about the co-operation needed between the Art and Technical schools concerning the delivery of subjects common to both building and architecture. In December 1930, the Royal Institute of British Architects (RIBA) gave the Department (which it called School) the important status of recognition "...for exemption from the Testimonies of Study for the RIBA Intermediate Examination". Inter-RIBA exemption had been claimed for the architecture course in the Plymouth Education Directory, 1916/17, but had presumably lapsed.[36] One solution, seriously discussed in 1930, and effective after World War II, was for a school (meaning department) of architecture and building straddling the Art and Technical Colleges but under a under a single head.

A somewhat similar situation existed in the 1920s for two other subject areas, commercial subjects and 'women's and girls' subjects. Almost inevitably there was a confused situation between junior and more advanced levels and between day and evening work. The teaching of domestic subjects had slowly developed from the early years of the century, in the junior and evening institutes, including some overseen by the Principal of the Technical Schools. By 1923 there was some day work partly in the Plymouth technical school building, and partly nearby in Portland Place.[37] The most popular subjects were cookery and dressmaking and the section was managed by a headmistress. In 1926 the work was moved completely into converted houses in Portland Square and it became known as the School of Housecraft. This accommodation was the subject of the most scathing of comments by the HMIs when they inspected further education provision in Plymouth in 1937.[38] Nevertheless, having emerged as a separate establishment under the local authority, it was to remain in the same location until merged with the College of Further Education following the re-organisation of 1970. Commercial education evolved in the lower level evening institutes, some of which were the responsibility of the Principal of the Technical College. By 1933 there was a Central Commercial Institute and there were some advanced classes in the Technical College, but the relationship between the various sets of classes was confused.[39] By 1937 commercial studies were more firmly established in the technical college, but there was no head of department. At the most advanced level a few students were working for the intermediate examination for the Bachelor of Commerce degree. The one year full time day course included shorthand, typing and book-keeping as the main subjects with options in English, arithmetic, commerce, geography, economics, French and German. The HMIs recommended that more status be given to commercial mathematics, statistics, geography and English.[40]

With Britain beginning to draw out of the great depression, the Government planned an additional expenditure of £12,000,000 to carry through its development programmes for technical and art education across the country. Local authorities like Plymouth, which had been so often criticised for their inadequate facilities and confused tertiary education structures, could begin to look for central financial aid to put matters right. But, as part of the Board of Education evaluation, Plymouth was subjected to the inspection not only of its further education provision in 1937, but also of its art provision in 1938.[41] As only marginal progress had by then

CITY OF PLYMOUTH
EDUCATION COMMITTEE

PLYMOUTH & DEVONPORT
TECHNICAL COLLEGE
CALENDAR FOR THE
SESSION, 1939—1940

DATES OF OPENING
DAY COURSES
THURSDAY, 7th SEPTEMBER
EVENING COURSES
THURSDAY, 14th SEPTEMBER
1939

*3.15 The College had just published its
prospectus for the coming session, when war
broke out, putting a halt to the improvements
to the building and facilities which has been
recommended and disrupting the routine
delivery of courses.*

[PCL-LS]

been achieved, the reports again constituted a full catalogue of deficiencies in accommodation, facilities and equipment. The principals and staff of the colleges were absolved from responsibility as invariably they were achieving all that was possible in the circumstances. Effectively, the HMI recommendations comprised a blueprint for the complete reconstitution of tertiary education in Plymouth. With new or additional accommodation the Art School should extend its range of subjects to include commercial art (commercial photography and typography to be added to existing facilities), dress-design and millinery, display, a junior art department, and printing (if that was not developed by the Technical College). The Technical College should abandon the moribund link with the UCSWE, and the LEA should build a new central college building to accommodate all the work, relegating the Devonport building to other uses. This implied demolishing the Plymouth building, a recommendation made by Principal Boeree in 1935.[42] The engineering courses would require three engineering laboratories and workshops for automobile work, metallurgy, welding founding and forging. Electrical courses should have three electrical laboratories and workshops for installations and repairs. These and the building course would share at least two drawing offices. Woodwork, plumbing and brickwork each required a workshop; there should be a building science laboratory, a materials and samples room, and three general classrooms. A strong commercial department should be developed, but there were no special comments on accommodation. The School of Navigation, which had been merged with the PDTC in 1932, needed a seamanship room, chartroom, signals room and a lecture room, and it should develop a pre-sea course. Science courses should have laboratories for inorganic, organic and physical chemistry, preparation, balance and store rooms, and several classrooms; for physics there was need for an elementary room, and electrical and heat laboratories, and two lecture rooms. Medical courses needed physiology and biology laboratories, while pharmacy needed a dispensary, a materia medica room and a technical laboratory. For general use there was need of an assembly hall, gymnasium, library, common rooms and administrative accommodation. Wherever printing was developed, it would need four workshops to include ones for composition and letterpress machinery.

Although the Second World War was to postpone the redevelopment of technical education for some fifteen years, the Plymouth authority had initiated some of the essential preliminary moves. With the acquisition of the former military hospital in Stoke it was able to move the girls secondary school out of the Devonport building releasing the space for day-time use by the Technical College. On the Plymouth site it had long ago purchased land adjacent to the College known as the Shute Park Estate and also held a second plot, the former cattle market, but this together was insufficient to accommodate a new technical college building and also provide for the College of Housecraft and the College of Art. Further, there was the threat that the Council's need for a new bus station and car park

3.16 A lecture theatre at the Technical College's Devonport building in the 1920s.

[PWDRO]

might compromise these sites for educational use. £5000 had been earmarked for the long needed heat engines laboratory, and the Plymouth building had been renovated.[43] A start had also been made on improving links with local industry and commerce through the Government-approved approach of advisory committees for each of the main subject areas. By 1938, such committees had been formed for breadmaking and confectionary, pharmacy, meat trades, milk and dairy trades, printing and typography, and architecture.[44]

By the end of the 1930s then, some improvement in the physical environment experienced by students and staff at PDTC had been achieved and some of the structures associated with technical colleges in the period after World War II were emerging. College internal structures are always to some extent fluid, depending upon the varying size of subject areas, the number of management positions a funding authority such as the LEA might be willing to support, and policy which might take into account factors such as recognition by professional or learned institutions. By 1939, the College was describing quite small subjects areas as departments, though there were only six designated heads of department, for the Departments of Mathematics and Mechanics, Chemistry, Civil and Mechanical Engineering, Electrical Engineering, Building and Pharmacy. Four of these were reasonably substantial departments with full and part-time staff numbers totalling, 11, 26, 11 and 25. Chemistry had only three staff and Pharmacy one. The existence of a Pharmacy Department was a condition of recognition by the Pharmaceutical Society. The departments of Physics, Biology, Gas Engineering, Navigation and Commerce merited only lecturers-in-charge directly under the Principal. In all the staff numbered 110, but about three quarters of these would have been teaching part-time.[45] Apart from the industrial advisory committees which would have met once or twice a year, the only formal committee at the College was the Board of Studies which seems to have contained one or two staff nominees in addition to the heads

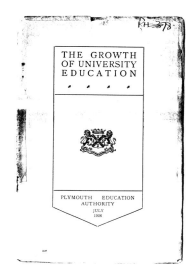

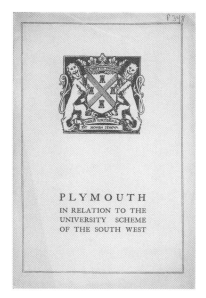

3.17, 3.18 As part of its support for a technology faculty of the UCSWE at Plymouth, these two booklets were issued by Plymouth's Council, one soliciting donations to the UCSWE development appeal, the other arguing the case.

[PCL-LS]

of department and the more important lecturers-in-charge. Principal Murray from UCSWE was also a member, demonstrating that links with Exeter were still being maintained, and the PDTC registrar also attended.

The situation had changed little by 1943 when the Director of Education for Plymouth, Dr Andrew Scotland reviewed the internal organisation of PDTC for the HESC. This report gives the weekly student hours generated in each department, and shows that the normal work of the College, about 260,000 hours per annum, was at roughly the same level as in the late 1930s. This was doubled by special training courses associated with the war effort, for which the Board of Education had issued special guidance in 1939.[46] For the dockyard and naval radio courses special staff must have been taken on. Mathematics had lost its head of department, and the table shows that remuneration did not necessarily accord with responsibility. Although Dr Scotland contemplated the possibility of renaming the lecturers in charge of departments as acting heads of departments (without additional remuneration), he effectively recommended no action. After the war it was likely that Plymouth would assume a regional role, and was likely to develop an internal organisation involving a faculty structure similar to that of universities. In the event, a faculty structure would not be adopted until 1980.

Table 3.4

Plymouth and Devonport Technical College, 1943 Departmental Weekly Student Hours & Heads/Lecturer-in-Charge Annual Salaries.

Department	Student Hours/Week			Status	Annual Salary (£)
	Normal Work	War Work	Total		
Civil & Mechanical Engineering	2184	775	2959	HoD	414
Electrical Engineering	782	164	946	HoD	530
Building	746		746	HoD	530
Chemistry	456	164	620	HoD	530
Pharmacy	180		180	HoD	494
Mathematics	954	224	1178	LiC	480
Physics	595	222	817	LiC	480
Commerce	521		521	LiC	342
Biology	401		401	LiC	354
Navigation	254		254	LiC	384
Dockyard Labour Course		2280	2280		
Naval Radio Course		3605	3605		
Totals	7073	7434	14507		

Source, PRO, ED51/161, Memorandum on Organisation of Technical College, November 1943. The Principal's annual salary was £950. HoD: head of department; LiC: lecturer-in-charge.

Plymouth and the University College of the South West

In 1938 Plymouth LEA assumed full control of all the university level work in Plymouth, which had been provisionally ceded to the UCSWE in the mid-1920s, thus ending a relationship which had never been properly supported or financed, either nationally or locally.[47] From the end of the nineteenth century it had been possible to sit London University External Degree examinations in Plymouth, a long-standing facility that was not dependent on the link with the UCSWE. However, in the period early in the

3.19 The Devonport Technical College building was to be Plymouth's main contribution to the creation of a technology faculty of the UCSWE in Plymouth.

[PWDRO]

twentieth century when the Albert Memorial College at Exeter aspired to designation as a university college, it seemed that a stronger case could be made on a regional basis, by associating the local authorities and educational establishments which were involved in advanced work. Perhaps the ideas owed something to the federal University of Wales created in 1893. Looking back it is difficult to avoid the parallels with the multi-campus University of Plymouth assembled in 1988/9.

With both Plymouth and Exeter associated with the university extension movement in the latter part of the nineteenth century, aspirations for a more substantial establishment would have been in the minds of local people interested in higher education. The drive at Exeter was much stronger than at Plymouth, and the Albert Memorial Building, well established as the tertiary education centre in the City for Science and Art classes, was advanced in the direction of university college status by embracing the university extension approach, becoming the Technical and University Extension College in the 1890s.[48] With the addition of teacher education from 1901, it was increasingly regarded, unofficially, as a university college. Indeed such a development had been mentioned by the then president of the Board of Education in 1914, in a response to a deputation from the College at Exeter.[49] In contrast, as already noted in Chapter 2, it was a struggle in Plymouth to sustain extension classes at all, and even with the merged college from 1914 the local perception did not extend to collegiate status. Thus before Plymouth had appointed a principal to its newly merged college, it was the Principal of the Royal Albert Memorial College at Exeter (the name in use from 1901), A.W. Clayden, who, in 1915 put forward the outline of a multi-site university college for the South West of England. Clearly the main campus would be at Exeter which had a focus in the arts and sciences, but the subject base would be extended through the association of centres: Plymouth for engineering and marine biology, Camborne for mining, Newton Abbot for agriculture at

E. CHANDLER COOK, F.C.I.S., Esq.
PLYMOUTH

3.20, E. Chandler Cook was the long serving Education Secretary (ie. director of education or chief education officer) for Plymouth, who was at the heart of the Plymouth drive to be associated with the UCSWE in the 1920s and 1930s. His base was in the Education Offices (now the University's Reynold's Building), in Coburg Street, very close to the Plymouth Technical College building.

[PCL-LS, C.W. Brachen (ed.) The Book of Plymouth (London, Jack, 1910) 6.]

the new Seale-Hayne College (see Chapter 6), together with the teacher training provision at Truro and at Exeter (St. Luke's College).[50] This concept was brought to the attention of the Higher Education Sub-Committee at Plymouth in 1915 in the review which it had ordered of educational provision in the new County Borough.[51] This review suggested a teacher training college in Plymouth as a stimulus to university level teaching, and in time, Plymouth emerging as an element in such a scheme as outlined by Clayden. However it could only come once secondary and technical education had been organised and developed. It would not be cheap. By 1918 the list of subject areas at Plymouth had been extended to include a medical school based on the long-established naval and military hospitals and later there was even mention of a fisheries school.[52]

At Exeter the drive gathered momentum, with the formation of a Committee for the Furtherance of University Education in 1917. Chaired by the Chairman of Devon County Council, Sir Henry Massey Lopes, this included the Plymouth solicitor, W.L. Munday. Committee members toured Devon drumming up support for a University College in the region. A delegation to the President of the Board of Education in 1918 received an unfavourable reception. However the Board of Education, which at that time had little understanding of the university college idea, agreed to inspect university work at Exeter. Overall this report was favourable, though a university college was unlikely to emerge immediately. Nevertheless the College at Exeter made an application for recognition for the receipt of treasury grants. A further delegation to the Board of Education in 1920, was also rebuffed, the proponents' case not being helped by the unwillingness of the Plymouth and Cornwall representatives to indicate financial support from those authorities (Devon and Exeter councils were already making substantial grants to the Exeter college). Meanwhile, Exeter had secured promises of financial donations from private sources to allow the purchase of the Streatham Estate on the edge of town as the new location for the development of the university college. In 1921 Plymouth promised the proceeds of a penny rate annually and Cornwall promised £1000. Eventually the recently formed University Grants Committee (UGC), following a visit to Exeter, was persuaded to make a grant from August 1922, and so the University College of the South West of England came into being. But despite the Plymouth and Cornwall annual grants, there was no provision for associating the technical schools at Plymouth in the receipt of UGC grants, which were for university work in arts and sciences at Exeter only.[53]

Despite the setbacks inflicted by the Board of Education in London on the university college movement in the South West and, particularly, on the provisions for a federal approach, representatives of Plymouth had been involved from 1917. In 1921 a joint committee with the Exeter college had been formed to work out details of relationship with the Plymouth and Devonport technical College including allocation of subjects, teaching and residential accommodation, teaching support in Plymouth by Exeter staff, overall control, and financial implications. The involvement of the Plymouth

ASTOR HALL OF RESIDENCE

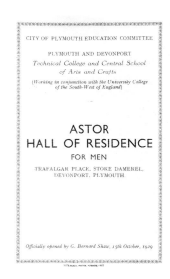

Officially opened by G. Bernard Shaw, 15th October, 1929

authority in developing these arrangements was justified partly on the basis of the 1902 Education Act which had brought tertiary as well as secondary education within its oversight, and partly on a clause in the 1918 Education Act which allowed local authorities to form a federation for the joint delivery of advanced education where development by a single authority alone was not financially or educationally viable. The hopes that the UGC and Board of Education would eventually relent, must have been sufficiently strong throughout the 1920s for the Exeter college and Plymouth to put a scheme into effect and to operate it into the 1930s.

So what was the nature of this scheme, which, for whatever reason, appears to have been actively promoted by Principal Hetherington whilst in charge of the College at Exeter between 1920 and 1924? In his perception the Plymouth section of the University College organisation (largely agreed by the Plymouth authority) would comprise:[54]

"(a) A full Faculty of Engineering, including departments of Mechanical, Electrical, Marine, Motor (and Aeronautical) Engineering.
(b) Ancillary to this Faculty, there would be Departments of Pure and Applied Mathematics, Physics and Chemistry.
(c) A full Department of Economics and Commerce.
(d) Ancillary to this, the necessary teaching in Modern Languages, Geography, History, etc.
(e) A Department of Law (as at present).
(f) Some provision for the conduct of tutorial classes and similar extra-mural activities.
(g) The Department of Pharmacy.
(h) First -year Medical and Dental Course (general science preliminary, Biology, Chemistry, Physics)"

The idea of a medical school would have to be held over until the right time, but it should be at Plymouth. The cost would not be cheap, certainly not less than £13,000 in start up expenses and a similar sum annually in running costs. The UCSWE would assume responsibility for all post-matriculation (ie.post-university entry) work in Plymouth, and appropriate Plymouth academic staff would also transfer. As an interim arrangement, until the Plymouth section could be fully vested in the UCSWE, the management of the provisional scheme was delegated to a 'Branch' committee having four

3.21, 3.22 The Astor Hall of Residence for 'university' students, who belonged to the PDTC and the University College of the South West of England, was only a minute's walk from the Devonport building. This picture was taken after the building of the extension in the 1930s, and the scene is unchanged today. It is now the base of the Plymouth and District Disabled Fellowship.

[PCL-LS, Astor Hall prospectus, 1936]

3.23 Funds for the purchase, refurbishment and furnishing of the Astor Hall of Residence were donated by Lord and Lady Astor, and the official opening was performed by the playwright George Bernard Shaw on October 1929.

[PCL-LS, Western Independent (13 October 1929)]

3.24 In the late 1940s and 1950s, PDTC Students' Union issued the student magazine Tekel, which, compared to modern equivalents, was a very staid, though informative and well produced publication. The designer of the cover included a variation on the Plymouth coat of arms (probably without permission). The motto translates 'Knowledge is power'.

[PCL-LS]

3.25 A Student's Union had functioned at PDTC in the 1930s and it was certainly functioning soon after World War II. This is a picture of the Executive Committee in 1948.

[PCL-LS, Tekel (June 1948)]

3.26 This group of students participated in the PDTC Annual Sports day in 1948

[Miss D. Potter].

members from the HESC at Plymouth and four from the Council of the University College.[55] This would "...dissect and prepare the work of the Technical Schools for the fuller development foreshadowed ...". The internal management of the Plymouth technical school in the interim period was placed jointly under the Principal of the UCSWE and the Principal of PDTC, with the former being called the Supervisor in recognition of Principal Templeton's formal appointment from 1916.[56]

This curious, essentially private, arrangement between Plymouth LEA and the UCSWE was in the end not to progress beyond the interim stage. Yet the actions and plans of both parties convey the impression that university level work at Plymouth would be fully integrated with the University College. Plymouth committed itself to handing over the Devonport Building (suitably extended), once the girls school could be moved out. That was valued at £65,000. It would also make an annual contribution to the University College to support the Plymouth section of £10,000 from the rates. Furniture and equipment to the value of £10,000 would also be handed over. In 1929 it also provided the Astor Hall of Residence. Altogether the Plymouth financial contribution was capitalised as at least £333,000. Plymouth would "...acquire a definite place in the University College Scheme for the South West....", with a full Faculty of Engineering and the University Departments noted above. Exeter's contribution was the transfer of the Pharmacy Department in 1924, teaching and administrative support and recognition. Principal Hetherington and his successors certainly divided their time between Exeter and Plymouth, on occasion travelling two days each week. Further, the UCSWE Court (160 representatives including 21 from Plymouth) and its Council (40 representatives including 5 from Plymouth) met alternately in Plymouth and Exeter. Lecturing staff, particularly in law and economics, travelled several times each week to teach at Plymouth, and in 1929 a member of the Exeter staff became resident warden of Astor Hall, travelling three days each week to Exeter to give his classes there.[57]

That the partners developed the schemes so far is remarkable. Not only were the parties rebuffed at the start as noted above, but they could hardly have been ignorant of continued opposition from London which had not waned in the mid-1930s. An official in 1925 commented:[58]

"This is not a Scheme which the University Grants Committee are anxious or able to assist.... The College [Exeter] got onto our grant list by the skin of its teeth and a deciding factor with the Committee was that it did no technological work... the unpopular task of pouring cold and sensible water will inevitably fall to the central departments...Mr. Hetherington [the Exeter principal]... thought that since the Exeter College had the chance of getting control at Plymouth, it would be unwise not to take it....Apart from the pretence of a 'University connection', Plymouth can get little in the way of tangible academic advantage out of the Scheme... there is no use in allowing vague aspirations and ambitions to blind one to the facts.... a federation of a heterogeneous group of second-rate colleges...might give a university degree, but could not give a university education.... for the Plymouth college... the range of subjects proposed is not far short of that provided by a small independent university...which... would cost nearer £100,000 than £10,000 per year... work of lower grade needs to be carried out to a much higher point in the Plymouth area, before Plymouth can hope to bring into existence a technical institution of university standard."

Plymouth's ambitions were laid out by Chandler Cook in 1927 in a pamphlet in support of the Mayor of Plymouth's appeal for a building and endowment fund for University education. Throughout the inter-war period UCSWE was running an appeal to develop its Streatham Estate, to which collections in Plymouth had already contributed £3506 by June 1927. Presumably this Mayor's Appeal was in aid of developing the Plymouth section, as, given the failure of Plymouth, noted in the discussion on PDTC in this period, to undertake the development deemed necessary by the HMIs, it hardly seems possible that Plymouth could have fulfilled the anticipated outlay on University work in the Borough.[59] The arrival of Principal John Murray at Exeter in 1926 coincided with an increase in the UGC grant, and it seems that by the 1930s the Plymouth dimension was becoming much less important to the UCSWE. Although Murray continued the interim arrangements and even provided a member of staff for the Astor Hall, he took much less interest than Hetherington, delegating the Supervisor's role to his Deputy. In practice little of the service teaching at Plymouth was to degree students, and when the new Principal of PDTC also assumed the role of Warden at Astor Hall, it must have been obvious that the link with the UCSWE would not be developed.

Clapp observes that "Astor Hall symbolised the federal nature of the University movement in the South West". Certainly it was the only physical entity to materialise, and was probably the only product of the Mayor of Plymouth's appeal. Even then it was the gift of £10,000 from Lord Astor which secured this single feature of a University for Plymouth. A former home for the blind in Stoke was purchased and renovated for 32 students, a resident warden and matron. Subsequently it was extend to accommodate 40 men students in 26 study bedrooms, ten of which were single rooms. The communal rooms included a dining hall, common room and library and in the grounds two tennis courts were laid out. In 1939/40 full board was set at £1 12s. 6d. per week, with laundry and common room subscriptions being extra. Residence was compulsory for students whose homes were outside the City

3.27 Although Tekel appears to have lapsed, the Overseas Students' Association appears to have sustained student publishing with The Wanderers, which appeared in the late 1950s. The existence of this student society shows that Plymouth was already attracting a nucleus of students from abroad.

[PCL-LS]

INTERMEDIATE SCIENCE.						PURE SCIENCE FOR B.Sc.							
	MONDAY.		TUESDAY.		WEDNESDAY.		THURSDAY.		FRIDAY.		SATURDAY.		
Time.	Subject.	†Room.	Subject.	†Room.	Subject.	†Room.	Subject.	†Room.	Subject.	†Room.	Subject.	†Room.	
9¼–10¼	Physics L.	P29	Mechanics *or* Zoology L.	P11b P18	Mathematics *or* Botany L.	P31 P21	Chemistry L. *or* Mathematics	P5 P11a	Mathematics *or* Zoology L.	P11a P18	Physics L.	P29	
10¼–11¼	Mathematics *or* Botany L.	P11a P18	Mechanics *or* Zoology Pr.	P11b P21	Mathematics *or* Botany Pr.	P31 P21	Mathematics *or* Botany L.	P11a P18	Mechanics *or* Zoology Pr.	P11a P21	Mathematics *or* Physics Pr. *or* Botany Pr.	P11a P30 P21	
11¼–12¼	Chemistry *or* Mathematics	P14 P11a	Mathematics *or* Zoology Pr.	P27 P21	French & German *or* Botany Pr.	P11b P21	Physics L.	P29					
2–3							Botany L. *or* Mechanics L.	P18 D10 *or* P11a	Organic or Physical Chem. L.	P14			
3–4	Physics Pr.	P30	Chem. Pr.	P13 & P14			Mech. L. & Pr. *or*	D10	Chem. Pr.	P13 & P14			
4–5							Physics Pr.	P.29 & P30					

INTERMEDIATE SCIENCE (Alternative Courses).
  This Course is suitable for Students who wish to take their London Intermediate, the First Medical or Dental Examination for London M.B. or B.Sc. (Veterinary Science), and for entrance Scholarships to the London Hospitals. Students for these courses will be given individual time tables from the above.

3.28 The 1947-48 intermediate level day class time table for University of London external degree students. The one and a half hour break for lunch, was, by the late 1990s a very distant memory.

[PDTC Prospectus, 1947-48]

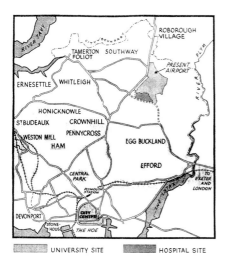

UNIVERSITY SITE   HOSPITAL SITE

3.29 By the 1960s, Plymouth City Council had a site at Derriford, adjacent to the airport, which it had designated for university development. In the end this was taken by the College of St. Mark and St. John which moved from London in the early 1970s.

[PCL-LS, press cuttings file]

boundaries. The opening, by the playwright George Bernard Shaw in 1929, was a grand affair. His enigmatic address, in which he alternately denigrated and complimented the role of universities in front of the assembled dignitaries from the UCSWE and City of Plymouth councils, was broadcast live (the only way at that time) by the local radio station in Plymouth.[60]

Table 3.5

**Plymouth and Devonport Technical College 1923-38
Student Achievement (passes) in External Examinations.**

Examination	1923/4	1924/5	1935/6	1936/7	1937/8
BSc (Gen.) Final	1	2	3	2	
BSc (Eng.) Final			6		3
BA Final	1				
BComm Final			1		
Inter BSc (Gen.)	3	3		4	6
Inter BSc (Eng.)	4	1	2	5	4
Inter BComm			1		1
Matriculation (Lond)	8	5	10	8	3
HNC (Mech.Eng.)	3	4			
HNC (Elec.Eng)			2	2	
HNC (Naval Arch.)			2		1
HNC (Building)			3	1	3
ONC (Mech.Eng.)			2	3	1
ONC (Elec.Eng.)		2	5	6	1
ONC (Naval Arch.)				4	
ONC (Building)			7	5	6
Inter RIBA			4		
Pharmaceutical Prelim		1	19	6	5
Pharmaceutical Final			17	11	16
Other professional			21	12	16
1st Medical/Dental	7	2		3	2

Source: UPPLY, Principal's Annual Reports

The numbers passing the more advanced external examinations, University of London degree, national certificates and professional body assessments, remained quite small during the inter-war period (Table 3.5), though comparing the early 1920s with the late 1930s there was clearly an increase. The great majority of students attending PDTC were taking lower level qualifications for the City and Guilds of London Institute (CGLI), the Royal Society of Arts (RSA) or the College's own internal examinations. Classes for the more advanced studies were of course larger than the pass data indicates, taking into account failures and non-completing students. Whether the growth in the 1930s can be attributed to the link with the UCSWE rather than to the general increase in the number of students attending technical colleges must remain an open question.

The demise of the interim scheme did not mean that the idea of a university level establishment at Plymouth, either an engineering faculty under UCSWE, or an independent establishment, had finally been laid to rest. The idea seems to have become engraved in the minds of successive generations of Plymouth education office officials and of long serving councillors, to be raised at every occasion when the development of tertiary education in the Borough was under consideration. It was taken into account in *A Plan for Plymouth* produced during the 1939-45 war, and re-emerged in 1948 in an unsuccessful bid by the UCSWE, for university status.[61] In a *volte face* from his pre-war attitude, Principal Murray, resurrected the old federal idea, and led a deputation of regional representatives, including Plymouth, to the UGC, whose Chairman in 1948 was Sir Walter Moberly, Murray's predecessor as Principal at Exeter, 1925-6. No ground preparation had been attempted. London opposition to the federal concept resurfaced, and the overture was rejected out of hand. Exeter's successful petition to the Privy Council, carefully prepared in 1954-5, avoided the federal concept. The UCSWE received its charter as the University of Exeter in December 1955.

Plymouth's aspirations for a university reappeared again in 1960, with a green-field site of 193 acres at Derriford, three miles north of the City centre replacing the Devonport building as the main location.[62] This was a period when it was widely recognised that a rapid expansion of university provision was urgently needed. The numbers in sixth forms had more than doubled in the past decade; the bulge in the birth rate following the war was now feeding through into tertiary education; expansion might correct the persistent imbalance of opportunity for the offspring of semi-skilled and unskilled workers; Britain still lagged behind other countries in the proportion of the population entering higher education; a connection between higher education and economic growth was recognised.[63] This was the context in which the Government was preparing to announce the creation of a number of completely new universities, in the knowledge that both industry and the opposition supported the expansion. So Plymouth prepared its case, made sure that Exeter would not oppose the idea, and submitted its bid to the University Grants Committee in December 1960.[64] Both Plymouth's merits as a university city and the choice of site were widely debated in the local press. Arguments against picking Plymouth included the lack of good research libraries in the area (the MBA library excepted), the lowering of academic standards as only failed 'Oxbridge' applicants would opt for Plymouth, and the small local population base. The merits of a location in the vicinity of the City Museum and Library, instead of a green-field site, included the area's designation by the planners as a cultural zone, proximity to transport hubs and the fuller life and more realistic experience of a city centre location.[65] By the end of 1961, it was clear that Plymouth, as with several other towns, had missed out to the stronger cases made for Norwich, Brighton, York, Colchester, Canterbury, Coventry and finally Lancaster. Hopes were raised again with the appearance of the Robbins Report in 1963-4. But larger population centres were in favour. In June 1967 a *Western Morning News* headline read "Concentrate on Polytechnic - University 'a long dead corpse".[66]

Towards a Regional College

Although the Government had promoted some development of technical education in the late 1930s, it was the second world war which ensured that further education generally, and higher technical and scientific education in

3.30 *For most of its existence from the 1920s, the School of Housecraft, later called the College of Domestic Science, occupied houses on the east side of Portland Square (now University property). It merged with the College of Further Education in the early 1970s.*

[PCL-LS, press cuttings/ephemera files]

Table 3.6

Plymouth College of Technology, Teaching Staff, Autumn 1963.

Department	Grade	SL	L	AL (B)	AL (A)	PT (D)	PT (E)	Total
Mechanical Engineering	IV	5*	10	6	3	7	37	68
Physics & Mathematics	III	3	8	5	2	3	24	45
Commerce and Admin.	III	1	7	14	12	4	52	90
Electrical Engineering	III	5*	9	10	1	9	8	42
Chemistry & Biology	II	2	7	7	2	10	11	39
Navigation	III	2	8	11	-	1	7	29
Building	II+	1	2	8	1	5	22	39
Heads of Department		7						7
Total		7	19	51	61	21	39	161	359

Source: PRO, ED 114/1531, HMI Report, 1963. Notes: * includes one principal lecturer. + The HoD Building worked part-time, being also head of Architecture in the College of Art. Departmental grading related to the academic level of teaching, and defined the staffing levels and remuneration. Abbreviations: SL senior lecturer; L lecturer, AL (B) assistant lecturer (grade B); AL(A) assistant lecturer (grade A); PT (D) part-time (day); PT(E) part-time (evening only).

particular, would be much higher on the list of government priorities in the post-war period. The war itself saw significant developments in science and technology which called for a better educated work force, and this emphasis was sustained subsequently through the arms race of the cold war, and through developments in the production and use of manufactured goods. Such factors, together with the need to retrain large numbers of ex-service personnel, ensured that technical colleges across the country continued with significantly larger student bodies immediately after the war than they had catered for in the 1930s, and that there would be a steady expansion thereafter. However it was to be over a decade of severe economic constraint before the aspirations of the post-war planners and the recommendations of investigating committees would lead to a major reconstruction of further and higher education provision in Britain.

The general pattern of development in Plymouth appears to be typical of the rest of the country.[67] By 1948/9 PDTC was enrolling three times the number of students compared with ten years earlier, though this only represented a doubling of student hours (Table 3.3, charts 3.1 and 3.2). With numbers of full-time students remaining comparatively small well into the 1960s, the college continued to cater mainly for part-time students, with the

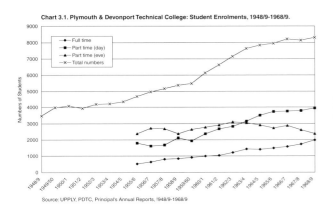

Chart 3.1. Plymouth & Devonport Technical College: Student Enrolments, 1948/9-1968/9.

Source: UPPLY, PDTC, Principal's Annual Reports, 1948/9-1968/9

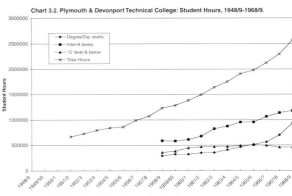

Chart 3.2. Plymouth & Devonport Technical College: Student Hours, 1948/9-1968/9.

Source: UPPLY, PDTC, Principal's Annual Reports, 1948/9-1968/9

most significant development being the expansion of day-release study as employers increasingly came to recognise the value of a better educated work force. Total student hours was to reach three times pre-war levels by the time the first of the College's new buildings became available in 1954. In such circumstances, the College was desperately short of teaching accommodation, a situation which would persist well into the 1960s. The transfer of the College of Art to Palace Court in 1950 released space but over the next two decades less advanced courses in particular were moved out to a variety of temporary locations across the city. As early as 1946, for example, the School of Navigation found itself in the former military hospital in Stoke, while in the mid 1960s Electrical Engineering's wiring training occupied a former supermarket at Drake's Circus for two years. In this context, the continued survival of the unloved Plymouth building assumed an unanticipated importance to the PDTC despite the progressive phases of new college building development which came into use during the 1960s. The College found itself in conflict with the re-development plans at the north eastern edge of the new city centre. The new peripheral road system demanded a roundabout at the lower end of North Hill further down than the Museum/Public Library building. The 1892 Technical College building was now scheduled for demolition to make way for the roundabout with its pedestrian underpass which was to become the main route for staff and students alike between the college site and the city centre shops. The final phase of new building, occupied by the College in the mid 1960s, in the end offered only replacement teaching accommodation instead of the augmentation which had been anticipated.[68]

In the late 1940s, however, although the redevelopment of Plymouth's further and higher education was on the agenda, the pattern of development which would be in place twenty years later, was by no means clear. Like all other LEAs, Plymouth was required to draw up a plan for the future development all sectors of post-school educational provision in the Borough, taking account of the provisions of the 1944 Education Act. In the interplay between the LEA and officials of the Ministry of Education, development plans rarely start with a completely clean sheet. Invariably the baggage of previous discussions carries forward, with the Ministry particularly, being capable of resurrecting unresolved matters from the distant past, and the LEA always seeking to reduce the impact on the rates of any new initiative. Often local understanding was found to be out of step with that of Ministry officials. Thus in Plymouth's 1948 scheme, much play was made of PDTC becoming a regional college which implied Cornwall and Devon making significant financial contributions. Yet the idea that 'technical, commercial and women's work' should be separate persisted despite the opinion of the HMI Report of 1937, endorsed by an inspection in 1949, that, particularly where advanced work was concerned, this should all be part of a single establishment.[69] The plan had at that time to embrace the 1944 Act's idea of County Colleges, but was still distorted by the idea of involvement in the UCSWE. It also had to deal with art education, evening institutes,

3.31 Dr. John Graymore, Principal from 1947, was wont to pursue his research in the Chemical Laboratory of the 1892 Plymouth building, though the odours permeated into the nearby secretarial offices.

[PCL-LS, The Wanderers (March 1959), 4; Miss D. Potter]

3.32 The Duchess of Kent visited Plymouth in 1952 to lay the foundation stone of the first of the technical college buildings to be erected since the 1890s.

[Photo: Dave Griffiths]

3.33 Work on the first of the post-war College buildings, the Engineering Block (now Smeaton Building) started in 1952. The accommodation situation was so desperate that classes were being held on the ground floor before the building had been completed.

[PCL-LA, Tekel (1953), photo J.J. Andry]

3.34 This areial view of the College site was taken in the late 1950s. The Engineering Block is completed and the housing on the west side of Portland Square has been cleared in readiness for the Workshop Block. The reservoir (top left), Sherwell Church, the Public Secondary School and the Education Offices survive from this period, but most of the housing has been demolished.

[PCL-LS, photo: D.P. Fitzgerald]

community centres, the youth service, correspondence tuition, residential study, and other forms of adult education, and it is perhaps not surprising that London found the 1948 scheme confused and insufficiently worked through. It took until August 1954 for a reworked scheme to be granted ministerial approval. Nevertheless, the Colleges of Art and Housecraft continued to be seen as separate establishments, while the proposed link with the UCSWE remained prominent. The plan still failed to address the detail of PDTC subjects, referring instead only to an engineering school, a building school and a commercial school. The engineering school would inevitably be interactive with the UCSWE engineering faculty were it to materialise. The commercial department of the college did become a significant development, but the building department, already in existence, did not develop the strength and significance anticipated in the HMI reports. Although

3.35, 3.36 This model and artist's impression depict the compact educational zone anticipated in the mid-1950s. Portland Square is preserved as a green space at the heart of the campus. Existing buildings: 1 Sherwell Church, 2 Museum, Art Gallery & Public Library, 3 Education Offices, 4 Public Secondary School, 5 Engineering Block. Planned buildings: 6 Workshop Block, 7 College of Housecraft, 8 Hostel block, 9 Assembley Hall, 10 Science and Commerce Block, 11 Administration and Communal block, 12 Exercise block, 13 Gymnasium, 14 Swimming Pool, 15 College of Art.

[PCL-LS, photos: Western Morning News (1957).

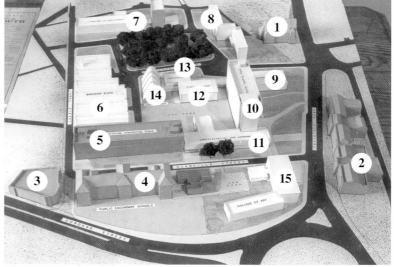

ministerial minutes of the period allude in passing to the development of the navigation school, the Plymouth scheme completely fails to anticipate the major expansion of the Merchant Navy education and training in Plymouth from the late 1950s.[70] However, Plymouth was not without backing for PDTC becoming a regional college, having achieved the endorsement of the South West Regional Council for Further Education in 1949, and agreement that costs would be shared by Devon, Cornwall and Plymouth LEAs in proportion to student hours. However, a reformed Governing Body for 'Plymouth Colleges of Further Education' (including Plymouth, Devon, Cornwall and industrial representatives), did not meet until October 1957, at the time that PDTC status was raised to that of a regional college in the wake of the seminal white paper, *Technical Education, 1956.*[71] Government recognition was confirmed in 1961 when the College was allowed to change its name to Plymouth College of Technology.[72]

3.37 By 1959, new buildings to the north and east of Portland Square appear to have been dropped from the plan, though the nuclear laboratory has been added.

[UPPLY, PDTC Prospectus (1959/60)]

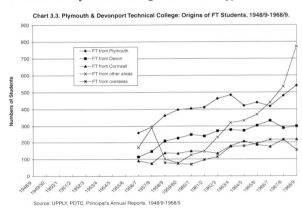

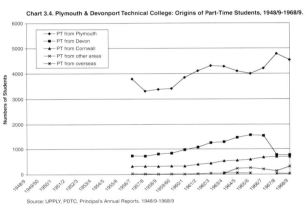

Some idea of the relative significance of the College's regional role in this period may be gleaned from charts 3.3 and 3.4, which separate students funded by Plymouth, Cornwall and Devon from other areas and overseas financed students. Throughout the period to 1969, more full-time students came from Devon than Cornwall, but both these were significantly exceeded by those belonging to Plymouth. The most notable feature of chart. 3.3 is the rapid increase, as the 1960s progress, in the numbers of full-time students from the parts of Britain than Devon and Cornwall. Predictably the great majority of part-time students (Chart. 3.4) came from Plymouth. Again Devon produced more students than Cornwall, but in both cases such students would have lived within relatively easy commuting distance of the college, or worked for Plymouth employers. This point is made by the sharp decline in the numbers of part-time students from Devon between 1966/7 and 1967/8 and the corresponding increase in those from Plymouth, which may be attributed to the extension of Plymouth's boundaries in 1967 when the suburbs of Plymstock and Plympton were absorbed from Devon.

Important in achieving official designation as a regional college was a significant proportion of high level work with staff, facilities and equipment to match. The breakdown for Plymouth, expressed in student hours, is shown in Chart. 3.2. During the 1950s and 1960s, the dominant category at the

3.38 Mr. Eric Bailey, who succeeded Dr Graymore as Principal in 1959, was to see the College through a period of rapid change. This included its designation as a regional College of Technology and then as a Polytechnic, the completion of the post war set of buildings and the move towards much more full-time day study.

[PCL-LS, The Wanderers (March 1960), 4.]

3.39 In this view (ca 1961) of the second phase of new College buildings, the nissen huts, which had provided temporary accommodation for bombed out shops, are being demolished. On the opposite side of Glanville Street is the old technical college building which was also soon to be pulled down.

[PCL-LS, photo: Modern Portraits]

3.40 By 1964 the Science section of the eight story teaching block had been completed. The outline superimposed indicates the northern section, intended for the Commerce Department, and the Assembly Hall, which constituted the third and final phase of the development.

[UPPLY, PDTC Prospectus (1964/65)]

College was the intermediate level, which included 'A' level, Ordinary National Diploma, Ordinary National Certificate and a range of professional body studies, about 50 per cent of its work in 1962/3.[73] 'O' level, craft and similar 'school' level teaching amounted to about 29 per cent of work in 1962/3, with degree, diploma, Higher National Diploma, Higher National Certificate and some professional body teaching accounting for about 21 per cent of work in the same year. University level work shows a significant increase towards the end of the 1960s, part of the justification for the granting of polytechnic status, but the proportion at the end of the 1950s must have been barely sufficient for achieving recognition as a regional college of technology. Nevertheless, by 1963 the transfer of school and part-time intermediate work (work inappropriate to a regional college) to a new further education college in Plymouth, was openly under discussion, and recommended by the HMIs:[74]

3.41 This picture of the old College, with Science Block behind it, was taken in 1966, just before demolition started and while the roundabout , for which it had to make way, was being constructed.

[Photo: A. Kennerley]

3.42 A view of the Assembly Hall and Science/Commerce Block soon after completion. The changing names and logos on the east wall of the Assembly Hall marked the changing status of the establishment over the next 30 years.

[UPPLY, PDTC Prospectus (1967/68)]

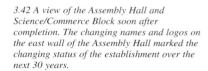

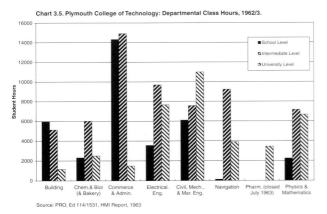

Chart 3.5. Plymouth College of Technology: Departmental Class Hours, 1962/3.

Source: PRO, Ed 114/1531, HMI Report, 1963

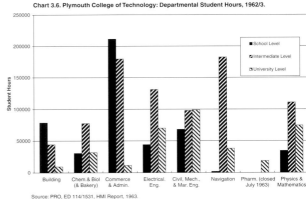

Chart 3.6. Plymouth College of Technology: Departmental Student Hours, 1962/3.

Source: PRO, ED 114/1531, HMI Report, 1963.

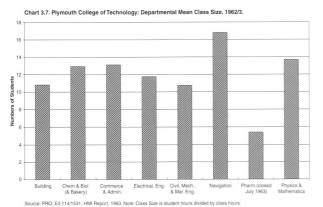

Chart 3.7. Plymouth College of Technology: Departmental Mean Class Size, 1962/3.

Source: PRO, Ed 114/1531, HMI Report, 1963. Note: Class Size is student hours divided by class hours

"It is the main recommendation of this report that the college should gradually cease to attempt to cover the whole range of technical and commercial education and that every effort should be made to expand the advanced work in all appropriate fields where there is a reasonable demand regionally and even, in certain specialised spheres, nationally."

The effect that such a transfer might have on individual departments is shown by Chart. 3.5 and 3.6, which give the three levels of work in each department in terms of class hours and student hours. By 1962/3 commerce was the largest department, but as with the smallest department, building (pharmacy closed that year), the bulk of its work would transfer to a new lower level college. About half the work of the engineering departments and mathematics and physics would be retained while the navigation and chemistry and biology departments would retain rather smaller proportions of their work. The College at that time was working with a mean class size of about 12 students (Chart. 3.7), though navigation, almost all of whose students were in full-time day attendance, achieved a mean size of 16. Finally, before leaving this snapshot of the state of the College in 1962/3, Table 3.6 provides data on the numbers and grading of academic staff. Full-time staff had increased to 160 who would have certainly carried the major proportion of the teaching load, and probably almost all of the advanced teaching. Nevertheless, the College still relied heavily on 200 part-time staff, particularly for the lower level evening work. The level of work in each department is reflected in the staff and departmental grading.

3.43, 3.44 The opening of the Communal Block provided a new student canteen and a new library.

[UPPLY, PDTC Prospectus (1963/64, 1964/65)]

For an understanding of some of the problems faced by those working and studying at PDTC in the 1940s and 1950s, it is necessary to return to the war years. As noted earlier, throughout the war 'normal' classes were maintained at PDTC at much the same scale as in 1938, and a significant amount of war-related training was undertaken. Principal Boeree and the Head of Civil and Mechanical Engineering, Major Hambling, were amongst the staff absent on war service, and no doubt Principal Duckett of the School of Arts and Crafts, who was also acting as PDTC principal, made up his staff as best he could using temporary and part-time appointments. Conditions for staff and students alike, by no means ideal before the war, inevitably deteriorated as the war progressed. The Plymouth building, already in a sorry state despite the limited refurbishment just before the war, somehow managed to survive the bombing, though many properties nearby were hit. No doubt all who knew it, secretly hoped it would become total loss, perhaps bringing nearer the long-contemplated replacement.

The physical conditions in which classes had to take place were, during the 1940s and 1950s, often primitive, partly owing to conditions brought about by the war, and partly through the use of unsuitable temporary premises in an effort to accommodate expansion. Those teaching and studying at Plymouth in that period vividly remember the conditions.[75] Nearby bomb hits may have missed the 'tech' but of course the blast blew out the windows, practical work was carried out in laboratories from which the sky lights were missing. The typical staff work load was twenty-six and a half hours class-contact per week, and some staff regularly had to hold down two classes simultaneously, delivering a lecture while supervising a practical in an adjacent laboratory. Evening classes could involve as many as eight separate streams, all of which meant separate preparation and oversight. Rushed repairs to the building were often 'botched', as in the case of the replastered ceiling which promptly collapsed owing to the weight of 'dustmo' (sweepings) which had accumulated from the floor above. No eating in class rooms was allowed as the building was heavily infested with mice. In 1949 it was found that switching on the lights in the Biology Laboratory fused the lights in an adjacent laboratory. The electrical insulation had rotted leaving runs of bare wiring. Rewiring the following session managed to leave many lights unconnected as there were no wiring diagrams for the building. One class room seemed to make people feel ill, until it was realised that carbon monoxide was leaking through a hole from the boiler room below, whereupon the room was closed off. Soon after he arrived in 1947 Principal Graymore turned one room in the building into a student canteen. Well meaning though this was, it did not help teaching as the building was devoid of sound proofing and the noise from the canteen interfered with teaching. Pressure on accommodation was so great by the 1950s that classes were held in the unfinished open ground floor of the new block in Glanville Street (Engineering, now the Smeaton Building), with two teachers lecturing at each end of the same undivided space.[76]

Before work could be started on the modern buildings, property not already in the hands of the City Council had to be purchased, and then all the old buildings in the area selected had to be demolished. Meanwhile, negotiations with the officials in the education ministry in London will have been ongoing perhaps over several years. Almost every detail was subject to ministerial approval including the site itself, outline and detail of the design and equipment, tenders and selection of builders, and finally the payments to the various contractors subject to certification that the work had been done to a satisfactory standard. Finance controlled the whole process. From the mid-1950s there was always some construction work taking place at the PDTC sites, but hardly any of the major developments reached completion without delays and amendment, usually associated with the state of the Country's finances. Commonly, starts to approved projects could be held back for a year or two, or some cut in the design could be enforced, to bring a project within a new financial target.

Work on the Engineering block, which was the first element in the complete redevelopment of PDTC (now following the plan to concentrate technical college work on the Plymouth site), started in 1951. Early on, as noted above, it had to serve as a multi-purpose building. So the ground floor, intended as workshops for automobile, bricklaying, plastering and plumbing students, initially housed engineering machinery pending the erection of the workshop block. The first floor, Engineering Science, included three classrooms, two proper drawing offices, four laboratories, and balance, features and fine measurements rooms. There was also a small college library. The second floor was given over to building, with seven class rooms, five drawing rooms, a building science laboratory and materials and balance rooms. Until 1970, the top floor of the four story building was occupied by the School of Navigation and the Bakery section. The latter was provided with two classrooms, food testing, icing and piping rooms. The smell of fresh bread and cakes permeated the building, drawing staff and students up to the two bakeries soon after four p.m. each day when the efforts of the students

3.45 This view of the workshop block today is very little changed from the scene in the late 1960s, except for the re-clad engineering block with the satellite dish on its roof.

[Photo: A. Kennerley]

went on sale at advantageous prices. The School of Navigation at the other end of the floor could hardly match that temptation, though it had four classrooms, instruments, chart and seamanship rooms, its own library and a small room for master mariners. On the roof sprouted its mast, compasses and other ships' instruments. According to members of the college in that period it was the extrovert head of Navigation, Captain Johnson, who carried the administrative burden in the College for bringing the Engineering block, 'modernistic in design', decor and furnishing, to fruition.[77]

The workshop block (now the Brunel Workshops), which ought to have been ready within a year of the Engineering Block, was not completed until 1960. Once fitted out, the workshops catered for the practical training, demonstration and experimental work in mechanical and civil engineering. There was a new heat engines workshop, another full of lathes and similar machine tools for workshop training, laboratories for structures, fluid dynamics and civil engineering surveying, and facilities for testing concrete cubes for local civil engineering contractors. This last produced a steady income for the College of some £500 annually. A late addition to the design, the Nucleonics Laboratory housing an electron microscope, was completed in 1961.[78] This was linked to the north end of the workshop block. Meanwhile, work had started on the southern half of the eight story Science block facing the City Museum across North Hill. Physics and Biology moved in 1962, and the Chemistry floors were occupied in 1963. Work on the administration (Link) block had also started. This was occupied in 1962. This at last gave the College a modern set of ancillary facilities, not found in the 1890s buildings. The ground floor provided administrative offices for the Principal, the registrar and clerical staff, and for the first time a proper staff room. The first floor provided the College's first purpose built library, with seating for 80 though as yet with only 10,000 volumes.[79] On the second floor was the new self service canteen for use by both students and staff, seating 280. This block lay along the north side of Glanville Street in line with the Engineering block and at right angles to the Science block with which it was integrated. A bridge at first floor level linked it with the Engineering block. In 1964 work started on the northern half of the Science block, to be used initially by the Commerce department, together with the extension eastwards for the Assembly Hall, with its television galleries and a large lecture theatre at first floor level. Phase three of the development plan, as this was called, was completed in 1966, and it was then that the original 1892 building was demolished. Planning provided for a further block, extending westwards from the north end of the Science block, but this idea was dropped. The plan also allowed for a students' union complex, but this did not materialise until 1976.[80] However, agreement had been reached early in the 1960s for the building of a residential nautical college on Portland Square, and a new seamanship centre at Coxside. The latter was completed in 1967 and the former in 1970. These and other buildings occupied by the School of Navigation are discussed in Chapter 4.

The One thing that the College had always lacked, proper recreational facilities for student use, was also rectified in the late 1960s. Since the 1920s, principals' reports had bewailed the failure of the local authority to provide dedicated playing fields for the College. Certainly the Council owned numerous playing fields, but first priority always went to its schools leaving the College teams to pick up on isolated vacancies. In particular clubs found that they could rarely offer home fixtures, and were often condemned to arranging away matches only. Considerable assistance was given over the years by the local armed services who co-operated by allowing the use of their own pitches. Eventually in 1963, the City Council allocated land, though it turned out to be something of a poisoned chalice. The College playing fields at Ernesettle, some six miles from the City Centre, with all the travelling such a distance implies, are on the banks of the River Tamar on a former waste disposal site. Although roughly levelled with a surface dressing of soil, drainage was very poor. Certainly in the early years of College use, the pitches laid out there were unplayable for much of the student year. However, at least the clubs had a home. The College built a recreation hall on the site which opened in 1967 and the Student's Union funded the building of a pavilion which opened the same year, and an extension opened in 1969.

Despite the condition of the playing fields, the facility at Ernesettle provided a focus for a rapid increase in student recreational activity, becoming available at a time when the numbers of full-time and day release students was beginning to increase rapidly. While the College had had a high proportion of part-time and evening students it had never been easy to sustain a full student life, and the provision of facilities for student activity had been given very little attention. However student union officers had the use of a room in the old Plymouth building, and by 1963 had "...the good fortune to possess a pleasant suite of rooms of its own..." according to the HMIs.[81] This was in the new Administration block, and included a games room, separate commonrooms for men and women, a student committee room and a rest room. The refectory and library were in the same block.[82] But within a few years activity had grown such that this had become desperately over crowded. Student activities were increasingly successful. The proceeds from the annual rag grew from £500 in 1958/9 to over £2000 in 1963/4. In 1961/2 a referendum produced a majority in favour of compulsory membership, a move subsequently endorsed by the College governors. However, this was an issue which did not find universal favour particularly among more mature students taking short full-time courses and students being taught in the increasing number of annexes who had little contact with the main building. Another measure of student activity was the increase in the number and range of student clubs and societies. In the mid-1960s they numbered eighteen: Soccer, Rugby, Tennis, Cricket, Hockey, Table Tennis, Badminton, Basketball, Fencing, Weight Lifting, Drama, Music, Film, Engineering, Bakery, Biology, Christian Union, Overseas Students. Students were also active in raising the profile of the college through assistance with the open fortnight and careers convention for prospective students, which became a regular feature of the annual cycle in this period.

3.46, 3.47 In the early 1960s student sports teams still relied on borrowed facilities. Then playing fields at Ernesettle were acquired. The pavilion and sports hall were built towards the end of that decade.

[UPPLY, The Wanderers (May 1961); photo: Western Morning News, A.Kennerley]

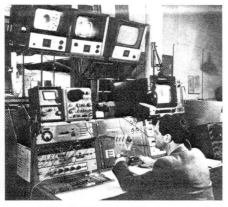

3.48, 3.49, 3.50 In the 1960s the Work of the Department of Electrical Engineering ranged widely. It included experimental television, marine radio training and turbo generation, illustrated in these pictures.

[UPPLY, PDTC/PCoT Prospectus (1958/59, 1959/60,1966/67)]

The College's improving association with schools in the area was enhanced by the creation of television links from the College television studio in the Science block. This was part of an initiative by the Electrical Engineering Department to provide training for the television industry and to develop a specialism in Educational Technology, marking the College as a national leader in that field. The same session, 1963/4, saw this Department organising conferences on Computers in Schools which attracted teachers from no less than 86 schools, and for the Association of Marine Radio Schools, and running short courses on electronics in schools. The following session saw 90 teachers from local schools taking a course in television teaching and contributing to the local educational television network. From these beginnings emerged a one term full time course. Even groups of HMIs came to Plymouth for short courses in the new subject. By 1968 an Educational Technology group had been formed within the Department, which had in a few short years achieved a national reputation for innovation in the subject, confirmed by the appointment of the Head of Electrical Engineering, Mr. B.R Webster, to the National Council for Educational Technology.

Of course the Electrical Engineering Department was developing rapidly in other fields. Throughout the 1960s new full time and day release courses were being introduced particularly at the more advanced levels to match the trend away from evening class work. These included the HND (sandwich) in Electrical Engineering and an option in Communication Engineering, the College Diploma in Electrical Engineering rated at honours degree standard, and from 1969, the first CNAA Degree in Communication Engineering. This last course identified another grouping within the Department. A significant feature in this area was the development of courses for marine radio operators and courses in radio and radar maintenance. The former were also pre-sea courses, and with an element of occupational socialisation in mind, the decision was taken in 1961/62 that the 78 students then enrolled should wear Merchant Navy uniforms during their studies, emulating the practice in the School of Navigation whose cadets had worn uniform since the 1940s. The Department also pioneered work with computers, designing and building its own analogue machine in 1961, which was featured on local television. Naturally, special courses in this new field of computing and control engineering were provided. In 1965 two new computers were purchased and a service provided to other departments of the College and externally, for example, in connection with medical research. This period of rapid change of course involved the staff in major stages of laboratory development with the department moving from the Devonport building and expanding as successive phases of the building plan were completed. As well as its range of fourteen full-time and the short courses mentioned above, Electrical Engineering also continued to offer part-time courses, thirteen in 1967/68.

Developments in Civil and Mechanical Engineering may have lacked the profile of the world of electronics, but nevertheless there was a similar range of course changes and increases in the numbers of full-time and day release students. In 1963, London University again revalidated the Department for

3.51, 3.52, 3.53 Student practical work in the Department of Civil and Mechanical Engineering included hydraulic measurement, steam turbine performance testing and concrete beam destruction testing.

[UPPLY, PDTC/PCoT Prospectus (1959/60, 1961/62, 1964/65)]

teaching the external degrees in civil and mechanical engineering, and the Plymouth staff made visits to London to be briefed on the revised regulations London University had introduced. In 1961 the College Diploma in Civil Engineering as well as the degree were delivered involving new sandwich arrangements with local employers, and the former was rated as equivalent to an honours degree. Such was the basis for applications to the CNAA (1964) to be validated for the awards of that new body. In the event, the process turned out to be more tortuous than might have been expected, and approval for the degrees in Civil and Mechanical Engineering was only achieved for starts in 1969. In the area of marine engineering, the OND (dating from 1957) was joined by a course for Part A of the government examinations, making marine engineering students a significant grouping in the department. There was also expansion in less advanced mechanical engineering courses which put pressure on the workshop facilities. This was eased at the end of the 1960s with an arrangement with HMS *Fisgard* at Torpoint, for the use of their workshop facilities. As well as full-time courses, the Department continued to offer an extensive range of part-time courses in engineering subjects, twenty-one in 1967/68. That session it also offered eight short courses.

The work of the Department of Chemistry and Biology largely continued the established courses for the science degree awards of London University. However, an accreditation visit by the Royal Institute of Chemists, with the plans for a nucleonics laboratory well in hand, secured approval for a course for the Graduateship of that Institute. As an addition to its national certificate course in Chemistry, the development the HND in Biological Technology proved to be a particularly successful initiative, as was the HND in Applied Biology from 1968. Unfortunately the attempts to establish a CNAA masters' degree in crystallography did not find favour, and the CNAA also rejected proposals for a degree in applied chemistry. Perhaps that decision was

3.54, 3.55, 3.56 These illustrations show the practical work of students studying biology and chemistry: practical zoology, biological dissection and first year students working on chemical experiments.

[UPPLY, PCoT Prospectus (1962/63, 1963/64)]

influenced by over supply in the country, as the Department's application for an HND in applied chemistry was rejected by the DES in 1969. However, as noted below, the department's research led the way in the College.

Although the other science department, Physics and Mathematics, had a similarly increasing pattern of London University external degree work, the bulk of its teaching was in the service of courses in the two engineering departments and in the School of Navigation. Almost all their courses included physics and mathematics as foundations for the understanding of the applied content, so that the service teaching expanded with the growth in numbers of technology students and the development of new courses. However the Physics and Mathematics department was not without its own initiatives which included the Diploma in Mathematics for in-service teachers and the National Certificate in Applied Physics, both dating from 1960. It was also involved in developments in computing, offering short courses with its analogue computer, and was at the forefront of the initiative to obtain permission and funding for the College to purchase a modern digital instrument. This was successful in 1967/68 when an IBM 1130 machine was installed in time for students on the new HND in Computer Mathematics to use it for practical work. The Department was also the base for the development of new subject areas. Geology was built up from 1959/60 initially with one lecturer as a service for engineering courses but increasingly as a subject in its own right as it was not widely offered in Britain at that time. Another subject beginning to achieve a separate identity in this period was statistics, and from 1967/68 Geography was added to Geology and Physics as subjects which could be studied for London external degrees. These developments were facilitated by new laboratories in the Science block and the redeployment of the Pharmacy suite when that department was closed in 1963, the College not being able to offer pharmacy degrees. Like other departments, Physics and Mathematics made a CNAA degree proposal, in Applied Physics, but failed to gain the necessary approval from the DES who turned it down on economic grounds.

3.57, 3.58, 3.59 *The study by pharmaceutical students of chemistry and microbiology, which had started at the College in the mid-1920s, was about to cease with the closure of Pharmacy Department in 1963. At that time a significant proportion of pharmacists practising in Devon and Cornwall had trained at the College.*

[UPPLY, PCoT Prospectus (1961/62, 1962/63); photo: A.Kennerley]

The unification of commercial and associated subjects within the PDTC was a long-advocated initiative of the late 1940s. By the 1960s the Commerce and Administration Department had grown into the largest department of the College, though with a high proportion of lower level work. Because the College had no departments dedicated to the arts, humanities or social subjects, this Department increasingly delivered a diverse range of subjects which did not fit in with the other departments where the focus was on technical and scientific subjects. Close links were maintained with local businesses and to the core work of secretarial and office subjects, various aspects of business studies were developed as short or part-time courses. These included courses for particular trades such as fish, meat or drinks, courses for training and personnel officers, and subjects such as human relations in industry, work study and ergonomics. It was not until the mid-1960s that integrated business course began to gain acceptance, by which time the ONC in Business Studies and the HNC in Business Administration had been developed. The HND in Business Studies was offered from 1967/8 and the first small group of students attend the Diploma in Management Studies (DMS) course about the same time. Also at the more advanced level were the long-established courses for the financial world, banking, accountancy, insurance. The mid-1960s also saw the introduction of health visitor training, child care and social work courses for the Central Council of Social Work, and management courses for nursing and hospital staff. Some of these courses were delivered using programmed instruction with the 'Tutor' teaching machines. Language teaching also underwent development with the installation of a language laboratory used for training language teachers in schools and in connection with the general studies being introduced into national diploma and CNAA degree courses. Indeed, general (liberal or complementary studies) had a high profile at the end of the 1960s and the

3.60, 3.61, Secretarial training, also with origins in Plymouth in the 1920s, had by the 1960s become a significant part of the work of the Commerce Department. Along with bakery (which provided local training for the baking and confectionery industries) it was to transfer to the College of Further Education in 1970.

[UPPLY, PCoT Prospectus (1961/62, 1962/63)]

technical departments of the college in particular turned to the Commerce Department to deliver this element of their courses. Finally, the opening of the College sports facility at Ernesettle added sports teaching to the diverse range of subjects which fell to the Department to provide. In 1967/68 there were over sixty courses on offer of which twelve were full-time.

Despite the encouragement given by HMIs in earlier periods, much of the work of the Building Department (from 1965 Department of Construction Studies), was at craft level and mostly part-time throughout the 1950s and 1960s, serving the building trade crafts such as brick laying, carpentry, plumbing, plastering, gas fitting. Small numbers of students progressed to the more advanced courses leading to the membership grades of the Institute of Building, often via the Department's ONC, HNC and OND courses. The arrangement in which the head of department was also head of Architecture in the College of Art was ended in 1964, and there was some development of construction management for administrators of building firms. But, by 1969, the Department was preparing to move to Wyndham Street in anticipation of joining the new College of Further Education. This path would also be taken by the Bakery sub-department (reported with Chemistry and Biology) when the new CFE building was completed.

The growth of work in the main engineering, science and commercial departments put considerable stresses on the existing staff, despite the numbers of additional teaching staff which were taken on. With more advanced teaching, better qualified staff were required. New appointments helped but many existing staff sought higher qualifications through part-time study and research, while a few were allowed leave of absence to take full-time courses at universities. The 1965/66 Burnham review of the teaching establishment at colleges, led to five of the seven Plymouth College of Technology departments being upgraded, though as yet the College did not qualify for a full-time vice principal. Technician support was also far from adequate; salaries were depressed, and a new scheme planned in the same year was delayed owing to the current constraint on spending. Indeed at this time the DES issued instructions that classes under ten in size should be

3.62, 3.63 The Department of Construction Studies was the only full department of PcoT to be completely absorbed by the new College of Further Education in 1970. It occupied a lot of workshop space. The illustrations show training in decorative brick laying and prefabrication joinery.

[UPPLY, PDTC/PCoT Prospectus (1958/59, 1962/63)]

3.64, 3.65 The facilities in the Science Block in the 1960s included a number of lecture theatres, some of which are still in use. In the third phase of the building, the College was able to include a television Studio, used to train technicians for the television industry and by the Students Union Television group.

[UPPLY, PCoT Prospectus (1964/65, 1967/68)]

disbanded, affecting a number at the College. But the long-running under-provision of secretarial staff was seriously hindering all aspects of the work of the College. It was expressed by the Head of Electrical Engineering in the following words:

"After continuous requests for more secretarial help over many years, we are still paying the highest rates for the most inefficient typists in Plymouth, but it is hardly their fault, as they are supposed to be Senior and Principal Lecturers."

In 1967, when this comment was made, the College employed only seventeen office staff, which allowed most departments only one clerical assistant. Canteen staff numbered 21, and there were ten in the maintenance and caretaking section. Amongst the factors limiting the employment of support staff was the way in which the Government funded education. Essentially local authorities received funding for the provision of education, buildings, equipment, and teaching staff. Non-educational support had to be met from other sources, normally the rates, which accounted for the reluctance of local councils to expand their commitments. Additionally, because support staff working in educational establishments, were simply a sub-group under a single employer, their gradings fell within a much larger remuneration hierarchy where the higher grades were invariably in the local authority's central administration. In simple terms the college registrar, no matter how great the responsibilities, was subordinate to the senior staff in the education office and the post inevitably carried a lower grading.

With the division of the College already planned before the Government's binary policy on further and higher education was announced in 1965, the need for the College to develop its research portfolio had been recommended by the HMIs and recognised by the College. There had long been a trickle of research publications particularly in the science departments. A grant from the Department of Scientific and Industrial Research had allowed the purchase of x-ray diffraction equipment in 1958, and there was a research studentship in the Chemistry and Biology department in 1960. Research in subsequent years was carried out for English China Clays, Imperial Chemical Industries and the Medical Research Council, and a Science Research Council grant of £2,500 came in 1964. But recognition of the role of research came in 1967 with the research assistantship scheme and the appointment of six research assistants. The following year the first research groups in the college were recognised: soil science and marine science. Research activity in other departments tended to be projects for local organisations, and the technical departments were active in consultancy, providing advice to industry. So the scene was set for metamorphosis into a polytechnic.

3.66: Development Diagram

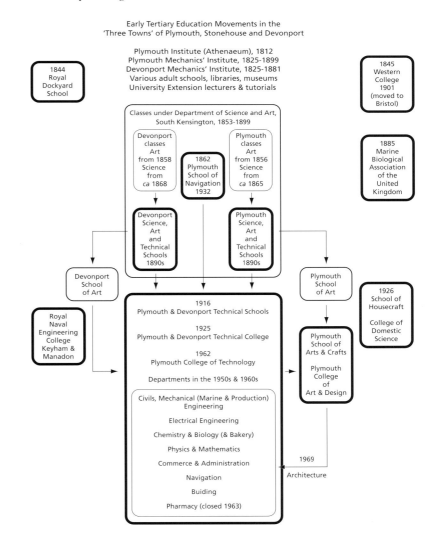

Early Tertiary Education Movements in the
'Three Towns' of Plymouth, Stonehouse and Devonport

Plymouth Institute (Athenaeum), 1812
Plymouth Mechanics' Institute, 1825-1899
Devonport Mechanics' Institute, 1825-1881
Various adult schools, libraries, museums
University Extension lecturers & tutorials

1844
Royal
Dockyard
School

1845
Western
College
1901
(moved to
Bristol)

Classes under Department of Science and Art,
South Kensington, 1853-1899

Devonport
classes
Art
from 1858
Science
from
ca 1868

1862
Plymouth
School of
Navigation
1932

Plymouth
classes
Art
from 1856
Science
from
ca 1865

1885
Marine
Biological
Association
of the
United
Kingdom

Devonport
Science,
Art
and
Technical
Schools
1890s

Plymouth
Science,
Art
and
Technical
Schools
1890s

Devonport
School
of Art

Plymouth
School
of Art

1926
School of
Housecraft

College of
Domestic
Science

Royal
Naval
Engineering
College
Keyham &
Manadon

1916
Plymouth & Devonport Technical Schools

1925
Plymouth & Devonport Technical College

1962
Plymouth College of Technology

Departments in the 1950s & 1960s

Plymouth
School of
Arts & Crafts

Plymouth
College
of
Art & Design

Civils, Mechanical (Marine & Production)
Engineering

Electrical Engineering

Chemistry & Biology (& Bakery)

Physics & Mathematics

Commerce & Administration

Navigation

Buiding

Pharmacy (closed 1963)

1969

Architecture

4.1 The cap badge adopted for the pre-sea cadet course in the late 1940s carried an image of the Golden Hinde, the ship in which Sir Francis Drake completed his circumnavigation in 1577-80.

Plymouth School of Navigation

C H A P T E R F O U R

Of the various elements which came together on the Plymouth campus of the University of Plymouth, the most venerable is the large department now known as the Institute of Marine Studies.[1] Dating from 1862, and with a clear lineage to its present position, it retained its trade mark title 'School of Navigation' until the late 1960s, when the series of maritime educational initiatives which was to change it into a world-scale maritime teaching and research establishment, began to gather momentum. Of course, investigation and writing was by no means a new departure for the staff of the School. Although its main function was the vocational preparation of merchant seafarers for their professional qualifications, the School especially through and as a legacy of its first head, Dr. John Merrifield, had a tradition of advanced study of maritime subjects through research and publishing.

Given its vocational relationship with the merchant shipping industry, the School of Navigation was inevitably more part of the national scene of nautical education, training and licensing, than of any provision for local industry as was the case with most vocational work in what were to become

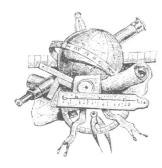

known as technical colleges. Indeed, its foundation was very much an outcome of national concerns about the quality of merchant ship officers, and in particular their ability to navigate ships on ocean voyages. In this sense the School was a relatively late addition to a national network of state-aided navigation schools, merchant shipping being one of the first industries for which special educational and training provision was made by the state.

Before this development, the advanced nature of the knowledge and skills needed by ocean navigators had led, from the seventeenth century, to teaching ashore. Navigation was taught in proprietary, endowed and charity schools, of navigation as a higher study for boys who had progressed sufficiently in what would today be called their secondary education. It was studied either before boys went to sea, or by serving seafarers between voyages.[2] Becoming proficient in navigation involved the mastery of a number of foundation scientific subjects which finally came together in the practice of navigation and nautical astronomy. Arithmetic, geometry, trigonometry, spherical trigonometry, geography, astronomy, meteorology, tides and ocean circulation (many of them subjects which today are very much degree level studies), all had to be addressed, together with the associated range of measuring instruments and resultant complex mathematical calculations. Indeed, such was the importance of navigation that the word 'mathematics' was synonymous with navigation, and the specialists ashore who combined teaching with nautical instrument making, nautical research and writing were known as mathematical practitioners.[3] Many schools also offered what today would be called international maritime business, as shipmasters were invariably involved in commercial transactions. From the nineteenth century, other seafaring subjects were progressively added to the curriculum of navigation schools, including ship construction, ship stability, marine engines, maritime law and state regulation, seamanship, cargo handling and stowage, magnetism, electricity and electronics and finally, man management, so that the navigation schools of the mid-twentieth century, such as that at Plymouth, were concerned with a very wide spectrum of knowledge, and Merchant Navy officers received a very broadly based education and training.

While parents, ambitious for their sons, or seafarers set on advancement, might seek out local navigation teachers in order to progress their nautical education, until 1851 there was no legal requirement for mates and masters of merchant ships to have attained certain standards or for them to be licensed. Judgments on fitness to command merchant ships were made by the owners and at times by insurers. In the circumstance of a rapidly expanding shipping industry by the middle decades of the nineteenth century, increasing numbers of under-qualified seafarers were reaching positions of authority. Although inadequate education and training was by no means the only factor, the numbers of merchant ships being lost each year became something of a national scandal in the 1830s. An influential parliamentary investigation which reported in 1836 identified educational standards as a factor and recommended the introduction of licensing and the provision of cheap nautical schools.[4]

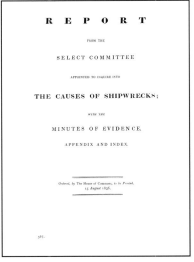

4.2 Although it took many years, almost all of the recommendations of the Select Committee on Shipwrecks, 1836, were acted upon, including state licences for mercantile marine mates and masters, and the establishment of a state system of nautical schools

[BPP, 1836, XVII]

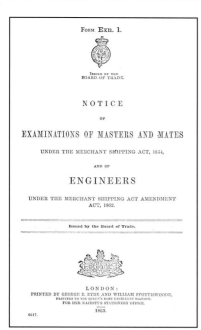

FORM EXN. 1.

ISSUED BY THE
BOARD OF TRADE.

N O T I C E

OF

EXAMINATIONS OF MASTERS AND MATES

UNDER THE MERCHANT SHIPPING ACT, 1854,

AND OF

ENGINEERS

UNDER THE MERCHANT SHIPPING ACT AMENDMENT
ACT, 1862.

Issued by the Board of Trade.

LONDON:
PRINTED BY GEORGE E. EYRE AND WILLIAM SPOTTISWOODE,
PRINTERS TO THE QUEEN'S MOST EXCELLENT MAJESTY,
FOR HER MAJESTY'S STATIONERY OFFICE.
1863.
6617.

4.3 Though not the first edition (which appeared in December 1850) of the regulations governing the masters and officers in the British mercantile marine, this version from 1863 exemplifies the management of the licensing system by the Marine Department of the Board of Trade which was to dominate the work of the Plymouth School of Navigation from its foundation in 1862 to the end of the 1960s.

[PRO, MT9/24]

These were changes which would not come immediately. The Government had only just made its first small grant-in-aid of elementary education (in 1833), and such technical education as there was, came through self-help bodies such as mechanics' institutes. The powerful ship-owning lobby was against state interference in matters it considered its own preserve, and the introduction of examinations and licensing had major administrative implications. A preliminary step in the direction of state oversight came with a voluntary examination and licensing system administer by Trinity House (London), which included Plymouth as an examination centre, between 1845 and 1850.[5] There was no incentive for seafarers to submit themselves to examination and less than 3,000 certificates had been issued when, in a development against the trend (the Navigation Laws had just been repealed), the necessary structures for a state system were introduced from 1 January 1851.[6] A new department in the Board of Trade (BoT), soon to be known as the Mercantile Marine Department, was given central control, while new bodies, Local Marine Boards (LMB), were created in the main ports, including Plymouth, to over see the local maritime safety administration including the examinations. That the thinking behind this change related particularly to oceanic voyages is shown by the omission of the then very large British coastal trade from the requirements for ships to carry certificated officers which, initially, meant masters and mates. However the requirement was soon extended to include coastal passenger shipping, and foreign-going ships were from 1862 also required to carry certificated engineers. But it was some 130 years before the remainder of coastal shipping was brought within the licensing regulations.[7]

By The Lords of the Committee of Privy
Council for Trade.

Certificate of Competency

as

MASTER

OF A FOREIGN-GOING SHIP.

To William George Wainwright

Whereas it has been reported to us that you have been found duly qualified to fulfil the duties of Master of a Foreign-going Ship in the Merchant Service, we do hereby, in pursuance of the Merchant Shipping Act, 1894, grant you this Certificate of Competency

By Order of the Board of Trade,
this 12th day of September 1896

Countersigned,
Ingram B Walker { One of the
Assis¹ Secretaries
to the
Board of Trade.

Mark Hall
Registrar General

Registered at the Office of the Registrar General of Shipping and Seamen.

4.4 Captain W.G. Wainwright's Certificate of Competency as a Master Mariner (foreign-going), allowed him to command British ships of any size anywhere in the world.

[author's collection]

The licensing requirements created opportunities for educational entrepreneurs. Although courses in preparation for the examinations were not a prerequisite, all but the most confident of prospective candidates felt the need for support. In most ports existing nautical school provision was soon augmented by proprietary teachers and schools concentrating on the bare essentials which would secure a pass. There was also an upsurge in new text books written to assist the process. Known as 'cramming', this approach was by no means unique to examination in the nautical profession, though it is widely condemned in the theoretical literature on how merchant service officers should achieve their education and training. In Devon, most ports had supported navigation teaching in the eighteenth and early nineteenth century. In 1852 there were at least four teachers in Plymouth, Stonehouse and Devonport where however, they could also cater for the needs of naval officers.[8]

The 1836 recommendation that something should be done to subsidise nautical education was not forgotten, though developing and sustaining 'cheap nautical schools' was to be plagued by the debate of education versus training and the view that industry should finance the latter. There was an acceptance that, because the state had imposed licensing, it should also aid nautical education. But because of the rapid development of cramming it was easier to identify nautical education in schools offering pre-sea vocational education, and to lump all in-service education (which inevitably meant examination preparation), regardless of a teacher's approach, with the crammers. There is no doubt that the intention was to create a network of nautical schools in the main British ports. In 1849, at the request of the BoT, one of the government's inspectors of schools, the Revd. Henry Moseley, formerly Professor of Astronomy at King's College in London, submitted a scheme to the President of the Board of Trade. The navigation schools he proposed were to be mainly pre-sea establishments accepting boys up to the age of 14 years, though with evening class provision for merchant service apprentices who happened to be in port.[9] Plymouth was not included in his list of the twelve significant commercial ports where schools should be built each capable of accepting 100 boys. The teacher should be suitably qualified by knowledge and experience, and be assisted by two pupil-teachers. Drawing on the ideas of Sir James Kay-Shuttleworth, which the Committee of Privy Council on Education had adopted in 1846, this was clearly the model for the arrangement made by the Marine Department of the Board of Trade with the sailors' homes at London and Liverpool for schools under its auspices in 1853 and 1854.[10] But the BoT initiative was overtaken by the creation of the Department of Science and Art (DSA) in 1853, to which responsibility for navigation schools was transferred in 1857.[11] In its Science section the extension of the network of navigation schools was amongst the earliest tasks undertaken by the DSA. Including that at Plymouth (the last in 1862), seventeen Science and Art navigation schools came into existence either as new creations or through reforming existing schools. The DSA provided financial support, but still expected reduced fees to be charged.

4.5 Well into the twentieth century, Plymouth School of Navigation was in competition with private navigation schools in other ports such as this one in London, as it by no means relied on a clientele which was resident locally.

[Brown's Nautical Almanac, 1904]

4.6 The Department of Science and Art would only finance qualified teachers at the schools and classes it supported. John Merrifield, founding headmaster of the Plymouth School of Navigation attended the Exeter Diocesan Training College for two years and was finally in 1862 awarded his certificate after six years teaching at Mary Tavy National School just before taking up his appointment at Plymouth.

[PCL-LS, Merrifield file]

4.7 Captain F.W. Johnson giving individual instruction in magnetic compass correction using the 'deviascope', when the Plymouth School of Navigation occupied a former operating theatre in the old military hospital in Stoke in the late 1940s. The small mixed class of students following different programmes of study leading to the state certificates of competency must have been typical of navigation schools throughout the country in the nineteenth century.

[PWDRO, School of Navigation deposit]

Most navigation schools soon became involved in preparing candidates for the BoT examinations where the real demand and fee income lay. However, a further report, by Captain A.P. Ryder, RN, in 1858, supported the policy of focusing on pre-sea nautical education. He calculated a need for some 1,300 officer apprentices to join the mercantile marine each year, which meant a pre-sea nautical school population numbering 4,000, and as many as thirty navigation schools in which to educate them.[12]

With the cost to the state of supporting education (Science and Art classes as well as elementary schooling) a matter of growing concern towards the end of the 1850s, the DSA was increasingly looking for ways of reducing the expenditure to which it was being committed by the rapidly growing numbers of Science and Art classes it was aiding across the country. So the DSA tried out methods of making its grants dependent upon "...the results of the instruction afforded".[13] Initially it specified minimum class sizes; then it required the teachers to have passed its examinations for teachers, certificates in designated 'nautical' subjects (navigation, nautical astronomy, mathematics, physical geography, steam), with the level of payment linked to the grade of pass. The system of 'payment-by-results' was rounded out with a requirement that for the teacher to claim the payments, pre-sea boys must have attended 40 lessons and in-service students 20 lessons. The full rigour of this approach was applied to the navigation schools from 1 January 1864, with the result that within a very few years all but three of the schools dropped out of the Science and Art system, either closing or surviving on their fee income largely deriving from students preparing for the BoT certificate of competency examinations.[14]

Plymouth School of Navigation in the Nineteenth Century

On 24 October 1862 the *Western Morning News* reported to its readers:

"We understand that the Plymouth Local Marine Boards have at last decided to establish a Nautical School in connection with the Mercantile Marine department of the Board of Trade, under the superintendence of a duly qualified and certificated master, at which the highest amount of nautical instruction will be given at the lowest possible cost."

The existence in the mid-nineteenth century of proprietary nautical schools in the vicinity of the Three Towns has already been noted, but it seems likely that navigation teaching in endowed schools to pre-sea boys in the far south west of England had died out, making the new Plymouth School of Navigation the only establishment where subsidised teaching was made available. But this new initiative was not the first time that the issue of nautical training had come before the leading citizens in the area. The perennial concern over the supply of seamen for the Royal Navy in time of war, almost a national phobia, continued throughout the nineteenth century. Early in the century (when the war with France was uppermost in people's minds), in a petition from the Borough of Plymouth, dated 6 July 1803, against a Bill for "Creating a company for the more effectually supplying the Metropolis with fish...", a major argument read:

"That the advantages arising from the British Fisheries to the nation in providing a nursery for seamen for the Royal Navy are so obvious as to need no observations from your petitioners and they conceive that the bill now under consideration will materially prevent any increase in the numbers of fishing vessels..."[15]

In 1810 the Mayor of Plymouth called a meeting to consider a bill 'to increase the numbers of persons to be bred to the sea service'.[16] Then in 1816 came a suggestion from a group of 'the most respectable of merchants' in Liverpool who had established a Marine School there in 1815, with a copy of the annual report (circulated to 'every considerable port' in the United Kingdom) urging the establishment of similar institutions. Probably the local private teachers, noted earlier, satisfied the demand, but the introduction of examinations for certificates of competency with the south western examination centre at Plymouth (Bristol or Southampton were the nearest alternatives), must have created an opening for a new navigation school there.

No local records relating to the new Navigation School in the last century have been located, but from the way such schools were founded elsewhere, together with references in local newspapers, it is reasonable to

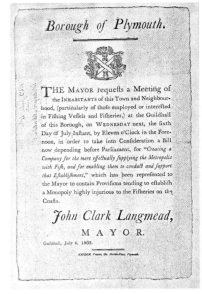

4.8, 4.9 Throughout much of the nineteenth century the supply and training of seafarers was a national concern. These posters from the period when Britain was often at war with France, Plymouth people engaging in the national debate. Later in the century Plymouth would become a major centre for naval training, and in the mid-twentieth century it would support one of the leading establishments for mercantile marine training.

[PWDRO, W668T]

4.10 13½ Gascoyne Place, adjacent to Beaumont Park, was the home of the Plymouth School of Navigation from its foundation in 1862 until 1922 when it moved to Durnford Street. Both John Merrifield and his successor as headmaster, Charles Morris, lived at the School.

[Photo: A. Kennerley]

deduce that a local committee would have been formed, whose membership may have been almost synonymous with that of the Plymouth Local Marine Board. No doubt the Mayor of the day was an *ex officio* member. Thomas Restarick was the first Chairman, and William Bennet Cumming, the Secretary. Cumming, a 'surveyor of shipping', was a typical member drawn from the maritime interest. He was still a member of the Local Marine Board in 1881, and had previously examined for Trinity House in Plymouth during the period of voluntary examinations.[17] The *Western Daily Mercury* recorded what was probably the first inspection, and might have been the official opening of the 'Plymouth New Navigation Schools' by its managers, "...the Schools having been properly furnished and prepared for use".[18] The use of the plural ('Schools') might suggest that a major establishment of considerable size had been set up, but this was not the case; there were simply different classes for the various levels of instruction. The return of the School to the DSA reveals:

"...the total number of students receiving instruction in or through the agency of the School during 1863 has been 240 [and] the entire number of adults and boys who have at any time paid fees during the year are: masters [ie studying for the certificate as master mariner] 39, chief mates 26, only mates 70, second mates 39, master home trade 1, mate home trade 1, seamen 10 apprentices, 6 boys [the pre-sea group] 22. The number of boys who have gone to sea during the year is 18... most of the students attend both day and evening classes."[19]

The fees to be paid by students were to vary between six pence and six shillings per week. The Torpoint Naval School (Mr Hall, Master, R.N.) was in the same year offering "advanced instruction in practical navigation, marine surveying and the use of nautical instruments" to " naval cadets, masters' assistants, masters and mates of the mercantile marine" for one guinea per month in advance.[20] The graduated subsidy at the navigation school provided the greatest support to seafarers at the start of their career, such as pre-sea boys and seamen/apprentices, while those studying for the master mariner certificate, with several years earning at higher levels, paid approximately the commercial rates for their instruction. This was of course in line with the policy of the DSA. The numbers of students present at any one time would have been highly variable. Presumably the pre-sea boys attended continuously until ships were found for them, but those already at sea could only attend between voyages, and only for so long as their accumulated income (unless supported by relatives) allowed them to live ashore. Opportunities to attempt the certificate examinations were available almost every week. The mean daily attendance was probably well under twenty students.[21]

To qualify for DSA support the local committee in Plymouth had to find the funding to acquire and furnish the building which the Plymouth School of Navigation was to occupy for the next 60 years, 13½ Gascoyne Place, a convenient location less than fifteen minutes walk from Sutton Harbour and close to Friary Station. Certainly the local merchant shipping interest was supportive:

..."the members of the Board and shipowners of the port liberally supplied the school with apparatus, books, and every other requisite, and appointed a certificated teacher to conduct the school."[22]

The DSA probably provided support for teaching aids, and would normally have guaranteed the salary of the teacher initially while such a school was being built up. Particular attention would have been paid by the DSA to the appointment of the teacher, as the qualifications and training of navigation school teachers was one of the criteria for recognition.

John Merrifield (1834-1891), a local man from the Tavistock area, who would go on to make his mark locally and nationally, certainly met the DSA expectations for the headship of the Plymouth Science and Art Navigation School. Following a pupil-teachership in an elementary school, he had received his training at the Exeter Diocesan Training College (St. Luke's College, now merged with the University of Exeter), 1854 to 1856, achieving good results especially in scientific subjects. He became head of Mary Tavy National School and by 1861 had obtained the Schoolmaster's Certificate from the Committee of Privy Council on Education based partly on inspectors' reports over five years at that school. He had also obtained the DSA teachers' certificates in chemistry and steam (1861, 1862). After his appointment to the School of Navigation he had obtained DSA certificates in mathematics, navigation, nautical astronomy, physical geography and stability by 1865; a gold medal for applied mechanics and a bronze for theoretical mechanics (1867), and gold medals for magnetism and electricity, and nautical astronomy, and a bronze for navigation (1868). Thus he was exceptionally well qualified for his post, and like the heads of the other navigation schools, quite young and without seafaring experience.[23]

In augmenting his range of qualifications, Merrifield achieved several objectives. He maximised his ability to qualify for DSA payments for the stipulated subjects in navigation schools, and he was able to benefit in a similar manner by teaching other Science and Art classes in Plymouth. The breadth would certainly have benefited his teaching in the navigation school, but it also laid a foundation for his more advanced writing and research in the marine sciences which was to bring him national recognition. An early initiative was to establish a meteorological observing station at the School of Navigation. Admiral Robert Fitzroy's Meteorological Department of the Board of Trade supplied the School with a complete set of meteorological instruments, registers and meteorological reports in October 1864, and for the rest of the nineteenth century the School telegraphed meteorological data to London each day.[24] The data became the basis for a number of meteorological summaries by Merrifield. In 1868 he published his first text book on navigation and nautical astronomy, and in 1872 his studies of magnetism and compass deviation led to a book, *Magnetism and Deviation of the Compass*, translated into a number of languages, which brought him to the attention of an international audience.[25] A paper on a 'New Method of Clearing the Lunar Distance' was published by the Royal Astronomical Society and a design for an artificial horizon attracted the interest of the American government. In the early 1870s he was awarded a doctorate by a university at Philadelphia, and fellowships of the Royal Astronomical Society and the Meteorological Society. From 1877-80 he was a member of

Dr MERRIFIELD

4.11 John Merrifield used this illustration with his election address when standing for membership of the Plymouth School Board in 1880. he was opposed to sectarian teaching and in favour of education which had a bearing on future vocation.

[PCL-LS, Western Figaro (8 January 1880)]

MAGNETISM

AND

DEVIATION OF THE COMPASS.

FOR THE USE OF STUDENTS
IN
NAVIGATION AND SCIENCE SCHOOLS

BY

JOHN MERRIFIELD, LL.D., F.R.A.S.

Joint Author of 'Navigation and Nautical Astronomy'; Head Master of the Plymouth Navigation School; and Teacher of Mathematics, Mechanics, Steam, &c. in the Plymouth Science School

NEW EDITION.

LONDON:
LONGMANS, GREEN, AND CO.

All rights reserved.

4.12 This little book, published in 1872, helped establish Merrifield internationally as a marine scientist. It was a recommended text in the United States Navy and, and was also translated into a number of languages.

[author's collection]

4.13 The heading of the earliest known printed document from the Plymouth School of Navigation, an instructional leaflet on navigation, found pasted into Thomas Slade's copy of Norie's Epitome of Navigation. Slade passed his master's certificate in August 1866. It was discovered by Helen Doe, Slade's great-grand-daughter.

[Helen Doe]

Science   Navigation

and Art   School,

GASCOYNE PLACE, PLYMOUTH.

a British Association committee chaired by Sir William Thompson (Lord Kelvin), which studied the tides in the English Channel. International invitations included observing the transit of Venus in India and joining the British government delegation to the Vienna Exhibition.[26]

During its first decade, enrolments at the School of Navigation appear to have grown to in excess of some 300 annually. A figure of 344 was reported by the DSA in 1868, 192 in 1871, but only 8 in 1872. However, this decline almost certainly reflects the changes in policy noted earlier with only those students qualifying for DSA payments to teachers being listed in the returns for the rest of the century. Although there is no evidence that the School had significant numbers of boys taking a pre-sea course, Plymouth was one of three navigation schools which continued to receive payments from the DSA until the end of the century when the DSA ceased to exist.[27] That the real work of the school was with certificate candidates is evident from a comment made in November, 1871:

"This School seems to have been eminently successful in promoting the object for which it was established; and the inspectors who have visited it say it is among the best adapted for the purpose of any in England. Since its establishment about 2,100 officers have received certificates after having been prepared in this school; and many belonging to the Royal Navy have found it advantageous to attend; but we believe very few of the students ever presented themselves for the Department [DSA] examinations, owing, no doubt, to the nature of the employment of those attending."[28]

The figure for BoT examination passes suggests about 200 successful seafarer students annually. One of these was Thomas Slade, master of the schooners *Alert* and *Jane Slade* (1870-92), who passed his master's examination in August 1866. The School provided him with its own printed summary of the steps to be followed in making the main navigational calculations, and appears at that date to have recommended the well established textbook on navigation by Norie.[29] Much of the instruction must have been tutorial in approach, akin to student-centred guided learning, long a feature of navigation school teaching because small members attempting different grades had to be taught together. It is unlikely that Merrifield had to manage on his own for very long. Assistant teachers would have been essential for him to sustain his widening range of activity, which in addition to study, research and publishing included teaching in the Plymouth Science schools and, in due course, political work as a member of the Plymouth School Board. The DSA directories list J.W.White in 1872, Charles Morris from 1874, W.V. Merrifield (John Merrifield's son) from 1877. S.S. Merrifield and R.H Merrifield are listed in 1878 and 1879, and E.M. Minhinnick in 1881. W.V. Merrifield was a Cambridge graduate and had clearly made nautical teaching his career; in the 1890s he joined the staff of the Liverpool Nautical College and soon succeeded to its headship. In the 1891 census John Merrifield's occupation is given as 'navigation teacher retired', only few months before his death at the age of 56. Charles Morris (with his family) was resident at the Navigation School, and may have succeeded to the headship towards the end of the 1880s.[30]

Although the regulations concerning Science and Arts grants were eased towards the end of the century, the path of the Plymouth School of Navigation well into the twentieth century was set by the events of the 1860s. It was to be mainly concerned with preparing seafaring students for the Board of Trade's certificates of competency, work which would be augmented only in a small way by pre-sea students and occasional students of other maritime topics. Because it had its own local management committee it remained unaffected by the complex educational developments of the 1890s which saw the centralisation of the 'Plymouth Science, Art and Technical Schools' in its new building in 1892 opposite the museum and public library (on the southern corner of the site now occupied by the University of Plymouth). With the new county and county borough councils (1888) managing local technical education from 1889, the incorporation of the Science and Art Department in the Board of Education in 1899, the transfer of the powers of the School Boards to the local education authorities in 1902, and the winding up of local marine boards in 1908, the small navigation school was increasingly an anomaly.[31] So that year the management of the school was transferred to Plymouth local education authority.[32]

Local Authority Control, Decline and Merger

With Plymouth LEA receiving the fees paid by students and assuming responsibility for maintenance, equipment and staff salaries, the School of Navigation had become part of a much larger management structure, having potential benefit but also carrying dangers. At this stage there seems to have been no threat to its independent existence. In 1911, its work was endorsed in an HMI report noteworthy for its brevity:

"The main object of the School is the preparation of candidates for the certificates of competency of the Board of trade for master, mates and for engineers, though pupils may receive instruction in special subjects without a view to examination. The number on the books for the present session is a little under a hundred. Students attend for varying periods, but the average number in attendance at a given time is 10-15. Students are expected to come with regularity while in attendance, to put in full attendance amounting to six hours daily, three in the morning and three in the afternoon, and on Saturday morning. The School is satisfactorily equipped for the purpose. The work is necessarily tutorial in character, and is characterised by steady application on the part of the pupils. The teachers are assiduous in their attention and do not begrudge extra time with willing pupils."[33]

4.14 Like his predecessor as Headmaster of the Plymouth School of Navigation, Charles Morris lectured at the Plymouth Institution. A report of his address on Deviation read: "Mr. Charles Morris, F.R.M.S., lectured at the Plymouth Institution on the "Deviation of the Compass" before a good attendance of members. He dealt exhaustively with the complex issues of the variation and deviation of the compass, touching first on its action when only under the influence of the earth, and then when under the influence of earth and ship. He also explained how soft iron was magnetised, and elaborately dealt with sub-permanent, induced, retentive, semi-circular and quadrilateral magnetism, and heeling error. In the discussion Mr. C.S. Jago pointed out that the wrecks of the Schiller, Serpent and Roumania occurred after boisterous weather, and asked whether it was possible that the ships got out of their courses by the compass being affected by the heavy rolling. Dr Oxland mentioned that several years ago the late Captain Walker, R.N., speaking at that institution, quoted instances of vessels being wrecked on the coast of France at a time when their commanders imagined the position to be near the Needles. Captain Walker attributed those disasters to heeling error. the lecturer was complimented on his paper, and the hope was generally expressed that he would contribute another paper on navigation at an early date."

[author's collection; photo: F.W. Motouth]

4.15 In 1922 the School of Navigation was moved to the former Durnford Hotel in Durnford Street, Stonehouse, where it shared the building with the Junior Technical School.

[photo: A.Kennerley]

In 1917, the head, Charles Morris, was allowed to attend a conference on nautical education in Liverpool, and in 1918 he was able to visit the Board of Trade. In 1920 the need for additional accommodation for the school was recognised and the Education Committee acquired the Durnford Hotel, in Durnford Street, Stonehouse, into which the school was moved. But in 1922, with the Council under financial pressure, a proposal was made to close the School of Navigation as an economy measure. The move was successfully resisted using the arguments that:

"The School is in a flourishing condition in spite of the fact that there has been for the last year or two a slump in shipping; that the tradition which has been built up during the sixty years of its existence is being maintained; and that the students from other towns who reside in Plymouth while attending the School undoubtedly contribute to the welfare of the town by the money they spend."[34]

In 1920/21 the School had enrolled 123 day and 30 evening students, and, of 88 who had attempted BoT examinations, 71 had passed. However, with the decline in admissions in the early 1930s (Table 4.1), at the depth of the depression, the inevitable step was taken in 1932 of merging the School with the Plymouth and Devonport Technical College. Initially a free standing unit, it was later managed as a section of the Department of Mathematics and Physics.

Table 4.1 demonstrates clearly that the School's main function was BoT examination preparation. Holders of master's certificates, were studying for the Extra Master qualification; first mates were studying for the master's certificate, second mates for the first mate's certificate, and apprentices, cadets and ABs for the second mate's certificate. There were a few pre-sea students taking a two term course. The fishermen would be preparing for the BoT skipper or second hand certificates. The evening students came from the Dockyard for a course in seamanship. Students came from all over Devon and Cornwall, with a few from further afield. Many found accommodation in Stonehouse, eight houses in Durnford street alone taking in navigation school students as lodgers. At this time the standard fees were: second mate's course £4, first mate £5, master £6, extra master £7 10s (or 10s per week), pre-sea £3 10s per term. Unemployed students were allowed to run up arrears.

Table 4.1

Enrolments at Plymouth School of Navigation, 1928-36.

	Annual enrolments			Certificates held on entry/previous occupations								
Year	Day	Carry -over	Even -ing	Master	First Mate	Second Mate	Apprentices Cadets	Pre-Sea	Able Seamen	Fishermen	Other occup- ations	Total Fees Paid £
1928/29	142	21	10	3	37	44	42	5	9		2	623
1929/30	146	25	6	4	42	42	37	5	13	2	1	826
1930/31	107	27	7	6	39	21	28	3	7	3		511
1931/32	76	16	7	6	17	14	31	2	2	2	2	409
1932/33	51	5	9	2	14	7	15	5	2	5	1	195
1933/34	30	9	8		8	4	13	3	2			
1934/35	28	3		1	14	4	3		2	1	2	
1935/36	37	5		3	9	10	7	2		4	2	

Source: PWDRO, School of Navigation Register Book, 1928-36. Other occupations includes 4 engineers, a student, an extra master, a marine optician, an electrical engineer, a retired RN captain, a flight lieutenant.

Early in the 1930s, Mr R. Stitson attended the Navigation School in the Durnford Street premises it shared with the Junior Technical School, and confirms the educational culture that the HMIs had found twenty years earlier.

"I think 4 or 5 rooms were used - seamanship room on the ground floor...back upstairs room with large bay window overlooking the river also useful for sextant practice. Furnishing sufficient but by no means lavish.... [Teaching aids included] sextants, wooden models for rule of the road...barometers...charts....Can't ever remember any boat drill or practical boat work at school...Chiefly working exam papers - lectures on meteorology, seamanship, etc., practice with models...signalling practice....Think Extra Masters and Masters studied together and we Mates and 2nd Mates were usually together. Lectures given by all three masters, but Capt Frost-Smith took seamanship. Masters made subjects very interesting - all three were very approachable and extremely helpful. Mr Liddicoat gave the impression of being a born teacher with a mass of knowledge..."[35]

But it was soon after Mr Stitson's experience that the School of Navigation declined to its lowest ebb. It lost its key full-time members of staff. Mr Liddicoat, Head since 1919, moved to a headship of an elementary school at the time of the merger. This loss was followed a year later by the death of his successor, Mr Frost-Smith. For the next decade, though managed by a lecturer-in-charge, H. Keast, the School was kept going through the use of a succession of part-time teachers. It also lost its reasonably spacious accommodation in Durnford Street and was confined to two rooms in the main technical college building in Tavistock Road, a situation condemned as poor by the HMIs in 1937, who specified a minimum of five rooms totalling some 4,000 square feet.[36] They also suggested to the authority that it might be beneficial for a proper pre-sea course to be opened; ten years later that was the initiative which would start the revival of the School. The inspectorate also pointed in the late 1930s to the national competition faced by all navigation schools, when it was noted that the fees imposed by Plymouth LEA for courses at the School of Navigation were significantly higher than those charged at other ports.

Recovery through Merchant Navy officer cadet training

Given the state of technical education in Plymouth in the 1930s, it is unlikely that the authority would have taken any action on behalf of its Navigation School in response to the prodding of the HMIs. Perhaps some seeds had been sown, but if so they were to lie dormant as World War II soon intervened. Although a minor player compared with, for example, Liverpool,

4.16 Mr. W.J. Liddicoat, Headmaster of Plymouth School of Navigation, 1919-1932, in his office in the Durnford Street building. The author of a textbook on navigation and highly respected as a teacher, he was a loss to nautical education on the absorbtion of the School into the technical college in 1932, when he accepted the headship of an elementary school in Plymouth.

[photo: Mr Philip Liddicoat]

4.17, 4.18 The development of a pre-sea cadet course had been recommended before World War II. Adopting the Merchant Navy uniform raised the profile and provided photo opportunities. This group in the late 1940s was one for the first to wear uniform, while later groups were often required to form guards of honour at college events, such as the official opening of the engineering block (now Smeaton Building) in Glanville Street.

[PWDRO, School of Navigation deposit; photos: Devon Commercial Photos, Western Morning News]

4.19 In the 1960s a bus full of Plymouth cadets made the journey to London to parade at the Merchant Navy memorial at Tower Hill for the service of remembrance in November. This group attended in 1963.

[PWDRO, School of Navigation deposit; photo: Shell Film Service]

4.20 Captain Johnson took every opportunity to publicise the School of Navigation. In this 'excursion' he took the mayoral party afloat in one of the School's boats to visit the Dayspring, then being used to give pre-sea cadets some practical training afloat. the Mayor's mace bearer is in the bow; Alderman Perry is shading his eyes from the sun; the Mayor is in conversation with Captain Johnson who has taken the helm.

[PWDRO, School of Navigation deposit]

the School at Plymouth was needed in its well established role of preparing students for the certificate examinations. Merchant Navy mates and masters still had to be qualified, and the demand for merchant shipping meant that there were never sufficient seafarers available.[37] The enemy campaign against merchant ships, which led to over 30,000 merchant seafarer deaths out of a population of about 140,000, seriously exacerbated the supply situation. State control of labour meant that very limited periods ashore in preparation for the examinations were allowed, though probably the examinations became somewhat less rigorous.

While the School of Navigation managed as best it could, in Plymouth as well as London thoughts were turning as early as 1942 to post war reconstruction, which was to lead to new beginnings in many areas, not least in technical education. The shipping industry organisation concerned with training was that year reconstituted as the Merchant Navy Training Board, improvements in seamen's welfare provision in ports had a high profile, and in the Board of Education (soon to become a Ministry) the nautical inspectors were looking to the creation of a national college for the training of Merchant Navy officers.[38] A single national college for officers did not emerge, but in time Plymouth was to become one of seven or eight regional centres for nautical education, with the basis for this being laid in the immediate post-war period. The developments must be seen as part of the state drive to boost British technical education, though from the perspective of the long history of vocational education for merchant seafarers, they can be seen as picking up from where the Science and Art Department had left off in the 1860s. Models for the development of cadet work at Plymouth were to be found, for example, in pre-sea school ships HMS *Conway* (River Mersey/Menai Straits) and HMS *Worcester* (River Thames), and Southampton School of Navigation (Warsash). The Associations of Navigation Schools and of Marine Engineering Schools provided opportunities for the exchange of experience at their annual conferences, and of course the HMIs specialising in nautical education were in close contact. Staff also maintained links with the examiners of master, mates and engineers, and with the shipping industry through the Merchant Navy

4.21 In the 1950s The school of Navigation was attracting increasing numbers of students to is masters' and mates' courses. This group was photographed on the steps of the engineering block (Smeaton Building) in 1955. Some of the staff are seated in the front.

[PWDRO, School of Navigation deposit; photo: Arcadian photos]

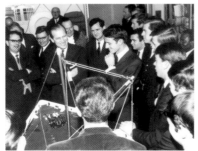

4.22 During his visit to the School of Navigation on 8 March 1968, HRH Prince Philip Duke of Edinburgh met several groups of students, including these from the mates' and masters' classes

[PWDRO, School of Navigation deposit]

4.23 This group of master mariner students are seen making the observations and calculations for magnetic compass correction using the deviascope under the supervision of Captain David Moreby.

[Plymouth College of Technology prospectus, 1963/64]

Training Board and, particularly, the training officers appointed by the shipping companies which carried cadets or apprentices on their ships.

It is convenient to date the new initiative in Plymouth from 1944 when a new head of the School of Navigation, Captain F.W. Johnson was appointed. The first of a series of heads drawn from a merchant seafaring background, Johnson's outgoing personality was suited to the task of moving the school forward. Locally, he soon became a well known figure. In 1945 the School was moved into rooms in the former Stoke Military Hospital and in 1947 a pre-sea cadet course was started. Such was the shipping industry's shortage of officer trainees at that time, that many cadets went to sea before completing the full length of the year long course.[39] From 1948 cadets wore the Merchant Navy apprentices' uniform, though with a Plymouth School of Navigation cap badge, a move which at the time is thought to have widened the appeal of the course in the south western counties.[40] The new accommodation may have brought space for expansion, but owing to bomb damage, there was no heating and many windows were broken, so that, especially during the severe winter of 1947, attending 'nav school' was no rest cure.

Running a properly organised pre-sea cadet section was far more demanding administratively than delivering the class-room based short courses for the professional certificates. Dealing with sixteen year olds straight from school who would attend for a year, meant that the staff of the School were *in loco parentis*. With increasing numbers being drawn from locations beyond daily commuting distance by public transport, the cadet section was soon developing as a boarding operation. For ten years the School's network of local lodgings served the purpose, but eventually the local authority accepted the logic of establishing a hall of residence. In 1958 Merrifield Hall opened as the first of eight *ad hoc* halls in which in due course over three hundred cadets at a time were to be housed. To get Merrifield Hall started, Captain Johnson and his wife (accompanied by their four daughters!) moved in as resident warden and matron/house keeper, until suitable staff could be appointed. Tragically, Captain Johnson died within a few months, but his wife stayed on in that role with the School for many years, and is well remembered by many generations of former Plymouth cadets.[41]

Cadet work also meant the development of practical work, seamanship and boatwork, for which a waterside site was required. The little fishing harbour of Mutton Cove, immediately seaward of the naval dockyard, offered huts to store equipment and the shelter for the boats which the School acquired, and so became the base, despite the strong and treacherous tidal streams which ran past the entrance to the harbour. State promotion of nautical education, which peaked in the 1960s, provided Plymouth with a purpose-built Seamanship Centre in a more suitable location at Queen Anne's Battery, Coxside, which was opened by the Duke of Edinburgh in 1967. With the provision of proper facilities for seamanship the School became the recognised local centre at which the statutory Efficient Deck Hand, Certificated Lifeboatman and Survival at Sea courses and

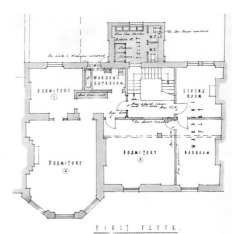

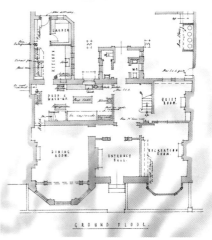

4.24, 4.25. These plans illustrate the conversion in 1962 of 22 Portland Square into a hall of residence for the School of Navigation. Previously occupied for over 100 years by the Square/Elliot family of medical practitioners, it had been used by the City Engineer during the 1940s and 1950s. The fine entrance hall, wood panelling and other decorative features have, so far, survived these changes of use.

[PWDRO, School of Navigation deposit]

4.26 Merrifield Hall, Greenbank, became the School's first hall of residence for Merchant Navy cadets in 1958, with Captain and Mrs Johnson as the first warden and matron. Cadets received full board, even returning there from classes for their midday meal.

[photo: A.Kennerley]

4.27 The School of Navigation occupied huts for its first Seamanship Centre at the little fishing harbour, Mutton Cove, just outside Devonport Dockyard perimeter wall, between 1950 and 1967.

[photo, A.Kennerley]

4.28 School of Navigation watersports day at Mutton Cove, 1966. The School's training ketch Tectona is alongside the breakwater and teams of cadets are competing in the sheerlegs/breeches buoy competition for the fastest time to 'rescue' a man from a 'sinking ship'.

[photo: A.Kennerley]

4.29 On 8 March 1968, HRH Prince Philip, Duke of Edinburgh, visited the School to unveil the foundation stone of the Residential Nautical College, and made time to visit the Seamanship Centre. He is seen here in the seamanship classroom with receiving an explanation from Captain Keith Hyde, the lecturer in charge of the Centre.

[PWDRO, School of Navigation deposit.]

4.30, 4.31 In 1967 the School moved into its new seamanship centre at Queen Anne's Battery (Coxside), which included a large boat store, workshops for maintenance and a seamanship classroom, a private slipway, davits for lifeboat training and a sampson post, derrick and winch for cargo handling training. Boat training and racing was controlled from its own 'bridge' lookout, with signal mast and morse equipment.

[photos: A.Kennerley]

examinations were held. Character building, perhaps influenced by Kurt Hahn's Outward Bound Movement, was also very much to the fore at this time. Like several other British nautical colleges, in 1964 the School of Navigation purchased its own sea-going training vessel, the 80 ton ketch, *Tectona*, and until 1980, when the ship was sold, both deck and engineer cadets were timetabled to spend up to a week cruising in the Channel. On land this was paralleled with short expeditions in small teams across Dartmoor. For several years the School entered teams in the Ten Tors event. The School also had a camp on Drake's Island, and included canoeing, rock climbing and abseiling in the activities on offer. In 1962 the contribution of cadets in rescuing farm animals from the moor during the severe winter snows was recognised by the presentation of a certificate. The seamanlike conduct of cadets involved in the annual race to Fowey, at the time of the disastrous Fasnet Race of 1971, earned a commendation from the Navy.

The expansion of the cadet section in the 1950s and 1960s was in response to a series of national developments in nautical education which led shipowners to contract with colleges for the in-service education and training of apprentices and cadets that they had employed. The most significant contract secured was that with Shell Tankers, who for a good number of years sent their cadets exclusively to Plymouth in groups. At its height in the late 1960s this meant that four terms, in two phases, were being spent in College by deck cadets before attempting the first professional certificate. Other companies making similar arrangements at Plymouth included British and Commonwealth, Irish Shipping, BP, Cunard, P & O, Blue Star and the Royal Fleet Auxiliary. The desire to train engineer cadets together with deck cadets led to the School of Navigation absorbing marine engineering courses from the engineering department in the mid-1960s. Here there was an element of social engineering in anticipation that the time might come when the two roles aboard ship might merge. However, as engineer cadets spent two years at college before going to sea (except for trips aboard *Tectona* and ship visits) there was a significant disparity in maritime experience. The evolution of the sandwich arrangements had started with introduction of mid-apprenticeship release (MAR) courses from 1960. From 1962 the pre-sea cadet course was gradually merged with MAR courses to produce phased training which was continued in various forms until cadet work ended early in the 1990s. At the same time the academic content of the courses was recognised through validation by the Joint Committee system dating from 1922, but with new committees for Nautical Sciences and Marine

4.32, 4.33 The School of Navigation training ketch, Tectona (80 tons), purchased in 1964, was built in Calicut, India, in 1932. She anchored off Fisher's Nose on 8 March 1968 while prince Philip was visiting the Seamanship centre. During the summer months parties of cadets went on training voyages in the English Channel for up to a week. She is seen under full sail in Plymouth Sound off Jennycliff Bay.

[PWDRO, School of Navigation deposit; A.Kennerley]

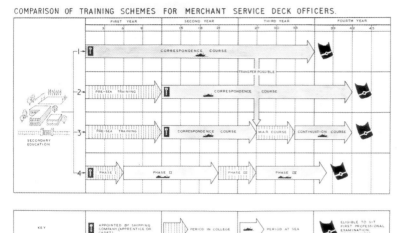

COMPARISON OF TRAINING SCHEMES FOR MERCHANT SERVICE DECK OFFICERS.

4.34 There had always been more than one route for a youngster to become a Merchant Navy Officer. In the 1960s patterns of apprentice/cadet training multiplied as shown in this diagram. The fourths scheme, phased training, was pioneered at Plymouth in collaboration with the Shell tanker Company.

[PWDRO, School of Navigation deposit.]

Engineering.[42] These validated the award of Ordinary National Certificates (ONC) and Diplomas (OND), and subsequently for Higher National Certificates (HNC), to Merchant Navy cadets, and were later absorbed into the Business and Technician Education Council (BTEC) system of national certificates. Though bearing the same name and addressing the same subject matter, BTEC qualifications were significantly different in approach from the earlier system which had achieved a high level of acceptance amongst employers.

4.35 Merchant Navy trainees received ample small boat experience   during their courses at Plymouth, in training sessions in the School's dinghies (here being launched at Mutton Cove), and in the School's cutters and whalers (here a whaler competing in the race for service boats).

[Plymouth College of technology prospectus, 1964/65; A.Kennerley, July 1968]

The philosophy of integrating time spent in Colleges following tailored vocational education and training courses with service on merchant ships at sea was that cadets would be better equipped for work on the increasingly technologically advanced ships that were coming into service, and would be better able, through the broadening effect of the course content, to fit in with life at sea. Further, to a large extent college provision satisfied the abortive aspirations of the 1918 and 1944 Education Acts for post-school part-time continuation education for 16 to 18 year olds. In practice pre-sea courses had long been recognised by the board of examiners of the Marine Department (now the Maritime and Coastguard Agency) for remission of the sea time demanded before the second mate's examination could be attempted.[43] Plymouth's pre-sea course had been granted six months remission in 1951.

4.36 In the 1960s and 1970s, the highlight of the social calendar for the School's cadets and officer students were the end of term dinner dances and balls, which needed the largest venue in Plymouth. At Christmas 1966 Chief Cadet Captain Salmon (left) made up a party to attend the ball in the Plymouth Guildhall

[PWDRO, School of Navigation deposit: Express Photos.]

4.37 The guest after dinner speaker invariably came from the world of shipping. In the summer of 1968 it was Captain Treasure Jones, formerly master of the Queen Mary, here being presented with a momento of the occasion.

[PWDRO, School of Navigation deposit: Express Photos.]

PLYMOUTH SCHOOL OF MARITIME STUDIES

Mayflower 70 Ball

Plymouth Guildhall - Wednesday, 8th July, 1970

from 2030 until 0130

Bob Miller and The Millermen

Rod Mason and the Tamar Valley Jazz Band

Uniform or Dinner Jacket

exchanged for Buffet Ticket on presentation at door

4.38 In 1970, the School made its contribution to Plymouth's commemoration of 350th anniversary of the sailing of the Pilgrim Fathers in the Mayflower to America in 1620, by inviting the Captain Superintendent of the United States Merchant Marine Academy, King's Point, New York, to be its guest of honour at its Mayflower Ball, with dancing to leading national and local bands.

[author's collection]

4.39 In planning from 1961, Plymouth's 'Residential Nautical College' (the architect's working title) was finally ready in 1970. The suite of four building included the ten story tower block to accommodate 200 cadets, a communal block with kitchens, dining rooms, common rooms, and study bedrooms for research students, a teaching block and the planetarium.

[UPPLY, maritime collection]

Now under the phased training arrangements the whole of the time in college qualified for remission, but it carried the implication that, as on a ship, cadets' time would be heavily regulated. The weekly contact hours amounted to no fewer than thirty eight and a half hours, achieved through running a three session day (morning, afternoon and evening) Monday to Friday. Additionally there were classes on Saturday morning and games in the afternoon. Of course by deducting the time devoted to the out-door activities noted above and a programme of Liberal Studies (three hours per week), the time devoted to vocational subjects matched that of other full time courses at the College.

With groups of deck cadets arriving and departing each term, and thus breaking continuity, much of the organisation of sporting activity and some of the social activity, fell to the School of Navigation staff. The co-operation of local organisations, especially the Navy, gave access to playing fields, and the School was able to field teams in the popular sports of football and rugby which were very much a match for teams in the locality. Cadets were also competitive in local yachting and rowing events. Lecturing staff served as wardens and as all meals were taken communally in the halls of residence, there was ample informal contact with staff. The main formal social events were the School of Navigation dinners and dances, attended by cadets, senior students and staff, girl friends and wives. Originally small termly events, they were later held at Christmas and in the summer. These formal events involved leading figures from the shipping industry as after dinner speakers, and were regularly attended by the Lord Mayor of Plymouth and the Principal of the College. Bands of national standing were engaged, and at the peak of their success only the Plymouth Guildhall was large enough to accommodate the event at which, on one occasion, 450 people sat down to dinner. Cadets may have been subject to a full and disciplined regime, but they still managed to make their mark on the city. For example on more than one occasion the civic flag staff in Armada Way received nocturnal attention.

Their uniform and short hair cuts also marked them out to local youths and a number of cadets were assaulted when out on the town. The substitution of blazers and flannels for the Merchant Navy uniform in the late 1970s reflected a more relaxed approach at the time that the cadet body began to shrink in the wake of the decline of the British shipping industry.

The growing size of the cadet section in the 1960s, meant of course that the staff had to be expanded rapidly to cover both the additional teaching and the other work that fell to the staff. Many of the new staff found that a condition of appointment was to assume the role of a warden in one of the halls of residence, for which some reduction of teaching duties was allowed. The School's training ketch, *Tectona*, was also officered on the same basis, though the master of the vessel was a regular appointment. As well as residential accommodation, teaching space became problematic. With the opening of the first of the technical college's new buildings in 1954 (now called the Smeaton Building) the School of Navigation had become a separate department, and had moved into a set of well equipped rooms on the top floor of the building. Within a few years the cadet section moved out to occupy the former North Road School building, and from there it moved in 1967 to the derelict former Notre Dame girls school building in Wyndham Street. Meanwhile, planning had started in 1961 for a purpose built set of buildings, for the School of Navigation, as the regional nautical education facility the Ministry of Education/Department of Education and Science (DES) was funding. Delays meant that the Residential Nautical College at Plymouth was not ready until 1970. Together with the Seamanship Centre, this provided a massive upgrading of the facilities for nautical education. Several of the *ad hoc* halls of residence were replaced by the residential block (now Mary Newman Hall) for 200 cadets in mainly six berth rooms. There were hobbies rooms on the ground floor, a sick bay, and two 'bungalows' on the roof for the wardens. The service block (now the Isaac Foot Building) offered kitchens and a cadet dining room (waitress service), student common rooms, staff dining and common rooms and fifteen study bedrooms for short course students. The teaching block (now the Fitzroy Building) housed a manoeuvring tank, laboratories for hydrostatics, naval architecture, electronics, oceanography, navigation aids and compass work, a radar simulator, chartrooms, a mock ship's bridge and a maritime library, as well as general classrooms. A special building provided the only planetarium in the South West, the William Day Planetarium.

While the building brought the maritime work together on one site and offered major improvements in specialist facilities and equipment, its delayed completion and financial cuts meant that the teaching block was less than well suited to its purpose. The loss of a central staircase produced a cramped entrance. The ship's bridge was never used for its intended purpose and was soon adapted as a meteorology laboratory. However, it was change in government policy on post-school education which rendered the new facility less than ideal. This involved the separation of less advanced work from higher level work with the creation of the polytechnics and colleges of

4.40, 4.41 This floor plan of the residential block, and view of one of the six berth dormitories then considered appropriate for Merchant Navy cadet as reflecting the conditions they were likely to experience afloat.

[UPPLY, maritime collection; photo: Plymouth College of Art]

4.42 The maritime teaching block was equipped with several laboratories. In the Naval Architecture laboratory this 1970s Phase I cadet group is undertaking a stability practical using a 'box vessel' in the stability tank.

[UPPLY, maritime collection]

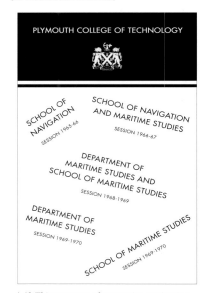

4.43 This montage of successive navigation school prospectuses shows the confusing series of name changes felt necessary as the School adapted to new national qualifications and degree level studies

[author's collection]

4.44, 4.45 One of the most distinctive small buildings on the Plymouth campus is the William Day Planetarium, which since 1970 has been host to numerous adult and children's groups from the region, in addition to its primary role as nautical astronomical teaching and research instrument. Inside, orientation is provided through the Plymouth night horizon around the circumference of the dome.

[Photos: A.Kennerley, Plymouth Polytechnic Prospectus, 1975/6]

4.46 The late Captain William Day, creator of the planetarium, with the 10 inch reflecting telescope used to observe the total eclipse of the moon on 18 November 1975, and, of course, many other astronomical events.

[UPPLY, Spectrum (December 1975)]

further education (Chapter 8). In the establishment of Plymouth Polytechnic and Plymouth College of Further Education (CFE) in 1970, all the departments of the old College of Technology (as it had become from 1962) were divided according to level of work. So the former School of Navigation, which had adopted the title Maritime Studies in 1967, became two departments of Maritime Studies, with certificate courses and degree work in the Polytechnic and cadet courses in the CFE. But the cadets still occupied the residential accommodation; rooms in the teaching block were allocated to one or other of the two departments, and on the ground floor of the accommodation block two heads of departments' offices were on opposite sides of a corridor. Even when the CFE acquired its new building at King's Road, Devonport, provision was made for teaching only the engineer cadets.

This divided situation lasted until 1984, by which time the numbers of cadets required for the shrinking British merchant fleet had markedly reduced. Four of the cadet staff were made redundant, and the remainder were transferred from the CFE back into what had become the Faculty of Maritime Studies. Soon after Plymouth was approached by Shell Tankers and the Department of Transport to pioneer a combined navigating and engineer officer training scheme, with a four year dual training programme being initiated in 1986. By the early the 1990s, the shipping industry was recruiting under one hundred cadets annually, though with 130 cadets on its books the cadet section had remained a significant provider of cadet courses. In 1992, at the time the Polytechnic was emerging as a university, professional maritime courses at Plymouth were discontinued with the remaining cadets being transferred to other colleges. As the Department had for many years been active in the development of other maritime courses, staffing had been progressively re-oriented or had taken the opportunities offered for early retirement. The blow was cushioned, however, by the introduction of the HND in Marine Operations, which ran successfully until at the end of the 1990s the University settled on the policy of fostering Higher National Diploma (HND) initiatives at its partner colleges. Maritime work at this level continues at Falmouth Marine School. In recent years co-operation in course development with partner colleges has greatly improved, and the outcome might have been much more positive had present conditions existed eight years ago.

The Development of Maritime Higher Education at Plymouth

The rise and decline of Merchant Navy cadet courses at Plymouth illustrates both the advantages and disadvantages to a tertiary education establishment of close links with a particular industry even at a national level. Nevertheless, there is little doubt that cadet courses had a significant impact on the viability of certificate and later degree courses. As well as generating students living in the South West who would return for further study, the cadet courses brought young people to Plymouth from all over the country and from overseas, who when studying for the mates' or master's certificates chose to return to the familiar territory of Plymouth in preference to other nautical colleges. Social matters played a part as well through marriages to local girls, including two of Captain Johnson's daughters. Further, with Plymouth once again on the national map, its growing reputation was a factor in bringing in students, while the absence of an examination centre at Plymouth (withdrawn in 1932 and a factor in the decline) was of less significance in a period of improving transport links. Further, a larger critical mass meant that examiners were more prepared to travel to Plymouth to conduct examinations. The numbers of senior certificate students present at any one time rose to about 100 in the 1960s and 1970s. Courses of study increased in length and owing to increased leave allowances following service at sea, many students were unable to achieve their master's certificates until their early thirties, compared with their mid-twenties in the 1950s and 1960s. Some students were effectively on the books for fifteen or more years.

The transfer of the Marine Department's written examining function to the Scottish Vocational Education Council (SCOTVEC) in the 1980s, and the development of the courses for mates and masters as BTEC HNDs, combined the state's licensing function with the issue of national qualifications. Students were now taking compulsory courses in preparation for qualifications in which, after over a century, the lecturers had some real input into the examining process. As well as designing the BTEC courses with continuous assessment in the BTEC model, several staff became moderators, revisers or examiners for the unseen examinations now administered by SCOTVEC under the oversight of Marine Department examiners. This closer relationship with the external examining system, might be seen as starting with the opening of the radar school at Fisher's Nose (now Dutton's cafe) in 1955, with School of Navigation staff authorised to teach and examine students for the compulsory Radar Observer's Certificate. Similarly, the installation of a radar simulator in 1970 in the main building allowed courses for the Radar Simulation Certificate. This was supplemented in 1978 by a second Navigation Simulator in the space once occupied by the Maritime Library, which allowed the delivery of the statutory Automatic Radar Plotting Aid (ARPA) course from 1982. A measure of the department's expansion in this period was the growing number of technicians required to support its technical and practical work. Also on the increase was the level of secretarial/clerical support which had

4.47 For 35 years from 1955 groups of students studying for the Second Mate's certificate attended two and three week courses at the School of Navigation's Radar School at Fisher's Nose in this building which provided a radar view out to the Eddystone Lighthouse, real shipping movements, and strong echoes from the gas holders at Cattedown and the wall on Staddon Heights.

[photo: A.Kennerley]

4.48 From the late 1960s, advances in electronics allowed the installation of a succession of the radar and then navigation simulators in the maritime teaching block (now Fitzroy building). This is some of the equipment in use in the 1970s.

[UPPLY, maritime collection]

4.49 Radar Simulator courses soon became compulsory for students qualifying as master mariners. In the Simulator Suite, Dr.Robbins, Director of Plymouth Polytechnic, presented the certificate to Mr David George, the 1000th successful Radar Simulator Course student at Plymouth, on 21 May 1981.

[UPPLY, maritime collection]

4.50 Amongst other short courses offered to Merchant Navy officers, was a voluntary course on the gyro compass, often taken by officers appointed to ranks at sea which carried responsibility for the maintenance of ship's compasses

[UPPLY, maritime collection]

4.51 The most advanced professional qualification for merchant seafarers, the Certificate as Extra Master, dates from 1851, but began to be superseded by Nautical Studies degrees were introduced from 1966.

[S.T. Harley]

4.52 Captain G. R. Hughes, who succeeded Captain Johnson in 1958, led the development of national qualifications for seafarers and organised the introduction of nautical and post-graduate maritime degrees and diplomas at Plymouth. He later became assistant director at Plymouth Polytechnic.

[Photo: Media Services]

been non-existent in the 1950s. In this way the Department kept abreast with the rapidly developing technical requirements demanded of colleges by the Marine Department and by international agreements on maritime training. Nevertheless, with declining Merchant Navy manpower, it was only a matter of time before the merit of offering vocational courses for merchant seafarers was questioned, and after 130 years, in 1992, these courses were discontinued. Plymouth was not alone: of the other regional centres, Hull had likewise discontinued professional courses, Leith Nautical College, King Edward VII Nautical College (London) and Merchant Navy College (Greenhithe, Kent) had closed, and the provision elsewhere was much reduced. The number of institutions offering the full range of vocational courses for the Merchant Navy fell from some seventeen to three.

With the benefit of hindsight, the decision to devise a nautical degree course following the creation of the Council for National Academic Awards (CNAA) in 1964 was far-sighted in the extreme. Progressively it would lead to other degrees, post graduate courses and to a much enhanced research profile, though staff teaching the certificate students had already embarked on personal research projects.[44] The desire to take nautical subjects to more advanced levels than those required for the standard certificates was by no means new. It was implicit in Merrifield's activity and explicit at the Liverpool Nautical College in the 1890s where a short-lived advanced diploma was offered.[45] It was also explicit in the provision made when certificates were originally introduced in 1850, for a voluntary extra certificate, known as Extra Master, for seafarers desirous of demonstrating their superior knowledge.[46] Extra Master became the recognised qualification for seafarers aspiring to positions ashore which were closely related to merchant shipping. It was a prerequisite for all Marine Department surveyors and examiners, useful for marine superintendents and harbour masters and a degree substitute for nautical college lecturers where in the 1960s it qualified for an increment on the salary scale. Indeed under the regulations in force in the 1950s it had become a rigorous, yet broadly-based qualification ranging across mathematics, magnetism and electricity, chart construction and marine surveying, commercial and legal knowledge, ship construction and maintenance, meteorology, oceanography and economic geography, theoretical naval architecture and hydrostatics.[47] The standard in each of these papers was at least third year degree if not beyond. The unusual title, unusual breadth and the absence of a compulsory course in preparation meant that the Extra Master Certificate was ill understood by people outside the shipping industry; as a certificate, and as a certificate of competency it was inevitably under-rated. Its very difficulty meant that relatively few certificates were issued each year. Most nautical colleges had rarely more than one or two students studying for it at any one time, though at Plymouth in the 1960s the numbers varied between seven and twelve. Yet it was this qualification which made the nautical lecturer so flexible when it came to subject teaching, and ensured a multidisciplinary approach in relation to the maritime world.

4.53, 4.54 In 1968 Sheila Edmundson, seen here studying chartwork at Plymouth, made the headlines as the first woman cadet in the Merchant Navy. In 1980 she became the first woman to be awarded a master's certificate, and was serving, after eleven years at sea, as second mate.

[UPPLY, maritime collection, photos: Robert Chapman; Western Morning News]

The idea of degree level studies was also in the minds of the nautical educationalists in the period following World War II when the development of technical education was being planned and promoted. They included the nautical HMIs, Bray and Edgar, and people like Albert Mansbridge, founder of the WEA and of the Seafarers' Education Service, and his successor as Director of the SES, Ronald Hope. Encouragement for nautical studies degrees also came from the influential Rochdale Inquiry into Shipping (1970), which looked forward to the day when the normal educational route for ships officers would include degree studies.[48] By the mid-1960s the time of the Nautical Studies degree had come and courses were developed for validation by the CNAA at Plymouth and Cardiff. Liverpool soon followed, and rather later South Shields and London. The degree initiative should be seen in the same context as the developments in cadet courses from the late 1950s, noted above. At Plymouth, the head of the School from 1958, Captain G.R. Hughes, had the insight to seize such new opportunities at an early stage, and to direct staff into the forward planning that was needed. The BSc at Plymouth, approved in 1966 for an entry that September, was the first to achieve recognition, and the first CNAA degree at the Plymouth College of Technology. Although initially conceived as an ordinary, sandwich degree, the first entry of twelve produced the first graduates in 1969. Qualification for entry was the master's certificate, and it was not long before nautical degrees usurped the role of the Extra Master Certificate. The original syllabus at Plymouth almost exactly emulated that of the Extra Master Certificate. In 1972, the very high standard to which the course had been taught, allowed the CNAA to validate an honours stream, and at the same time the course was opened up to 'A' level entrants. It was then found that students lacking the maritime background were hard pressed to cope with the breadth and the standard set. Subsequent revisions created second year alternatives, navigation with hydrography or maritime business as majors, and ocean science or naval architecture as minors. By the 1983 re-validation entry numbers had reached 50, of whom about 40 were fresh from school.

PLYMOUTH POLYTECHNIC

DEPARTMENT OF
MARITIME STUDIES

B.Sc. IN NAUTICAL STUDIES

Director: E. BAILEY, B.SC., F.R.I.C., A.M.I.CHEM.E.
Head of Department of Maritime Studies: CAPTAIN G. R. HUGHES, M.R.E., F.INST.NAV., EXTRA MASTER
Course Co-ordinator: L. W. J. FIFIELD, M.INST.NAV., A.M.INST.T., EXTRA MASTER

4.55 The BSc in Nautical Studies, the first CNAA to be approved at Plymouth College of Technology accepted its first entry in September 1966 and produced its first graduates in July 1969. However it was originally conceived as primarily a sandwich course with various entry routes, with the 'straight through' course as an exceptional alternative.

[UPPLY, maritime collection, course booklet]

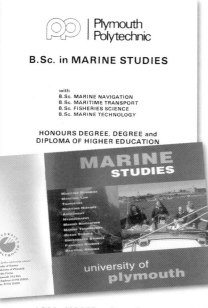

4.56 In 1986/87 undergraduate courses in the Faculty of Maritime Studies were merged into the Marine Studies Modular Scheme, offering several single subject awards and a number of combined award degree titles, arising out of the greatly increased opportunities for student choice which modular structures allowed.

[UPPLY, maritime collection]

4.57 Dr Ken George, a keen amateur player in Gilbert and Sullivan operettas, borrowed his costume as Captain Corcoran in HMS Pinafore, to deliver a lecture on the history of navigation to BSc Nautical Studies students on 31 October 1975.

[UPPLY, Spectrum (November 1975)

The development of undergraduate work continued with a degree in Fisheries Science in 1973 and pathways in oceanography, transport and astronomy from 1976 in the combined studies modular scheme. In 1987 the two internal degrees were merged into the Marine Studies Scheme offering degrees in Fisheries Science, Marine Navigation, Marine Technology, Maritime Business and Ocean Science. Subsequent developments saw the addition of degrees in Hydrography and Underwater Studies, additional pathways in technology and maritime history and the incorporation of the transport and astronomy pathways when the Combined Honours scheme was devolved to departments in the 1990s. By the mid-1990s, when admissions peaked in response to the Government's expansion of access to higher education, there were over 770 Marine Studies undergraduates in college. In recent years there has been some decline in admissions, reflecting changes in the funding mechanisms, the difficulty of recruiting to subjects unfamiliar to school leavers, a decline in mature students and the weakness imposed by the geographic position of Plymouth relative to major centres of population.

There were parallel developments in post-graduate taught courses. In the 1960s the School had offered short courses in aspects of maritime management for people working in the shipping industry ashore. It became apparent that there was an international demand for post-graduate/post-experience courses of a year's duration, satisfied by the successive development in the 1970s of a shipping Diploma in Management Studies and a master's degree in International Shipping. Subsequently the MSc in International Logistics was added and the diploma was absorbed into MSc structure. These courses have recruited well for many years and were extended by partnership links in the Netherlands and France. As a result Plymouth is extremely well known overseas and former Plymouth students may be found in senior shipping positions in most countries having maritime interests. The Diploma in Hydrographic Surveying was another successful initiative in the 1970s, providing the only course in the subject outside naval training, and recognised by the International Hydrographic Office. This has recently been integrated with a new MSc in Hydrography. Meanwhile the MSc in Applied Marine Science, validated in the early 1990s has also proved attractive to graduates. Taken together these courses now account for over 150 postgraduate students.

As noted earlier, the Institute of Marine Studies (the title for the department adopted in 1987) has long been involved in the provision of maritime short courses, both for serving seafarers and for people involved in the industry ashore. The close links of staff to the commercial shipping world in London produced the Galbraith Wrightson Shipping Course, devised at Plymouth delivered partly in Plymouth and partly in London. With leadership from Plymouth it ran from 1971 to 1992, and continues though now in the hands of others. Another initiative was the long series of courses in Maritime English dating from 1972, which originally brought teachers of English from overseas nautical colleges to Plymouth to learn the technical English of the sea. Staff also travelled extensively overseas to teach at

nautical colleges, some of which sent their students to Plymouth for short courses. There has also been a long series of short courses based on the navigation simulator, for marine pilots and for the staff of the Hydrographic Office in Taunton. Amongst recent developments have been courses in marine technical management, for marine superintendents.

4.58, 4.59 The Faculty's catamaran, Catfish, was designed and equipped for hydrographic and oceanographic field work afloat.

[UPPLY, Plymouth Polytechnic prospectus 1983/4]

To expand the work of the department on such a broad front, it was necessary for those staff originally recruited as nautical studies lecturers to develop specialisms. For many years a staff development policy was operated which allowed year-long sabbaticals to take taught masters degrees or to progress work on research degrees. This resulted in the great proportion of such staff achieving high level academic qualifications. From the late 1960s the nautical staff was increasingly augmented by staff entering with research backgrounds in specific aspects of maritime work. With the retirement of the staff recruited for maritime vocational work, it is the latter group which now dominates the department, which has become increasingly research oriented and increasingly able to compete for research funding. All the department's subject areas have been addressed at the doctoral or post doctoral levels either as personal research or through funded projects. In the department as a whole the number of research students has increased from one or two in the late 1960s to over forty at present.

As indicated earlier, a strength of the maritime staff at Plymouth since the 1960s has been their involvement with the maritime world nationally and internationally. Perhaps this is most evident in their work with professional

4.60 After over 30 years of offering nautical degrees, Plymouth maritime graduates are to be found all over the world in mostly occupations having a relationship with the sea. Lindsay Wilson, a Marine Studies graduate in 1992, immediately went on to serve as mate aboard the Lady Beaverbrook, seen here in Albert Dock, Liverpool, during the Tall Ships event that year.

[photo: A. Kennerley]

bodies, with lengthy and on-going representation on the councils and committees of the Chartered Institute of Transport, Royal Institute of Chartered Surveyors, Institute of Marine Engineers, Royal Institute of Naval Architects, International Commission for Maritime History. Staff have played leading roles in the formation of new bodies, notably The Nautical Institute (1972), The Hydrographic Society (1972), and the International Maritime Lecturers Association (1978). Such involvement has enhanced contacts with the maritime industries, helped achieve a wide range of professional institutional accreditation for the Department's courses, produced numerous employment opportunities for students and led to research and consultancy opportunities. Staff have given evidence to government investigations, such as the Rochdale Committee on British shipping, and done work for bodies such as the International Maritime Organisation, (IMO) the United Nations Conference as Trade and Development (UNCTAD) and the Food and Agriculture Organisation. Allied to research and consultancy has been a return to publishing. In the early decades of the Department's renaissance much of this effort was focused on producing new textbooks, in the traditional professional certificate subjects but also for wider maritime dimension increasingly being addressed by the Department. Graham Danton's *Theory and Practice of Seamanship* (1962), which has become a standard work, and David Moreby's *Personnel Management in Merchant Ships* (1968) represent the traditional and modern themes which were addressed. Consultancy work for government departments produced major reports such as those of the Sealife project and the Technology and Manning project. In more recent years maritime staff have become significant contributors of academic articles in refereed journals, and a number of research monographs have appeared.

The changed emphasis which has turned the School of Navigation/Institute of Marine Studies from a vocational department having a wide subject base into an academic department retaining that wide subject base has not of course been achieved without internal tensions and adjustments to the internal structure of the department. The fourteen year migration of the cadet section to the Plymouth College of Further Education has already been noted. Prior to 1970 there was a *de facto* subdivision between the senior and cadet sections, though it carried no official recognition in the Plymouth College of Technology. In the early Plymouth Polytechnic, as one of seven departments, perhaps the main internal distinction was that between Board of Trade certificate courses and the emergent work with undergraduate and post-graduate courses. Informal subject interests certainly existed, for example in shipping business or hydrographic survey, but many staff mixed in several areas, if only by virtue of the breadth of their subject teaching. Towards the end of the 1970s the Polytechnic adopted a system of teaching groups in recognition of distinct subject interests which had been built up in some of the departments. However, even the four groups identified in Maritime Studies represented some forcing together of maritime topics. From this, it was a natural step to create a faculty structure with separate subject departments in each faculty. One of the new faculties from 1980 was that of Maritime Studies, but with only three departments, Marine Science, Marine Technology and Shipping and Transport. This grouping by broad subject area was to be upset by the re-assimilation of the cadet section, leading to a re-organisation which put the vocational work into a Department of Shipping Operations, left the dominant Department of Shipping and Transport as it was, and put the remaining subject areas into a Department of Marine Science and Technology.

More change was in the offing. Although undergraduate work and post-graduate work was expanding, the declining scale of the traditional vocational work for the merchant shipping industry gave the impression that the whole Faculty was in decline. Further, although research had grown, the Faculty was not seen as sufficiently research oriented. Growth elsewhere in the Polytechnic made the Maritime Faculty appear comparatively small. An attempt to pull together marine work elsewhere in the Polytechnic, the Marine Science research laboratories in Plymouth and the Maritime Faculty produced a new over-arching title, Institute of Marine Studies and a new research thrust in oceanography, but otherwise had little effect. At the end of the 1980s the creation of a multi-campus Polytechnic added three vocationally oriented faculties, with the former agricultural college, Seale Hayne, in particular matching Marine Studies in size, industry links, and range of science, technology and business subjects addressed. Nevertheless, in 1991, at the time that the College was being designated University of Plymouth, the decision was taken to eliminate this Faculty on the Plymouth campus, by merging it into a single department within the Faculty of Science. At the oceanographic research level, the linkage with the pure sciences was an asset, but the move with respect to the larger proportion of the Institute of Marine Studies' work meant a less easy relationship, as was likely to have been the case if Marine Studies had been required to join, for example, the Plymouth Business School or the Faculty of Technology. Certainly there was a loss of identity

THE THEORY
AND PRACTICE
OF

Seamanship

REVISED METRIC EDITION

GRAHAM DANTON

4.61, 4.62 These books by Graham Danton and David Moreby from the 1960s marked the return to publishing by maritime staff after a lapse in the middle of the twentieth century.

[UPPLY, maritime collection]

particularly in group publicity with non-science subjects appearing under science headings. For the Marine Technology subject area, a key topic in the days of maritime vocational work, this problem was eased when the Bachelor of Engineering Degree in Marine Systems Technology was accredited by the Institute of Marine Engineers for Chartered Engineer status, and the section was transferred to the Faculty of Technology in 1998, into a new Department of Mechanical and Marine Engineering. With its work in marine navigation, hydrography, oceanography, meteorology, fisheries, maritime business, maritime law, and a new course in surf science and technology, the Institute of Marine Studies remains one of the largest departments in the University of Plymouth with about 100 staff in all, including some 34 academic staff, and some 850 students, 750 undergraduate and 100 post graduate.

4.63: Development Diagram

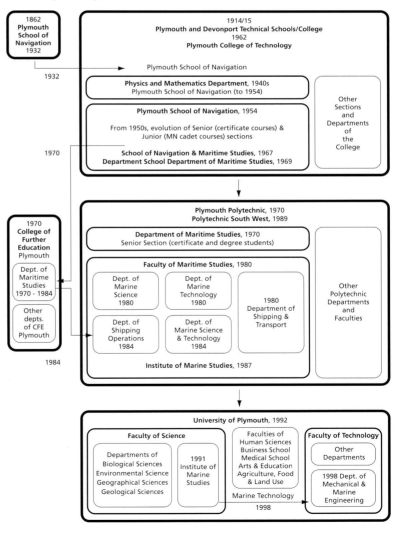

5.1 The City of Exeter Coat of Arms dates from 1564. The motto, Ever Faithful, was suggested by Elizabeth I in 1588 acknowledging a gift of money from the citizens of Exeter towards the shipping costs in resisting the Spanish Armada. [1]

Exeter School of Art

CHAPTER FIVE

by Helen James

The Exeter campus of the University of Plymouth may be traced back to the School of Art which was founded in Exeter in 1854. As one of the earlier applied subject areas to receive state encouragement and funding, art and design would, for over one hundred years, largely evolve as a separate and distinct sector of tertiary education, with its own administrative treatment at national level. Like teacher training, navigation and agriculture, it lay in a kind of tertiary 'no man's land' between school and university, and even when technical colleges had become well established in the twentieth century incorporating a wide range of subjects, art and design education continued its separate existence. Only towards the end of the century did the drive for all-embracing establishments of higher education lead to the Exeter college's merger with the University of Plymouth on the basis of its advanced work, while Plymouth College of Art and Design has remained a separate tertiary education establishment. It is one of the curiosities of higher education development in Devon, that the University of Exeter (1955) traces its earliest roots to this same School of Art, which, with its other roots, were associated under the same management until 1922, and even after that in occupancy of the same building.[2]

It was in the middle decades of the nineteenth century that training and education in design for industry became a matter of national concern leading to the rapid creation of an extensive network of schools and classes in art and design. After a less than easy start, the success of the initiative lay in the availability of pump-priming funding from the state, backed by central educational provision in London and a strong regulatory framework which was to be provided by the Department of Science and Art (DSA).

Despite Britain's early lead in industrialisation, by the 1830s, concern was growing about the level of reliance of manufacturing industry on imported designs, notably from France. So a Select Committee on Arts and Manufactures was appointed to "inquire into the best means of extending a knowledge of the Arts and of the principles of design among the people (especially the manufacturing population) of the country". Its report, in 1835, led to the founding by the Government of a School of Design in London in 1837, and to a number of similar schools in the provinces also funded by the state. The involvement of the young Devon landowner and Member of Parliament, Stafford Northcote, in the early distribution of grants to the schools of design was to have a bearing on initiatives locally in Exeter.[3] For the first decade or so the central administration of the small system of vocational education for design was of an *ad hoc* nature and erratic. By 1851 the annual sum involved had reached £15,000. The schools of design now became the responsibility of a new section of the Board of Trade, the Department of Practical Art, created in 1852. But almost immediately in 1853, partly as an outcome of the Great Exhibition of 1851 when the need to promote scientific education for the same reasons was re-emphasised, the new Department was reconstituted as the Department of Science and Art having two parallel sections. On the Art side the long term outcome has been that most of the surviving provincial schools of art have similar origins, while the School of Design in London has evolved into the Royal College of Art. Similarly, the importance of museum collections to the study of art and design gave rise both to provincial museums and to, particularly, a museum collection in London, with a basic holding of objects assembled by the School of Design augmented with items from the Great Exhibition. This would become the Victoria and Albert Museum.[4]

In the early years the two sections were managed centrally almost as separate organisations. Thus the Joint Secretary of the DSA and Superintendent of Art, Henry Cole, with a head start in his section owing to the existence of the schools of design, gave his attention to the regulatory framework under which state funding could be made available and to encouraging the spread of the network of art schools, which would number 120 two decades later.[5] By 1881 there were 160 schools of art catering for over 30,000 students and additionally there were nearly 600 separate art

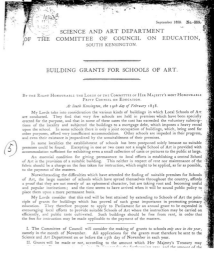

5.2 *The Department of Science and Art encouraged the building of dedicated premises for art schools, by making grants (considered repayable) to local committees such as that managing the School of Art at Exeter, which received £500 towards the cost of the Albert Memorial building, opened in 1868.*

[PRO, ED/17, DSA minutes]

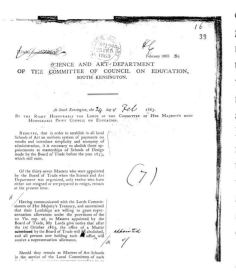

5.3 With this minute of 24 February 1863 the Department of Science and Art imposed the full rigour of 'payment-by-results' on all the schools of art which it recognised, in order to "...introduce simplicity and economy of administration...". The minute also notes that only twelve of the art teachers appointed ten years earlier subject to the original method of DSA allowances, have not resigned from their schools.

[PRO, ED/16, DSA minutes]

classes with some 23,000 students. In the 1850s, the new regime made the granting of state support dependent upon local fund raising and local management. It also exercised some constraint over the level of student fees to encourage the less well off to attend, though the hope that schools of art would rapidly become self supporting allowing the state to pull back was never to be realised. Perhaps as a result of the adoption of the term 'practical art' in the title of the 1852 department, which became simply 'art' when the DSA came into existence, the word 'design' dropped out of usage. This did not mean that the vocational and economic purpose of an art education and training was lost to sight. Art schools were not, and are not, solely concerned with what came to be known as 'fine art', that is painting and sculpture appealing to the sense of the beautiful, even though art teachers could draw a good proportion of their income from teaching recreational art to, especially, ladies who could afford the fees. The regulations for making 'Payments on Results of Instruction in Schools of Art' (1863) make this clear: drawing, painting, and modelling and designing for manufactures were the qualifying subjects.[6] In the twentieth century the vocational purpose of many art schools has been emphasised by the adoption of the phrase 'art and design' in their titles. While in the early years different regulations were applied in the two sections, of the DSA, Art and Science, they were at one in demanding that the teacher appointed to an art or science school should have been trained. One of the main functions of the central or normal school of design/art in London was the training of prospective art teachers who would then be directed to particular towns, often as the founding headmaster. Other aspects of the early regime included allowances for equipment and buildings, the payment of the salaries of pupil teachers where they were taken on, and payment for teaching children in local elementary schools. In addition there were, of course, regular visits by the art inspectors and annual reports to be made to London.

Over time there have inevitably been changes to the arrangements made in the 1850s. The uniform system for public art education introduced by Cole and his assistants consisted of the National Course of Instruction, the National Competition and National Graded Examinations in Art. The course comprised four divisions of instruction for drawing, painting, modeling and design, each of which were divided into stages, making 23 in all. The system became centralised around the National Competition with inspectors from the Department of Art visiting art schools in the provinces each year to select the best of students' work to be sent to London to compete for national medals and prizes. The system of graded examinations, provided for three grades. The third grade, the highest, was for the Art Master's Certificate and the second grade was for the teacher's certificate which allowed the holder to teach pupils studying for the first grade, or elementary school level. In 1913, the Board of Education (which had been formed in 1899 by the merging of the Departments of Science and Art and of Education) introduced a Drawing Certificate which replaced the many categories of drawings which had been required for the Art Master's Certificate. It was followed by certificates in painting, modeling, pictorial design and industrial design. Two years later the National Competition for schools of art was abolished. Over the years the standard of these national qualifications was gradually raised. Further changes came in 1933, when the Board of Education's Teaching Certificate for Teachers in Schools of Art was renamed the Art Teacher's Diploma (ATD). Then in 1946, the Ministry of Education replaced the Board's examinations in drawing by the Intermediate Examination in Arts and Crafts and introduced the National Diploma in Design (NDD) to replace the Art Teacher's Diploma This was to change with the introduction of the Diploma in Art and Design (DipAD) in 1961, which replaced the NDD. The 1970s saw the intoduction of degrees in subjects such as fine art and graphic design, in collaboration with local universities or through the Council for National Academic Awards (CNAA). But the Government's white paper, *A Plan for Polytechnics and Other Colleges* in 1966, was to see the amalgamation of many art colleges with polytechnics. In some areas of art education disquiet was felt at this development. The artist Patrick Heron wrote an article for *The Guardian,* 'Murder of the art schools' which spoke of the obliteration of the identity of the art schools which he said were 'being dismembered and swallowed piecemeal.'[7] However, Exeter College of Art and Design was to remain independent until its merger in 1988 with Polytechnic South West, which was to become the University of Plymouth in 1992.

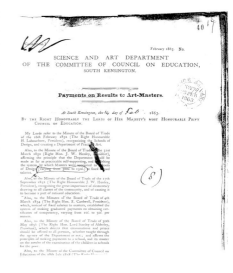

5.4 *With the introduction of the new system of financing art teaching in 1863, all the previous regulations had to be revised or cancelled. This DSA minute contains a summary of earlier practice.*

[PRO, ED/16, DSA minutes]

By the twentieth century, of course, most schools of art (not all survived) had been brought under the management of the local education authority and were supported partly by the local rates and partly through monies allocated by the state to local authorities for education, though for a long time student fees were an important element. But in the late 1850s it was new arrangements made by Cole for supporting art teaching that were to be the testing ground for the system of 'payment-by-results' which, in the 1860s, was applied to the schools and classes of science and to the elementary school system. As with the science schools, DSA support for art included classes in elementary schools as well as in named schools of art. Attempting to cover all local situations, the DSA would support:[8]

"(A) Unions for Art-teaching where no School of Art is established. Five Schools for the poor must be brought together…(B) Art-classes, formed under Local Committees, held in any premises approved by this Department. An evening class for artisans must be established meeting not less than three nights in each week, and the fee for such evening class must not be higher than 6d. per week…(C) …Art-schools held in premises approved by this department and exclusively and permanently devoted to Art instruction…"

The full force of payment-by-results was applied in 1863. Art teachers were required to claim from the DSA the payments which were linked to the passes achieved by their pupils and students in the annual examinations and competitions for certificates and medals. Thus for every child who passed a paper of the first grade a sum of one or two shillings could be claimed. At the top of the scale 50 shillings could be claimed for every work for which a national medallion was awarded and fifteen pounds for a student who had passed the Art Teacher's Certificate. The submission of the annual report on time was worth ten pounds. Payment-by-results

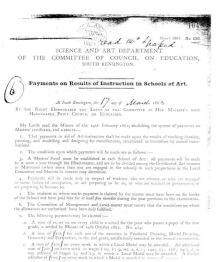

5.5 *This DSA minute of 17 March 1863 sets out the conditions under which art teachers could claim payments which now related to their students' success in examinations and the level of the qualification.*

[PRO, ED/16, DSA minutes]

remains controversial to the present day, and it was so at the time. Reporting in 1864, as the new rules were beginning to take effect, the Select Committee on the Schools of Art condemned the system as ill suited to schools of art, but to no avail.[9] Indeed Stephens, in his study of the Warrington School of Art, argues that payment-by-results did not have any particular negative effects on that School. It was already heavily influenced by the DSA regime, it was successful in gaining a fair proportion of the higher awards, sustained a balanced student body from the various classes including the working-classes and artisans, and numbers fluctuated no more than elsewhere, being particularly strong in the 1870s.[10] The strong emphasis on providing classes for local elementary teachers in the early period gradually reduced the necessity for the schools of art to be directly involved in teaching school children, and, towards the end of the 1860s, that requirement was dropped from the DSA regulations. Now the schools could be more clearly identified with the provision of art education and training for those who had left elementary school and, particularly, adults in employment seeking to upgrade their artistic skills. The relaxation of the regulations as the nineteenth century progressed meant that by the 1890s fixed salaries were being introduced. Then, following the creation of the county councils and the allocation of special funds for technical education, the schools of art began to be brought properly under the local education authorities, either as separate establishments or as sections of local technical colleges.

During the twentieth century the art school network remained an identifiable section as far as the central administration in London was concerned, and was subject to special regulation and policy making. Locally art schools were managed like the technical colleges by local authorities' technical, higher or further education sub-committees. In the 1930s the Board of Education attempted a rationalisation of the diverse arrangements for the provision of art education, which still included small isolated classes as well as numerous, large and small schools of art.[11] The Board recommended the establishment of central art colleges for each district which would become centres of excellence. It wished to avoid an unnecessary duplication of instruction, make good gaps in the provision of art education for each area, to "...ensure the best possible teaching, accommodation and equipment..." for advanced students, and to maintain close relations with local industries. Some success was achieved in the northern industrial cities, in the midlands and with a grouping in the coastal region of Hampshire/Dorset. In the south west the Plymouth School of Arts and Crafts was proposed for this role and the education authorities of Devon, Cornwall, Exeter and Torquay were invited to make use of courses there for advanced students. However, at that time it was considered either that there was no demand or that the offer could be taken up at a later stage, if necessary, so the spread of local art schools in the south west was to remain unaffected by this development. [12]

Table 5.1
Day Time Enrolments in Art Establishments (England & Wales), 1952/3.

Subject	FT	PT
Painting	1047	1779
Illustration and Commercial Design (incl. lithography, lettering)	1510	761
Printing and allied crafts (including book-binding)	62	3726
Dress & allied crafts (including embroidery)	1196	5524
Textile (printed & woven), & wallpaper design	287	225
Modelling, sculpture, lettercutting, etc.	228	278
Pottery and glass	184	254
Interior decoration and painting & decorating	133	4326
Silversmithing, jewellery and allied crafts	66	548
Furniture	75	550
Metals & plastics (design for mass production)	18	61
Display work	43	108
Photography	105	124
Other branches of design	167	81
Intermediate and general art courses	4921	2795
Architecture	1126	892
Teaching Course (final year for intending specialists)	468	174
Miscellaneous general crafts	106	8323
Total	11742	30529

Source: K. Holmes, 'Art', in Venables, *Technical Education, op.cit.,* 307.

In the early 1950s art education and training, as with other areas of technical education, was still largely a part-time and evening affair. Only one in twenty students was studying full-time during the day. That barely one tenth of these students were taught in separate art schools, demonstrates the extent that art education had been absorbed into technical education. About a third of students were studying part-time during the day while about two thirds were attending evening classes.[13] The range of subjects studied in art establishments by full-time students in the 1950s is representative of the subject scope developed during the nineteenth century (Table 5.1). The schools of art shared in the changes to technical education in the 1960s and 1970s, benefitting from the move from evening to day time study, from course development and from the building boom. The colleges of art at Exeter and Plymouth, for example, both gained new buildings. In the structural changes of the late twentieth century there were further mergers with larger establishments, though some colleges, such as those at Plymouth and Falmouth survive in the prevailing funding regime, as further education corporations.

Exeter School of Art in the Nineteenth Century

Though not amongst the first phase of art school foundations, the Exeter School of Art was established sufficiently early in the push of the 1850s, to indicate that the leading citizens of Exeter were alive to the opportunities and advantages offered under the new DSA arrangements. Of course Exeter was not alone in the south west. There were similar initiatives in many other centres of population, some of which seem rather unlikely to modern eyes. However it must be remembered that travel was not the easy thing it has now become, and small comparatively local establishments were inevitably the order of the day. Both the art schools at Tavistock and Exeter date from 1854,

5.6 For the DSA to support an art teacher, the local committee had to set up schools or classes in a structure which would be approved by the DSA. This minute of 8 July 1863, sets out the conditions which applied following the review of the whole structure of support for art education. .

[PRO, ED/12, DSA minutes]

though Exeter only admitted its first students in January 1855. They were preceded by Bath (1851) and Bristol, Penzance and Truro (1853), and followed soon after by Plymouth and Taunton (1856), and Devonport (1858). Amongst later foundations were Torquay (1866), Barnstaple (1868) and Tiverton (1879). At Exeter, unlike Plymouth, there was no mechanics' institute to underwrite the art school's foundation. Exeter's mechanics' institute had closed in 1835, owing to low membership and high subscriptions, whereas Plymouth's successful mechanic's institute in the 1850s provided art instruction in drawing, water colour and oil painting. Plymouth's School of Art was to close in 1858, and re-open again in 1862, while that at Devonport also had an uncertain start. The School of Art at Exeter was successful perhaps because there was a lack of alternative art training provided by a mechanics' institute art classes.[14]

Table 5.2

Exeter School of Art, Enrolments, Fees Paid and DSA Aid, 1855-90.

	Children	Teachers	Central School Day	Central School Evening	Central School Total	Grand Total	Fees £	DSA aid £
1855						784		
1860	1080	29	68	215	283	1392		164
1865	952	12	84	165	249	1201		169
1870			84	182	266	266	368	155
1875			67	202	269	269	437	164
1880			55	174	229	229		
1885					280	280	320	173
1890								184

Source: DSA Annual reports, 1855-1890

The premises obtained for the new art school were some rooms over the entrance to the Lower Market in Fore Street, Exeter, later destroyed in the 'Blitz' of 1942. Local donations and subscriptions together with a local committee enabled a start to be made. Sir Stafford Northcote was one of the Exeter School of Art's founders and became President of the School. Montague Wigzell, with one certificate from the DSA as his qualification, was appointed as headmaster. The inauguration was celebrated in style with a *soirée and conversazione*. The walls of the school were decorated with drawings and there was also a display of casts supplied by M. Brucciani of London, arranged with 'great taste' by Mr.Wigzell, and the Exeter artist, John Gendall (1768-1865). The following month, the *Exeter Flying Post* recorded the fact that many of the public went to see the exhibition and that 72 people joined the artisans' class, noting that "...the other classes are well attended and there can be little doubt that the school will be entirely successful."[15] At the School teaching was given during the day and evening, and organised in classes lettered from A to F. The artisans' class, C, was for people in occupations, and therefore took place in the evenings, with a charge of two shillings a month. Class E, for school masters, school teachers and pupil teachers also took place in the evenings. The ladies' class, A, took place during the day with a charge of a guinea a month. The number of students taught ranged from 784 in 1855 to 1160 in 1862, though these totals include a significant number of school children.[16] With the withdrawal of the requirement to teach school children, a clearer picture of the work of the central school during the latter part of the nineteenth century may be seen (Table 5.2). Typically the school enrolled about 260 students annually who paid about £400 in fees while the DSA grant amounted to about £170. The Exeter School of Art seems to have been of average size in this period, one of the larger schools to be found in the more rural parts of the country, but significantly smaller than those in the large centres of population. Before the move to the new Albert Memorial Museum, annual out-goings for rent amounted to £40, with £34 for heat and light. Repairs cost £29 and other payments amounted to £54 (data for 1862).[17] From the income, the teacher received half the student fees and half the DSA grant. Exhibitions of students' work have always been characteristic of art school activity, no less in the 1850s than the present. Indeed, they were expected by the DSA, who requred returns of the attendances by the general public. In addition in 1855 and 1859 it had exhibitions of works from London complemented by works by local artists, which were enthusiastically greeted by the public.[18]

5.7 *This plaque on the Queen Street façade of the Albert Memorial building commemorates the donor of the site, Richard Somers Card, MP, and the laying of the foundation stone on 30 October 1865.*

[Photo: A. Kennerley]

The early success left the School of Art in need of additional accommodation. Indeed over the years the inadequacy of the teaching accommodation available was almost a standing characteristic of art schools as it was of technical colleges, and frequently the subject of comment in HMI reports. The death of Albert, the Prince Consort and patron of the Great Exhibition, in December, 1861, was to be a trigger for fresh thought and activity on what was needed for Exeter. At the annual meeting of the School of Art at Exeter on 31 December that year, Sir Stafford Northcote referred to the devotion of Prince Albert to culture, and to the necessity for a great 'Art and Science Centre' in Exeter. The need to have better accommodation for the School of Art was also expressed. If it could not expand and grow it was in danger of dying, and there was "...one thing just then very much talked about and in everybody's mouth in this City of Exeter, and that was a Museum...". The first attempt to supply the need for a museum had been the establishment of the Devon and Exeter Institution in 1813 which had aimed to provide a library, reading room and museum. Although it was able to develop through various donations, this institution evolved as more a library and reading room, and its building was not adapted to provide a museum. The Exeter artist, John Gendall, was later to make that point when in 1853, William Cotton of Ivybridge had offered his collection of art to Exeter, and it had been reluctantly refused because of its lack of a museum. The collection went to the museum at Plymouth. Consequently, the proposal for a building at Exeter was not to make it "...entirely a School of Art...[but] to have the building partly used by the School, and partly by other institutions in the City...".[19] On 7 January, 1862, the Mayor of Exeter held a meeting of those interested in establishing a museum, resulting in donations amounting to £1,500. At a meeting the following month it was agreed that a Museum of Science and Art would be a fitting memorial to Prince Albert, and a committee was set up to procure a suitable site. R.S. Gard gave a piece of

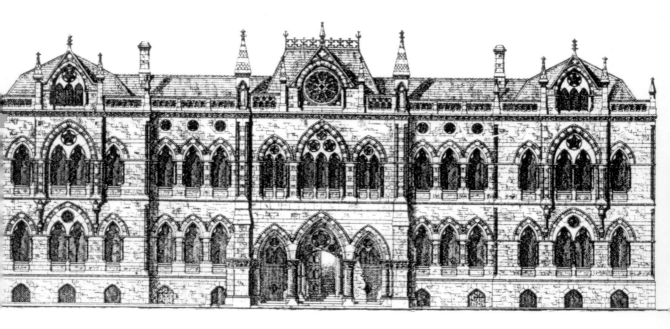

5.8 The competition for the design of the proposed Albert Memorial museum was won by a local architect, John Hayward, who produced this gothic style drawing for the front elevation opening onto Queen Street.

[West Country Studies Library]

land at Queen Street, 140 feet by 70 feet, behind which the Committee was able to buy an additional area. In 1864 it invited architects to submit plans for the proposed building. Those of John Hayward (1808-91), a local architect, were selected out of 24 sent in. The front block of the museum was built in 1865-8, and there were extensions in 1884, 1895 and 1899. George Dunisthorpe in 1868 described the building as being in the "...Gothic style of architecture [with a] considerable variety of outline and detail, the intention of the architect being to reproduce some of the picturesque character of the old city, without copying any of the old forms of its architecture... ".[20] So the School of Art, together with the School of Science (which had opened in 1853 at the Literary Society, 10, Bedford Circus) moved their premises to the Museum in 1868. The School of Art was allocated a space of 70 feet by 60 feet in the upper part of the building. The School of Science was situated in the basement, while the first floor was devoted to a Free Library and the second floor to the Museum.[21] Erecting this building was certainly far sighted. It can be regarded as a technical college building which was twenty years ahead of the period when such multi-function educational buildings were being erected elsewhere. Its existence undoubtedly helped the university extension movement in Exeter, and it is perhaps not stretching a point too far to suggest that such an early physical preparation, with its series of extensions, had a bearing of achieving university college status in the 1920s. So at Exeter, in contrast to some of the larger industrial cities where schools of art paid substantial rents to use the rooms of a library and museum, art students had the benefit of working in a newly created, sponsored and spacious Albert Memorial Museum and School of Art due to the generosity of local benefactors.[22]

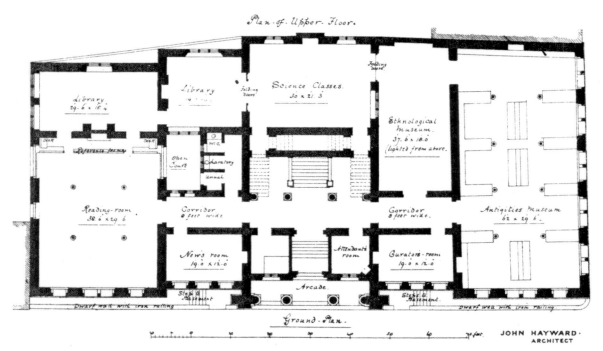

Table 5.3

Student Occupations at Exeter School of Art in 1862.

School children	35	Masons	3	Builders	19
Smiths	5	Metalworkers	2	Cabinet makers	4
Teachers/pupil teachers	3	House painters	5	Wood carver	1
Upholsterers	2	Plumber	1	Clerks	10
Ironmongers	2	Architects	6	Draper	1
Land surveyor	1	Artist	1	Engravers/etchers	4
Lithographer	1	Booksellers	3	Gardner	1

Source: Select Committee on Schools of Art, *BPP*, 1864, XII, Return of Exeter School
of Exeter School of Art.

5.9 The ground floor of the Hayward's design for the Albert Memorial building contained the library and reading room on the left, the antiquities and ethnological museum on the right. The Science School was allocated only one room at the rear of the building.

[West Country Studies Library]

It has always been the case in art schools that the staff should be seen to practice their professions as well as teaching. This has been so with all the headmasters and principals at Exeter, and was certainly the case with James Birkmyer who was appointed to succeeded Montague Wigzell as Headmaster of the School of Art in 1861. He was very well qualified with four DSA teacher's certificates. A landscape painter, he exhibited at the Royal Academy, the Royal Society of British Artists and the Royal Hibernian Academy between 1868 and 1898.[23] It was not long after his arrival that in 1863 the revised system of payment-by-results was introduced.[24] His return to the Select Committee on Schools of Art which reported in 1864, showed a wide variety of occupations represented amongst his students. Table 5.3 numbers 110 individuals, so it is likely that students who did not fall within the terms of the return are not represented. The average weekly attendance for males was 40 and for females 41. The duration of regular attendance varied between one month (24 males and four females) and ten months (23 males and 31 females). The most popular class at the School of Art was that

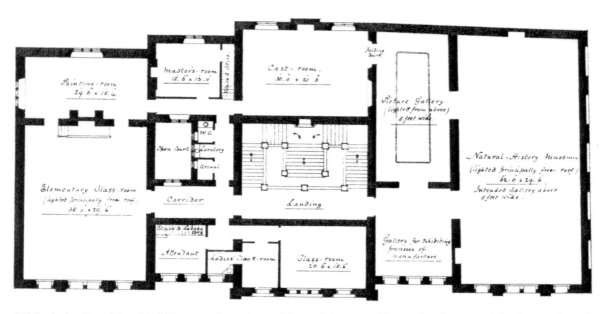

5.10 On the first floor of the original Albert Memorial building, Exeter School of Art was allocated two classrooms, a painting room, and a master's room. The museum occupied the remaining space on the right of the plan which included two rooms as art galleries and a natural history museum.

[West Country Studies Library]

for artisans. Most of these would attend twice a week in the evening after work. During the time of Henry Cole's period of office from 1852-73, the emphasis was on education in drawing rather than design and at this stage artisans' classes would have been referred to as night classes in drawing.[25] As well as teaching in local schools in the early years, the School also ran classes at the Exeter Diocesan Training College (1839) now the Saint Luke's Department of Education, University of Exeter, and in the 1890s a branch class in Exmouth.[26]

The annual reports of the School of Art at Exeter record the varying success rates of students throughout the years. That for 1874 stated "There can be no doubt that the School is growing in popularity, under the present able master, and is doing much useful work". That for 1877 reported that at the Second Grade exams, of the 90 students, about 75% were successful, and that Exeter stood "...first for success in competition of all towns which can be termed non-manufacturing". In contrast, the annual report for the preceding year expressed surprise and dissatisfaction, in common with other provincial art schools, at the levels of awards made by the DSA for the Second Grade examination. The marking had been inconsistent and the grades awarded were low. The Committee for the School of Art protested and after lengthy correspondence succeeded in obtaining a revision of these awards.[27] The minutes of the Schools of Science and Art Sub-Committee reported that Richard Redgrave, the Inspector General for Art, who had taken responsibility for the irregularities, resigned shortly after this, and it expressed more optimism for the future with the appointment of his successor, Edward John Poynter, RA[28] Poynter, in common with the artists Frederic Leighton and Lawrence Alma Tadema, was influenced by classical art and in favour of drawing from the nude model, and as such was to swing the movement in art education more towards fine art. The annual report for

1878 stated that "...the School of Art continues to progress satisfactorily, not withstanding the much higher standard of excellence required under the new direction at South Kensington...". Birkmyer's report that year, also referred to the "...great increase in the standard under the new direction of Mr. Poynter, R.A. at South Kensington."

Exeter School of Art was fortunate in having the support and interest of leading figures in the City. The role of Sir Stafford Northcote has already been mentioned. At the end of the century the landscape artist, Frederick J Widgery, who had studied at the School, was active in civic affairs, serving as Lord Mayor of Exeter, Chairman of the Governors of the Royal Albert Memorial College and Chairman of the Exeter School of Art Committee.[29] The annual reports for the 1870s also refer to the instigation of a new prize, the Sir John Bowring Prize. Sir John Bowring (1792 - 1872), an Exeter man, was a linguist, writer, traveller and diplomat who advocated Britain's adoption of the decimal currency. At Exeter he was the first president of the Devonshire Association for the Advancement of Science, Literature and the Arts (1862-3) and president of the Devon and Exeter Institution (1865-6).[30] He took an interest in the School of Art and the school's annual report for 1873 stated that that it missed the"...instrumentality of the late Sir John Bowring." The following year a prize fund of £100 was established, the interest from which was to be given annually for a prize in his memory. The prize continued as an annual award for special achievement until the 1980s.

The School was less successful during the last quarter of the nineteenth century. Enrolments of students at the School of Art were variable during the 1870s and 1880s. In 1867 there were 247 pupils.[31] Twelve years later the annual report for 1879 recorded 272 pupils. However, the annual report for 1881 recorded that for the past three years the School of Art had felt the effects of the depression of trade, that there had been a considerable decrease in the numbers of students, but that now the school was recovering itself. By

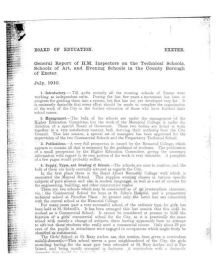

5.12 Exeter School of Art had been subject to regular visits and reports by DSA inspectors from its inception in the 1850. It was to be no different under the Board of Education and its successors, except that on some occasions as with this visit in 1910, the HMIs made an assessment of all the post-school educational provision in Exeter. Here they find the local management under separate committees of the University Extension College and the and School of Art (sharing the Albert memorial building) work together in a very satisfactory manner.

[PRO, 114/105]

1884, there had been a serious fall in the number of wealthier students although the artisan classes had still kept their numbers. Birkmyer reported a decline of fee income because of a decrease in the number of ladies attending the day elementary class, since the establishment of a high school for girls, elementary drawing being taught there with no extra fee charged. The source of income from the Diocesan Training College and the seven other schools had now ceased, as art teaching at these establishments was now undertaken by masters who had qualified at the School of Art. All this led to a decline of the income of the school and of its headmaster.[32]

In such a situation new initiatives might have been expected. Although at this stage there were ladies' advanced classes for watercolour and landscape painting, none were offered for men despite a demand for them. It was suggested that these could become mixed classes. The Headmaster, James Birkmyer, expressed the prevalent Victorian reserve about this issue, writing that the admission of male students would have a prejudicial effect. Although it might have been expected that the range of classes would have been extended, permission was refused to a Miss Agatha Middleton when she wished to open a class for ladies in wood-carving. In 1894, it had been recommended that a life class be offered in the Art School for those students who wished to join, but as late as 1900 a report criticised the School as being at a disadvantage compared with other schools because of the"...non-existence of an adequate life class." Under the regime of Henry Cole, drawing from the nude model had not been seen as an essential part of art education and in 1863 only one in eight Schools of Art had a life class. Until 1893, female students were not permitted to draw from the nude. Even after this they were not allowed to draw from the female nude, but only from a partially draped male nude.[33]

Exeter Technical and University Extension College

In 1893, the School of Art at Exeter, became part of a larger educational institution known as the Exeter Technical & University Extension College. A course of Cambridge Extension Lectures organised by a University Extension Committee had started in Exeter in 1886.[34] This was a new development in education for Exeter, something in addition to that offered by the Schools of Science and Art at the Albert Memorial, though as with the initiative 40 years earlier, it emulated educational developments taking place in other provincial centres. Like so many other applied subject areas, art and design were not then perceived as university subjects. From having been one of the principal reasons for building the Albert Memorial establishment and at the centre of activity there, the School of Art was now to be progressively side-lined as the University Extension College grew in strength and ambition. The culmination would be its separation in 1922.

At the heart of the changed environment was the introduction of a new management structure for central post-school education in Exeter. The regime required by the DSA had been for a management committee for each of the schools and classes it was prepared to support. The senior teacher in a science school or art school, the headmaster, reported to this committee. There could be, as it were, competing committees, though in time the logic was for a single committee in a locality to oversee all science and art activity in its area. These committees had not been automatically sub-committees of local town corporations. The re-structuring of local government in 1888 and the new arrangements for funding technical education from the early 1890s, meant that city and county councils absorbed the functions of the ad hoc committees, through the formation in some places of technical education committees. Having separate establishments occupying a single central building, was an unsatisfactory business. The erection of central technical college buildings throughout the country during the 1890s imposed a logic that all local authorities eventually followed of unifying technical education provision under a single head generally with the title, principal.

Exeter settled on this approach rather earlier than towns such as Plymouth and Devonport. The initiative is credited to Miss Jessie Montgomery, Secretary of the University Extension Committee from 1888. In 1893 she put forward an ambitious scheme to the Museum and Technical Education Committee that there should be a college with three departments working under a principal who should be a university graduate. The first department was to be a university extension college. The second was to be a department of technical schools continuing and extending the existing schools of science and art. The third department was to be a teachers' department for the training of teachers. At the meeting, the sentiment was expressed that "...if you can get the University Extension people and Science and Art School people to work harmoniously together, it will be a very good thing - an admirable thing..." and that co-operation was 'most desirable, and antagonism disastrous'.[35] Later that year, Mr. Arthur William Clayden, an M.A. from Christ College, Cambridge, was appointed Principal of Exeter University Extension and Technical College. His degree was in natural sciences and his specialism was geology. H. Lloyd Parry in his *History of the Royal Albert Memorial College, Exeter* (1946) also described him as being "...an expert photographer and a painter of merit...", and also as a man of 'an attractive disposition' who 'was held in affection by the students and all members of the staff'. His books *Cloud Studies* (1905) and *The History of Devonshire Scenery* (1906) were published after his appointment as Principal. *Cloud Studies* was one of the few books written on that aspect of meteorology at that time and was published in a second edition in 1925. It is interesting that, in his preface to the first edition, Clayden expressed his hope that the book would be of interest to the artist as well as the meteorologist by drawing "...attention to the variety and exquisite beauty of the sky...".[36] At the time of his appointment the College was divided into two departments, the Technical Department, consisting of the Schools of Science and Art, working under the Museum and Technical Instruction Committee, and the University Extension Department working under the University Extension Committee. The two departments were to hold classes in the same building and also to be administered by the same Principal. The teachers' department was developed at the end of the decade.

Adopted 15 . 5 . 20.

BOARD OF EDUCATION.   EXETER C.B.

Report of Inspection of EXETER, ROYAL ALBERT MEMORIAL COLLEGE SCHOOL OF ART, held on 25th, 26th, and 27th February, 1920.

Inspectors.—Mr. J. W. Allison, H.M.I.   Mr. F. Suddards, H.M.I.
                   Mr. W. B. Dalton, A.R.C.A.

LOCALITY.

The School serves the City and County Borough of Exeter and the surrounding parts of the Administrative County of Devonshire. About one-half of the students in day attendance reside in the County area.
Exeter had a population of 59,092 in 1911; the population was increased by some 11,000 in 1913 by the inclusion of the large suburb of Heavitree.
The School is organised as a department of the Royal Albert Memorial College, and is housed in the College premises. These premises are central, convenient of access from all parts of the city, and within easy reach of the principal railway stations.
The local industries on which the activities of the School can be brought to bear are the manufacture of stained-glass windows, ecclesiastical carving (wood and stone), metal working and embroidery; cabinet making; house painting and decorating; lithography, engraving and printing; dressmaking and millinery; photography, etc.
The aim of the School is to provide instruction for those who wish to qualify for an artistic profession, to train industrial art workers, to supplement the training of Elementary School Teachers, and to provide for those who desire a knowledge of art as part of a liberal education.

THE SCHOOL IN ITS RELATION TO THE LOCALITY.

Several firms are known to give monetary aid to enable their employees to attend the School. It is difficult to determine the actual number of these cases, as sometimes the direct payments are made by the students although part of the money is provided by the employer.

MANAGEMENT.

Pending the reorganisation of the College under a charter of incorporation, the institution has been placed under the temporary control of a Body of Governors composed of nine representatives of the Exeter City Council, nine of the Devon County Council, and six co-opted Governors. The Governing Body are assisted in the management of the School by an art sub-committee, composed of four Governors, one of whom is a woman. The sub-committee works under the chairmanship of a Governor who is an artist by profession.
The Principal of the College and the Chairman of the School of Art Sub-Committee visit the School occasionally.

5.13 When the HMIs visited in 1920 it concentrated exclusively on Exeter School of Art. Every aspect of the work of the School received close attention and comment. It is clear that the School was soon to be separated from the oversight of the Royal Albert Memorial College. The HMIs' main criticism was reserved for the inadequate accommodation in which the school had to function.

[PRO, ED 114/ 209]

5.14 Over the years quite a number of Exeter School of Art's former students have achieved national or international reputations. In 1920 John Angel completed this sculpture of the Last Supper for a church believed to be in New York. He subsequently settled and practised in the USA.

[UPEXE, School of Art collection]

The effect of the changed management structure was to demote the head of the School of Art to a head of section, in parallel with the science section of the newly designated department, though it is unclear whether there was a head of department over them. Probably the School of Art had become set in its ways given the lengthy service of its headmaster, James Birkmyer, and a shake up was needed. At the time the change took place it was suggested that the School of Art give more attention to design and decorative art, than to painting in oils and watercolours. It should have the 'usual' subjects of design and decorative work, modelling, wood carving and metal work, if possible. The establishment of the College appears to have benefited the School of Art and in 1895 a call was made for more teaching power. The number of enrolments had increased from 224 in 1893 to 273 in 1895 and there had been an increased interest in new subjects such as drawing and modelling from life. The early years could not have been easy for staff. During the first year of the College, its two departments were reported to have worked side by side, though with not much connection, but that during the second year there had been more fusion with students taking classes in both.[37] In the Albert Memorial College's aspiration for university college status (it changed its name in 1900),[38] it would have been inevitable that the very existence of sections concerned with practical as well as less advanced work would have raised questions about the merits of retaining such work within the same setting. But, in 1911, the right of the School of Art to be there was emphatically confirmed in a review of the trust deeds relating to the Albert Memorial building. In 1867 a condition of the building grant from the DSA (£500) had been that "…a portion of the said buildings, to be erected and filled up…should be held and appropriated by the Trustees or Managers exclusively for the purposes of a School of Art…until the full amount of said grant should be repaid to the Department…". This requirement was carried through a series of deeds, and in 1908 the Charity Commissioners restated the position "…that a portion of the premises appropriated exclusively for a School of Art were held solely for educational purposes until the full amount of the building grant was repaid."[39]

The death of James Birkmyer, in 1899, provided an opportunity for a new approach. Arthur Clayden, the Principal of the College, recommended a system where the School of Art was kept in touch with the current spirit of art and where students had opportunities of contact with specialists. The outcome was the appointment of two experts as Directors to visit the School of Art at intervals, to confer with staff there and to deliver occasional lectures. These were Alfred Drury, who acted Director of Modelling and Design, and Lewis Davis, who was to visit the School of Art to criticise students' work and advise staff. Davis, not in good health, was soon replaced by Glanville Fell. As visiting Directors their role may be seen as similar to that of external assessors today. Over the next few years, the Directors' reports seem to have been instrumental in pinpointing weakensses, achieving some improvement in the School's accommodation and in the introduction of new courses. Almost immediately the School was criticised for its inadequate life class, and and the use of models from London was recommended. They should stay a fortnight at a time, alternating between males and females.[40] As visiting Directors, Fell and Drury continued to play a valuable role in raising standards in the School. The School was praised for its situation and its assets of the museum and library on the premises, but criticised of the lack of a special modelling room, the distance of the 'life' room from the rest of the school and the lack of an enameling furnace. Such comments did effect changes. A new modelling room was acquired, and the course in enameling was started after a circular to employers asking them to allow apprentices to leave work an hour earlier two or three days a week to attend. Later reports praised the work of the students, "...the Design Work, especially showing the advantage of the living model, some of which was very good", and a letter from Alfred Drury found "...the progress of the Modelling School very satisfactory indeed, under the present conditions". The following year his report praised the "...progress of the students in Metal Work and Enamelling."

But the HMIs remained unimpressed with the accommodation allocated to the School of Art which they found scattered and detached. The courses organised by the new headmaster, John Shapland, for the training of students such as "...Painters, Modellers, Sculptors, Designers, Illustrators and Decorative Artists and Craftsmen..." were systematic and covered "...the ground of most of the subjects of the examinations of the Board of Education...". Generally the work was carefully planned and supervised by the Headmaster "...whose special experience in pictorial work gives vitality to the advanced Drawing, Painting and Life Study." The report was more critical of the teaching of the principles of design, which it said was in the care of "...teachers of moderate qualification and of less reliable accomplishments." Another aspect of concern was the branch school held in the St. Thomas district of the City. Closer co-operation in teaching was needed between the central and branch schools and the Headmaster needed time to visit there more frequently. At the time of the 1910 inspection it was anticipated the branch would be closed owing to poor attendances.[41]

5.15, 5.16, 5.17. Published by a staff and student group throughout the 1920s, the Exeter School of Art Magazine was an outlet for student work, which was highly commended for the standard of production achieved using the School's inadequate printing facility. Both these cover illustrations, in contrasting styles, appeared in 1922. The imprint block is from an issue in 1927.

[UPEXE, School of Art collection]

5.18, 5.19, 5.20 Examples of student work which appeared in the Exeter School of Art Magazine in the 1920s: design for a poster by L.F. Johnson (1922); an illumination by R.M. Wood (1923); Etching by F.M. Hayman (1927, Newton St. Cyres).

[UPEXE, School of Art collection]

ROYAL ALBERT MEMORIAL SCHOOL OF ART

·· ·· ··

DAY CLASSES

Every morning 01 30. to 1. except on Tues. & each afternoon 2 30. to 4 30. except Weds. & Saturdays.

NIGHT CLASSES

In all subjects from 7. to 9. except on Sats.

TERMS 1929.

January 7. to April 6. April 29. to July 22.

5.21 Class hours at the Exeter School of Art in 1929, publicised in the Exeter School of Art Magazine.

[UPEXE, School of Art collection]

The new energy at the School of Art was brought by John Shapland who was appointed as 'Art Master' in succession to Birkmyer, the other teachers in the School of Art being designated 'Assistant School Teachers'. His starting salary was put at £180 a year. He had been teaching at the School for some years and had studied for his Art Teacher's Certificate under Birkmyer. Shapland, Headmaster of the School 1899-1913, was a painter of figure subjects in oil and watercolour. He exhibited from 1901-14 at the Royal Academy, the Fine Art Society, the New Gallery, the Royal Institute of Painters in Water Colours, the Walker Art Gallery at Liverpool, and also at the Paris Salon and in the U.S.A.[42] By 1896 he was also acting as Assistant Teacher on the evenings of Monday, Tuesday and Thursday. The report of the Principal for 1897/8, stated that at this stage he was giving a larger part of his time to help James Birkmyer.[43] In April, 1913, William Burman-Morrall succeeded John Shapland as Headmaster. He had studied at the Schools of Art at York and Sunderland and at the Royal College of Art. He came to Exeter from London in October, 1903, and worked as second master at the School of Art, under John Shapland. He was a sculptor, modeller and mural decorator and an exhibitor at the Royal Academy and Paris Salon.[44]

World War I would certainly have impacted negatively on the School of Art, affecting staffing and numbers of students. Local records for the School of Art during the First World War have since been destroyed but after the war, in October, 1919, there were nearly 400 day students at the Albert Memorial College, including 110 at the School of Art.[45] By the time of the 1920 HMI inspection (February 1920), enrolments had increased to 185, with 173 in regular attendance. This report again raised the problem of the School's scattered premises within the Royal Albert Memorial buildings. It recommended that these should be rearranged, that there should be a better workshop accomodation, a suitable life room and a separate room for lithography and etching.[46] That no School of Art prospectus had been issued

EXETER SCHOOL OF ART MAGAZINE

for some years and there was little about it in the College prospectus may simply reflect the difficulties of the war years, though it may equally indicate the extent to which the School was irrelevant to the College's future. In general the tone of the report was satisfactory, though there was scope for improvement in most areas of work, and equipment needed up grading. The existence of a temporary body of governors including representatives from Exeter City and Devon County Councils, together with references in the Report to a university college, indicate that the moves to separate the School of Art were under consideration. In 1920, Arthur Clayden retired as Principal of the College. His vision in his 1915 address as President of the Devonshire Association on 'The Future of Higher Education in Devon', for a University for the South West encompassing establishments at Exeter and Plymouth was only partly fulfilled by the recognition granted in 1922 (see Chapter Three).[47] In the event, a merger between educational institutions located in different Devon towns, was not to take place until the formation of Polytechnic South West in 1988.

Exeter Municipal School of Art

The designation of the University College of the South West of England (UCSWE), in 1922, meant a rearrangement of the management structures of the various establishments. The administration of the Museum was placed under a different committee of Exeter City Council. The subjects of the former School of Science, now labelled technical subjects, had already been incorporated in 1918 in the Day Technical School; USCWE, of course, retained the university extension work and the teacher training department; and Exeter School of Art emerged as a separate establishment under the administration of Exeter City Council.[48] Collaboration between the University of Exeter and the School of Art was not to be resumed again until the development of the Combined Honours Degree between the institutions in 1967. The School of Art prospectus eventually produced in 1923 lists staff as the headmaster, the two visiting directors and six assistant art masters, a tiny establishment to modern eyes, but probably typical even then of art schools in smaller provincial towns and cities. The subjects offered included drawing, painting, modelling, architecture and design as general courses with lettering and illumination, lithography, etching, illustration, needlework, carving, painting and decorating and commercial engraving as evening vocational courses for students working at trades where draughtmanship and an artistic outlook were essential. Each was taught at elementary, intermediate and advanced levels.[49]

5.22 *This pen and ink drawing of the production team of the Exeter School of Art Magazine at work in 1926 could apply to student publications in any period. (R.M. Wood, 1926).*

[UPEXE, School of Art collection]

STAFF

PRINCIPAL : W. GREEN, A.R.C.A. (Lond.).
ASSISTANTS : W. RUSCOE, N.R.D.

Full Time :   *Senior Assistant.*
            General Art and Pottery.

          G. W. ADAMSON.
          Etching, Engraving, Illustration and General Art.

          C. FISHWICK, A.T.D.
          Painting, Drawing, Lithography.

          G. V. HAYWOOD, A.R.C.A. (Lond.) ; A.R.B.S. ; *Prix de Rome, Proxime Accessit ; R.C.A. medal (Sculpture) ; B.I. (Sculpture). Sculpture and Drawing.*

          MISS F. SWANN, A.R.C.A (Lond.).
          Design, Women's Crafts and Textile Printing.

Visiting :   MISS R. M. WOOD, N.R.D.
          Member of the Society of Scribes and Illuminators; Lettering, Typography, Advertising Art, Illuminating.

          G. T. REID.
          Painting, Decorating, Signwriting.

          MISS P. C. TUTTON.
          Weaving.

DEPARTMENT OF ARCHITECTURE
Lecturer :   H. M. R. DRURY, F.R.I.B.A., A.A. Diploma.

Building   E. SUCKSMITH, B.Sc.
Science :

                        Page three

5.23 *Exeter School of Art staff list in 1948.*

[UPEXE, School of Art collection, Prospectus, 1948/49]

MINISTRY OF EDUCATION **ISSUED**
                    16 SEP 1948

GENERAL REPORT BY H.M. INSPECTORS ON THE PROVISION OF TECHNICAL, COMMERCIAL AND ART EDUCATION IN THE CITY OF EXETER

For the Period ending 31st December, 1947

III—SCHOOL OF ART

16. The major Further Education provision for Art is centred in the School of Art and Crafts in the middle of the City. The School occupies some nine rooms, four of which are in the main building known as the Royal Albert Memorial, while the remainder are in the Annexe adjoining. All are small rooms, ill-adapted for the purposes of Art and Craft instruction with the possible exception of two in the main building, which are of more reasonable dimensions.

Apart from the small rooms used for Pottery, Modelling and Weaving all have to serve as multi-purpose rooms with the inevitable congestion and lack of opportunity for expansion and proper organisation which this entails. There are no common rooms for staff or students and there is no cloak-room provision. The sanitary offices are deplorably inadequate.

The School is a full-time institution of long standing, managed by a Governing Body which is a special Sub-Committee of the City Education Committee. The Governing Body meets terminally on the school premises. In addition to the manifold functions of a normal full-time Art School, it endeavours to foster an appreciation of the Arts among the general public by means of lectures and exhibitions. These activities are, however, severely handicapped by the lack of more suitable premises.

At the time of the review the total student roll was 348, of which number 190 were evening enrolments, made up of 138 from the City and 31 from the surrounding area up to distances as much as eighteen miles from the City Centre. The School offers the usual day classes and is open to evening students on five evenings a week and a very wide range of subjects is available. This includes General Drawing and Painting, Life Drawing and Painting, Etching and Engraving, Lithography, Commercial Art, Modelling and

13

5.24 *The 1947 inspection once again condemned the School's accommodation, while endorsing the direction it should take in the future*

[PRO, ED 196/8]

EVENING CLASSES TIME TABLE

MONDAY		TUESDAY		WEDNESDAY		THURSDAY		FRIDAY	
Life Drawing and Painting	F	ART APPRECIATION		Modelling and Sculpture	H	Special Courses for Teachers in	S	Modelling Life Painting, Still	H
Pottery	R	Public Lecture 7 p.m.		Pottery	R	Embroidery and Textile		Life	F
Weaving	G	See special Syllabus		Lithography		Design and		Textile Design	S
Dress Design				Advanced	F	Printing		and Printing	
DressMaking	S			Drawing				Weaving	T
General Art	A			Engraving		Sculpture	H	Advertising	
Architecture R.I.B.A.	D	Painting Still Life	F	Etching Illustration	A	Life Drawing Weaving	R G	Illuminating Art	R
		Sculpture, Modelling		Advertising Art		Pottery (n-11:0) Advertising	G R	Lettering Architecture R.I.B.A.	D
		Life	H	Lettering Illuminating	W	Art		Painting and	
		Pottery Engraving	R	Textile		Lettering Illuminating	W	Decorating Signwriting	G R
		Etching	A	Design and Printing	S	General Art Building	A		
		Illustration Painting and		Painting Decorating		Mechanics Painting and	E S	The Principal may be interviewed be-	
		Decorating Signwriting	G R	Signwriting	G R	Decorating Signwriting	G R	tween 7.30 and 8.30 on Fridays only	

● The letters in the narrow columns indicate the Teacher responsible for the Class, as follows: Mr. Green, G ; Mr. Adamson, A ; Mr. Drury, D ; Mr. Fishwick, F ; Mr. Ruscoe, R ; Mr. Reid, G.R. ; Miss Swann, S ; Miss Tutton, T ; Mr. Sucksmith, E S ; Miss Wood, W ; Mr. Haywood, H.
● Evening Classes are held from 6.30 to 8.30. Students may commence work before 6.30, but Classes close promptly at 8.30.
● Students are informed that the School Shop is closed on Wednesday evenings.

5.25 This timetable from the 1948/49 Prospectus, illustrates clearly the range of subjects which the School was able to offer at that time.

[UPEXE, School of Art collection]

5.26, 5.27 William Ruscoe demonstrating the potter's art to a group of students in the late 1940s, and a display of student pottery from the 1949/50 Prospectus.

[UPEXE, School of Art collection]

In the 1920's the school produced the *Exeter School of Art Magazine,* which provides an insight into the feelings and attainments of its students. Clearly there was some apprehension at the change of management. In 1923 the editor commented "we have now been under the Education authority for twelve months and are relieved to find that no 'new broom' has disturbed the tranquility of the School".[50] The magazines are interesting for their illustrations by the women artists, Joyce Dennys, Primrose Vera Pitman, Norah Pearse and Ruth Wood. Joyce Dennys, an illustrator and cartoonist, later wrote a book about her childhood *'And then there was one'* (1983), at the end of which she said, she left school and put up her hair and went to the Exeter Art School, where she "...had splendid teaching from a man called Burman Morrall".[51] Norah Pearse, was appointed as a part time teacher of lithography in 1926.[52] The HMI report in 1920 had criticised the employment of a lithographic printer rather than a lithographic artist as a teacher of lithography and the lack of a separate room for lithography. In 1923 the lithography class was given a new room.[53] Ruth Wood edited the magazine and was also first appointed as a part-time teacher in 1926. Her teaching hours were increased at different stages and she had a long teaching career, eventually resigning in 1963. A specialist in lettering, calligraphy and heraldry, she exhibited examples of her illuminating at the British Empire Exhibition, and had two examples of her work bought by the Victoria and Albert Museum for the National Loan Collection. The School's magazine also carried comment on the equipment provided. An article 'Making Bricks Without Straw - Triumph of a School of Art', an extract from *The British Printer* (February, 1924) observed "If the *Exeter School of Art Magazine* were produced by the aid of the latest developments in the arts of the painter, lithographer and etcher, it would still remain a piece of work noteworthy alike for its artistry of conception and beauty of craftsmanship" but goes on to say "...this publication achieves a unique interest when we are acquainted with the total inadequacy of the equipment at the disposal of its producers". In 1929, the Higher Education Sub-Committee recommended that a second-hand etching press be bought for £40, and the following year *Exeter School of Art Magazine* records a number of gifts including a lithographic press, and contributions towards a new kiln.[54]

The School of Art continued to occupy a section of the much extended Albert Memorial building, where the UCSWE was also based. During the inter-war period, Burman-Morrall gradually added to the range of subjects the School offered. In 1930 a course in dress design was started followed by another in hand printed textiles three years later.[55] He was keen to promote co-operation between the School and the University College arranged a successful series of public lectures. The idea of collaborating in a central college based in Plymouth, following the recommendations of the Board of Education in the 1930s, did not find favour, the response of Exeter's Higher Education Sub-Committee being non-committal.[56] He died in December, 1939,[57] and was succeeded as Principal in March, 1940, by William Green, under whom the School would begin to achieve a higher profile.

Green had previously been Principal of the School of Art at Wallasey. He was well known as a painter in water colours, exhibiting at the Royal Academy, the Royal West of England Academy and at Paris and also as a collector of English water colours.[58] Having taken charge early in the Second World War, Green did much to enrich the cultural climate of Exeter. He organised several concerts a year given by musicians of national and international repute during the war, which public queued to attend, a valuable contribution to raising local morale.[59] Green also organised exhibitions such as Modern British Paintings (1900-1940), held at the School of Art, from 13 October to 8 November, 1941. An article from a contemporary local newspaper wrote that although there had been "...a certain amount of criticism by those unaccustomed to the contemporary school of painting, the vast majority of visitors greatly appreciated the exhibition". In 1946, he arranged a loan exhibition of the Ford Art Collection, considered among the finest art collections of the country at that time. Some of the exhibitions such as 'Rebuilding Britain,' on loan from the National Gallery, also came with a related series of lectures.[60]

The Creation of a Modern College of Art and Design

Although the inter-war years had seen some small developments, Exeter School of Art continued to function in much the same way as in the latter part of the nineteenth century. The number of students enrolling was of the same order, between two and three hundred, with a significant proportion of part-time and evening work, It still occupied accommodation in the Royal Albert Memorial building augmented by scattered rooms nearby, and it was still cheek-by-jowl with the UCSWE. True, its funding through Exeter City Council offered improved stability compared with the system in the nineteenth century, but under the Higher Education Committee of the Council, it was just another small school competing for attention amongst all the other (mainly secondary) establishments. As in other parts of the country, there was no major investment. After World War II, although it would still be decades before its accommodation problems were given serious attention, the climate for tertiary education had changed and the School of Art would extend its subject scope and level of work as it kept pace with changes in art and design education taking place across the country.

Although the School found itself with an enrolment of 550 in 1946, owing to an influx of ex-service students, with only the Principal, four full-time and five part-time lecturers, it was really not as large as the emergency teacher training college which had just been set up down the road at Exmouth, though both were struggling with inappropriate accommodation. In a speech for the opening of an exhibition of students' work in that year, William Green spoke of the Exeter School of Art working in a 'mausoleum-like-atmosphere' and being faced with 'an almost ludicrous position in the matter of accommodation'.[61] The School of Art was, of course, still holding many more classes during the evenings than during the day, a situation which would prevail for some years. Indeed, it was the only location where

5.28, 5.29 Fine art classes from life at the Exeter School of Art in the late 1940s: sculpture and painting.

[UPEXE, School of Art collection]

5.30 William Green (top right), Principal of the Exeter School of Art from 1940 taking a weaving class.

[UPEXE, School of Art collection]

5.31, 5.32 Architecture (above) and painting and decorating students at work at the Exeter School of Art in the late 1940s.

[UPEXE, School of Art collection]

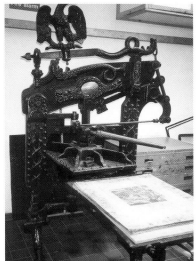

5.33, 5.34 Printing students in the 1970s had the use both of quite modern printing equipment, and of this 1851 printing press, still in working order and still used.

[UPEXE, School of Art collection, Prospectus, 1971/72; photo: A.Kennerley]

art education was available, as, although there were no less than nineteen evening class centres in Exeter where technical and commercial classes were available, none offered art and design subjects. Reporting on their inspection in 1947, the HMIs recommended the development of evening classes in art subjects in some of these centres, so as to relieve the School of Art of lower level work and to enable it to concentrate on the development of advanced work.[62] Predictably, the inspectors also commented on the inadequacy of the School's accommodation, noting the lack of common rooms and a cloakroom ("The sanitary offices are deplorably inadequate"), and recommending the immediate provision of additional space, and the inclusion of new and up-to-date premises for art education in long-term planning. At the time of the inspection, there were 348 students on the roll, which included 169 evening enrolments, of whom 138 were local and 31 from further afield, travelling as much as eighteen miles to attend classes. The Schools efforts to foster art appreciation among the general public were commended.

Even though improvements were unlikely to follow quickly as post-war austerity measures were still in place, the HMI report of 1947 put pressure on the local authority and provided encouragement to the staff by endorsing the direction the School should take over the coming years. The prospectus for 1948 pointed to a 'modern School of Art' able to give a 'sound training in the Arts generally' endeavouring to 'foster an appreciation of the Arts by means of Lectures and Exhibitions'. Emulating the approaches in the nineteenth century the School published an autumn and spring series of public lectures given by the Principal, William Green, and Clifford Fishwick, who was to succeed him as Principal, and six other lecturers.[63] Signs that improvements were beginning to appear could be found in small developments, such as the ability of staff and students to make visits to London to view exhibitions, and have their expenses paid.[64] The School was kept in the public eye in other ways, such as the building of a model of Thomas Sharp's plan for rebuilding Exeter after the war.[65] Another development which helped to improve the stature of the School was the introduction, in common with other art schools throughout the country, of courses for the National Diploma in Design (NDD) initiated by the Ministry of Education (which had replaced the Board of Education). This became the accepted qualification for teaching in art and for designing in industry. The School also offered the Intermediate Examination in Arts and Crafts which replaced the Board of Education Grouped Drawing Examinations dating from 1913.[66] Other arts schools in the region of course made similar moves. Those at Bideford, Penzance and Weston-Super-Mare were running the Intermediate course. Exeter, Falmouth, Newton Abbot, Plymouth, Taunton and Yeovil were also running the NDD course. However, the number of students was very small and those schools only survived by holding a range of non-advanced classes.[67]

During the late 1940s departments in architecture and in printing were developed. In 1946, arrangements for the establishment of a Department of Architecture were approved, and the following year arrangements for the provision of an additional class for the new Department to cover building science and mathematics was agreed.[68] Students were prepared for probationer, intermediate and final examinations of the Royal Institute of British Architects.[69] The department survived until 1963. Printing classes had taken place before the war at the Exe Island School. They were transferred to the School of Art in 1940. After the 'Blitz' of 1942 the classes had been closed down as the teachers were called up for military service and the machinery and equipment were loaned to printing companies affected by the blitz. In 1954, following discussions between local printing employers, LEA officials and the HMIs for printing schools, a Printing Department was opened at Burnthouse Lane, Exeter. 28 day-release students and 21 evening students enrolled. The Department gradually developed and in 1960 it was transferred from Burnthouse Lane to premises in The Mint at a site formerly occupied by St. Nicholas School.[70] The Department continued to flourish until the 1980's providing instruction graded to the requirements of the Technician Education Council, the City and Guilds of London Institute examinations and the British Printing Industries Federation courses.[71]

A major land-mark in the Development of Exeter School of Art was reached in 1951 when it was upgraded to the status of a college with the title of 'Exeter Central College of Art', following a decision from the Ministry of Education.[72] This was an endorsement of the progress made since the HMI visit in 1947, as well as an aspect of the Ministry's policy in fostering the development of central colleges of art engaged in advanced work. Of course the Ministry had reports of the standards being achieved at Exeter in the early 1950s. At an opening of the annual exhibition of students' work in July, 1953, William Green observed that "...few colleges and schools of art in the country could claim the equal of the 100 per cent success attained by the College's students in gaining national diplomas in the season 1951-52." In common with other art schools and colleges, there had been a great increase in student numbers in the six years following the war with men and women returning from service, though in the past year or two there had been a "...slight decline in the proportion of full-time students...", but that even so,

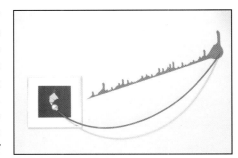

5.35, 5.36 As in the past, much of the College's publicity material continued to be designed by students, such as this invitation card and cover for the 1982/3 Prospectus.

[UPEXE, School of Art collection]

5.37 Over one hundred years after first occupying the Albert Memorial building the College still had accommodation at the rear of the much extended building, in Gandy Street.

[Photo: A. Kennerley]

5.38 This art studio in Gandy Street looks into the quadrangle at the rear of the Albert Memorial building.

[UPEXE, School of Art collection, Prospectus, 1964/5]

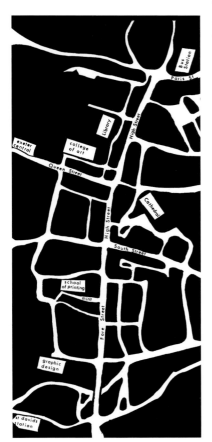

5.39 This map for students shows the location of the College's scattered premises in the 1960s and 1970s.

[UPEXE, School of Art collection]

"...it had nearly twice the number of full-time students it had before the war."[73] After his resignation in 1957, the Exeter Education Committee expressed their appreciation and gratitude for his valuable services during "...18 difficult and eventful years as Principal of the College of Art."[74]

In 1958, Clifford Fishwick was appointed as Principal of the College of Art.[75] During his lengthy tenure, he was to over see the re-incarnation of the College, with new premises, great improvements in equipment, the development of advanced courses of university level and a significant increase in the size of the student body. A very gifted painter, he sustained his output throughout this period, exhibiting frequently locally and in Liverpool. After his death in 1997, the Universities of Exeter and Plymouth, together with the Royal Albert Museum, celebrated his contribution by sponsoring exhibitions of his work.[76] By the time of his appointment, the UCSWE had achieved university status as the University of Exeter, and was well advanced in developing the Streatham Estate on the edge of the City as its main campus. This created some flexibility on the Albert Memorial site and, in 1959, it was agreed that the College of Art should be transferred to the York wing of the museum, after conversions had taken place. In 1960, its Printing Department transferred its premises to the Mint, which also became the site of the private press of the College, The Priory Press. The Graphic Design Department had its premises nearby at Bartholomew Street.[77]

By 1961, further changes in the qualification structure for art education, which would enable Exeter College of Art to raise the standard of its activity yet further, were being recommended. The National Advisory Council on Art Education (Chairman Sir William Coldstream) outlined requirements for a new higher award, the Diploma in Art and Design (DipAD) to replace the National Diploma in Design (NDD). This consisted of a pre-diploma course of one year, followed by a three year diploma course in one of four areas of specialisation: fine art, graphic design, three dimensional design and textiles/fashion. Fifteen per cent of the course was to be devoted to the history of art and complementary studies. The National Council for Diplomas in Art and Design (NCDAD), under the chairmanship of Sir John Summerson, was appointed to administer the award, and applications were invited for the new diploma courses.[78] In November, 1961, Clifford Fishwick recommended to the Further Education Sub-Committee (which had superseded the Higher Education Sub-Committee) the submission of proposals to the NCDAD, but it was agreed that, in the first instance, provision should be limited to a course in fine art, with the possibility of adding a course in graphic design at a later date. By July, 1963, NCDAD had approved "...the proposed course in the Fine Art area of study leading to the Diploma in Art and Design, a course of Honours Degree standard...[but] that such approval had been given to but 29 colleges in all."[79] Exeter was one of the first colleges to have its DipAD course accepted. Its prospectus of 1963 describes the course as "...broadly based-narrowing to specialisation in the later stages," saying it may be "...symbolically expressed as a triangle with a broad first year as its base." As the course progresses "...more responsibility rests upon the student for consistent individual work, with the aim of equipping the student 'practically and psychologically', for his/her future work as a practising artist."[80] It was to develop a strong reputation for Fine Art, and in 1974 its DipAD in Fine Art became a BA Honours degree.

The early and mid-1960s was to be a period of expansion with more staff appointments and upgradings, including the appointment of a vice-principal, William Ruscoe.[81] He specialised in teaching pottery and his book, *A Manual for the Potter,* was published in several editions.[82] He was succeeded as Vice-Principal in 1966 by Arthur Goodwin. The growing status of the College was recognised through visits by eminent artists and writers including, in 1966 alone, Trevor Bell, Robert Adams, David Leach, Ruari McLean, Edward Bawden, Al Alvarez and Ted Hughes.[83] By 1965, the College had its own gallery, the Exe Gallery at Gandy Street. This was sponsored by the Exeter Education Committee and managed by the College with students staffing it on a rota system. Its displays were to include work by staff and students and also by artists of international repute. It opened with an exhibition by Mark Tobey.[84] In 1967, in conjunction with the Exeter City Gallery it put on an exhibition of surrealist art The Enchanted Domain which included works by Dali, Duchamp, Ernst, Magritte, Miro and Picasso. During the 1970s John Bratby, Patrick Caulfield, Oskar Kokoschka and Conroy Maddox were some of the artists who exhibited there. The Gallery remained in existence until the late 1980's.

Similarly, in the early 1960's the College also had its own private press, 'The Priory Press,' based in the Graphic Department in Bartholomew Street. An extract from an early production *Children at Play: a Collection of Impressions and Observations of Exeter College of Art* (1962) was printed by James Townsend and produced as an insert for the *Penrose Annual* (vol. 56, 1962). Other examples of work by the Priory Press included *Poems and Woodcuts* by Jenny Ashmore (1968) and *The Rime of the Ancient Mariner* illustrated by a visiting German student, Reiner Burger (1969). In 1966 the Bartholomew Print Workshop was formed by the Printmaking Department. This produced books under the name of Bartholomew Books. One of the first was a book of poems by Ted Hughes illustrated with linocuts by Gavin Robbins in 1968. This was followed by books illustrated by students such as Grenville Cottingham, Adrian Jones and Brenda Barnard in the 1970's. In 1974, Alan Richards who taught in the Printmaking Department and who was to become head of Fine Art from 1979-89, produced a humorous book, *A Bestiary: Words and Linocuts.* These books were sold to the public by the Exe Gallery. Some were also given to local schools. Bob Clement, as county advisor for art education in Devon, expressed particular interest in the work and this led to the development of printmaking workshops for Devon teachers at Bartholomew Street. This was also a rich period of creative collaboration between artists and poets, with staff working with other private presses such as Out of the Ark Press and poets such as Charles Causley, Christopher Logue as well as Ted Hughes.[85]

5.40 Peter Brooke, Parliamentary Under Secretary of State for Education and Science, unveiling a commemorative plaque to open a studio extension at the Earl Richards Road North main College site.

[UPEXE, School of Art collection]

5.41 The SPACEX Gallery, providing exhibition and studio space for artists and art students, was supported by the College.

[Photo: A. Kennerley]

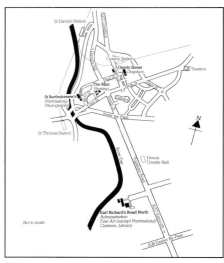

5.42 This map for students in the 1980s shows the relationship of the new site at Earl Richards Road North to the other sites in the centre of town.

[UPEXE, School of Art collection, Prospectus, 1982/83]

By the 1960s, student expectations of conditions in colleges had advanced, and, with a higher proportion of full-time students, student union activity at the College of Art was becoming more organised. However, not many colleges at that time had in place the staff/student liaison structures which now allow student concerns to be brough formally to the attention of the College authorities. The wave of student unrest in the summer of 1968 concerning the DipAD provided an opportunity for student at the Exeter College to focus on and protest about a range of issues, notably the continuing inadequacy of the College accommodation. It was in June, 1968, that students at Exeter College of Art emulated student disturbances taking place notably at the art colleges of Hornsey and Guildford but also at Brighton, Birmingham, Croydon, Wimbledon and Nottingham. An article by M.G. McNay in *The Guardian,* 8 June, 1968, discussed the nature of the students' dissatisfaction with the new Diploma in Art and Design, particularly the minimal entrance requirements of 5 GCE 'O' levels and the eventual conferring of a diploma giving academic respectability. At Exeter meetings were held to question the structure and organisation of education within the college. A staff/student association was formed to inquire into ways of making improvements. According to an article in the local Exeter paper, *Express & Echo* (17 June, 1968), half of the full time staff at the College had joined with the students in pressing for major changes, but an article in the same newspaper the following day, reported that most of the staff and students were not supporting the association. A decision to have a ballot of full time staff and students on how a committee of representation should be arranged was abandoned when 36 members of staff wrote to the Principal to say that they felt that they could not take part. The following month Clifford Fishwick sent a memo around the college to say that from the first week of the new term he intended to create staff/student bodies in each section of the college to deal with specific problems relating to courses, attendance and other issues.[86]

One of the causes of grievance at Exeter College of Art was its problem of scattered accommodation in different annexes. At this stage the College occupied not only the York wing of the Royal Albert Memorial Museum, but also premises at Bartholomew Street, Queen Street, Gandy Street, St. David's Hill and Paul Street. By November, 1966, the Further Education Committee of Exeter Council had finally reached the decision that the College of Art should be rehoused at the earliest opportunity and, in March, 1967, the Planning Committee agreed that the new college be built on a site at Earl Richards Road North. Even after this the matter remained fluid while alternative sites (one at Shilhay) were discussed and rejected. It took time for the site, building plans and finance to be approved by the Department of Education and Science (DES) as the Ministry of Education had become. Eventually in 1969 a start date in January, 1972, for the first phase, with the second phase to follow soon after, was agreed. After much controversy about the choice of site and many delays recorded in numerous articles and letters in the local newspapers it was in 1973 that a new building was completed to house the Fine Art, Combined Honours and Foundation courses, and central amenities and administration of the College. The Graphic Design Department, Printing Department and Schools of Printmaking and Photography remained in annexes, though they were expected to be re-housed in Phase 2 of the new building. Soon after the new building was occupied a revised title for the College, Exeter College of Art and Design, was approved.

5.44 Clifford Fishwick with his successor as Principal in 1984, David Jeremiah, on the occasion of an awards ceremony in 1986.

[UPEXE, School of Art collection]

The issue of the comparability of the DipAD, which had exercised the students in 1968, was to be overcome by upgrading that qualification to a degree. Exeter College of Art had achieved the ambition of earlier principals of collaboration with Exeter University, when, in 1967, it participated in offering a BA joint honours degree course in English with Fine Art. The course was to be divided equally between the study of the two subjects at the two institutions. At Exeter College of Art this was later to lead to a Department of Combined Studies and at Exeter University the course was to be expanded to include the study of French, Italian or Spanish with Fine Art. An important additional outcome was to be the introduction of a post-graduate course in publishing and book production at the College of Art. An

5.45 Subsequently named the Towne Building (1997), this was part of the second phase of building development on the Earl Richards Road North site.

[Photo: A.Kennerley]

5.46, 5.47 Student work at the end of the 1980s: a display of textiles and a critique of student work in illustration, in a studio cubicle.

[UPEXE, School of Art collection, Prospectus, 1988/89]

early aim in the undergraduate work was to have students' creative writing printed, and so the College's printing department became involved. In the process many students themselves became interested in the rudiments of printing, and this led to the formation of a private press, named Rougemont Press, in 1970. As well as printing student work, the Press also published works by Ted Hughes and Clifford Fishwick. It was wound up in 1984, but the post-graduate course, the first of its kind in the country, was started in 1976. Publicity attracted students from abroad, and the publishing house, Macmillans, made an annual grant and supported a student to attend the course.[87] Meanwhile, the creation of the Council for National Academic Awards (CNAA, 1964) and the development of the binary policy for higher education were to have important effects on art education. In September, 1974, NCDAD was amalgamated with the CNAA and the DipAD in Fine Art at Exeter was revalidated by the CNAA as a BA Honours degree. Soon after, in 1975, the degree in graphic design received its approval, and there could be no doubt that the Exeter College of Art had joined the ranks of institutions of higher education. Later advanced course developments were to include a degree course in three-dimensional design (1987).

Although the emphasis on fine art in the 1960s had greatly enhanced the College's reputation, the development of graphic design had by no means been neglected. Students taking the new degree course were soon to make their mark, and in their 1983 report the CNAA praised the course for its 'buoyancy'. In the same year the graphic design students exhibited work at the Young Blood exhibition at the Barbican Centre, London. The 1980s was also to be a successful period for graphic design students in national competitions.[88] Students were finalists in the Photographers and Illustrators' Gold Awards two years running. They also to took part in the annual Young Illustrators' Exhibition at this time. However the graphic design course was not to benefit from new accommodation until 1984 when Phase 2 of the campus at Earl Richards Road North was completed. The annexes for graphic design at the York Wing of the Royal Albert Museum and for printmaking at Bartholomew Street were vacated. Their courses were re-housed in a range of new studios in an extension opened on 7 November, 1984, by Peter Brooke, the then Under-Secretary of State for Education and Science. The photographic section of the graphic design department remained at 83, Queen Street, and it was envisaged that this would be added to the campus in Phase 2 (b).

During the 1970s, the College's involvement with and support of the wider community was by no means neglected. In 1974 the SPACEX complex at 45, Preston Street was opened. Its purpose was to provide studio space for artists and also to allow for for a range of creative activities on similar lines to S.P.A.C.E. which had been set up by Bridget Riley in London. SPACEX, Space Provision (Artistic Cultural Educational) Exeter Ltd. was registered as a limited company. The College of Art had a close involvement with a senior member of staff acting as chairman. First floor of the Spacex building remains in use as studio space for third year fine art students. In 1978 Spacex

5.48 *The studio, workshop and communal accomadation to the rear of the main building added in the 1980s, at Earls Richards Road North has, with the opening of the Veysey Building (see chapter 9) in 1997 become a view seen by every one using the campus library or visiting the Institute of Health Studies.*

[Photo: A. Kennerley]

Gallery was formed with the aim of showing contemporary art from established and up and coming artists. One of its first shows was a two man exhibition of the work of Mike Mayer and Alan Davie. In the 1990s it expanded considerably as the result of lottery funding, support which was marked by exhibitions of works by Bridget Riley and Richard Long, and the opening of a new workshop space, the David Sample Gallery.[89]

Although the College made great progress in the 1970s, one cloud was the Government's policy on higher education institutions. Small establishments seemed to be out of favour, and the period was one of college amalgamations and closures, teacher education being the sector which had the highest public profile. Rolle College at Exmouth was one of the establishments marked for closure (it eventually survived), and its saga must have influenced the thinking of Devon County Council, which had recently assumed responsibility for Exeter College of Art & Design under the local government re-organisation of 1974. Area provision of art education and the relationship of one college to another was once again under discussion. In 1975, the County's Further Education Sub-Committee resolved that agreement should be given in principle to a proposed amalgamation with Plymouth College of Art and Design, though this would be dependent on a report of the "...detailed arrangements and financial implications of such a merger". But by April, 1976, owing to the problems of such a merger, including distance between the two sites, the Committee had decided to abandon the idea, though it urged the colleges to continue to develop co-operative links.

Clifford Fishwick retired in December, 1984 and was succeeded as Principal by David Jeremiah in January, 1985. The new Principal, who like his predecessors was a practising artist and art historian, was responsible for the broadening of the college's horizons in a major way with the introduction of a range of new degree courses in studio and academic disciplines. At the time of his appointment, although the College was well established with 300 undergraduate students and 120 on diploma/certificate courses, it was vulnerable to national policy in higher education. Questions were being raised about the numbers of students in art and design, and what was perceived as an over provision in fine art. With its existing pattern of work,

5.49 Student work in fine art in 1991.

[UPEXE, School of Art collection]

Exeter realised that this had far reaching implications, and began to implement plans for a redistribution of student numbers which would substantially increase the existing graphic design course provision and support the introduction of a new undergraduate course in three-dimensional design. This was a demanding agenda to develop, for not only was it necessary to obtain CNAA academic approval, the College had to convince the LEA of the validity of these moves and negotiate the support of the Regional Council. Fortunately, the College was to be well supported by the Devon County Council Education Officers and, against a background of uncertainty the new initiatives began to take shape. At the same time the non-advanced course provision was under review and, although they were to prove short lived developments, the College introduced the new BTEC diploma courses, and played an important role in setting up a regional diploma scheme for Foundation Art & Design.

Despite the widespread support for the strategic plan, questions continued to be raised about the economic viability of the College. It was considered to have an over-generous staff/student ratio and, although the studio accommodation had been greatly improved, the College was still dependent on using a miscellaneous range of city centre buildings which were expensive and difficult to manage. Having become accustomed to substantial supplementary funding from the LEA to sustain its work, the decision to phase out this financial support brought about even greater cultural changes in the everyday life of the College. Many of these changes could be absorbed without too many problems, but others were to be greatly regretted, notably the closure of the Exe Gallery, which had played such a vital role in presenting contemporary work to the community. For the longer term planning for the future of higher education in art and design, by July 1986, the College's Academic Board was already anticipating that the College would become a constituent part of what was then being described as a Polytechnic University of Devon.

As all of this was taking place the College was preparing for a CNAA Institutional Review in the autumn, 1986. With a new academic plan in place, the administrative framework was reorganised, and the two established departments of Fine Art and Design were complemented by a new Department of Art, Design and Communication. The other initiative involved changes to the budget and terms of reference of the Research Committee. This committee had existed since 1977, and was now to take direct responsibility for six teaching/research fellowships, the funding of staff research projects, and act as the agency for the registration of higher degree students within the CNAA system. In terms of PhD projects, the College was to establish itself at the forefront of national planning for research that involved studio practice and critical inquiry, commencing what has remained a highly successful programme of post-graduate research across all its disciplines. The College's European exchange fellowships, which had started in Frankfurt in 1981, extended to include Rotterdam in 1984, and in June 1985 was run as a joint study programme with the participation also of

Dublin and Limerick. Taken together, it formed a presentation for the CNAA which was well received, confirming the optimism in the quality of the courses and the vision of the future role.

In September 1987, the College took its first intake of students for the BA Honours Degree in Three Dimensional Design. This provided a common grounding in design before moving to specialisms in two named awards, Designer Maker and Designer for Industry. During the academic year, the other course changes were taking place, with the phasing out of the printing vocational courses, and the validation of the Publishing and Book Production course as a post-graduate diploma, which introduced new technology and arranged student placements in the publishing industry. The discussions on the possibilities of institutional merger continued throughout the year, and at every stage of the negotations the College was greatly helped by the understanding and support of its governors, and the contribution made by David Sample, who had taken a short term appointment as Vice-Principal.

Merger and recent history

By the summer of 1988, the College was faced with the prospect of an institutional merger. What had begun as a proposal to establish a consortium of higher education was now put forward as a new polytechnic, Polytechnic South West, run from Plymouth. At this stage independence was not a realistic alternative, and while there were concerns that the reorganisation should not hamper the long-standing collaboration with the University of Exeter, the College unanimously agreed that it should become part of the new institution. Over the following months further discussions took place on the academic compositions of faculties to be formed from the merging colleges (Art and Design, Rolle and Seale-Hayne). By April 1989 the new structure of the Faculty of Art and Design was in place with David Jeremiah as Dean. This allowed for an internal structure of three departments: Arts, Design and Humanities, Performance and Media, the latter incorporating many of the areas of work developed at the College in the 1980s. The changes involved major re-adjustments both for academic staff and for all categories of support

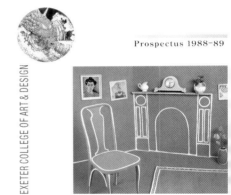

Prospectus 1988–89

EXETER COLLEGE OF ART & DESIGN

5.50 Exeter College of Art & Design, Prospectus cover, 1988/89.

[UPEXE, School of Art collection]

5.51 The Exeter School of Art & Design still occupies two premises in Queen Street close to the Royal Albert Museum.

[Photo: A.Kennerley]

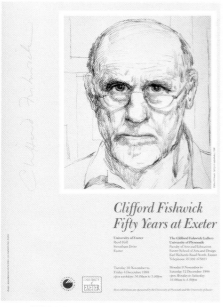

5.52, 5.53 In 1998, The University of Plymouth in association with the University of Exeter and the Museum staged exhibitions of Clifford Fishwick's work and the Clifford Fishwick Gallery was named in his memory at the University of Plymouth's Exeter Campus.

[UPEXE, School of Art collection; photo: Dave Griffiths.]

staff as they found themselves working in new groupings and subject to new regulatory frameworks. Rolle College emerged as the Rolle Faculty of Education, but it also had areas of work in the arts and humanities which it had developed in the 1970s and 1980s. The 1988/89 faculty structure left many of these overlapping areas unresolved in academic and resource terms, and it was soon realised that tensions between the two faculties would have to be eased through a further reorganisation. In 1994 the faculties merged to form the Faculty of Arts and Education spread across the campuses at Exeter and Exmouth. Four departments emerged, Exeter School of Art and Design, the School of Humanities and Cultural Interpretation, Rolle School of Education, and the School of Graduate Studies in Arts & Education, bringing together post-graduate and research work. With David Jeremiah concentrating on his research interests, the Dean of the new faculty from 1994 was Michael Newby.

Becoming part of a larger institution provided opportunities for new academic initiatives, which built on the established degree experience at Exeter with the fine arts and graphic design and at Exmouth with the integrated studies scheme in the arts and humanities. In the first instance developments took place around a revised BA Honours Combined Arts scheme complying with the Polytechnic structures. Major courses in English, history and theatre arts, which were run at the Exmouth campus, were now joined by two new subject areas, media and design arts (visual arts). Art history and heritage were then added, and towards the end of the 1990, courses in cultural practice and American studies. Research support took on a new significance as the work in the humanities and performance arts were incorporated into the scheme. An integrated strategy was put in place which encouraged the development of post-graduate research projects across all disciplines, and was the basis of the submission for the 1992 Research Assessment Exercise and the much more successful submissions in 1996, in the categories Art & Design and History of Art, Architecture & Design. These initiatives, particularly with the registration of PhD projects through creative practice, were greatly enhanced by the change from polytechnic to university status, and the understanding shown by the new processes of academic validation. Research studentships were created in English and theatre arts, and research grants provided for a number of projects, including funding a proposal which was to lead to the exhibition *Artist Visitors to Devon, 1750 - 1850,* at the Royal Albert Museum, Exeter and the University Gallery, Nottingham in 1995. Similarly important was the support for the fine art collaboration with the National Trust which resulted in the 1993 exhibition of contemporary sculpture, *The Ha-Ha,* at Killerton. Exeter had become the national centre for the Landscape Research Group in 1992, and two years later launched the *International Journal of Heritage Studies.*[90]

By the 1990s Exeter was recognised externally for its commitment to excellence across all its subject areas. International links were consolidated and it had also taken on a wider regional role. In 1991 the Faculty became the Erasmus Art and Design Coordinating Institution for 28 European colleges. Regionally, the part-time degree in fine art was introduced, and the Combined Arts scheme was expanded to the franchising of English and history courses to regional colleges. An Art and Design consortium of five participating colleges was formed in 1992, which resulted in an integrated modular scheme which gave the Faculty the prime responsibility for the validation and quality control of art and design courses, including four new HND courses, two new degree courses and the franchising of modules from existing programmes. By this time all the non-advanced courses in the Faculty had been phased out. The Foundation course was transferred from the Faculty to Exeter College and Plymouth College of Art and Design. The design courses also provided a wider range of specialisation with new named awards in design photography, illustration and typography.

The mid-1990s have seen a number of exciting developments. In 1996, the Erasmus scheme became part of the Socrates scheme which now involves 35 colleges. This enables students to take part in an international exchange programme in Europe spending from three to twelve months abroad. In addition links have been developed with universities and colleges in the United States, Japan and Australia. Regionally, SWADE, the South West Art and Design Education partnership, now covers a wide range of subjects taught in the School of Arts and Design at Exeter and at eight other institutions throughout the south west. It provides support for courses from Access to MPhil and PhD level. Within fine art, a new degree in contextual practice was started in 1997. This enables students to spend a proportion of their time working as artists in residence with outside agencies such as museums, hospitals and schools in this country and abroad. In the area of three dimensional design, the degree course has expanded from offering two to five named awards, with the inclusion of design/Italian which was validated in 1998. It has had a number of successes for students in national competitions with many RSA awards and awards from the Lighting Association. At postgraduate level, the Integrated Masters programme incorporated art and design modules from 1995s. It is focused on an enhancement of practice with a strong research element to it. The QAA Subject Review of 2000 praised it for its 'high quality' and for being 'innovative in all areas of provision'.

Research in the 1990s has of course been greatly influenced by external forces such as the RAE and the operations of research councils. In 1996 research within the School of Arts and Design was grouped around five themes as a result of the impact of the 1992 and 1996 RAEs on the art and design area which now had to compare its achievements with those of other institutions. The formation of the Arts and Humanities Research Board in 1999 also changed the climate to a comparative, competitive one. Within the School of Humanities and Cultural Interpretation support for research led to the organisation of the Art Historians Conference at Exeter and another exhibition at the museum at Exeter, *Going Modern and Being British - Art, Architecture and Design in Devon, c.1910 - 1960.* The following year it provided financial support for another conference, Crosscurrents.[91]

The broadening of educational activity in the 1990s on the Exeter campus also included another of the University of Plymouth's regional initiatives as the Exeter base for the Institute of Health in 1996 resulting from the incorporation of the Tor and South West College of Health. It occupied the first floor of the new Veysey Building. The ground floor was purpose-built for Academic and Information Services, Exeter, incorporating the library, media, computing, counselling and careers services, yet another twist in the saga of higher education in the area. Exeter, then, was one of the earliest localities to respond to a national educational initiative in art and design, and to take advantage of such state support as might be available. Its art school established a national profile and international links, and for almost 150 years the City has enjoyed access to a high level of art education, a tradition maintained to the present.

5.54: Development Diagram

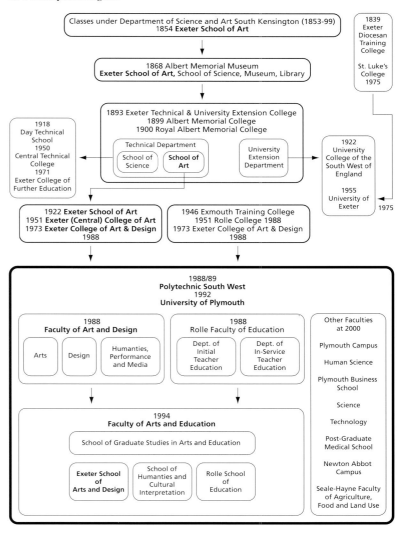

6.1 Wood carving of the Charles Hayne Seale-Hayne coat of arms over the fireplace in the former dining halls, now the staff room. The motto may be translated 'Salvation is in Heaven'.[1] [UPNAB, Seale-Hayne collection]

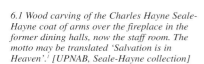

Seale-Hayne

CHAPTER SIX

The Newton Abbot campus of the University of Plymouth was, from its inception as Seale-Hayne College, clearly identified, locally and nationally, as an establishment concerned with vocational education and training for the agricultural industry. The college's gestation was prolonged, as was the debate over the level which was to be its main focus, but once it emerged as a fully fledged establishment Seale-Hayne soon established its place amongst the top echelon of agricultural colleges. Even before land had been purchased on which to build the college and develop the related college farm, Seale-Hayne had assumed a place in national agricultural education policy as the college for the south western region in a Board of Agriculture plan to expand the provision of more advanced agricultural education and training throughout England, in association with its expansion of scientific advisory services to the farming community. Thus Seale-Hayne always had a close involvement with Government departments, particularly the education and agricultural ministries, which, as the source of maintenance and development funding, were able to exert considerable control in what was always a state/voluntary college partnership.

Agriculture has never stood still. Always subject to variations in climate and soil quality, to natural disaster, to disease in crops and animals, the farming community has a long tradition of adaptation through example.[2] In like manner, the preparation of the next generation of farmers has long been rooted in apprenticeship approaches.[3] Nevertheless the industry has been increasingly influenced by scientific and technical thinking since the latter part of the seventeenth century. As yet structured education and training played no part. Rather it was the efforts of individuals in drainage, reclamation and enclosure, in new methods of breeding and farming techniques, which led the way, supported by literature and demonstrations, and, towards the end of the eighteenth century, by the formation of agricultural societies and farm co-operatives.[4] With chairs at Edinburgh and Oxford dating from the 1790s, and other initiatives in Scotland and Ireland, a very modest start to higher agricultural education had been made by the early decades of the nineteenth century. Additionally, the work of Liebig and others was laying the foundations of systematic scientific research in relation to agriculture.

The 1840s and 1850s, however, saw increasing interest in England in scientific and vocational education, with, for example, the schools of design and the work of the Science and Art Department, and the founding in 1845 of the first significant establishment for higher agricultural education, the Cirencester Agricultural College.[5] This soon established a reputation for its scientific work, and from 1869 its students were prepared for the new examinations of the Royal Agricultural Society, whose diplomas were to remain the highest mark of achievement for agricultural students until the

6.2 Charles Hayne Seale-Hayne, 1833-1903, founder. The M.P. for the area, he left £100,000 to build and endow the College for benefit of the people of Devon, but it was 1920 before the first proper agricultural students came into residence.

[UPNAB, Seale-Hayne collection

6.3 A view of the south face of the College building in the 1920s. The path on the right leads down to the College farm.

[UPNAB, Seale-Hayne collection]

1960s. From the 1870s the Science and Art Department made some contribution to Agricultural education at a lower level through its Normal School of Science and its classes in the provinces. However, increasingly, the need for lower level agricultural education and training which would deal with practical techniques for the working farmer and the more able labourers was being identified. This was a key element in the report of the Paget committee in 1888, which sat quite soon after Royal Commission on Technical Instruction had reported in 1884.[6] The latter had included a major section on agricultural education.

Although these reports produced no immediate results, one of those seminal changes of wide influence in British society was in the offing. It provided a spring board for the development in particular of agricultural education and training.[7] Through a combination of initiatives by local authorities and universities, individual endowment and Board of Agriculture promotion, the next two decades saw an expansion of mainly grant-aided provision of higher agricultural education, degrees, diplomas and other courses. However the involvement of the new county councils in the early years was not extensive, and the new Board of Agriculture was more in touch with the university departments concerned with agriculture, than other levels of progression. The growth in agricultural education was more marked in the period before 1914, as is indicated in Table 6.1

Table 6.1

Numbers of Agricultural Students in Grant-aided Establishments.

	1899/1900	*1912/1913*
No. colleges offering degree courses	3	10
No. of degree students	14	102
No. colleges offering diploma courses	5	14
No. of diploma students	85	642
No. colleges offering one year+ courses	6	9
No. of students taking one year+ courses	112	337
No. colleges offering short courses	8	12
No. of students taking short courses	421	46

Source: Brassley, *op.cit.,* Table 9.2. The Royal Agricultural College (Cirencester), not yet grant-aided, is not included here.

The numbers of students taking full time courses increased five fold from 211 in 1899-1900 to 1081 in 1912-13 to 1081. In 1900 the Royal Agricultural Society of England and the Highland and Agricultural Society of Scotland jointly launched the National Diploma in Agriculture which for the next 60 years, with the National Diploma in Dairying, was the pinnacle of agricultural qualifications for most students in higher agricultural colleges. Together with internal college diplomas, this was a pattern which Seale-Hayne would join after 1920. The emphasis on diplomas was already clear before 1914, despite the involvement of eight university departments.

There was a similar development, in the period from the 1880s to 1914, in the provision of lower level training courses, again through a combination of initiatives, typified by the label 'farm institute', many specialising in particular farm activities, and often having an attached farm in which to base practical experience. Thus there were travelling and fixed dairy schools (and even more specialised cheese schools), dairy institutes and horticultural colleges as well as institutes which took a more general agricultural approach. But it was the dairying specialism which dominated expansion at this level.[8]

6.4 Originally the foundation stone (in the north block) carried the builders' name Pethick, but Jenkins was substituted when that firm replaced Pethick to complete the building.

[Photo: A.Kennerley]

With the administration of state-supported educational provision in the hands of a number of governmental bodies, a potential for inter-departmental conflict was created in 1889 by the granting to the Board of Agriculture of powers to inspect and report on any schools, except public elementary schools, in which instruction on agricultural subjects, whether scientific or practical, was given, and to grant-aid such schools.[9] It could also aid lecture courses in agriculture and oversee examinations. At a wider level it was required to collect statistical data, oversee experiments and research and disseminate data.

The depressed state of farming in the 1880s and 1890s had produced three other parliamentary investigations of the industry which resulted in five reports over the period 1880 to 1896, so the Board of Agriculture was well provided with information on the industry as a whole.[10] But it lacked the administrative machinery, Cheesborough argues, to perform its role with lower level agricultural education and training provision. This was to be a major concern of the Reay report on agricultural education, 1908.[11] Meanwhile the 1902 Education Act widened the role of the Board of Education, created in 1899 to unify the central administration of education, heightening the overlap between the two departments. An attempt to clarify spheres of influence was made in 1906, but it was not until early in 1912 that the conflict was settled with the Board of Agriculture assuming responsibility for agricultural education for all students over the age of sixteen. That the laying of the foundation stone for the Seale-Hayne college buildings, for which grant-aid was considered essential, did not take place until the end of November 1912, was not unconnected with these circumstances.[12]

6.5 The original library was in the south wing where the painting of the founder (on the left) used to hang. It now hangs in the Great Hall.

[UPNAB, Seale-Hayne collection; photo, Middleton, Newton Abbot]

6.6 A view of Seale-Hayne College showing the south and eastern faces, and the service section on the right of the picture, from a postcard posted in 1939.

[UPNAB, Seale-Hayne collection]

The Reay committee's recommendations on a country wide network of farm institutes began to be put into effect in 1910, drawing on a new source of state funding as a result of the Development and Road Improvement Funds Act, 1909, which contained funding provision for both farm institutes and for higher level agricultural education. For the latter purpose the country was divided into twelve regions each having a focus in a university department or agricultural college, where agricultural specialists would be trained. The gap in the south west coverage was to be filled by Seale-Hayne, as specifically stated in the Reay report and in the subsequent planning of this network.[13] This three level approach, university degree courses, agricultural college diploma courses and farm institute courses, into which Seale-Hayne would be fitted, was to dominate agricultural education and training for the next 60 years. However, the demands of war meant that the new college's initial contribution was at the lowest level, the short course training of land girls.

The Origins and Founding of Seale-Hayne College

As has already been indicated, becoming fully operational as an agricultural college in 1920 was for Seale-Hayne College a very drawn out affair: some 30 years from the original date of the founder's will (1889), seventeen years from his death (1903), thirteen years from the purchase of the Howton Farm on which to locate the college (1907), ten years from the formation of the Governing Body and the appointment of the first principal (1909/10), eight years from the start of work on the college building (1912). The original, predictable delay was a feature of many educational endowments, and always bore the risk that changing circumstances would undermine the original intention. It took some years to sort out the legal complications, as did the application for grant aid. Then building delays, rampant inflation, and the demands of war took their toll for a further eight years.

6.7 The archway under the tower in the centre of the south face is still the imposing main entrance.

[UPNAB, Seale-Hayne collection]

Charles Hayne Seale-Hayne (1833-1903), a bachelor, was a member of the Devon landed gentry, descended from the Seale and Hayne families having long standing connections with the County, and particularly Dartmouth, and held offices locally as well as nationally. In 1885 he became Liberal member of parliament for Ashburton (mid-Devon), retaining his seat until his death, and was a member of the fourth Gladstone government as Paymaster General from 1892-95.[14] Given his local interests and his arrival in parliament while technical education was an issue of the day, the debates which led to the Technical Instruction Act in 1889 must surely have had a bearing on his decision to leave the bulk of his estate for the benefit of the people he represented:

"...to found establish and endow a college for the promotion of technical education of artisans and others without distinction of creed primarily and specially with reference to manufactures industries and products of the County of Devon, such college to be established in the neighbourhood of Newton Abbot..."[15]

He gave his executors

"...discretion to settle and adjust a scheme for the formation of such college in accordance with what they may in their absolute discretion think most nearly to correspond with what they may consider to be my views..."

His codicil in 1897 reinforced the application of the residue of his estate to a technical college to be free from ecclesiastical interference and not to be applied to any chapel for the college. It also appointed George Lambert, M.P. for the adjacent constituency of South Molton, as an executor.

From the will it seems fairly clear that Seale-Hayne had in mind the kind of multifaceted college like those science, art and technical college buildings which were to spring up all over the country in the 1890s. Agriculture, as a significant industry in Devon, was clearly included, but was it meant to be the sole focus? In 1902, events in Newton Abbot were to overtake the provisions Charles Seale-Hayne had made. In October that year the foundations were laid for the Newton Abbot Public Library and Newton Abbot Science Art and Technical School, on a site for which Seale-Hayne had used his influence to have released by the Local Government Board. This building, close to the centre of the town (and still in use today), was financed partly by Devon County Council and partly by local subscription with the library section funded with a donation by the philanthropist J. Passmore Edwards (whose mother was from Newton Abbot).[16] Given that Seale-Hayne knew of this initiative well over a year before his death, and that he must have discussed his intentions with George Lambert (leading exponent of Seale-Hayne College and life chairman of its governors) on more than one occasion, why was the will not changed to allow for an agricultural college?[17] There can be little doubt that the use of the endowment to found an agricultural college had become the intention. Seale-Hayne died on 22 November 1903, and on 18 December Lambert visited the Board of Agriculture to gather information about grants for agricultural education and

6.8 Charles Seale-Hayne smoothed the way for the Newton Abbot Science, Art and Technical School (opened 1904), a year before his death. The initiative must have limited his own idea to found a similar establishment 'in the vicinity of Newton Abbot'.

[Photo: A. Kennerley]

6.9 J. Passmore Edwards (1824-1911), a publisher, donated money for public educational buildings throughout Devon and Cornwall, including the library at Newton Abbot, part of the same development as the Science, Art and Technical Schools.

[Chart and Compass, 33 (1911), 104]

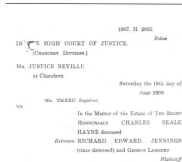

*6.10 This judgement established the
Seale-Hayne charity, released the Seale-Hayne
legacy and approved the scheme for managing
the College.*

[Public Record Office, ED 37/407]

*6.11 The Scheme for establishing and
regulating the College at last, over six years
after the founder's death, allowed George
Lambert to set about bringing the College
into existence. It was not to be until 1920 that
the College received its first proper
agricultural students.*

[Public Record Office, ED 37/407]

on provision in Britain and overseas. The Board's officials made it very clear that they hoped the endowment would be used to fill the gap in the network of agricultural colleges "...between Reading and Land's End...".[18]

Seale-Hayne's estate was valued at £119,505 gross, which left about £100,000, after disbursements, to found the college. It would take time to draw up a trust deed which would need the approval not only of the charity commissioners, but also of the Board of Education, which had a duty to oversee educational trusts. No doubt George Lambert became impatient about the rate of progress, but it seems likely that one sticking point was the distinction between a technical college and an agricultural college. The approval of the purchase of the Howton Farm (230 acres) in 1907 for £10,000 was held up, and it is also clear that the officials at the Board of Education were intent on having the college emerge as a farm institute with a strong emphasis on basic practical training, rather than a more academic establishment like the Harper Adams College (1901) in Shropshire.[19] The trustees, in reality George Lambert, took out an action in the Chancery Division in 1907, against the Attorney General to force approval of the purchase of the farm and of the scheme for establishing the college. The Seale-Hayne proposal appears to have become a pawn in the strained relations between the Board of Education and the Board of Agriculture, and the action dragged on throughout 1908. At one point a Board of Education official commented that it was

"...a bare-faced attempt to defeat the decision of Parliament over the jurisdiction of the Board of Education over charitable trusts. The Scheme seems to vest this control in the Board of Agriculture and Fisheries."[20]

Finally, on 19 June 1909, a judge approved the "Scheme for the Establishment and Regulation of the College for Agricultural and Technical Education...".[21] The purchase of the farm was approved, and the property vested in the Official Trustee of Charity Lands for the Foundation. The governors were allowed to realise £20,000 to fund the building and equipment, but £33,333 had to be held in trust to fund an annuity of £1000, which would revert to the endowment on the death of the annuitant.[22] The balance of funds was vested in the Official Trustee of Charitable Funds to produce an investment income for the college.

Although the way had now been cleared for establishing the college, it was already apparent that the endowment was unlikely to prove adequate to complete the physical development of the college and farm to the standard desired or to cover annual operating expenses, if fees were not to be set at unacceptable levels. Nevertheless, with the Scheme's 83 clauses providing detailed guidance on the appointment and proceedings of the governors, the deposition of property, teaching arrangements, pupils and college fees, instruction and examination, and the provisions from the will about religious matters, Lambert set about forming the Governing Body, which held its first meeting on 3 September 1909.[23] Lambert was appointed a governor for life and required to appoint four co-optive governors about whom he must notify the Board of Education. The Board of Agriculture was to appoint one governor and Devon County Council three, essential appointments if the college was to bid for grants from those sources. Much of the early work of the governors was taken up with the administrative demands of creating a new establishment. In November they appointed the first Principal, Mr Bernard N. Wale, previously Senior Lecturer in Agriculture at the South Eastern Agricultural College at Wye in Kent.[24]

From the start there were always two major dimensions under the general oversight of the Governors and under them of the Principal, the college and the college farm, which had to be developed and upgraded roughly in parallel in response to the outside pressures to which each was subject. As far as possible the farm had to pay its way as a commercial enterprise, yet to perform its role as a teaching aid (albeit on the most grand scale). The educational and research demands placed on it would inevitably detract from its operation as a normal commercial farm. Farms do not stand still, and it was important to develop the College Farm, which was badly run down, while the College was being built so that it could function as an educational tool when the first students started their courses. It seems likely therefore, that Wale's experience of managing the College farm in Kent played a part in his

6.12 George Lambert (1866-1958), fellow MP for a Devon constituency and protege of Seale-Hayne, carried through the benefactor's intentions confident that the intention had become that of founding an agricultural college. He was chairman of the Governors for fifty years.

[UPNAB, Seale-Hayne collection]

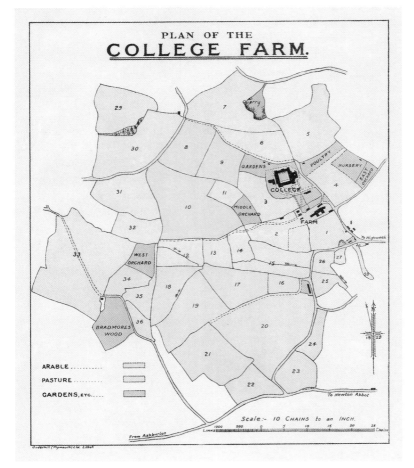

6.13 In this plan of the college farm in 1922, almost all the land was part of the original purchase of Howton Farm in 1907. George Lambert chose the site for the college above the farm buildings and well back from the main road at the foot of the plan.

[UPNAB, Seale-Hayne collection]

6.14 View of the north side of Seale-Hayne College buildings in the 1920s long before the development of the Frank Parkinaon halls of residence up hill of the original complex. Note the farm buildings to the right of the picture.

[UPNAB, Seale-Hayne collection]

appointment. On the farm front the new Principal was immediately embroiled in forming policy on staffing (the outgoing tenant farmer was appointed bailiff temporarily), purchase of stock and equipment, cropping, and a research project on cereals testing. On the college front he had to draw up an outline plan for the categories of accommodation required which would form the basis of instructions to architects, with the brief of 50 resident students and twenty day students, and within the cost limit of £20,000.[25]

Throughout much of his tenure Wale must have functioned as a general factotum in progressing the development of the college, and frequently on his own as there were no other academic members of staff. He would not have been without advisers, as it seems likely that the Governors constituted a 'local committee' to address issues in detail, which would have met between formal meetings. There would also have been meetings with education and agriculture ministry officials and with those of the county council, as well as with interest groups such as Devon farmers. But the governors were by no means always available as all had diverse interests and commitments. For example, the Chairman, George Lambert (1866-1958), who clearly must have been very closely involved, was a successful 'yeoman' farmer but his work in parliament must often have kept him in London. He was a public figure for much of his life. By 1889, aged only 23 he had become a Devon County Councillor, and in 1891 he won a by-election at South Molton, holding the seat until 1924 and again between 1929 and 1945. He was Civil Lord of the Admiralty between 1905 and 1915, and chairman of the Liberal Party in 1919-21. On retirement from parliament in 1945, he was made a viscount, no doubt at the suggestion of Churchill under whom he had served when Churchill was at the Admiralty. One of his earliest tasks in Parliament had been to serve on the Royal Commission on Agricultural Depression (1893), which together with his farming background, must have influenced the orientation of the Seale-Hayne bequest towards agricultural education. He was not without influence in government circles, but in trying to secure the future of the college, he did not always endear himself to ministerial officials. The writer of his entry in the Dictionary of National Biography comments:[26]

6.15 The Principal's house, now known as Howton House, was to become the commanding officer's and nursing sisters' residence in 1918-19 during the period the College was requisitioned as a military hospital.

[UPNAB, Seale-Hayne collection]

"A man of strong convictions who knew his own mind and spoke it. He was not given to subtlety of speech or opinion, but he was downright, steadfast and incorruptible: a force to be reckoned with by party leaders."

Whether Lambert's judgement in selecting the Howton Farm for the College, was as sound as his credentials might suggest was to be questioned. In the future its unsuitability for horticulture was to be the cause of the College's failure to develop that dimension of the work satisfactorily. Early in 1911 the Governors considered selling in order to move closer to Newton Abbot, but could not find an alternative. Selecting a suitable site on the farm for the College's buildings did not prove easy, and in the end it was left to the Chairman.[27] Meanwhile a competition for the design of the College buildings had been announced with Prizes of £100, £50 and £30, and in July 1911 the Governors had 35 sets of plans to consider.[28] Messrs Mitchell, Son and Gutteridge's design for a building on the university quadrangle style, was selected for the first prize and in due course Mr F. Gutteridge was appointed College architect. This Southampton-based partnership was well established in institutional building design, with amongst others, Southampton Sailors' Home (1908), in its portfolio. It took another year for the details of erecting a building on a green-field site to be sorted out, including for example services such as water supply and sewage, access roads, and for the building itself, the type of stone and central heating rather than open fires. Underlying the decisions being taken was the Governors' determination to have a building of high quality in which external appearance was an important factor. In July 1912, the tender of Messrs Pethick (a Plymouth building contractor) for £21,674 was accepted for the erection of the west, north and east sides of the building, with the south side to follow at the same rate if agreed within the coming year. So, on 15 October 1912, with a suitable bout of publicity, the foundation stone was laid by the President of the Board of Agriculture and Fisheries, Sir Walter Runciman.[29]

6.16 Seale Hayne College farm yard during the 1914-18 war, when the college was running short courses training members of the Women's Land Army in practical farm work. The farm buildings were still in a very run down condition.

[Brooks, Newton Abbot, 1917; UPNAB, Seale-Hayne collection]

With the Board of Education having oversight of educational endowments and of operational grants-in-aid in the period from 1909, at the same time as developing the building plans, it was necessary to develop the details of the courses to be offered and of the staffing. From the perspective of Education officials they needed to consider this side before giving their blessing to the building plans. The early proposals were for: winter agricultural courses of 14 to 20 weeks for men; summer courses for women (two to six weeks) in dairying, poultry, horticulture, beekeeping; summer vacation courses for elementary school teachers. The college should develop as an Agricultural College, and the minimum student age should be sixteen.[30] The staff proposed implied an annual salary bill approaching £3,000: principal (£450), assistant (£150), chemist (£400), assistant (£120), botanist (£400), assistant (£100), entomologist (£100) veterinary subjects teacher (£350), non-technical subjects teacher (£300), horticulture teacher (£180), poultry teacher(£120), dairying teacher (£150). Had agricultural education remained with the Board of Education, Seale-Hayne might well have emerged as a farm institute, which the Board was prepared to support with annual grants totalling £500. Its officials noted the dichotomy between the courses proposed, which they interpreted as farm schooling, and the staffing proposed which was more suited to an agricultural college.[31] That level of grant was well below what the Governors were seeking. They estimated staffing and running costs at £4,450, fee income at £880 and endowment income at £1,700, leaving a short fall, to be met by a hoped-for grant, of £1,940. Their application for funding from the Development Fund was made in October 1910, and rejected by the Board of Education in August 1911. Fortunately the transfer of post sixteen agricultural education to the Board of Agriculture early in 1912 removed the dead hand of the Board of Education and in March 1912, the Governors were notified that they would be eligible for grants from both the Development Fund and from county councils.[32] There was also to be a grant of £1,000 annually for farm advisory and

6.17 Women's Land Army trainees at Seale-Hayne enjoyed the release from the pre-war social constraints,but raised the ire of Devon's Women's War Agricultural Committee who complained that they smoked and did not attend church on Sundays.

[UPNAB, Seale-Hayne collection]

6.18 Women's Land Army trainees making hay at Seale-Hayne College, 13 July 1917.

[UPNAB, Seale-Hayne collection]

6.19, 6.20 One of the main activities for
inmates at Seale-Hayne Hospital in 1918-19,
was occupational therapy. The group with the
officer in the College farmyard have been
posed holding animals. As well as working at
farm activities, indoor activities, such as
basket making, were also provided.

[UPNAB, Seale-Hayne collection]

technical work, which, with agricultural research, was of particular interest
to Lambert. This helped to ensure the Seale-Hayne's ultimate development
as an agricultural college and as a base for advisory services. In December
1912, a building grant of £9,000 was agreed (augmented in May 1914 by
£1,825), relieving the Governors' worries to some extent about eating into
the endowment.[33] However, access to funding brought with it demands for
increased representation on the Governing body. In 1915 a revised regulatory
scheme was approved which would remain the basis for governing the
college to the 1980s. Lambert could now co-opt nine governors; nominated
governors now included one from the Board of Agriculture, and three each
from Devon and Cornwall County Councils. Staff appointments and
dismissals were vested in the Governors instead of the Principal and
provision was made for a Board of Studies of college staff.[34]

Having overcome the funding issues, the College was let down by its
builder so that it failed to become operational before the disruption caused
by the 1914-18 war. On more than one occasion the builder was warned for
making slow progress, and progress was further impeded by the use of faulty
bricks which had to be replaced. By August 1913, only £4,000 worth of the
contracted work (£22,000) had been completed. The contract with Pethick
was cancelled, and Messrs Jenkins of Southampton contracted at an increase
of 6.5% on the original tender, which, taking into account of inflation,
brought the cost to £26,290. In addition, Jenkins' tender of £11,680 for the
south side was accepted.[35] The College building was not completed until the
summer of 1916, though much of it became available during the previous
year. Meanwhile the Governors had successfully resisted a breach of contract
suit from its original builders, and had extended their land holding by the
purchase of the adjacent Ingsdon Estate at £13,000, for which investments
were realised with the reluctant agreement of the Board of Education which
retained oversight of the endowments.[36] Plans for a range of new farm
buildings had to be set aside owing to the war, but the Governors went ahead
with the erection of six labourers' cottages which were urgently needed.[37]

6.21 Lt. Col. D.R. Edwardes-Ker, Principal
1919-1933, topped the list of 54 leading
agricultural scientists who applied for the
position. His selection was certainly influenced
by MAFF, which vetted the list, and knew of
him as Vice-Principal of Wye College in Kent
and for his war work in chemical warfare.

[UPNAB, Seale-Hayne collection]

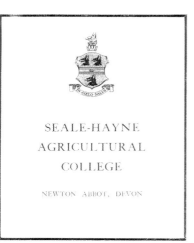

SEALE-HAYNE
AGRICULTURAL
COLLEGE

NEWTON ABBOT, DEVON

*6.22 The first prospectus for agricultural
students was issued in 1919. It was
substantially unchanged from that prepared by
Edwardes-Ker's predecessor, Bernard Wale, a
year or two earlier.*

[Public Record Office, MAF 33/47/TE158]

Governing Body
1920

Chairman:
THE RIGHT HON. GEORGE LAMBERT, M.P., Spreyton, Bow, Devon.

Co-opted Governors:
Miss S. CALMADY-HAMLYN, Bidlake Vean, Bridestowe, Devon.
R. ERNEST COCKS, ESQ., J.P., 20 Portland Villas, Plymouth.
ALFRED T. LORAM, ESQ., J.P., Rosamondford, Aylesbeare, Exeter.
EDWIN C. PERRY, ESQ., J.P., 9 Upper Knollys Terrace, Plymouth.
ARTHUR S. RENDELL, ESQ., F.S.I., Newton Abbot.
W. ROWSE, ESQ., J.P., Town Mills, Okehampton, Devon.
LIEUT.-COL. H. ST. MAUR, D.L., J.P., Stover, Newton Abbot.
WILLIAM VICARY, ESQ., J.P., C.A., The Knoll, Newton Abbot.

Appointed by the Board of Agriculture and Fisheries:
THE RIGHT HON. F. D. ACLAND, M.P., Sprydoncote, Silverton, Exeter.

Appointed by the Devon County Council:
W. P. HIERN, ESQ., J.P., C.A., F.R.S., The Castle, Barnstaple.
A. J. MURRIN, ESQ., J.P., C.A., to Powderham Road, Newton Abbot.
COL. R. A. MOORE-STEVENS, C.C., Winscott, Torrington.

Appointed by the Cornwall County Council:
BT.-COL. SIR COURTENAY VYVYAN, C.B., C.M.G., D.L., J.P., Trelowarren, Mawgan-in-Meneage, Cornwall.
W. HAWK, ESQ., J.P., C.A., Kernock, St. Mellion S.O., Cornwall.
E. H. HOSKIN, ESQ., C.C., Cartuther Barton, Liskeard.

*6.23 The constitution of the Governors of
Seale-Hayne College from the first Prospectus
in 1920, reflects the provisions in the
regulatory scheme as modified in 1915. The
Ministry of Agriculture Fisheries and Food,
however had far more influence on the college
than their single member might suggest.*

[Public Record Office, MAF 33/47/TE158]

It seems likely that the College first functioned in an academic role through research projects carried out at the College farm under the direction of the Principal, though their nature is unclear. A project contemplated in 1912 was an investigation of the financial aspects of washing sheep before shearing.[38] The Principal may also have been providing technical advice to farmers, but a more substantial service under the Board of Agriculture scheme to provide advice to the industry was the appointment in December, 1913, of a Livestock Officer who would be based in the College.[39] The first students, in the spring of 1916, saw the College operating at the level of a farm institute. Using two Dairy Instructresses seconded from Devon County Council, groups of women came to the College for short residential courses in farm work, of four weeks duration. Though the demand waned during 1917, there were women students at the college until April, 1918, and altogether some 350 women attended the college during the war.[40] The presence and behaviour of women (whose ages ranged from 23 to 35) at the college were the cause of some gossip picked up by the Women's War Agricultural Committee in Devon, who complained to the Board of Agriculture about the internal discipline at the College, especially about smoking, non-attendance at a place of worship on Sundays and irregularity of meals. In this clash of the old order represented by the genteel ladies of the Committee and the social changes being brought about by the war, the ladies were firmly rebuffed at a meeting attended by a Board of Agriculture inspector, the Small Holdings Commissioner, Governors, Principal, Matron and her assistant.[41]

This tentative start to the work of the College was brought to an abrupt halt when it was requisitioned by the War Office from April 1918 for use as a military hospital. The Governors themselves had anticipated this form of war use when in September 1915 they had agreed to offer the buildings to the War Office for just that purpose. Given the College's precarious financial situation they would have looked at any usage capable of generating income. George Lambert again offered the buildings in September 1917 for "neurasthenic cases", and this led to a serious assessment of the site for neurological/shell shock cases in which farm work would be part of the therapy. Unfortunately in pressing for a rental of £2,000 per annum, Lambert overplayed his hand in the process alienating both War Office and Agriculture officials. Requisitioning completely removed the authority of the Governors, who were forced to dismiss their staff, though some farm staff were retained by the Army. Lambert's protests to the President of the Board of Agriculture about the treatment of the Governors in these circumstances received a curt, unsympathetic response.[42]

The man in charge of Seale-Hayne Neurological Hospital, 1918-1919, was Major A.F. Hurst, RAMC. His scheme provided for 300 patients, 17 officers and 283 men, including 36 in isolation rooms.[43] Conversion was to be minimal. Additional latrine and wash house accommodation would be necessary, and he was allowed £1,000 to erect a recreation hut and convert outbuildings into handicraft work shops. The farm would provide "...a great variety of suitable employment for convalescent patients." His staff were to include four medical officers, a chaplain, and adjutant ("...Lt Lunniss, an expert farmer..."), a matron, four sisters, nine nurses, six ward maids, a dozen NCOs and orderlies, and four tradesmen.[44] Bernard Wale had to vacate his house which was to be occupied over by Hurst and the nursing sisters. When the army finally pulled out in the Autumn of 1919, it handed over the buildings it had erected. The Governors were left with the task of refurbishing much of the accommodation after the wear and tear of the war years.

The tortured emergence of Seale-Hayne College was to see one final twist before the first proper agricultural students were to arrive early in 1920, the replacement of the Principal. During the military occupation, Principal Wale had been paid a retainer of £50 per annum by the Governors to watch over the College's interests, and there appears to have been no suggestion that he would not be reinstated when the buildings were handed back. However, at the Board of Agriculture, officials were discussing his position, an internal debate which was coloured by their relationships with George Lambert. In January, 1917, they were concerned about the excessive costs of the building and commented that the Governors knew little about finance; in February 1918, when Lambert was pressing for a rent, they found him a very difficult person to deal with; in May 1919, they commented on the need for a suitable new principal, hinting that the Board of Education should approve the appointment; and in July 1919, they approved the choice of the new Principal commenting that he had the strength to stand up to Lambert.[45] Wale's resignation was accepted by the Governors in Lambert's absence on 11 June 1919. He appears to have been persuaded to go with verbal promises of support from the Board as well as the Governors in finding a new appointment, promises which were repudiated subsequently when he wrote seeking their help. Lambert certainly concurred, commenting that Wale was "...not fitted but useful...", and must surely have asked Wale for his resignation.[46] There is much that these files do not reveal, but it is difficult not to feel some sympathy for the first Principal who had held office in the most unusual and difficult of circumstances, and whose preparations were to be put into effect by his successor.

Staff

PRINCIPAL:
D. R. EDWARDES-KER, O.B.E., M.A. (Oxon.), B.Sc. (Lond.).

COLLEGE WARDEN:
E. W. FENTON, M.A., B.Sc. (Aberdeen).

Agriculture :
THE PRINCIPAL.
P. A. M'WILLIAM, N.D.A., N.D.D., C.D.A., C.D.D. (Glasgow).
T. J. SHAW, N.D.A.

Agricultural Chemistry :
THE PRINCIPAL.
E. VANSTONE, D.SC., M.SC., F.I.C., F.C.S.

Agricultural Botany :
E. W. FENTON, M.A., B.Sc.

Fruit and Vegetable Growing :
C. T. MACKINTOSH, Dip.R.H.S.

Dairying :
P. A. M'WILLIAM, N.D.A., N.D.D., C.D.A., C.D.D.

Surveying and Building Construction :
J. J. FLOWER, B.A. (Dublin), P.A.S.I., B.A.I. (Dublin).

Poultry Keeping :
C. CROSSE.

Book-keeping :
N. F. RICHARDSON.

Forestry :
E. W. FENTON, M.A., B.Sc.

Secretary and Bursar :
N. F. RICHARDSON.

6.24 The College opened for its first cohort of 37 agricultural students in 1920 with this academic staff of nine listed in the first prospectus.

[Public Record Office, MAF 33/47/TE158]

6.25 The College dining hall in the 1920s, looking north towards the high table. Note the Seale-Hayne crest above the fireplaces. The place settings appear to be for high tea.

[UPNAB, Seale-Hayne collection]

6.26 The Principal's enthusiasm for tennis (he was a county standard player) soon led to the laying out of tennis courts on the lawns in the College quadrangle.

[UPNAB, Seale-Hayne collection]

With the opening of Seale-Hayne to real agricultural students now firmly in sight, the long delayed decision on its character and level now became urgent. In May 1919, Lord Ernle, President of the Board of Agriculture, responded to Lambert that it should function initially as both an agricultural college and a farm institute, the former in the two winter sessions and the latter in the summer, but that eventually it would function at the higher level.[47] The possible linking of Seale-Hayne with plans for a university college of the South West was also in the Board's mind. So the new Principal had a clear direction and could pick up the course plans which had been developed by his predecessor to draft prospectus level, simply adding the names of staff once they had been appointed.

A College at Last

The Board of Agriculture clearly had a behind-the-scenes influence on the selection of the new Principal. They were supplied with a full list of the 54 applicants, which seems to have included a good proportion of current agricultural scientists/educators. No doubt the officials sounded their colleagues about the most likely candidates, and they certainly approved of Lt. Col. D.R. Edwards-Ker, the Governors' choice from a short list of eight, who had "...done famous war work..." in chemical warfare, but also came with a sound academic record from his position as vice-principal at Wye College in Kent, a front rank agricultural college soon to become a constituent college of the University of London. So commenced this new phase which would see Seale-Hayne established as one of the leading set of agricultural colleges, and undergoing almost continuous physical development with the support of Board of Agriculture grants. The timing was opportune. As a result of the war experience agriculture had been revitalised and there was a surge of interest in agricultural employment. In January 1919, the Board of Agriculture issued a circular asking local authorities to prepare schemes for agricultural education to include: a higher agricultural education institution, county agricultural instructors and organisers, a farm institute, a technical advisory service for farmers, short courses of instruction, local lectures and demonstrations.[48] Backed with £2,500,000 over five years, this was to set the pattern of agricultural education for the next half century. This funding included block grants to agricultural colleges from which Seale-Hayne was to benefit so much, and came with a policy of encouraging full-time two and three year courses leading to the national certificates and diplomas, and in time to degrees. With this enhanced role, the Board became the Ministry of Agriculture and Fisheries (MAF) later that year.

Edwards-Ker took up his appointment in September 1919, facing the urgent task of finalising all the courses, appointing staff, setting the fees, advertising, issuing the prospectus, and making sure the renovations were completed in time to receive students in January 1920. The negotiations for annual grants from Devon and Cornwall required provision to be made for reduced fees for students from those counties. Board and tuition fees were set at £45 per annum for residents of Devon and Cornwall, £105 for other United kingdom counties, and £150 for overseas students. The definition of Devon and Cornwall residents tried to cover most angles:

"...a bona fide resident of Devon and Cornwall be one who has resided for the whole of the twelve months immediately preceding the admission of the student in the geographical county of Devon or Cornwall, and that a candidate who fulfilled the above conditions, or whose parents or guardian fulfilled the above conditions, would be regarded as eligible for reduced fees."

The courses advertised in the first prospectus were: The College Diploma Course in Agriculture & Sciences (CDA)(three years, nine terms); The College Certificate Course in Agriculture (CCA) (or Horticulture, CCH) & Sciences (two years, six terms); separate short courses (ten weeks) in Dairying with butter and cheese making, Poultry-keeping, Horticulture and Bee-keeping. College Diploma students could also prepare for the National Diploma in Agriculture (NDA) and the National Diploma in Dairying (NDD). There were to be four terms, with men students being accepted only for three, and the fourth (the mid summer term) being reserved for women

6.27 A motor cycle rally held at Seale-Hayne in the inter-war years, presumably organised by the Motor Club. At the rear of the group a board with the word Dunlop is being held up, which suggests an element of sponsorship.

[UPNAB, Seale-Hayne collection]

6.28 From the early 1920s, Seale Hayne College interacted with the farming community through events at the College, attending markets and through taking stands at agricultural shows.

[UPNAB, Seale-Hayne collection]

students. The syllabus for the agriculture courses covered: soils, manures, crops, livestock, botany, general science, farm book-keeping, mensuration/ surveying/building construction, veterinary science/hygiene, agricultural engineering, woodwork, iron work. Prospective students, who could be accepted from the age of sixteen years, were warned:[49]

"A certain proportion of each student's time will be devoted to practical work on the farm and in the dairy, workshops, etc. This practical work is compulsory for all students, the object being not to make students labourers, but to give them the opportunity of learning how practical operations should be performed, so qualifying them to give efficient instructions to their own work men."

The practical farm work had to be passed in addition to residence and academic success, in order to be awarded the College's certificates and diplomas. The rigour was softened by references to centrally heated rooms, electric lightings, common rooms, teaching facilities and the colleges' programme of experimentation.

6.29 The Devon County Agricultural Association held its show at Seale-Hayne College in 1934. Taken on 22 May, the picture shows the College agricultural labourers cottages to the right of the show marquees on field no. 20. Note also the orchard laid out on field no. 24 (see fig. 6.13).

[UPNAB, Seale-Hayne collection; Sport and General Press Agency, London]

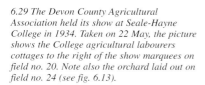

The College opened with eight academic staff in addition to the Principal, and a first entry of 37 students. Both faced an arduous baptism in making up for the term which had been lost though extra classes, because much of the college including the teaching spaces had not yet been properly furnished and because the farm was still very run down.[50] A temporary loan of furniture was made by the technical college in Newton Abbot. With a projected annual short fall in income of over £3000, the financial situation would remain difficult until county and MAF maintenance grants became available and the annual financial cycle became properly established. In April 1920 the MAF annual maintenance grant was set at £2,300; the annual grants from Devon and Cornwall were set at £3,000 and £1,000 respectively. A bid to MAF to fund new farm buildings produced a grant of £4,000.[51] In order to progress the improvement programme, a part of the Ingsdon Estate was sold off. However a condition of realising capital, was that the value should be returned to the endowment on an annual instalment basis over thirty years.

In these early years there was some turnover of staff as the college settled down, and in particular it proved difficult to fill the position as head of agriculture. As well as the full-time courses already noted, a programme of short courses was developed rapidly, including special ones for ex-servicemen. The four term year was quickly reduced to the more conventional three terms, abandoning the idea of a special term for women students, which was replaced by a number of short courses. Apart from this restriction, the student body could hardly have been more mixed, with ages ranging from fifteen to men in their forties, farm workers' sons to those from the landed gentry, men from the forces to those from families in the agricultural support industries. Despite the lack of amenity, it was not long before the Seale-Hayne College Union Club had been formed, and social events were taking place. Here the Principal was influential and socialising was one of his strengths.[52] Another was tennis, for which provision was soon made with the laying out of tennis courts. As the routine life of the college became established, the pace of student life steadied. Writing of 1921/23 Kevin Fitzgerald records:[53]

6.30 Frank Horne, Head of Biology, was a leading plant breeding reseacher in the 1930s and 1940s, specialising in rye grasses and broccoli.

[UPNAB, Seale-Hayne collection, 1934 college photograph]

"It was all very leisurely. We were either there on county grants or because our parents could afford it. Few of us had any idea of what we wanted to do when we left. Every morning was devoted to lectures and two or three afternoons a week to laboratory work. But we had a lot of time off for games, for cross-country and road running. There was a good deal of motor cycle activity, some quite serious rowing on the Teign, serious Rugby football in the winter, desultory cricket and tennis in the summer, much "binting", as the pursuit of local ladies was called, and quite a lot of us made serious botanical and zoological collections. In our second year, a lot of us began to work quite seriously for the National Diploma..."

Student recreational activity was reported in the *Seale-Hayne College Magazine,* which seems to have appeared three times a year from 1920, containing a mix of student compositions and poetry, old students reports of their work (several from abroad) and of course club and society reports. In 1931 the list comprised the Union Club (the umbrella organisation) Rugby, Association Football, Boating, Billiards, Entertainments, Cricket, Tennis, Boxing, Table Tennis, Motor, Hockey, Wireless, Discussion. The College Concert appears to have been a regular feature, perhaps organised by the entertainments committee, from at least 1922. Another early and significant development was the formation of the Old Seale-Haynian Club, which held its first general meeting on 23 October 1923. This has turned out to be a significant influence on the College in sustaining the network, publicising the college and contributing to improving the facilities.[54]

The fact that Seale-Hayne was up and running was soon impressed on the farming community. Of course publicity for its courses was a dimension, but the practical work of students also achieved this, through for example attendance at the local market. The presence of the college at farming industry events was significant. In March 1921 farm tractor trials were held at the college, with the Governors' Gold Medal being awarded to the International Junior tractor. As early as 1922 Seale-Hayne had exhibitions at the Bath and West Agricultural Show, the Devon County and the Royal Cornwall Shows; in 1923 there was a student team at the cattle judging competition at the London Dairy Show; later the College was at the Chelsea Flower Show. As the 1920s progressed the College was used for major conferences and as the location for agricultural shows.[55]

The college also benefitted through the basing on its premises of MAF advisory services to farmers in the South West. As noted earlier with the livestock adviser, this had been amongst Seale-Hayne's earliest roles. From 1923 the range was progressively extended to include advisers for entomology, mycology, chemistry, economics, bacteriology and veterinary science. Between them, the advisers touched all aspects of farming activity spending much time travelling to visit farms, analysing innumerable specimens in the laboratories at the College, and overseeing and reporting on some major agricultural investigations. Research and publishing was also part of the work of many of the teaching staff. Amongst the most notable was Frank Horne, Head of Biology, who made major contributions over many years in plant-breeding, working particularly with broccoli and rye grass. There was also industry-funded work such as the East Devon Manure experiment financed by Messrs Niham and county funded work, such as the Devon County Cockerel scheme.[56]

Surrounded by and often involved in this impressive array of activity, the full-time students were well placed to benefit from the enthusiasms of the staff as well as from the teaching offered. This soon began to show in the results, not just in passing the College examinations but with significant success in the external national diploma examinations. In 1922, Seale-Hayne student success placed it second in the league of twelve colleges, and it was not long before its students topped the list. From 1927 Seale-Hayne full time courses were expanded to include preparation for the BSc (Agriculture) intermediate and final examinations of the University of London, which was no mean recognition of the academic status which had been achieved, and soon its students were topping the list in those examinations.[57] Table 6.2 provides an overview of student success in this period; the numbers might seem small, but it must be remembered that having small monotechnic colleges was the accepted approach for the delivery of advanced vocational education. The table combines students who only attended for one year with two year diploma students and includes those who stayed on to take supplementary courses, of which the NDD was the most common. The short courses offered varied considerably in duration as well as subject, from two days to twenty weeks, and some became well established, being repeated for many years. The list of themes included dairying, poultry, rural science for schoolmasters, sanitary inspectors' course, bee keeping, butter milk, and tropical agriculture. The latter reflected the contact with overseas farming which had become established, and included student overseas visits and exchange, and visits of farmers from many parts of the British Empire.[58]

6.31 As well as serving as a laboratory for scientific experiment, the College Farm allowed ample scope for practical farming experience, in which all students were expected to participate, though to varying extents. Here students are seen turning hay or straw to encourage drying before is could be gathered in.

[UPNAB, Seale-Hayne collection]

6.32 Student social life at Seale-Hayne College soon became well developed in the 1920s. Motoring was an abiding interest and amongst the student clubs and societies there was a well supported motor club. The car in this picture certainly attracted a lot of interest.

[UPNAB, Seale-Hayne collection]

Table 6.2

Seale-Hayne Students, 1920-33: Courses Taken & Subsequent Occupations.

Courses taken		*Subsequent occupation*		*Subsequent occupation*	
Short course	180	Farming own farms (home)	106	Employed by other ag. firms	21
Certificate	142	Farming own farms abroad	34	Lecturers/instructors	32
Diploma	148	Farm Managers, agents	26	General agents abroad,	
Degree	20	Farming with fathers	77	other occ. abroad	74
Farm pupils	29	Farm pupils, assistants	24	Non agricultural work	56
Inter P.A.S.I.	5	Employed by dairy firms	17	Movement unknown	11
Total	524				524

Source: PRO, MAF 33/49/TE14644. MAF brief for visit of Block Grant Reassessment Committee to college, 1934. Numbers of students at time of departure and highest course level taken.

With such a level of exposure to the outside world, it was important that the College farm be brought into and maintained in good order. New farm buildings, including a new dairy, and six farm workers cottages, barns, piggeries, cow house, estate workshop and forge, shippon, granary, cart sheds, were erected in the 1920s, but other facilities were delayed for many years owing to financial stringency. The farm stocking policy was reshaped. Herds of dairy cattle, ewes and sows were developed, with the South Devon milking herd being particularly successful by the 1930s and achieving registration. The milking and breeding programmes were, of course, carefully recorded and reported. A substantial proportion of the farm was given over to grazing, but on the remainder a variety of crops in rotation were produced, and the farm was of course also used for plant breeding and crop trials. As already indicated, the farm featured significantly in the experience of the students. This was particularly so in the case of the farm pupils, who, although they lived in college buildings and had access to the facilities like other students, spent most of their time on the farm learning the practical work of farming under the farm staff who were their main instructors.[59] This arrangement continued until 1948 when the farm pupil course was disbanded.

6.33, 6.34 The annual sports day formed part of the College publicity and attracted a good crowd of visitors, judging from the number of motor cars parked around the perimeter of the sports field. There was a full range of track and field events.

[UPNAB, Seale-Hayne collection]

6.35 Following the resignation of Principal Edwardes-Ker, Seale-Hayne Governors acted quickly in 1933 to appoint a replacement as Principal, Mr Henderson Hogg, who had recently retired as a senior inspector for the Ministry of Agriculture and Fisheries.

[UPNAB, Seale-Hayne collection, from a group photograph by E. Brooks, Newton Abbot]

Although so much had been achieved in putting Seale-Hayne College on the map, the public image concealed stresses which would eventually break out and demand a major revision of the overall management of the College. The circumstances which now have to be discussed call into question the placing of the credit for the achievements of the 1920s. What proportion should lie with the Governors, with the Principal and with the staff team? Dedicated staff pressed on with their work for the benefit of the students and the reputation of the establishment, but signs of tensions in the relationships amongst the staff had reached the Governors early in 1922 and caused them to interview all staff. They hoped that their action then had overcome the problem. Amongst the top management financial worries were never far away and there were periods in the mid 1920s and early 1930s when cut backs were ordered.[60] The matter was set alight by the disappearance of the account ledgers, invoices, etc., from the Bursar's office, about 6 August 1932. The material was never found and no culprit was identified. The Governors' internal enquiries must have convinced them of the need for drastic action as they appointed an independent investigation under a high court judge in January 1933.[61]

"To ascertain whether the relations between certain members of the staff and an absence of team work are such as to disturb the efficient working of the college, and also whether the general financial position of the College is satisfactory and whether savings could be made without detriment to its utility as an educational institution."

The financial study showed that the College had carried an excess of liquid liabilities over liquid assets of in each of the past five years, never less than £2,000, over £5,000 in 1931 and £2,707 in 1932 mainly caused by building and improvement expenditure and largely offset by a legacy of £2,000. Even if planned economies of £1,800 were achieved, in the current downturn the annual debit on the current account would approach £1,000. An evaluation of the fixed assets showed a small loss of £170 since 1920. The main report recognised the successes of the College noted above, but concluded that there was "...a lack of organised control over expenditure which can no longer...be allowed to continue without grave danger..." and the absence of team work was bound to have an increasingly deleterious effect unless a better spirit was created. No one, Governors, principal or staff team came out of the investigation without some adverse comment. The Governors were castigated for their detachment from the management of the college, including the failure to operate properly the sub-committees which were supposed to exist (such as the finance committee), and the failure to insist on formal approval of financial decisions. They put much of the current difficulty down to uncosted, direct-labour building works, identifying twelve items for which approval was not recorded in the minutes of the Governors' meetings. The financial management of the farm was similarly conducted on a hand-to-mouth basis. Turning to relations with staff, the investigation found that the Board of Studies required by the College scheme had been instituted but allowed to lapse for several years. Though recently reconstituted it was

6.36 *One of the long-running specialist short courses run by the College in the inter-war period, was the Bee course. This was the group that attended in 1935.*

[UPNAB, Seale-Hayne collection, photo E. Brooks, Newton Abbot]

not serving as an adequate forum. Staff meetings were rare and there was no real channel for staff to the Governors. There was only one comment on educational facilities: the library was a disgrace! It was inevitable that, being at the heart of the operation of the College, the Principal would come in for adverse comment chiefly in relation to his style of man management. There were thirteen recommendations aimed at correcting the deficiencies, and they particularly picked out the Bursar for favourable comment as capable of seeing through the corrective measures. The principal resigned as did one of the long serving members of the Governors, who had acted in the role of executive vice-chairman.[62]

Seale-Hayne College in the 1930s and 1940s

Following this low point in the fortunes of the college, which mirrored the situation in Britain generally, came a steady but undramatic recovery until the outbreak of World War II created a new phase of uncertainty. Student numbers which had increased towards the end of the 1920s (in 1930 there were 83 on courses lasting more than six months), had fallen back to 52 (degree course 5, diploma courses 19, short courses 8, poultry course 5, special course 5, farm pupils 11) 22 short of the maximum.[63] The cuts which had been made in the grants from Devon and Cornwall were progressively restored. The staff contribution to the financial crisis had been in taking salary cuts of 7.5% and 5%, and these were restored in 1934. The overdraft at the bank had been cleared through the sale of stock. The MAF annual grant was fixed at £2,500 plus £500 for development schemes for the five years from 1935. Meanwhile, the governors had set up a reorganisation committee to address the recommendations of the investigating committee, and they had moved promptly to replace the Principal, appointing Mr W. Henderson Hogg temporary acting principal in April 1933, and making him permanent in October that year.[64] He had recently retired as Senior Divisional Inspector of the Ministry of Agriculture and Fisheries, and it is difficult not to see MAF involvement in putting his name forward.

6.37 The admission of women to Seale-Hayne courses in the 1930s raised the problem of separate accommodation. First they lived in Howton House, then the east block of the main building was set aside. Neither was really satisfactory given the social conventions of the period. So women students were moved out to this house, Daracombe, in Highweek village, which was purchased in 1943, as a women's hall of residence. It remains in use.

[UPNAB, Seale-Hayne collection, photo, N. Horne, Totnes]

There had been no interruption to the work of the College in its three spheres of teaching, research and advisory services, and these were sustained until the outbreak of war. It continued to attract the conferences of bodies such as the Agricultural Education Association, the British Grassland Society and the National Pig Society. It was also used in the vacation between 1926 and 1938 by the Co-operative Holidays Association. Educational developments included the recognition of Seale-Hayne as a centre for the Estate Agents and Auctioneers examinations, and for students to take the Royal Horticultural Society examinations; in 1937 a special one year course in Agriculture in co-operation with Cornwall was introduced, and 1938 a new course for Rural Science teachers.[65]

Both the College buildings and the farm underwent a range of physical improvements. The electrical supply was completely rewired with extensions to buildings not previously connected. The telephone connection was laid underground, and the college was connected to the gas supply. The kitchens were re-equipped, hot water system improved, study bedrooms were refurnished and improvements were made to the college roads. New building included piggeries, a glass house, post-mortem house, a grass drier for research, and an arboretum. A plan for an extension to the college, set aside in the late 1920s, was resurrected, but again set aside in December 1938 on the advice of MAF.[66]

One area in which progress was made was in the re-introduction of women students, who had not been admitted since the separate term arrangements of 1920. The issue had arisen later in the nineteen twenties, but identifying suitable separate accommodation from the men always proved the obstacle. The possibility of using Brooklands (a house not too far from the College) as a hostel was explored in 1927, and the extension plans of 1929 also allowed for women students. In 1934 arrangements were made for the accommodation of women at Howton House, after which the east side of the main building was set aside for female students. Finally in 1943, the Governors purchased Daracombe in nearby Highweek Village, which became the women's hall of residence.[67] Table 6.3 indicates the balance in October 1943.

Table 6.3

Students Registered at Seale-Hayne College, October 1943.

Course	*Male*	*Female*	*Total*
Farm pupils	23	7	30
College Diploma in Agriculture Year 1	41	2	43
College Diploma in Agriculture year 2	12	1	13
College Diploma in Dairying Year 1	3	4	7
College Diploma in Dairying Year 2	1	3	4
Horticulture Year 1	3	3	6
College Certificate in Poultry year 2	2	1	3
Husbandry	1	1	2
Totals	86	22	108

Source: PRO, MAF 33/356

With the Government assuming control of all manpower and resources at the outbreak of war, the College found itself with an unpredictable future under the direct control of MAF. Forward planning for war had implied that Seale-Hayne, along with most other agricultural colleges and institutes, would be used for the training of members of the Women's Land Army (WLA), with existing students being sent to the University of Reading to complete their courses. WLA trainees failing to materialise initially, the College reopened for normal courses on 6 November 1939 with MAF approval, recalling its students from Reading. Having lost key staff to other war duties, teaching had to be managed on an ad hoc basis using such staff and visitors as became available. WLA trainees eventually turned up and by December 1942, some 800 had passed through Seale-Hayne and on to work on farms. Additionally, the staff was able to handle four short courses on silage making. The pressure on farming to feed the nation meant that there was a shortage of trained agriculturalists, and a reason for allowing students deferment of military service. As a further measure to increase the supply, the College Diploma Course in Agriculture was reduced from three to two years. MAF again ordered closure from June 1940, but allowed the college to resume its educational role in October.[68]

War promotes scientific and technological development, and this was no less the case for Seale-Hayne. Well established as a centre for MAF advisory services to farming, this activity increased, and was the College's most significant contribution. The introduction of free milk for children and expectant mothers greatly increased the work of the bacteriologist, who handled the testing scheme for Devon and Cornwall. The veterinary officer became more heavily involved in testing for cattle disease, while the advisory chemist tested huge numbers of soil samples, linked no doubt with increasing yields. The entomologist conducted a five year long wireworm survey, particularly of land brought into production by the war need. The Government also needed vast amounts of economic information, which the Department of the Agricultural Economics (which had been formed in 1926) at Seale-Hayne was well placed to handle for the South West Region. Thus it produced a detailed survey of derelict land in Devon and contributed to the National Farm Survey of England and Wales, analysing the data on some 26,000 farms in Devon and Cornwall.[69]

6.38, 6.39 During World War II, Seale-Hayne College reverted to its earliest role of 1916, the training of women for work in farming. These pictures were taken in the quadrangle. There were certainly a residue of men students in the college at that time.

[UPNAB, Seale-Hayne collection]

6.40, 6.41 Student groups, even those on short courses, certainly enjoyed their time at the College, and were not backward in expressing their appreciation, though they were not usually quite so bountiful as this group in 1946 which added the clock tower to the north wing.

[Photos: A.Kennerley]

The rapid changes in policy about the role of Seale-Hayne together with the extra demands being made on its staff and in terms of usage were hardly conducive to the balanced educational experience which would have been expected in more normal times. It is not surprising that when the Luxmoor (later Loveday) Committee on Higher Agricultural Education visited in 1941 and 1942 there should be some adverse comment. The farm was considered less than satisfactory and adverse comment was made about the lack of discipline and the decline in student social life. The Principal had not protested when the playing fields had been ploughed up on the order of the War Agricultural Executive Committee. The annual sports had been discontinued and student clubs had closed down. Commenting in July 1943, MAF officials felt that the rot had set in five years previously. They thought it time that the Principal, who, they believed "...did not appreciate the need for a healthy and active social life as a basis for discipline...", be relieved. They suggested that he be replaced by Mr F.W. Hankinson, who had been appointed Head of Agriculture and Vice Principal in 1933, but was then away working for the Cornwall War Agricultural Executive Committee. The Governors on this occasion supported their Principal, but had a change forced upon them when Mr Henderson Hogg died unexpectedly on 29 July 1943. There was no scope for the normal processes in making the new appointment. For reasons which are not clear, the Governors resisted the appointment of Hankinson, but were virtually forced to accept the alternative nominated by MAF, Mr A.W. Ling. He was appointed Temporary Principal following an interview on 11 August 1943, on secondment from Bristol University where he had been Agricultural Officer until his transfer to MAF for war work. He was not confirmed as Principal until February 1946.[70] Although the war years offered little opportunity to improve facilities, the Governors were able to buy up adjacent land and properties which came on the market. In addition to Daracombe, they acquired Mallands, a 52 acres holding with house in 1942.

The end of the war brought new demands and opportunities. The retraining of ex-service personnel demanded an expansion of student numbers, for some of whom accommodation was created in the north block, while others were non-resident. In June 1947, there were 180 students (142 men, 38 women; 127 resident, 53 non-resident), of whom 90 were ex service personnel. There were some special short courses. The MAF annual maintenance grant was increased to £4,000, and the county grants were reinstated. £600 was granted by MAF for machinery purchase, and £910 for Broccoli research. Those of the advisory staff who were now formally structured in the National Agricultural Advisory Service, moved to a new base at Starcross, but in other respects the pre-war usage of the College for agricultural meetings and events was resumed. However, one outcome of the ending of hostilities, which would have a negative effect on Seale-Hayne, was the establishment at Bicton, South Devon, of a temporary agricultural training institute for ex-servicemen with an emphasis on horticulture. When this was made a permanent college under the County Council, filling a gap

6.42 The arrival of Dr Ian Moore as Principal in 1948, saw the drafting of a far-reaching development scheme, which led Seale-Hayne College into expansion and new levels of attainment in its three areas of agricultural education, research and advisory services.

[UPNAB, Seale-Hayne collection, photo N. Horne, Newton Abbot]

in the area for that level of college, Seale-Hayne agreed to discontinue its horticultural course.[71] Perhaps this was something of a relief, as the college farm land was not really suitable for horticulture.

An important initiative at this time which reinforced Seale-Hayne's status as an institution concerned with higher education was the resumption of links with the University College of the South West at Exeter. As long ago as 1920 the College had been mentioned in a petition to the President of the Board of Education to establish a university college, as a possible constituent faculty. In 1927, relationships with Exeter got as far as a draft scheme to facilitate co-operation and intercourse, the preparation of students for the Degree of BSc (Agric) and the interchange of staff and students. Although a few Seale-Hayne students did take degree courses, the scheme got no further, despite Exeter's receipt of an endowment for a chair of agriculture. Principal Murray of UCSW initiated the new moves for co-operation in 1944. Discussions led to Principal Ling being designated Professor of Agriculture and to an agreement that a degree in agriculture would be offered to Seale-Hayne students from 1949.[72]

Revitalisation, redevelopment and expansion

The adjustments of the immediate post war years had not been easy for Seale Hayne; there had been several staff changes and, with barely a 50% pass rate, the student performance had yet to return to the standard achieved between the wars. The resignation of Principal Ling in April 1948, probably came as no surprise to the Governors, and it was anticipated at MAF.[73] For the first time since 1919, the Governors were able to go through the selection process for their Principal under normal circumstances. Their choice, Dr H.I. Moore of Leeds University, was to prove to be just what the college needed to bring it to a high level of attainment in a period when the Government was prepared to spend money on vocational and technical education. Twenty three years later he would retire leaving the College very much in his debt.

6.43, 6.44, 6.45 The use of the College farm for student practical instruction offered considerable variety. These three illustrations show butter and cheese making, and poultry dissection.

[UPNAB, Seale-Hayne collection, photo: Fox Photos]

Principal Moore quickly embarked on a complete re-evaluation of the educational work of the college, a survey of college premises and facilities and an assessment of the condition of the farm, buildings and equipment. Ten years of austerity and state control of resources had taken their toll. His reports showed that in many areas the need for remedial action had become critical and could not wait for the MAF funding evaluations to run their course. In the College, for example, the paths in the quadrangle were so badly potholed as to constitute a danger to students, while the lack of changing and bathing facilities was a major obstacle to the conduct of student sporting activities as well as an embarrassment when receiving visiting teams. On the farm, the farm tracks were ankle deep in mud, while the crop of lucerne grass was ready for cutting but there were no pit silos, so he had purchased two sectional silos to allow the crop to be ensiled without further delay. Altogether there were ten college items and eleven farm items, estimated at £4,912 and £7,361 respectively, in Stage I of the Principal's scheme. Stage II applying to the farm only included five further items estimated at £2,800, while Stage III resurrected the plan for a new wing to the college (in excess of £20,000) mainly to provide accommodation for the 60 students staying in Newton Abbot. The Governors hoped that MAF would fund half the cost of the scheme, but would need permission to borrow to finance their share.[74] The educational dimension of the Principal's assessment included retaining the college diplomas in agriculture and dairying, re-instating the degree in agriculture, a post-graduate course in dairy husbandry, and short courses for farmers and teachers. The educational role of the farm should take the form of a demonstration unit, a research centre and example of progressive farming. But with only ten academic staff in post there was an urgent need to strengthen the team. Moore's request for four new staff was promptly agreed and they were in post early in 1949.[75]

As a result of this programme, student numbers were progressively increased from 145 when Moore arrived to 259 in 1956/57, settling at about 250 until the 1970s. By 1954 there were some eighteen academic staff and altogether some 90 college employees (Table 6.4).

Table 6.4

Seale-Hayne Agricultural College Staff, 1954.

Academic		*Non-Academic*		*Farm/Estate*	
Principal	1	Tech Asst	1	Bailiff	1
Burser/SL	1	Scientific(NIAB)	3	Farm workers	12
Warden	1	Lab. Assistants	8	Head Gardener	1
Sen. Lecturers	3	Administrative	4	Horticultural	6
Lecturers	6	Steward, Matron,			
Nurse	3	Skilled	4		
Asst/PT Lect.	6	Catering, Cleaning	28	General	2
Totals	18		47		26

Source: PRO, ED 174/158, a return from the college dated May 1954. Note: the NIAB staff were, of course, externally funded.

6.46 This view shows the student common room as it was in the 1950s.

[UPNAB, Seale-Hayne collection, photo: Fox Photos]

The Principal's interest in educational matters, arising from his lengthy experience at Leeds University, was expressed in another early innovation, a personal tutorial system linking designated students with particular members of staff for personal support in social as well as academic matters. He also reintroduced the annual speech day, promoted student sporting and society activity, and instituted an annual staff dance. He sought to instil in Seale-Hayne students a sense of direction and motivation from the moment they arrived, through his description of a painting, "The Avenue":[76]

"There is a long straight avenue with people proceeding to the principal building at the end - a building of mellow red brick closely resembling our own College - here is a portrayal of purpose. And then in the side-walk you will find a man and woman chatting - this denotes fellowship. In the middle foreground a man, gun over his shoulder and a dog at his heel seeks the sport and enjoyment of country pursuits. Another is busily engaged at his daily toil pruning trees, a routine job, but one which requires knowledge and skill. And so, portrayed on canvas in mellow colours, we visualise our goal, our daily work, our leisure and out friendships all blended into a perfect whole, a superb work of art, masterly in conception, scintillating with the sheer joy of craftsmanship and left behind for posterity. What are we doing today - working with a purpose? What are we going to leave behind - something of real value? Will the land be in better heart for our endeavours? I firmly believe the College is fulfilling her vital role of responsibility and abundant confirmation of this belief comes from my daily post bag. It is necessary to keep the picture of "The Avenue", the straight road leading to the goal, constantly in mind."

6.47, 6.48 In the 1950s and 1960s the College gained a number of new buildings, included the Great Hall, a general purpose theatre/hall the lack of which in earlier years must have inhibited the indoor presentation of events for large audiences.

[UPNAB, Seale-Hayne collection, photo: A. Kennerley]

In many respects the student experience in this period would not have been too different from that in the 1930s. The majority were residential and many of the same student led activities were continued especially the sports: rugby, soccer, hockey, boating, cricket, tennis, running. Squash, rifle caving and indoor sports were also available. Other societies included Agriculture, debating, motor, birdwatching, Christian Union, photography, and social entertainments. The College magazine, The Sealehaynian, now appeared once a year with content very similar to its pre-war predecessor, including a section about the Old Sealehaynians.[77]

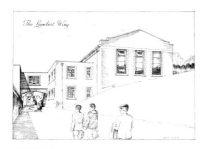

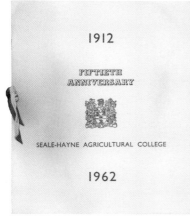

1912

FIFTIETH
ANNIVERSARY

SEALE-HAYNE AGRICULTURAL COLLEGE

1962

ERECTED IN CELEBRATION OF
THE GOLDEN JUBILEE OF THE COLLEGE AND TO COMMEMORATE THE WORK OF
GEORGE, VISCOUNT LAMBERT, P.C.
FOUNDATION CHAIRMAN OF THE GOVERNING BODY
FROM 1912 UNTIL HIS DEATH IN 1958.
THIS BUILDING WAS OPENED ON 28TH NOVEMBER 1962 BY
JAMES SCOTT HOPKINS ESQ., M.P.
JOINT PARLIAMENTARY SECRETARY TO THE MINISTRY
OF AGRICULTURE FISHERIES AND FOOD.

*6.49, 6.50, 6.51 This extension, the Lambert
Wing, proposed in the 1930s, finally came to
fruition in 1962. Its name commemorates the
founding chairman of the Governors, who had
died in 1958.*

[UPNAB, Seale-Hayne collection, photo: A. Kennerley]

The goal for most students was to remain for some time the two year
college diplomas (the three years course was not reinstated after the war)
with the opportunity to sit the national examinations as before. The
Principal's aim to offer a degree course in agriculture was to be frustrated,
although plans with UCSW at Exeter were sufficiently advanced to plan an
entry for 1950 and an honours entry in 1952. However officials at MAF were
concerned about the initiative even in 1948, and in 1947 the report of the
Loveday Committee firmly emphasised the segregation of agricultural
education at the three levels of institute, college and university department,
with colleges like Seale-Hayne offering diplomas. However, Seale Hayne
was allowed in 1953 to introduce a post diploma course in Farm
Management, which came in for much praise when the Murray Quinquennial
Grants Committee visited the College in 1955. This course owed much to the
Principal's involvement in a similar course when he was at Leeds University.
Educational policy was becoming increasingly short lived, and in 1958 the
De La Warr Committee on Farm Institutes suggested that colleges should run
three year courses. When the Robbins and Bosanquet committees reported,
Seale Hayne had already moved to three year courses. The Principal felt that
the College was already well advanced with its course development, and that
these last two reports would not impact on the college to any extent. With the
build up of a long waiting list towards the end of the 1950s, the College was
well aware of one of Robbins' conclusions, the need for graduates in
agricultural education. The Principal gave evidence to the next committee to
look at Agricultural education, the Pilkington Committee (1964), but the
proposal for a three years course in Dairy Technology at HND level, a topic
favoured by Pilkington, ran into difficulties with the Department of
Education and Science which had assumed responsibility for agricultural
education from MAF in 1964. The development of courses carrying national
qualifications was finally agreed with the DES at the end of 1968. This
allowed for a three year HND in agriculture, a diploma in agricultural
business and management studies, a diploma in milk production technology
and an OND in food technology. In 1970 the college was in debate with
Plymouth Polytechnic over a DMS (agriculture) and with Bristol Polytechnic
over an HND in Applied Biology.[78]

THE THOMPSON BEQUEST
THIS BUILDING WAS OPENED ON 14TH OCTOBER 1967
BY
SIR FERDINAND CAVENDISH-BENTINCK K.B.E. C.M.G. M.C.
FOUNDER OF THE TRUST FUND.
SIR GEORGE C. HAYTER-HAMES, C.B.E.   H. IAN MOORE, C.B.E. M.SC.
M.A. LL.B. D.L. J.P. C.A.   PH.D. N.D.A. Dip. Agric. Sc.
CHAIRMAN OF THE GOVERNING BODY   PRINCIPAL

TO THE MEMORY OF
WILLIAM BROWNRIGG THOMPSON
1880 TO 1952
A SETTLER WHOSE BELIEF IN AND SUPPORT FOR
EUROPEAN SETTLEMENT IN THE HIGHLANDS OF KENYA
MADE POSSIBLE THE ERECTION OF THIS BUILDING

*6.52, 6.53 As well as receiving Government
grants for new building, the College benefited
from bequests, such as this building for the
Thompson School of Animal Health.*

[Photos, A. Kennerley]

6.54, 6.55 *Another bequest, from Frank Parkinson, allowed the building of the Frank Parkinson Hall of Residence, and a later extension.*

[Photos, A. Kennerley]

There were also ups and downs in the redevelopment programme, though there was never a year in which some new building or renovation was not taking place. The oft proposed new wing to the college was yet again postponed, to be finally completed in 1962. It was opened on the fiftieth anniversary of the laying of the college foundation stone, 28 November 1962, and named after George Lambert who had died in 1958. However, four staff houses were completed in 1951, and the Great Hall in 1954. The National Institute of Agricultural Botany building opened in 1955 and the college laboratories were re-equipped in 1956. A further building programme was drawn up in 1960, which in addition to the Lambert wing, produced the college chapel (with significant donations from Old Sealehaynians), 1966, the Thompson School of Animal Health, 1968, and the student union building, the Moore building, 1969. In 1971 a start was made on a new library and teaching block. As before these had been achieved through funding supported by the DES. But a major donation amounting to over £200,000 from the Frank Parkinson Trust, allowed the building, progressively, of a student accommodation block, 1958 (centre block), east and west wings in 1965. A north wing proposed in 1971 did not materialise.[79]

On the College farm, the programme of improvement included six workmen's cottages (1952), re-equipping the dairy (1955), a balance and mill room and a sewage scheme (1958), a cattle building (1965) and a machinery management hall (1971). The South Devon herd was sold in 1957 when a beef herd was being developed, and a zero cropping policy was adopted in 1958. The herd had to be slaughtered early in 1968 owing to the out break of foot and mouth disease, which for a time severely affected college activity owing to the restrictions imposed on movement. Additions to the estate included the purchase of Blackmore Farm in 1964.[80]

6.56 *Seale-Hayne College was honoured on a number of occasions by royal visits. As early as 1932 it had received a visit by the then Duke of Kent. In May, 1969 it played host to Her Majesty, Queen Elizabeth the Queen Mother, seen her with Principal Moore (right).*

[UPNAB, Seale-Hayne collection]

Research and publishing remained an important part of the academic work throughout this period, with grants for example being received for grassland research (the Cambridge Plant Breeding Institute maintained an outpost at the College) and mastitis studies. There was a steady flow of research publications and the College yearbook achieved wide recognition. A feature in the calendar was the lecture series sponsored by the Devon Agricultural Association, and others, which were regularly published. The College continued to be used for conferences and other agricultural events. There were innumerable visits, notably from overseas where the College enjoyed a good reputation. A highlight was the visit of Queen Elizabeth, the Queen Mother, in May 1969.[81]

6.57 *In April, 1984, H.R.H. the Prince of Wales chaired a conference on land use at the at Seale-Hayne, and returned in April, 1986, to visit the College, seen here with catering staff.*

[UPNAB, Seale-Hayne collection; photo, Sunday Independent]

6.58 Dr. D.J. Dowrick succeeded Professor Moore as Principal of Seale-Hayne Agricultural College in 1971.

[UPNAB, Seale-Hayne collection; photo: N. Horne]

Further expansion, partnership and merger

It might seem curious to link loss of independence (1989) with the physical developments of the 1970s and the trebling of student numbers to 1,000, but such were the changes in the state approaches to higher education in the next two decades, that despite enlargement, Seale-Hayne would become increasingly vulnerable, and eventually have to face merging or closing. With the benefit of hindsight, it is possible to identify the start of the inexorable process which was to draw Seale-Hayne College fully into the state higher education system, with the last years of Professor Moore's term as Principal. For agricultural education the Pilkington report had started the move towards national qualifications under the joint committee system. Though he warned of the dangers to College independence, Principal Moore thought it could manage the change and supported the development of a degree under the Council for National Academic Awards (established 1964), as a means of sustaining that independence. However, successful though his tenure had been, in the much larger educational world of the DES (compared with MAF), Seale-Hayne was just one of a large number of small colleges which were looking increasingly old fashioned in scale, funding, courses and internal management. Certainly the loose internal management structure was really little changed from what had existed in the inter-war years.

Perhaps he wanted to make his mark, but the new Principal from September 1971, Dr. G.J. Dowrick, lost no time in spelling out to the Governors the reality of their relationship to the DES. They could make no decision on new courses without DES agreement, and they could take no decision resulting in change to financial expenditure without DES consent. These key elements in the direction of the College were outside their control. The Governors had control over things not requiring DES permission: "...essentially those matters over which the DES do not wish to exert control...such as internal organisation...".[82] Even here it would not be long before state measures would impinge on the internal organisation of colleges. In this respect Dr Dowrick's proposals for internal changes were abreast of, if not ahead of, national developments. There should be clearly defined departments and sub-sections, nominated course directors and tutors. The Board of Studies should be re-organised and an academic board established. There should be a staff/student academic committee. He looked to expand the College rapidly to 450 students over the coming five years.

The planned changes were introduced over the next year or two, as was the substitution of national awards for the various college awards upon which the reputation of Seale-Hayne had been developed so strongly. By 1974 the portfolio of courses included the OND (Agriculture), which proved to be very successful, HND (Agriculture), HND (Applied Biology), HND (Natural Resources/Rural Economy), OND (Food Technology), a post diploma course in farm management, and a DMS (Agriculture). The list of courses was soon extended to include an HND in Food Technology and a post diploma course

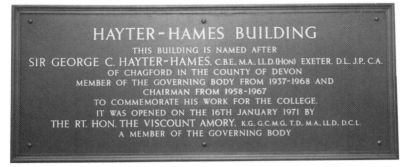

HAYTER-HAMES BUILDING
THIS BUILDING IS NAMED AFTER
SIR GEORGE C. HAYTER-HAMES, C.B.E., M.A., LL.D.(Hon) EXETER, D.L., J.P., C.A.
OF CHAGFORD IN THE COUNTY OF DEVON
MEMBER OF THE GOVERNING BODY FROM 1937-1968 AND
CHAIRMAN FROM 1958-1967
TO COMMEMORATE HIS WORK FOR THE COLLEGE.
IT WAS OPENED ON THE 16TH JANUARY 1971 BY
THE RT. HON. THE VISCOUNT AMORY, K.G., G.C.M.G., T.D., M.A., LL.D., D.C.L.
A MEMBER OF THE GOVERNING BODY

6.59, 6.60 The Hayter-Hames Building, concerned with machinery management, opened in 1971. One of its lecture theatres was equipped with a turntable and barn-sized doors so that farm machinery could be brought in to allow demonstrations.

[UPNAB, Seale-Hayne collection; plaque: A.Kennerley]

in Work Organisation and Planning. With a change in attitude at the DES, and encouragement from the HMI most closely connected with the College, Seale-Hayne could at last contemplate offering degree courses. However, the initial exploration of a degree proposal with the University of Bath in 1975 did not bear fruit. But by January 1977, this time working with Plymouth Polytechnic, the DES was being sounded on its attitude to a CNAA degree. A successful CNAA visit was made in June 1978, and the BSc Agriculture was approved in September, just in time for an HMI inspection. The first entry in September 1979 were following an ordinary degree, but by 1982 an honours stream had been approved. In 1988, in anticipation of merging with Plymouth Polytechnic, a BSc Combined Honours with options in Food Resource Management and Rural Resource Management was validated. These were the courses which, after further revalidations and inspections, were to see Seale-Hayne through to the end of the 1980s. By 1982, the eight courses then being offered mostly oversubscribed and the SSR was at the level of 12.8 students to one member of staff. These course developments together with improved facilities allowed numbers to be expanded to 622 students by 1988/89.[83]

Of course, the expansion in student numbers could not have been achieved without additional accommodation, and in any case there was still a need to enhance the range of other facilities to bring Seale-Hayne up to modern standards for a teaching institution. Fortunately, in the 1970s, the Government was still prepared to carry most of the funding for capital developments. The Hayter-Hames Building, devoted to machinery management, was opened in 1971. Essential for upgrading the level of courses was the new library/teaching block, which was completed in 1972. This was named the Devon Building in honour of the centenary of the Devonshire Agricultural Association. The Sports Hall was completed in 1974, the Food Technology Laboratories, and in 1977 a new accommodation block at Daracombe, Hosking House, was opened. In 1979 a bequest financed a set of squash courts. The Science block was completed in 1981, three years after it was allocated finance by the DES. The new refectory was ready for use in 1982, and in 1986 an extension to the Food Technology Laboratory.[84]

From the 1970s the students were allowed much more control over their affairs, for example in running the College bar themselves. The Sports Hall,

THE DEVON CENTENARY BUILDING
THIS BUILDING IS NAMED TO COMMEMORATE THE CENTENARY
OF THE DEVON AGRICULTURAL ASSOCIATION IN 1972
AND WAS OPENED ON 7TH OCTOBER, 1972
BY HER MAJESTY'S LORD LIEUTENANT OF DEVON
THE LORD ROBOROUGH, J.P. Hon. LL.D. C.A.
PRESIDENT OF THE ASSOCIATION AND MEMBER OF THE GOVERNING BODY

6.61, 6.62. In the 1930s the College Library had been severely criticised. The College finally gained a proper facility with the opening of the Devon Building in 1972.

[UPNAB, Seale-Hayne collection; photos: A.Kennerley]

6.63, 6.64 As in earlier periods student experience on the College Farm remained an important part of their education. Here students are seen learning hedge laying and studying ploughing.

[UPNAB, Seale-Hayne collection)

which came into use in 1974, provided opportunities for new sports, including judo, volley ball, net ball and archery, which joined the extensive list noted earlier. Women were also achieving greater prominence in student affairs, though for many years care had been taken to ensure female representation on the student union committee. In the 1980s the Seale-Hayne Rag week was increasingly successful, raising, in 1987, a massive £14,500 for the selected charities. The Old Seale Haynian Club continued to recruit a significant membership from amongst leaving students thereby helping to sustain a strong alumni association.[85]

Despite the diversification in courses offered, the College farm remained an important adjunct to the work of the College, although the building programme and road improvement of course meant a small loss of its acreage. In a review following the appointment of Dr Dowrick, the farm's unsuitablilty for arable crops was again noted and its grassland function

6.65 The final meeting of the Governors of Seale-Hayne Agricultural College was held on 25 February 1989. Back row: Lord Morley, S. Ward, T, Culley, Dr. R.M. Orr (staff), Lord Falmouth; middle row: J. Hosking, Prof V. Beynon, dr J.A. Kirk (staff), D.W. Sibley (staff); front row: G.R. Stallard, R.J. Michelmore, Miss J.M. Cleverdon (staff), C.A. Ansell (Chairman), Miss E.A. Gallup, Dr. R.F. M. Robbins (Director Plymouth Polytechnic), Dr. F. Harper (last Principal of Sseale-Hayne College/first Dean of Seale-Hayne Faculty), J. Scannell.

[UPNAB, Seale-Hayne collection, photo N. Horne, Newton Abbot]

endorsed: the College really needed to acquire a farm of about 400 acres suitable for arable crops. It had been expanded in 1969 with the purchase of the adjacent 78 acre Oaklands farm, and in 1976 the sale of Oaklands farmhouse realised £20,500 which was used towards farm improvements. Improvements in the 1970s included several items associated with milking and calf-rearing and the milking herd numbered 75 in the mid-1970s. The pig units were also improved, the breeding herd being about 55 sows. The farm also kept about 400 ewes. But an investigation in 1982 found that the pig and ewe operations were not particularly efficient. Indeed the DES subjected the farm and the College endowment to a detailed costings analysis in 1983, with a view to identifying funds for farm improvement. A major investment was made in the pig enterprise, from 1985, and there were a number of other improvements to farm facilities. In 1989 the dairy herd numbered 100, with 40 followers, beef cattle 40 animals, sheep 220 ewes and 190 lambs, and there were 1000 pigs. About 40 hectares were devoted to arable crops and some 1000 tons of silage was produced from the grassland.[86]

Despite the successful building programme and increase in numbers, those responsible for managing Seale-Hayne must have been increasingly concerned about the future of the College given the increasing number of changes which were being made by the Government to the provision, funding and management of higher education. In this process the position of the remaining ten or so direct grant colleges (of which three were agricultural colleges) became increasingly out of step. As early as 1973 the DES expected the College's expenditure on accommodation and catering to be balanced by the income from residential fees, which meant an increase in fees. This became a requirement in 1980, implying a possible increase of 39% in the charges. Also in the early 1970s state funded colleges were being required to adopt instruments and articles of government. The voluntary colleges such as Seale-Hayne already had regulating schemes for their management, but there were significant differences. Seale-Hayne Governors decided to bring their arrangements into line, which meant revising the 1915 scheme. They met under the 1978 scheme from 30 September 1978, and the following year and instrument and articles of governance were adopted. The 1980s were years of increasing difficulty. Responsibility for agricultural colleges was moved to the Higher Education Branch of the DES, but the creation of the National Advisory Body for Higher Education (NAB), to which responsibility for the agricultural education would be transferred from 1 February 1985, introduced more uncertainty. NAB created a subject board to review agricultural education provision in 1983, the year that Seale-Hayne's grant was cut by 5%. The following year funding on a 'unit of resource' basis was introduced. Then the white paper on the future of higher education, which proposed giving polytechnics their independence, indicated the ending of direct grant status.[87]

In this climate Seale-Hayne governors faced a dilemma: could they take the chance of a very uncertain future, become wholly independent and risk losing the state funding on which the College had always been dependent; or should they explore the possibility of merger with the chance of survival and

6.66, 6.67 These pictures from the 1990s show a Seale-Hayne bull on display at market, and students studying winter wheat growth on the College farm.

[UPNAB, Seale-Hayne collection]

enhanced opportunity for development as part of a larger organisation but with its implied loss of identity? The late 1940s ideas of links with what was now the University of Exeter had evaporated. The only realistic possibility was to join Plymouth Polytechnic with whom there were already close connections and which had already expressed interest. The issue was under discussion at least from 1984, and in 1986 Seale-Hayne participated in a meeting on a possible collegiate polytechnic with the DES, NAB, DCC, the Charity Commissioners and Plymouth Polytechnic. Clearly by then the Governors were seriously considering a merger, although at least one other agricultural college would opt for independence. Their main concern was for the survival of the Seale-Hayne name and for a strong faculty council of external advisers. In 1987 it became clear that the complicated merger would involve, in addition to Seale-Hayne and Plymouth Polytechnic, Rolle College at Exmouth and Exeter College of Art and Design. Seale-Hayne, as a charity, could only merge with another charity, so the other three colleges merged in 1988 as Polytechnic South West, and were joined from 3 April 1989 by Seale-Hayne once the new Polytechnic charity had been established. The Governors met for the last time on 25 February, 1989. Meanwhile Principal Dowrick, who had been made Professor of Agriculture by Plymouth Polytechnic, had resigned in 1988 on his appointment as a Deputy Director at the Polytechnic. His successor, from September 1988, was Professor F. Harper, who had been vice principal at Harper Adams Agricultural College in Shropshire. He would continue as the first dean of the Seale-Hayne Faculty of Agriculture, Food and Land Use.[88]

Seale-Hayne in the 1990s

As with the other colleges involved in the merger, no member of College staff and no aspect of College life remained unaffected. In his few months as Principal, Professor Harper identified six key areas of difficulty. The scheme overseen by the Charity Commissioners for the Seale-Hayne trust

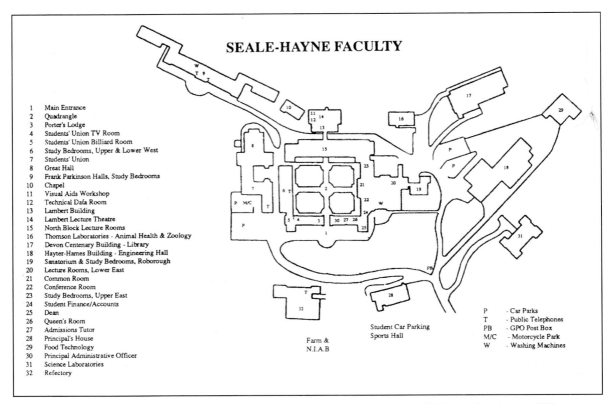

SEALE-HAYNE FACULTY

1   Main Entrance
2   Quadrangle
3   Porter's Lodge
4   Students' Union TV Room
5   Students' Union Billiard Room
6   Study Bedrooms, Upper & Lower West
7   Students' Union
8   Great Hall
9   Frank Parkinson Halls, Study Bedrooms
10 Chapel
11 Visual Aids Workshop
12 Technical Data Room
13 Lambert Building
14 Lambert Lecture Theatre
15 North Block Lecture Rooms
16 Thomson Laboratories - Animal Health & Zoology
17 Devon Centenary Building - Library
18 Hayter-Hames Building - Engineering Hall
19 Sanatorium & Study Bedrooms, Roborough
20 Lecture Rooms, Lower East
21 Common Room
22 Conference Room
23 Study Bedrooms, Upper East
24 Student Finance/Accounts
25 Dean
26 Queen's Room
27 Admissions Tutor
28 Principal's House
29 Food Technology
30 Principal Administrative Officer
31 Science Laboratories
32 Refectory

Farm & N.I.A.B

Student Car Parking
Sports Hall

P   - Car Parks
T   - Public Telephones
PB   - GPO Post Box
M/C - Motorcycle Park
W   - Washing Machines

6.68 This plan from the early 1990s shows the locations of Seale-Hayne buildings north of the College farm.

[UPNAB, Seale-Hayne collection]

was far from settled despite numerous drafts. Eventually, all the elements, land, buildings, prize funds, etc., became elements of a single scheme in which Polytechnic South West became the trustee. However, one or two aspects of the charitable arrangement involving Seale-Hayne were not finally cleared up until 1999. They included one safeguard concerning the disposal of land, which could be sold, exchanged or otherwise disposed of, subject to the agreement of the Faculty Council. This was not the Faculty Board but an advisory body to the Dean on the work of the Faculty. Five of the governors of the defunct Seale-Hayne governing body agreed to serve on this new body, which included academic staff and student representatives, the Dean and the Director of the Polytechnic, and representatives other outside interests. The position of Seale-Hayne staff was secured, with the agreement of the unions, by a transfer to the new employer at the same conditions and salary scales, with only the positions of the Principal, Vice Principal and Administrative Officer being seriously affected. The Polytechnic's system of funding, involving a top-slice of income to fund central services, was a threat to a college used to handling its own finances, but the agreement to waive this for a short period, secured the situation during the early period of adjustment. Another problem was the merging of four student unions into a single body, but the presidents involved worked out a new constitution which left Seale-Hayne students a good measure of autonomy to conduct their own affairs. In contrast, the freedom of the new Dean to manage all matters affecting the Seale-Hayne

6.69 This scene in the mid 1990s, of students moving between classes, is not so very different from a similar grouping from the mid-1920s.

[UPNAB, Seale-Hayne collection]

site was reduced to maintaining an oversight of campus functions and facilities. Perhaps the matter which caused most upset amongst people at Seale-Hayne concerned the image of the new faculty to the outside world, which was seen as something of a trademark. The less than sensitive imposition of new signs and note paper which down graded the words Seale-Hayne caused quite a reaction.[89]

In terms of diversification and course development the merger rapidly brought about a number of additional degrees, within the modular undergraduate scheme, which as noted above already conformed to the Polytechnic model. In response to changes in agriculture and land use, from 1990 Agriculture could be combined with Countryside Management, and there were new awards in Food Production and Rural Estate Management. A course in Hospitality Management was approved in 1991. In 1993 came a degree in Food Quality with Product Development and one in Tourism Management. Then from 1995 Agriculture could also be combined with the Environment and with Rural Estate Management, while to the Food portfolio of awards was added Food Biology. A post-graduate diploma/MSc course in Rural Development was also approved in 1995, to join Seale-Hayne's long established advanced course in Agricultural Business Management. By 1992/93 student numbers had increased to 857, and growth to over 1000 was anticipated through the additional courses. These were all four year sandwich courses, during which a year was spent in supervised work experience. In addition the Faculty continued to offer three HND courses of three years duration, including a year in industry. Of course the original focus in traditional agriculture was inevitably taking a smaller place in the work of the Faculty. A useful feeder for these courses has been the Extended Engineering course run in partnership at Bicton College of Agriculture from 1992. But Agriculture, like several other traditional industries in Britain, was going through increasingly difficult times, and with many farmers changing direction or leaving the industry, a decline in the numbers of agricultural students was inevitable.[90]

Research has also received a boost through the merger. Seale-Hayne has the longest tradition of continuous applied research of all the elements which now comprise the University of Plymouth. Nevertheless there was scope for much development in research and publishing. The great majority of academic staff now have research projects and the numbers of research fellows, masters and doctoral research students is increasing. The Faculty continues to serve the agricultural industry, in ways which would have been fully recognised by earlier members of its staff, through its research programme with studies such a the nutrition of pigs, management of uplands and soil nutrient studies.[91] The Faculty farm, run as a separate business without financial support from the Faculty, continues with much the same animal crop stocking as noted above. It remains the base for the NIAB in the south west. As a real business, it provides ample opportunities for a wide range of student case studies.

In 1993 the Faculty's courses were being delivered by 43 academic staff, approximately the same number as in 1980 when there were about 570 students. In recent years its HND courses have been phased out as collaborative arrangements with partner colleges have been developed. This now involves 24 programmes. However, with the development of more advanced work has come an increase in the number of students studying at masters level. 1997 saw the quality of the Faculty's teaching endorsed through an excellent rating following the teaching quality inspection. This covered all areas of work except tourism which was not part of the assessment.

The problems affecting the agricultural industry have not left Seale-Hayne unaffected. To counter the effects diversification has been essential.

New programmes in tourism and hospitality management have been developed, while under the agriculture heading animal behaviour and welfare are now subjects for study. Competition is severe in most areas of the Faculty's expertise and the differing social and employment expectations of today's students are making their impact. With a relatively isolated campus the continuing effort to improve facilities is important. A much greater proportion of students now live out, as the Faculty only has some 200 hall of residence places, though this is less of a problem than in the past with so many students now owning their own transport. Overall the Faculty presents a modern face to the prospective student with good recreational facilities and a full student life, yet within the rather special, indeed pleasant rural environment of what may still be termed a green field site.

6.70: Development Diagram

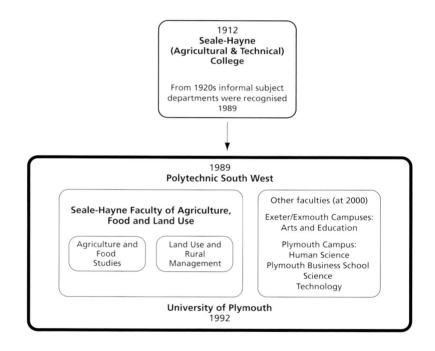

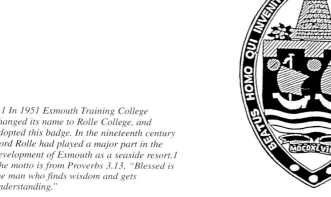

*7.1 In 1951 Exmouth Training College
changed its name to Rolle College, and
adopted this badge. In the nineteenth century
Lord Rolle had played a major part in the
development of Exmouth as a seaside resort.1
The motto is from Proverbs 3.13, "Blessed is
the man who finds wisdom and gets
understanding."*

Rolle

CHAPTER SEVEN

Although the range of higher education offered at the Exmouth Campus of the University of Plymouth, has broadened considerably in recent years, it is with the professional education of school teachers that Rolle has been concerned for the bulk of its existence since teacher training came to the town, unexpectedly, at the end of World War II. In many respects, its history over the past fifty years is inextricably linked with developments in Government policy on teacher education. Yet, from nothing there was rapidly developed an institution of national standing having innovative approaches to teacher education and offering a very satisfactory cultural experience to its students. For many years Rolle was able to maintain a position for applications at the top of the list of teacher education colleges. There was also a significant impact on Exmouth as a town in economic and social terms, the college being its first and almost only experience of an establishment of tertiary education. But Rolle did not exist in isolation. Only a few miles away at Exeter, there was a focus on education at the University College and at St. Luke's, while administratively its development was very much intertwined with the County Council, where in the early years it was the only institution of higher education under that local authority's oversight.

The professional education of teachers was no new idea in the 1940s. Leaving aside a short-lived university college at the end of the medieval period, teacher training colleges had existed in Britain for over one hundred years.[2] The Exeter Diocesan Training College, St. Luke's (1839), was amongst the first phase of foundations, which were the product of religious and voluntary effort and were concerned with elementary school teachers. The only other college in the South West from this early period was the Truro Diocesan Training College (1857). A limited training provision for teachers in service through evening classes held under the local science and art regime at Plymouth and Exeter was made also from mid-century, and full-time courses were developed in 1901 at the Royal Albert Memorial College, Exeter.[3] A further set of foundations came in the wake of the 1902 Education Act which allowed local authorities to operate teacher training colleges, though there was no initiative in Devon at that time. Rolle has its origins amongst the next collection of foundations in the wake of the 1939-1945 war.

Teacher education and training has always been something of a political football, but especially so in the context of state funding. This is not surprising. In more modern times teaching has been one of the few occupations of which everyone has had lengthy observational experience. Everyone has educational stories to tell, and a great many people are concerned about the quality and nature of the influences to which the next generation are exposed. With such a pivotal position in society, how teachers are prepared for their careers ought to be a key issue. Surprisingly, perhaps, there had been few significant government reviews of teacher training since the first set of foundations: Kay-Shuttleworth in 1846 (pupil teachers), the Cross Commission in 1888 (university involvement), the Departmental Committee in 1925, and in 1944 the McNair Report.[4] This last was of considerable influence in the relationships which Rolle would establish with its near neighbours in Exeter.

With a history of diverse approaches to and policy about the nature and content of teacher education and training, the debate on the balance between subject knowledge and vocational training has been ongoing and at times heated. At one end of the scale was the youth apprenticeship approach which meant that perforce training colleges devoted a significant proportion of courses to upgrading subject knowledge. At the other, a university degree, providing the subject basis, could be followed by a vocational course in a university education department or at a training college. By the 1940s, the former had disappeared, but only a minority of training was via the latter. The Exmouth Training College was destined to join the eighty existing training colleges which accepted students having basic school leaving qualifications, such as the school certificate, and which, in the two year course then standard, provided a combination of the two dimensions. In addition, on the vocational side, opinions varied about the importance of teaching practice in schools, and about the role of the colleges in developing the general culture of training college students.[5]

7.2, 7.3 The Southlands/Fairfield housing complex, previously the principal buildings of Southlands School, offered a convenient site for an emergency teacher training college at the end of World War II. The upper floors of Fairfield were adapted for the Principal's flat and provided study bedrooms for 39 students.

[UPEXM, Rolle Collection; Fairfield photo: R. N. G. Heanley.]

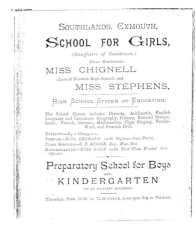

7.4 This late nineteenth century advertisement shows that Southlands had been a proprietary secondary girls school.

[UPEXM, Rolle collection]

7.5, 7.6 The former School's gymnasium and laboratory were put to immediate use in when the Exmouth Emergency Training College opened in 1946.

[UPEXM, Rolle collection]

7.7, 7.8 Brockhurst and Eldin were taken over from Southlands School, and adapted as halls of residence. Brockhurst was demolished in 1957 to make way for the Daw Building. Eldin remains in use as the Students' Union Building.

[UPEXM, Rolle collection]

Emergency College

It was in the middle years of the war, when the situation was at its most bleak, that those in official circles in London started work on 'post-war planning', which was to touch almost all areas of human activity. Their overhaul of social welfare and education provision is probably among the best known results. It was recognised early that a huge and rapid expansion of the number of teachers in state schools was essential, and that drastic measures would have to be taken to achieve this.[6] The factors leading to this conclusion included the loss of teachers to the forces, a serious decline in the numbers, especially of men, being trained by the colleges, the numbers of teachers reaching and staying on beyond retirement age during the war, a rise in the birth rate, the reorganisation of primary and secondary education, the raising of the school leaving age, the reduction in class sizes. Perhaps 50,000 extra teachers would be needed.

The solution was to be something like a military operation.[7] It would involve men and women released from the forces (and reserved occupations), after a process of application, rigorous interview, selection and allocation conducted by the Board/Ministry of Education. Sensibilities, for example about relative status of the emergency trained teachers, had to be suppressed: the course had to be short (48 weeks) and confer full certificated teacher status. Finance would come entirely from the state, but the co-operation of the local authorities, existing training colleges and university departments of education, was essential. For students, tuition would be free. The expansion required could not be absorbed by the existing colleges which had their normal work to do and were in any case rundown and depleted as a result of the war. New establishments were needed which had to be dispersed geographically because of the implications for teaching practice. In all 55 temporary colleges with 13,500 places, came into existence, which had to be found premises, residential accommodation, educational and social facilities, and needed to be staffed. This is where the local dimension was critical, although the staffing was partly satisfied by ex-service personnel who had previously been in teaching. About three quarters of the college staff came from secondary schools.

The Ministry of Education dictated the curriculum, the size of the student body (about 200), and thus the numbers of staff who would be needed at a staff/student ratio (SSR) of 1:11. Fourteen weeks was to be spent in schools on teaching practice. The remaining 34 weeks in college was divided between professional training study (principles of education, teaching method and visual aids, philosophy of education, psychology, health education, English language usage), and the study of general and cultural subjects (normally one major and one subsidiary subject from English literature, history, religious knowledge, geography, modern languages, mathematics, general science, physics, chemistry, biology, rural science, gardening, music, art, craft and physical education). There was detailed guidance on interpretation of the work in schools and in the college. In particular formal examinations were not considered appropriate: continuous assessment was to apply and guided private study time should be significant. The award was simply to be pass, refer or fail.

After initial publicity in 1944, the scheme was rapidly driven forward. By the summer of 1945 the locations for emergency colleges had been chosen, including the site of the former Southlands School at Exmouth. Exmouth Training College opened on 14 February 1946. Southlands had been a proprietary school for girls, which in the 1880s offered the 'high school system of education'.[8] In adjacent buildings there had been an associated preparatory school for boys and a kindergarten. Having closed prior to the war, with neglected, run down, but available buildings, this was the kind of site being sought for emergency colleges, and probably one of the more suitable ones. Apart from the problem of expansion in a suburb of large detached private houses, the location had much to commend it for a permanent establishment: close to the centre of the town yet by the sea and near the country, and within easy communication of the provincial centre, Exeter, where teacher education was well established and where the local authority was based. Probably only the most essential of repairs were undertaken before mostly second-hand furniture and equipment was delivered and the first batch of students moved in.[9]

Meanwhile, the search for staff had been going on: first the principal and then the teaching staff, to cover the subject range laid down.[10] Support staff was minimal, but nevertheless some help was required with medical, administrative, catering and site aspects. None of the appointments was to be permanent, as once the emergency scheme had completed its task, over three or four years, the majority of the colleges would be closed down. Early planning in London, however, had anticipated a need for a handful being kept on permanently to augment the provision pre-war.[11] The Principal, W.F. Morris, a geographer, had connections at Reading University, but it seems that the member of staff who made the most impression on the early students was the larger than life P.J. Floyd, a mathematician. In a brilliant caricature of Pepys' Diary,[12] he was described as "...one greatly capable of taking his pint." Floyd was taking the diarist to visit the "...colleg newly set up in these parts..." when they

"...were met by three rascallie knaves...Floyd...did assure me they were tutors by the name Burns, Gay and Dimond....We did later meet with one Mistress Bowen...a comlie woman

7.9 *Ryll Court was one of several large private houses off the Southlands site which were acquired by the College as halls of residents.*

[UPEXM, Rolle collection]

7.10 *Principal Morris took on the task of establishing the new college at the end of 1945. For the two years of his tenure, before it became a permanent establishment, he ran a relaxed regime for his almost entirely mature, mixed ex-service student body.*

[UPEXM, Rolle Call (1947)]

7.11 *Emergency college students took a one year intensive course to qualify as teachers. This is the 1947-48 group photograph.*

[Miss M. Perraton, Plymouth; photo: Eric C. Castle]

7.12 P. J. Floyd, caricatured in 'Pepys' Diary', was an early appointment by Principal Morris, who served the College for many years as head of mathematics.

[UPEXM, Rolle collection]

7.13 Open days, more for the townspeople of Exmouth than for prospective students, were a feature of the College calendar from the early days as an emergency college.

[UPEXM, Rolle collection]

7.14 Hear, O Israel, was one of not less than six production mounted by the theatre club in 1947-48.

[UPEXM, Rolle collection]

7.15 Sporting activity had become well established in the Emergency College period. Women's sports survived the change, and were well supported. The Hockey Club had 30 members in 1949-50. The team won six and lost two games.

[UPEXM, Rolle collection, Exmouth College Magazine (1949-50), 9]

withal and a great woman at Science and the studie of Biologie, a strange thing indeed. I did resolve to learn more upon that...the colleg...do consist of several houses new converted for the purpose...the scholars...were clean and seemly people and withal enthusiastick for the cause. Did find the Principal closeted with some strange people whom Mistress Bowen did assure me were H.M.I.'s. She did show me a fair room strangely equipped withal, and a machine called an epidioskop which do reflect cuts from print books on to a fair white sheet for the students to admire att, and such like figures as the insides of frogs and onions of Spain and the like. I did mightily wonder at itt and do resolve to have one if I can come at one cheap. From there to the librarie, a fair room in which the students do labour long hours. Led then to a commodious room wherein men stripp'd do disport themselves in a strange manner...Of evenings the students do retire themselves to this room and there dance mighty pretty as square bashing...Did meet the Principal here, a genial man withal, and a great man at cartographie...The whole buildings did take my eye for beauty and I do indeed believ that there is hardly the like among what they do call in these day Training Colleges."

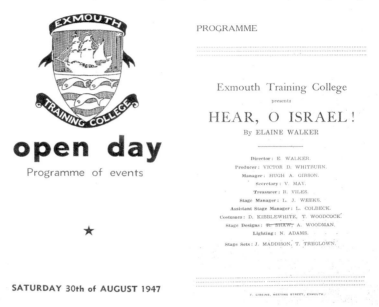

The old school buildings had provided the educational space but it was necessary to take over nearby properties as boarding houses. In Brockhurst, for example, in the summer of 1946 there were 31 students of whom 29 were married (37 offspring between them).[13] The students average age was 37 years. As they had numbered 33 on arrival on 21 February, presumably two had withdrawn. The Ministry had originally set the age range at 21 to 35, so this example indicates that the upper limit had been waived to admit a significant proportion of older people. In September 1946, resident students numbered 111 men and 69 women, and day students numbered 35 men and four women, in all 219 students.[14] Including the Principal there were fourteen male academic staff and five female; thirteen married tutors were residential. Contact between staff, including the Principal who was 'often around',[15] and students was excellent, and key factor in the life of a college where there was no overlap of successive student bodies.

So collegiate life became established very rapidly. Not only was there a student magazine within a few months and dances, as the extract from the June/July (1946) issue of *ETC* (Exmouth Training College) shows, but student societies were beginning to flourish: geographical, historical, music, debating, socialist, photographic, soccer, cricket, hockey, swimming, sailing. A sports day had been arranged for 10th August. A students' union was formed in 1947.[16] The Theatre Club was extremely active, with no less than six productions in 1947/48.[17] This enthusiasm was typical of all the emergency colleges. Service experience taught interpersonal and organisational skills and the necessity of making things work quickly, while the relative deprivation of their war experience meant, that, as well as a tolerance of the austere living conditions, these students were people in a hurry to get back to normal life. However, war service had its negative features, manifesting itself, for example, in the difficulty of adjusting to self directed academic study out of class. No doubt the benign regime was appropriate to the circumstances, particularly the recent experiences of the students, though at least one considered that discipline was a little too relaxed.[18] So the College was soon ready for its formal opening on 15 June 1946, which was performed by the Minister for Education, Miss Ellen Wilkinson.[19] Already behind the scenes, Devon County Council officials were opening the debate with civil servants in the Ministry, about the possibility of Exmouth Emergency Training College becoming one of the select few to be made permanent institutions.

7.16 Miss G. M. Croft was appointed principal of Exmouth\Training College in the summer of 1948 with a brief to develop the College as an all women establishment.

[UPEXM, Rolle collection, Rolle College Magazine (1959)]

7.17 The first timetable for the women's training college in September, 1948, shows that students had relatively little time to themselves.

[UPEXM, Rolle collection (re-typed)]

r Students			EXMOUTH TRAINING COLLEGE						Autumn Term, 1948	

TIMETABLE

	Division	9	1 9.20-10.00	2 10.10-10.50	3 11.10-1150	4 12.00-12.40	5 2.00-2.40	6 2.45-3.25	7 3.30-4.10	8 4.30-5.10	Voluntary classes
y	1											
	2	P		Special Courses			Private Study - Special Courses					
day	3						Tutorials - Visits - Field Work - Etc.					
	4											
	1	R	Psychology	History of Ed.		Physical Ed.						
	2		History of Ed.	Physical Ed.	Psychology		Private Study - Education					
day	3			Psychology	Physical Ed.	History of Ed	Tutorials - Special School Visits - Etc.					
	4	A	Physical Ed.		History of Ed.	Psychology						
	1						Physical Ed.	Health Ed.	English		Advanced
	2		General Courses				Health Ed.	Physical Ed.		English	Puppetry
esday	3	Y					English		Health Ed.	Physical Ed.	
	4							English	Physical Ed.	Health Ed.	Gardening
	1		Physical Ed.									
	2	E				Physical Ed.		Games			Gymnastics
sday	3		Educational Craft		Physical Ed.						5.15-6.00
	4			Physical Ed.	Educational Craft						
	1	R	Techniques of Teaching			Religious Ed.					Visiting
	2			Religious Ed.	Techniques of Teaching			General Interests			Lecturers
lay	3		Techniques of Teaching		Religious Ed.			Student's Societies - Etc			or
	4	S	Religious Ed.		Techniques of Teaching						Choral Soc
rday			Visiting lecturers or Choral Society								

Permanent College

Permanency raised issues and implications which had not had to be considered in the context of the war-driven, centrally controlled emergency training system. National considerations included forecasting the numbers of teachers needed, male and female, the geographical spread, the length and nature of courses, relationships to other educational developments, and, of course, finance in the context of the national economy. Local considerations included ownership and management, impact on local finances, the relationship with the local teacher training college and the university college education department, and the local effect of national policy decisions. So far Devon County Council had acted largely as the agent for the Ministry of Education though it appears to have acquired the title to some of the houses used by the training college, on its own initiative.[20]

7.18 The centre section of the 1949 College group photograph has staff seated in the second row from the front, amongst whom were some who had been re-appointed when the Emergency College was closed in 1948.

[UPEXM, Rolle collection]

DEVON COUNTY EDUCATION COMMITTEE

PROSPECTUS
OF THE

*Exmouth Training College
for Women*

ROLLE ROAD : EXMOUTH
1949

7.19 The Education Act, 1902, allowed local authorities to operate training colleges, but Exmouth Training College was the first such establishment to be run by Devon County Council.

[UPEXM, Rolle collection]

7.20 The dining hall in 1950 before renovation as part of Rolle College's first development plan.

[UPEXM, Rolle collection; photo, Henry Wykes, Heath & Praduse]

The merits of a local authority college in the South West were debated as though the emergency college at Exmouth did not exist. The areas around Bristol, Cheltenham and Salisbury were over-supplied with colleges, whereas the far South West was thinly provided, the Truro Diocesan Training College (women) having been closed in 1938 in a Church-instigated rationalisation programme. Since setting up the emergency scheme, biased towards men, the numbers of male teachers returning from the forces had exceeded expectations and there was now a shortage in the supply of female teachers: as St Luke's was a male college, the Ministry officials saw a case for a female college in the area. Undue competition with the Education Department at the University College at Exeter or the emergency college at Exmouth would be avoided if the emphasis was on the primary level. A new college should not be too far from Exeter or Barnstaple. The officials in Devon were certainly interested. Much of the running was made by the Director of Education for Devon, Elmsley Philip, who was to be a key figure facilitating the College's development in the early period. The idea was for a two year college (like most of the other training colleges), taking at least fifty students. Might it specialise in Physical Education? The Devon organiser for PE was very keen, but the cost of equipment was a disadvantage. The University College of the South West was also watching developments. Principal Murray wanted an umbrella school of education, dominated of course by his university college, as advocated in the proposals for area training organisations in the McNair Report. Thus the women's college should be located at Exeter.

7.21 This early 1950s development plan for the College shows the buildings inherited from Southlands School on the main site, and the phased addition of new buildings in the grounds.

[PRO, ED 78/228]

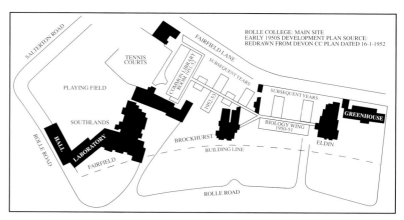

By October, 1946, the idea of making the Exmouth Training College permanent was put firmly on the agenda with a formal invitation from the Ministry to Devon County Council to consider the proposal, but it took until April, 1947, for the Council formally to express interest. The Minister endorsed the idea in October but haggling over numbers of students and finance took until the end of January, 1948, when numbers were fixed at 160/170 and the Ministry stipulated that at least fifty per cent of the output of teachers should be infant trained. Matters now moved ahead rapidly. The emergency college was already set to close in May, 1948, in anticipation of the opening of the women's college in September. Staffing was immediately an issue: would the existing staff be offered permanent appointments and should the Principal be a man or a women? There was apparently an undercurrent in the college in favour of a woman; the ministry thought a male appointment acceptable though unlikely, but it insisted that both men and women should be considered. Perhaps because Principal Morris was nearing retirement, the local authority seems to have settled on a change of leadership, and indeed all the staff were given notice. Twelve, including five men, wished to be considered for appointments in the new college. Exmouth Training College was transferred to Devon County Council on 31 July 1948.

The first task faced by Miss C.M. Croft following her appointment as Principal in the summer of 1948, was the tricky problem of appointing a full staff, in order to be ready to admit the first two year students in the autumn. Matters were complicated for her by the insistence of the Ministry of Education that the college take in a final entry of 75 one year emergency students at the same time. A strong nucleus of emergency college staff received permanent appointments in the new college, including Mr. Floyd who was to give lengthy service as head of Mathematics, but Miss Croft was to be disappointed in two of the staff she had hoped to retain on their appointment as heads of secondary schools. Nevertheless the permanent college owed much to the legacy of the temporary college developed by Principal Morris.

Principal Croft's background was such that it was quite possible that she was 'head-hunted' for the appointment. In World War I, in her twenties, she had risen rapidly to the rank of Commandant in the Voluntary Aid Detachment and had been awarded the O.B.E.[21] After studies at the London School of Economics and Exeter, she had been head of an evening institute in London, a lecturer at Rhodes University, South Africa, and Senior Lecturer and Warden at Avery Hill Training College in London. In World War II she was a Chief Commander of the Auxiliary Territorial Service, but had returned to Avery Hill before her move to Exmouth. This was a useful preparation for the struggles ahead. The male-dominated mixed ex-service student body was being replaced by young women school leavers. There was a new course to be introduced. The college was in competition with some one hundred other establishments, and could only offer roughly patched up run-down facilities. Raising the quality of the environment, establishing sound academic standards, and providing a rounded cultural experience were to dominate the eleven years of her tenure.

7.22, 7.23, 7.24 These three pictures of the Junior Common Room, the Biology Laboratory and the Art Room in the mid-1950s offer an impression of the improved facilities which became available under the early development plan.

[UPEXM, Rolle collection]

7.25 Rolle students at work in the science garden. Rural science was part of the curriculum in primary schools, and in the 1950s teacher training students gained experience by tending the College gardens.

[UPEXM, Rolle collection, Prospectus (1958)]

7.26, 7.27, 7.28 To accommodate increasing numbers of students, the College acquired more private houses in the area, including Hasledene and Dunsinane, shown here with one of the latter's study bedrooms.

[UPEXM, Rolle collection, Prospectus (1954)]

THE CHAIRMAN AND THE GOVERNORS
requests the pleasure of the company of
Miss V Daw
at the opening of
THE DAW BUILDING
ROLLE COLLEGE, EXMOUTH
on Thursday, 2nd July, 1959, at 3 p.m.
by
THE VERY REVEREND NORMAN SYKES, D.Litt., F.B.A.
DEAN OF WINCHESTER

7.29, 7.30 The Daw Building, on the site of Brockhurst, was the most substantial new building of the 1950s, providing additional educational accommodation including a new library.

[UPEXM, Rolle collection, Prospectus (1959)]

In the relationships between a college and its controlling authority, finance, both for running expenses and for improvement projects, always loomed large. As the legal employer, the local authority was involved in personnel matters and it had a duty to oversee the curriculum and general running of the college. At the same time the Government in London dictated much of the general policy on teacher education and training, allocating numbers of students, authorising the curriculum, distributing finance and inspecting delivery of training. Inevitably local authorities were sensitive about the levels of intervention by the Ministry of Education, in what was supposed to be their own operation. Principal Croft was far from satisfied with the local responsiveness to the physical condition of the College. In her first annual report (November, 1949) she did not mince her words:[22]

"I am, however, finding it very difficult to convince my Staff and the Students that I am representing to the Governors with sufficient emphasis the difficulties under which some of the Staff have to work in their cramped ill-equipped Class Rooms, and the basic discomforts and lack of essentials, quite apart from amenities, under which the Students have to live. I feel I am quite unable to impress the Governors with the really urgent need there is to remedy these matters."

Dry rot was rampant in three buildings, roofs were leaking making some rooms untenable on wet days, two gas boilers had been certified as dangerous. The reputation of the College was being affected, applications having fallen seriously.

In contrast, academically, the first year had been a great success, while the overlap of the temporary college had been a positive asset, socially and culturally, through the excellent example set by the temporary students. Miss Croft had been relatively free to design the curriculum, for which that at University College, Nottingham, had provided an example, but she had taken the precaution of submitting it informally to the Ministry of Education. The response had been positive and helpful. The course offered for Infant, Junior and Secondary work was:[23]

I   Basic Requirements (compulsory):
     a. English Language.   b. Physical Education.   c. Health education

II   Religious Education. Exemptions will be granted.

III The Principles and Practice of Education

IV   Special Courses Each student will pursue one well defined course of study including a piece of individual work chosen from the following:

English Language and Literature	Mathematics	History	Divinity
Physical Science	Geography	Arts & Craft	
Biological and Rural Science	Music	Needlecraft	

V   General Courses. Each student will normally take two general courses , one in each year, chosen from those set out in Section IV.

VI   General Interests. Each student is expected to take a live interest in some activity outside her coursework.

An important dimension of the emergency scheme continued in the permanent college was the introduction of continuous assessment, a departure from general practice at other two-year training colleges, though the unseen final examination was not abandoned until 1952.[24] Certainly, the absence of unseen examinations would become a factor in some student applications for places at Exmouth. Nevertheless, the initiative was fully endorsed by the glowing reports of the external examiners, who must have looked very closely at the innovation:[25]

"I can say with the utmost conviction and pleasure that both in its conception and in the way in which it was being carried out, the work, both in Mathematics and Physical Science, was most enlightened....Exmouth Training College has been able to put into operation things which I have advocated for many years and which have not been fully considered in other colleges in another area with which I am associated as external examiner."

"The work is satisfactory...and much to be commended. But I was particularly impressed by the attitude of all concerned...by the initiative and enterprise shown in the planning of the Course, and by the students interest in Child Study..."

"The work I saw...seemed to me one of the best things I have seen....They have what I think a good experiment"

"I should think that their standard and progress is equal to that of an older established college."

The HMIs were also impressed with the high standard of work at the final teaching practice and at the final exhibition of College work. Principal Croft was not impressed by the failure of any of the Governors to attend the exhibition! Another contribution to the image of the College was to be a change in name, to Rolle College, following the agreement of Lord Clinton, whose family had inherited the Rolle mantle, in the summer of 1951.[26]

7.31 Part of the new Rolle College library, opened at the end of the 1950s

[UPEXM, Rolle collection, Prospectus (1959)]

7.32, 7.33, Musical and dramatic events continued to be an important feature of College life in the 1950s. The annual 'fixture list' or programme included bookings by leading musical groups such as the Aeolian String Quartet.

[UPEXM, Rolle collection]

•. ROLLE COLLEGE

Douglas Avenue, Exmouth

★

OPEN DAY

The Principal, Staff and Students invite all who are interested to visit the College and its gardens on

Saturday, 3rd July

11.0 a.m. - 12.30 p.m.
2.0 p.m. - 4.0 p.m.
5.0 p.m. - 7.0 p.m.

★

A play centre for children under seven will be provided

7.34 Open days became major events in the 1950s. The provision of a Saturday play centre for local children greatly impressed Her Majesty's Inspectors.

[UPEXM, Rolle collection]

The real test of arrangements at the College was to come in May, 1955, when a team of thirteen HMIs probed every aspect of work and life, including continuous assessment. They "...were impressed with the thoroughness with which the College staff has planned the assessment arrangements..." and noted the support of the staff for the arrangements. They were not convinced, however, that students were making the best use of the time they were allowed for private study and recommended that students be instructed in study techniques. Similarly, although

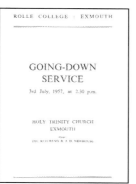

ROLLE COLLEGE : EXMOUTH

**GOING-DOWN
SERVICE**

3rd July, 1957, at 2.30 p.m.

HOLY TRINITY CHURCH
EXMOUTH

*7.35 Along with daily prayers, religious
events, such as the going-down service, were
voluntary activities which were well attended
in the 1950s.*

[UPEXM, Rolle collection]

*7.36 Miss D. E. L. Spicer, Principal throughout
the 1960s changed the whole atmosphere at the
College, seeing through physical and
organisational improvements which both
catered for expansion and made the
establishment an institution of higher education.*

[UPEXM, Rolle collection, Rolle College Magazine
(1960)]

*7.37 Rolle College was not without its local
dramas. On 17 May 1960, its Carlton Hall
(student residence) was burned down,
fortunately without any casualties.*

[UPEXM, Rolle collection]

undertaking a dissertation on an educational topic was an excellent innovation, student's choice of topics needed to be more strongly directed. But in general, on most aspects of its work the College came very well out of the inspection. The inspectors noted the huge improvements made in buildings, furnishings and equipment, but were worried about the disturbance caused by building operations which would continue for some time, and it noted the limitations on physical education due to the lack of adequate playing fields.

While the inadequacy of the College's sport facilities, a concern from the start, had yet to be resolved, great progress had been made in renovating buildings and grounds and in acquiring additional properties. Perhaps Principal Croft's criticism of the Governors in her first year did not make adequate allowance for the very severe problems facing local authorities in the immediate post war years. Certainly in subsequent years she made a point of emphasising their support in her public statements. The processes of securing approval for building work and the allocation of funds were tortuous, with numerous stages as discussion moved from between the College and local authority officials, the Governors, the county education and finance committees, and between these and the Ministry of Education as central finance was usually involved. Even once contracts had been allocated after tender, projects often seemed to get delayed well beyond their planned completion dates. The £12,000 allocated for the College in the 1950/51 County Council building programme suggests that the Education Committee "...had no idea how bad were conditions...expenditure would not be from the rates but from the national pool...there were only four class rooms at the college which needed fifteen..."[27] But the allocations for 1951/52 demonstrate movement on the building plan with estimates of nearly £100,000 to cover renovations and refurnishing of current properties, the acquisition of and equipping of additional houses and the building of educational blocks.[28] A further round of building development, at £80,000 was approved for 1956/57. The most significant structure resulting from this, the Daw Building, was opened by the Dean of Winchester on 2 July 1959. The foundation stone had been laid by Sir John Daw, former chairman of Devon County Council, on 26 March 1957.

While the College was certainly contributing to the economy of Exmouth, local people were not entirely happy about its continuing absorbtion of nearby property. This was associated with the acquisition by the County Council of other properties in the town for other purposes, dubbed by the newspapers County Council land-grabbing. Fears were expressed for the image of the town, which saw itself as a genteel resort, though the agitation may have been fanned by the belief that these were unnecessary expenses on the rates. Apparently, with respect to the College, the fact that the cost was poolable and largely a charge on the state, was not understood locally, as county councillors had repeatedly to explain the funding arrangements. Each house acquired by the College, of course, had an impact on adjacent private houses, but it was the proposal to acquire land at the rear of some private properties, currently used as allotments, which caused the greatest stir, and went to a public enquiry. In the event the college gained its playing fields in 1955.[29]

By the time of her retirement in 1959 Principal Croft had a two-year college in good order in most respects, with much of the cultural and academic achievement being due to the interest and enthusiasm of the academic staff in those formative years. Perhaps the management and operational style was a little too regimented, leading in the later years to tensions and turnover among staff.[30] Nevertheless, if the letters to Miss Croft from students who had recently completed their courses are a guide, most students were very appreciative of their time at the College, and of the roles played by the Principal and the staff. Student organisations were actively encouraged, not least by allowing a half day on the timetable for societies and clubs. Amongst the sports hockey, tennis, swimming, badminton, netball, had continuous support. The cultural societies which were well established included Geography, History, Music, Student Christian Movement, Art, Dance, Drama, Guide, Social Service. There was also a Social Committee and Student Representative Council. The 'fixture list' of events published in the annual magazine shows some forty cultural events: several visiting speakers, dances, student drama performances, music recitals, society special events and outings. Many were open to the public and the Principal put the college on the local map through invitations to attend these events.[31] In this period, the college day started with a short student and staff-led voluntary act of worship, which, the HMIs reported, was well attended. At Christmas there was a carol service and the year ended with a going-down dinner and service in Exmouth Parish Church. A student initiative which caught the attention of the inspectors in 1955 was the Play Centre run each week for local children in the College grounds. The inspectors concluded that "... the students find a very satisfactory community life in College and that they do not find the College rules unduly irksome".

Growth and Status

The change of Principal came at an opportune moment, and her more relaxed style was appropriate for the 1960s. There were new opportunities on the horizon. Miss D.E.L. Spicer arrived to see through a new phase of

7.38 The former heart of the College, the Fairfield/Southland buildings were demolished early in the 1960s to make way for the administrative/communal building which now occupies the western end of the main site.

[UPEXM, Rolle collection]

7.39, 7.40 The main entrance to the College is largely unchanged since its completion nearly 40 years ago. The new student common room in the mid-1960s, remains the link between the administrative and student sections of the building.

[UPEXM, Rolle collection; photos: A. Kennerley, Prospectus (1965)]

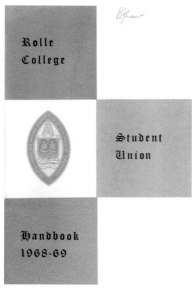

7.41 By the late 1960s Rolle College Student Union was offering the full range of services and activities including a bar and a shop. Though self-governing, it still had something to learn about managing its activities.

[UPEXM, Rolle collection]

expansion in response to developments in national policy[32]. In the mid-1950s the supply of teachers at last began to catch up with the demand caused by the growing school population, and a 'window' seemed to be appearing in which the long held aspiration of extending the length of the course to three years might be inaugurated. After taking advice from the National Advisory Council for the Training and Supply of Teachers (NACTST), the Government settled on September, 1960, for the start of the three year course. In simple terms, the training college population would have to expand by fifty per cent. But there were other factors. There had been a great increase in in-service professional development for teachers, through short courses and sabbaticals at training colleges, including Rolle, and there was the other long standing target of reducing class sizes. More significantly, the birth rate began to increase again and more children were staying on beyond school leaving age, then fifteen. The Government announced an immediate building programme to start the expansion of college places in 1958 and by early 1960 had authorised an expansion of 24,000 additional places and the target of completing the programme by September, 1966. Once again the debate on the nature and balance of courses raged, though ministry advice favoured increased the emphasis on academic work. In general though, the existing approaches were simply enlarged.[33]

Rolle was asked to expand to 400 students, and at the end of her first year Principal Spicer outlined the building plans drawn up by the County Council:[34]

"...a large social centre comprising student and staff common-rooms, two dining halls, kitchen, a fully equipped gymnasium and a new Hall fitted with an up-to-date stage... a new Science and Geography block, and additional Art and Craft rooms. The present new building will have to be adapted to extend the Library facilities, and make a centre for music activities. Residential accommodation will be supplemented by the erection of about ninety study bedrooms in the blocks on the Hasledene, Dunisnane and Seacroft sites."

For the first time since the days of the Emergency College, some students, about a third, would live in approved lodgings. Inevitably this new era would bring significant change in the life of the College.

The drama of 1959/60 had been the burning down of the Carlton Hill hall of residence, fortunately without casualties. The following year it was to be the Exmouth floods, in which the assistance of the College, students and staff, had not gone unnoticed. The playing fields in 1960/61 were waterlogged and unusable most of the time, but there were plans for acquiring additional playing fields. At least the pavilion was nearing completion.

400 was not to be the limit of the expansion. Discussions between the County and the Ministry were on-going. The County thought that Rolle was suitable for major expansion perhaps to 600, and in August, 1963, the Ministry set the numbers at 700 as that was within the capital outlay already allocated of £110,000. To growth was now added the aim of becoming co-educational, raised by Miss Spicer with the Department of Education and Science in June, 1964. A formal request to admit men as well as women and to expand to 900 was made in January, 1965, and the Department agreed in May, the change to be initiated in the 1966/67 session; men were to be thirty per cent of annual

intake.[35] Expansion to 840 students was not approved until 1969, and it was not until 1971 that the numbers of students at Rolle reached 886.

Hand in hand with the planning and development of the site, urgent consideration had to be given to the new curriculum, staffing and academic organisation for delivering the three year course to the rapidly enlarging student body. Full-time academic staff had numbered sixteen for much of the 1950s, and there had been one or two part-timers. Numbers began to increase in 1958. By 1964 there were 45 full-time and 6 part-time and by 1969, 81 full-time and 9 part-time. Add to these increases in support staff, clerical, caretaking, technical, catering, and others, as well as, of course, students, and it will be clear that the college of the 1960s was changing out of recognition from its earlier form. Another outcome of the government's expansion policy was to be an increased emphasis on primary training. For Rolle, this meant that the already minor proportion of students training for secondary schools would be further reduced. An innovation which started in 1961, was a collaboration with Dartington College of Arts, for specialist teachers of music. The creative arts had often featured low down the order of schools' priorities, and frequently such teaching was a part-time activity for artists and musicians who had not been too successful in their main interest. Dartington was producing teachers of the expressive arts "...for whom teaching was as important as their artistic achievements."[36] In the arrangement with Rolle College, the first year would be at Dartington, with the final two years at Rolle. In 1963 Rolle would offer a one year course for students already qualified in music. A final group of two-year students came to the College in 1961, but these were older people changing careers for whom special provision had been made.[37]

Meanwhile, in 1963, the Robbins Committee on Higher Education reported. As well as recommending the significant expansion of the numbers

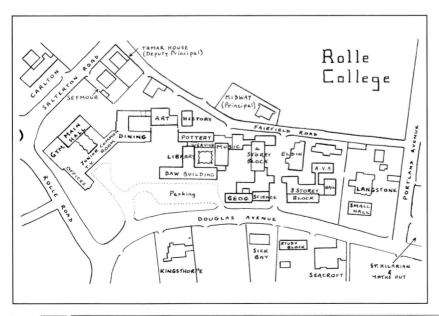

7.42 By the 1970s, the building programme on the main Rolle College site had been completed, so that this plan is as valid in 2000 as it was thirty years ago, apart from the relocation of some activities.

[UPEXM, Rolle collection, SU Handbook (1969-70)]

7.43 The Rolle College orchestra rehearsing under the head of music, Reginald Pocock.

[UPEXM, Rolle collection, Prospectus (1976-77)

7.44 Language training at Rolle College in the 1970s.

[UPEXM, Rolle collection, Prospectus (1976-77)

of universities, it made a number of recommendations designed to raise the status of teacher training colleges, including a closer association with a university through membership of the local Institute of Education, and the ability to offer four-year courses leading to the Bachelor of Education degree awarded by the associated university, for 'selected students'.[38] Rolle offered this opportunity in its 1968 Prospectus. The University of Exeter had created a School of Education, a federal relationship of its Department of Education, with St Luke's College and Rolle College. Registration of the first students was possible from September 1966, and a Board of Studies had been created to take responsibility for the academic arrangements. Students were required to have completed 'satisfactorily', one year of the Certificate of Education course, after which they might register for the three year B.Ed.[39] Education would be studied throughout these three years, together with a principal academic subject and an additional academic subject during the first two years. The academic subjects might be selected from: biology, chemistry, drama, economics, English, fine art, French, geography, history, music, pure mathematics, applied mathematics, physics, theology and physical education. Breaking Rolle's practice of continuous assessment, there were to be final examinations. Staff opinion was mixed. Miss Spicer "...felt that there was a certain value in occasional formal examinations...[and] any system of continuous assessment was open to criticism." However, one senior member of staff had doubts about the objectivity of examinations.[40] The dissertation, long a feature of work at Rolle, was part of the assessment for many subjects. Admission to the examination was dependant on having demonstrated 'competence in teaching' and having completed all other requirements of the course. The first twenty students were awarded their degrees in 1971. Involvement as part of higher education took another step forward when Rolle was invited by the DES to start a post-graduate training course from September 1971.[41]

Signs that there might be links further afield than those at Exeter and Dartington, came in 1967 when the DES asked the College to establish an outpost for mature students at Plymouth. Discussions did not progress well, and were overtaken by the offer of the London-based College of St Mark and St John, which set up the out-post.[42] The involvement of this college had long term-implications, as it was eventually offered Plymouth's 'site for a university' and moved there from Chelsea in 1973.

Student society at Rolle in the late 1960s had to adapt to the arrival of male students as well as to increased numbers. This was most obvious in sport where clubs for football, rugby and cricket were re-established. Men were certainly active in the students union where, in 1968/69, they held thirteen of the twenty-one official positions.[43] Most of the long standing union-recognised clubs were still operating, though the Student Christian Movement had given way to the Christian Union, and, of course, the Guide Club had become the Scout and Guide Club. The Principal made a point of emphasising that the student body was self-governing. Presumably students concurred with regulations which required them to sign a late pass book if they were going to be out of their halls of residence between 10.30 pm and midnight, and to apply two days in advance if they wished to request late leave beyond midnight. Friends 'of the opposite sex' could be entertained in student's rooms between 2.00 pm and 7.00 pm on Saturdays and Sundays. In addition to half term, two weekends away were allowed each term if application was made in advance. Absence through illness had to be supported with a medical note. Each hall of residence had its own student committee dealing with day to day matters in consultation with its warden. The Student Union was increasing in significance: it was already running a stationery shop and opened a bar in Autumn, 1968.

Fight for Survival

The expansion of Rolle, students, staff and facilities, continued through to Principal Spicer's retirement at the end of the 1971/72 session. Once again a change of Principal occurred when the future seemed healthy. The government had at last decided that all teachers in maintained primary and secondary schools, must be trained, which meant that graduates taking up teaching in secondary schools had first to take a professional course.[44] Then in 1972 the James Committee reported on its study of teacher education and training, and at the end of that year the white paper *Education: a Framework for Expansion*, accepted key aspects of the James report, including proposals for an all-graduate profession, expanding in-service training, further education teacher training and improved control of teacher training and supply.[45] However, the white paper also anticipated that some colleges would develop into major institutions in the public sector and widen their scope by catering for other social professions, though it allowed that this might be achieved through merger and that some colleges might merge with universities.

Small colleges felt threatened by this talk of merger, but Rolle had begun to think of itself as a large college and looked to developing as a free standing college. In May 1973, D.E.S. Circular 7/73, *Development of Higher Education in the non-University Sector* appeared, emphasising the 'binary' divide in higher education between the universities and establishments like polytechnics and colleges of education in the public sector. Local education authorities were required to submit proposals for the colleges under their control in April, 1974. Devon only had Rolle to consider, though of course it had a Polytechnic some distance away at Plymouth. At Rolle, thought was given to closer co-operation with St. Luke's, and even the possibility of merger was mentioned.[46] By September 1974, it was becoming clear that the Government was intent on reducing the numbers of teacher training places, and developing other higher education courses. It was not in favour of monotechnic establishments. Both Rolle and St. Luke's were very dubious about the merits and practicality of merging. Meanwhile St. Luke's was having discussions with the University of Exeter which were to lead to agreement on a merger, in 1975. However, the College of St Mark and St John had moved from London to Plymouth in 1973, and had joined the Area Training Organisation becoming a local factor in the allocation of training places, as well as an institution with whom liaison

7.45 *The shock inclusion of Rolle College early in 1977 amongst the teacher education colleges to lose their funding, led to an epic fight led by Principal Cammaerts to avert closure. It was closely followed and supported by the local press, but restoration of teacher education funding was not the end of the battle. Now the College had to diversify and prove itself in a range of new courses in the liberal arts.*

[WCSL, press cuttings collection: Express and Echo (Exeter)]

7.46 Francis Cammaerts, Rolle College Principal from 1972, was the right man at the right time to lead the fight for the College's survival in 1977/78. With the backing of Devon County Council, Governors, staff and students, and the press, every conceivable means of effecting a reprieve was tried, though the change of heart when it came was unexpected.

[WCSL, press cuttings; Express and Echo]

might be needed over new initiatives. But as a link with Plymouth Polytechnic had been rejected owing to the distance apart, the absorption of St. Luke's by Exeter University effectively left Rolle on its own. With the prediction that Rolle's share of the reduction of teacher training numbers would cause a decline from the present 890 to 600 places by 1981, the future seemed somewhat less secure.[47]

When the Government announced a general decision on the way forward in August 1975, following its consideration of LEA proposals, it was also faced with another factor, the declining birth rate, which was causing it repeatedly to reduce its allocation of numbers of teacher training places. Some colleges were not to be allocated any initial teacher training places. This meant that unless they had managed a significant level of diversification, they would be forced to close. Nearly eighteen months were to pass before the proposed fate of individual colleges was made public. The specialisms in teacher education which had been developed at Rolle and its geographical location, appeared to those associated with the college, and its staff, key factors which demanded its retention. So it was a considerable shock at the end of January, 1977, to find Rolle included in the Government's list of locations at which there would be no allocation of initial teacher training places after 1978.

The Principal from 1972, Mr F.C.A. Cammaerts, immediately called his staff together and announced an all-out battle to have Rolle's name removed from the list. There was widespread local support for the continuation of the college, and Devon County Council was fully behind the college in securing that objective.[48] In particular, the Chairman of the Governors, J.W. Stork, for whom the Stork Building is named, was to prove 'a tower of strength' throughout Mr Cammaerts' time at the College. The Principal had already pinpointed a weakness in the DES decision in relation to criteria in its general policy statements:

"...in terms of the impact on schools generally and particularly in terms of the importance of the in-service element in institutions doing initial teacher training, the geographical spread of institutions was of great importance...this part of England is very thinly provided with institutions of teacher education...

...we are the most sought-after college in the whole country...it was of great importance (to the D.E.S.) that colleges should be in a position to attract students and suitably qualified staff.

...they are concerned with preparing teachers for the shortage subjects, and our output of music teachers is one of the major features...if we were to cease initial teacher training [the effect] would be to reduce by 30%-35% the number of music teachers produced in the country."

Reputation was also important and Mr Cammaerts had no doubt that a 'pretty impressive list' of schools prepared to bombard the DES with protests could be produced; the impact would be powerful. People in Exmouth were certainly supportive. One resident asserted that Rolle was "... the only thing that keeps Exmouth alive."[49] Local parents valued the Saturday morning facility run by students, taking up to 400 children for out-of-school activities. There was extensive coverage of the fight back in the local press.

Defending the future of Rolle involved considerable behind-the-scenes activity co-ordinating protests, lobbying and preparing the closely-argued case for retaining initial teacher training at the College. The documentation developed the key points through a detailed national statistical analysis to demonstrate that the sub-region of Devon, Somerset and Cornwall merited special area treatment in relation to student places per school, student places per 1000 school children and student places per 1000 practising teachers, in each of which the region was significantly below the national average. Also drawn into the argument were Rolle's links with Dartington College of Arts, its overseas connections, its pre-school training emphasis as well as its primary emphasis, and the effect of closure on the local economy. Protests involving staff and students were mounted at County Hall and at Parliament in London where MPs were lobbied. The Secretary of State and Minister of State were lobbied at events in Exeter, Eastbourne, Torquay and Honiton.[50] A deputation from the College and Devon County Council, received at the D.E.S. in March, did nothing to brighten the prospect as little sympathy for Rolle's case was found amongst the civil servants present. Despite this reception, the courtesy of students and staff (notably a member of the non-academic staff during a demonstration at the DES offices) had impressed at the highest level (Shirley Williams was Secretary of State at the DES).[51] Eventually the sustained appeal was effective as, on 27 June 1977, the Secretary of State announced a reprieve, with a much reduced allocation of 350 places. Eighty per cent of these places were allowed for initial training, the remainder was to be devoted to in-service training. The implications were still severe, but with diversification the Governors thought it might be possible to sustain a figure of 800 students. However the County Council made it clear that it was essential that costs were cut, something most easily achieved through a reduction in staff.[52] There is no doubt that Principal Cammaerts' role in the survival of the College had been decisive.

It was the growth and scale of in-service education and training that were, in this difficult period, to give the College a new sense of direction and, of course, a new specialism. Indeed, by 1988 in-service education was sufficiently important to merit departmental status following Rolle's merger with Plymouth Polytechnic. Rolle staff became much more heavily involved in visiting schools to tutor and observe teachers undergoing in-service training, but the process also brought many teachers to the College for short courses or for short periods of research connected with educational projects. This was to lead the way teachers to undertake post-graduate study for diplomas and research degrees under the supervision of Rolle staff.

It took several years for the impact of changes in policy to work their way through at college level. Staff changes through resignation and retirement were on-going and the reduction in student numbers was progressive as earlier larger student cohorts successively completed their courses. Some staff were simply not replaced. A target for reduction to 66 to 69 academic staff was set for September 1979. By June 1978 it was known that fourteen staff were interested in voluntary redundancy. In the summer of 1979, ten

7.47, 7.48 Building developments of the late 1970s included the Spicer Building (above) and the Stork Building named in recognition of the contribution s made by the former Principal and the Chairman of the Governors.

[Photos: A. Kennerley]

staff posts were made redundant, but as part of the restructuring involved in introducing non-teacher training courses, four new positions were created.[53]

The diversification of courses also demanded an extended lead time, and the staff had been engaged in developing ideas and planning from the beginning of 1973. The college was in no more control of its destiny than it was with teacher education courses. The pitfalls were numerous. The staffing situation meant that it was in general limited to the subject capability of its staff, which, of course, was similar to most of the other teacher education colleges, subjects which were widely offered in universities. Rolle had no charter enabling it to offer its own awards, so it was dependent on validation by some other institution. Logically this was the University of Exeter with which it already had close relations, but on more than one occasion it contemplated turning to the Council for National Academic Awards (CNAA), established in 1964, which validated most Polytechnic awards. Validation established academic credibility and the award, but the course then had to get the support of the Regional Advisory Council for Further Education (RACFE) before undergoing the economic test at the DES: was there a demand and had unnecessary duplication been avoided? Even in giving its approval, usually in the first instance for a limited period, the DES dictated the numbers to be admitted. The duplication test applied locally as well. Rolle needed to offer courses which were different from those at nearby colleges, while the University of Exeter was certainly not going to validate any course which would compete with its own offerings. The circular nature of the processes meant that a college could expend an enormous effort in developing a course, only to have it turned down at the final hurdle, as the DES would only evaluate courses which had been fully developed academically.

Rolle staff worked on no less than nine new courses in the 1970s.[54] As well as re-designing the education degree, proposals included degrees in North American studies, expressive arts, urban studies, Russian/European literature, mathematics and society, community studies, environmental studies, and a certificate in theological studies. Though some proposals failed at the earlier hurdles, many were eventually incorporated as pathways in the modular BA in Combined Studies. The first course to pass all the hurdles was the BA in Urban Studies, to which nine students were admitted in 1978. It had originally been refused approval in 1976, when the expressive arts course was also turned down. Meanwhile the Combined Studies course was making progress, achieving RACFE support and DES approval in 1978. The first 51 students were admitted in 1979. Urban Studies admitted twelve students in 1979, but DES approval was withdrawn for 1980. The African studies course was submitted to the CNAA in 1979, but was not successful. The effect of the cuts became marked in the 1978/79 session when the total student body numbered 535, compared with 735 the previous session. However the diversification had not yet really become effective as the Table 7.1.

Table 7.1
Student Numbers as at 26 February 1979.

	Men	Women	Total	(1978)
Teacher Education Yr 1	11	59	70	(123)
Teacher Education Yr 2	19	97	116	(195)
Teacher Education Yr 2 (o/s)	19	1	20	(11)
Teacher Education Yr 3	27	152	179	(228)
Teacher Education Yr 3 (o/s)	11		11	(27)
Teacher Education Yr 4	14	37	51	(47)
One Yr. Prof Teachers	15	31	46	(68)
Teacher Education PG	11	21	32	(36)
BA Urban Studies Yr 1	6	3	9	
Special English	1		1	
Totals	135	400	535	(735)

Source: UPEXM, Governors minutes, 6 March 1979, College report.
o/s: overseas students (Kenyans).

The interest in American and African studies had been generated by links which had been built up with those areas. In the case of Africa the connection had been successful in bringing groups of students from Kenya and Botswana to study at Rolle; in America involvement with William and Mary College brought exchange students to England for periods of study at the College.

The student body, of course, had played its part in the fight for survival. Indeed in this period the significance of the Students' Union had been enhanced through the creation of the sabbatical presidency, representation on the Governing Body and Academic Board, and the allocation of its own building, the former hall of residence, Eldin, in 1976.[55] The Rolle College Club, which had existed as a financially separate student club bar, had been closely supervised by the Governors after being allowed to get into financial difficulty. Now properly incorporated within the Student Union under proper management, it was a profitable operation.[56] The Union also operated a shop and coffee bar and of course distributed financial support to approved student clubs and societies, which were as diverse and active as in earlier periods. Established annual events included the College rag week, regularly reported in the press, and the College open day in which student activity played a major part.[57]

7.49 Despite surviving the threat of closure in 1977, the future of Rolle College repeatedly came to the surface in the following years, as these newspaper headlines from 1984 testify. Indeed, behind the scenes discussions on the future of higher education in Devon (as elsewhere) were taking place throughout the 1980s.

[WCSL, press cuttings collection: Express and Echo and Western Morning News]

Restructuring and Merger

As the proportion of degree work expanded, the long standing staff structure of small subject departments devoted to teacher education approaches seemed increasingly inappropriate. Although part of the rationale in the development of BA courses was that some teaching would be joint with BEd. students, it was inevitable that staff became identified more with either the arts/humanities work or the teacher education work. The new Principal, Dr M. Preston, who succeeded Mr Cammaerts in 1981, therefore pushed through a re-organisation, with the support of the Governors, which created two faculties, one for the BA Combined Studies with 120 students, the other for Teacher Education with 480 students. He resisted the argument for a third faculty for in-service education.[58] If Rolle was to compete effectively with other establishments, it needed to be able to offer the highest undergraduate award, degrees with honours. Both the B.Ed. and the BA were revised in the 1980s, with the University of Exeter validating this higher level award. In the case of the BA award, the title Integrated Studies was adopted for a slimmed down set of pathways, the first entry of honours students being in 1985. This development went a long way to addressing some of the problems with the Combined Studies scheme, already identified by Rolle staff, which the HMI report noted in 1985. The previous year Rolle's initial teacher training courses, including the B.Ed., had a generally satisfactory report from a separate HMI investigation. By 1984/85 with 810 full time equivalent students (FTE) (335 full time teacher education students and 228 BA, 247 FTE in-service students), the College was recovering from the low point at the end of the 1970s.[59]

Despite the progress with diversification, there was to be no relief from the pressures created by changes in government policy. The exercise of state control was to change direction through cuts in the global sums set aside for public sector advanced further education and a move away from individual course approvals to institutional approvals. The latter favoured larger more broadly based establishments while the former forced all colleges to look closely at expenditure, as funding cuts were announced. The regional advisory councils would continue to offer the regional perspective, but a new body, the National Advisory Board (NAB) was given the job of recommending policy to the Secretary of State. At the same time it was becoming evident that some expansion in teacher education might be justified. In 1981, an HMI comment indicated some 4,000 unfilled vacancies for nursery teachers, and in November the Advisory Council on the Supply and Education of Teachers (ACSET) recognised the need for more teachers of younger children, Rolle's area of specialisation. But increased numbers had to be handled without increased income.

One effect of the funding changes was to move some expenditure charges from the central pool to local authorities. An example was college catering. This had long been a loss making area because of the variable student demand, caused by vacations and teaching practice. In 1980 the Rolle

7.50 By the time these headlines were written, Rolle College staff had already accepted that the future would be as part of a larger establishment, though the press picked up the unease amongst the staff about the nature of that future.

[WCSL, press cuttings collection: Express and Echo and Western Morning News]

College operation was losing £800 pounds per week. The local authority required the College to correct the situation. The College adopted a contract/voucher system which was used in many other colleges, in which all resident students were contracted to spend £5.00 per week in the refectory (non-residents £2.50). Turnover was increased to produce a trading surplus of £3,465 in 1982, but at the expense of a running conflict with the students. The issue boiled over in 1987 with a student boycott of the facilities, which led to the introduction of a credit card system, an annual contract of £345 for residents but with discount provisions. Without the guaranteed income the catering service might have been withdrawn, which the Student Union recognised by making up the losses during the boycott by £3,000.[60]

Ever since the closure crisis in 1977, the possibility that Rolle would merge with one or other of the institutions in Devon involved in higher education, was never far below the surface. Nationally, a succession of reports and policy developments relating to higher education in general, in addition to those specifically concerned with teacher education, had appeared having implications for the future of the College.[61] Certainly it appears from the minutes of the Governors and of Academic Board that it was increasingly being accepted that Rolle's future as a separate entity was limited. But concerns were expressed for the ability to continue at an appropriate scale the work which it saw as its own in teacher education and the liberal arts, within a larger institution. National initiatives of course create local responses, and from 1985 Devon County education officials worked on the development of a higher education strategy for the County which looked to an amalgamation of the maintained colleges of higher education. Merging with the College of St Mark and St John was certainly explored, but was not tenable owing to differences in legal status and the aspirations of the Church college for an independent future. In any case, Rolle's Principal, Dr Preston, wanted a guarantee of a subsequent merger with Plymouth Polytechnic, which had almost no work of the kind undertaken at Exmouth.[62] But on another front, the inclusion of Exeter College of Art and Design in the planning exercise, posed more of a problem as there was some overlap of liberal arts work.

By the summer of 1986, Rolle staff had accepted its future as part of a larger establishment, and the Academic Board agreed that:[63]

"The Polytechnic and Rolle College join together in a collegiate framework to provide on the Rolle site a Faculty of Education, Arts and Humanities, comprising a School of Education and a School of Arts and Humanities, with the possibility of Exeter College of Arts coming into association at a later date."

The endless round of planning meetings and consultation documentation, now taking place between the local authority and the institutions concerned, was complicated by the continued evolution of Government policy during 1987.[64] What had started as the unification of public sector higher education provision in Devon was to end with the creation of a self-regulatory establishment freed from local authority control, though still subject to close Government oversight through the allocation of student places and funding.

S.U.NEWS*CROP CIRCLES*XTV*ELECTION RESULTS* MUCH MUCH MORE

For those of you who haven't yet heard the results of the elections
or can't remember
here are the

**STUDENT UNION OFFICERS & EXECUTIVE
FOR SEPTEMBER 92**

SITE PRESIDENT: JAMES HERRING

WELFARE: HOWARD DAVIDSON

ACADEMIC OFFICER: ALISON CURRY & DAN PENFOLD

KAMPAIGNS: KRIS THOMAS

SOCIAL: VICKY & SARAH

WOMENS GROUP: LISA-JANE MOWBRAY & HANNAH THOMPSON

SECRETARY: JULIE CHALMERS

ENVIRONMENT: JIM KEW

CHAIRPERSON: FRASER MCALPINE

SPORTS AND SOCIETIES: RICHARD AVERY & NIC DAN

ROLLE UP: JULES BARNES & ADRIAN WANDSWORTH

RAG CHAIR: MATT & CATH

BAR SHOP: JO & MIKE

MATURE STUDENTS: JOHN RABETTS

PUBLICITY: ANNELIE WILLIAMS & SALLY MADDIN

OVERSEAS OFFICER: MARK MARSDEN

We still need somebody for the post of **Finance Officer** so anybody with a good head for figures and heaps of excellent fundraising ideas see Tean as soon as possible...

7. 51, 7.52 Though a part of the University of Plymouth Students' Union, a branch union was maintained on the Exmouth campus to administer the local facilities and services, with its own local executive and publications.

[UPEXM, Rolle collection, Rolle UP (1992)]

7.53 The research portfolio in the Faculty expanded rapidly in the 1990s. In this collaborative project with the University of Exeter called EXEL, ways of helping primary children improve their reading and writing of non-fiction texts were tested and primary teachers helped to improved their teaching as part of the national literacy strategy.

[UPPLY, The Bulletin (November 1997)]

Following Government legislation, Rolle became part of the new Polytechnic South West (PSW) in September, 1988.

Whatever the circumstances, such a transition could never have been easy for anyone associated with the former college. On its own, Rolle would probably have retained its unity as the focus for education, arts and humanities in the expanded Polytechnic. But the simultaneous assimilation of nearby Exeter College of Art and Design, which also had significant work in arts and humanities, led to more elaborate restructuring. Rolle's arts and humanities work, involving about a third of its staff, was immediately transferred to the new Exeter Faculty of Arts and Design, joining the Department of Humanities, Performance and Media. The B.A. Integrated Studies was absorbed into the Polytechnic's Combined Studies Scheme, and would evolve as a Combined Arts sub-scheme. In practice, these staff and most students remained on what now became known as the Exmouth campus. Principal Preston took retirement in the summer of 1988 before any of these changes took effect, and it was not until January 1989 and the arrival of Professor Michael Newby as the Dean of the new Rolle Faculty of Education that the remainder of the former College was re-organised into two departments, Initial Teacher Education and In-Service Teacher Education, and a unit for research in education.[65] However, the new arrangements were not to prove permanent, though the In-Service Department was to provide the basis for the School of Graduate Studies following the re-organisation of 1994.

Perhaps student life was less affected by the changes. At Rolle it had long since evolved along the lines found in universities. The regulated life of the all-female college had given way to the freedoms of self-regulation and self-catering. Despite support for the college in difficult times, summer especially tended to produce complaints from residents near college premises about noisy behaviour, usually readily handled through warnings to students and an apology from the College. The caring side of student nature came through with a challenge to South West Water on the discharge of untreated waste into the Exe estuary, and with their support for disabled students.[66] With the encouragement of Principal Preston a Cheshire Foundation home had been built on the Kempston site in the hope that residents would be able to study at Rolle. One such student found Rolle very supportive, both staff and students.[67]

Exmouth Campus in the 1990s

Becoming part of a much larger educational establishment had a major impact on everything that went on at Rolle. The employment and management link with Devon County Council was broken when the Polytechnic assumed control. Ancillary staff and academic staff alike had to follow a steep learning curve to master new guidelines and processes. Participating in the operations of the Polytechnic, such as attending committee meetings, meant a large amount of travel for staff at all levels. Operations including finance, personnel, catering, library, media, and site management had to be integrated. The same was true of courses, though perhaps least affected were existing students following courses validated by the University of Exeter, which were allowed to complete their full cycle. So four years passed before Exeter awards were completely phased out. Meanwhile, every course had to be reviewed, revised and revalidated as CNAA courses, even those which had been reviewed just before the merger. On the achievement of self-validation, they of course became University of Plymouth courses. Perhaps it was fortunate for Rolle that there was some increase in the numbers of trained teachers required and the Faculty was allowed some extra places. In November 1991, there were 729 students taking BEd. courses, 75 taking the one-year PGCE and 26 following the new Articled Teacher Scheme.[68] In addition there was a significant number of in-service students taking a variety of short course and part-time programmes of study. These were very difficult years for the staff, and making the adjustment needed time for consolidation, before energies could turn to new initiatives.

At the time of the merger, a third of academic staff took the opportunity of the Crombie provisions to take retirement. The academic establishment of the new Faculty numbered some 50, and of course the re-structuring led to a number of regradings and new appointments. An important new initiative was the development of a structured programme of educational research which was to bear fruit in the 1996 Research Assessment Exercise (RAE), with a creditable grading leading to a financial award to further promote research in the Faculty. Similar success was achieved elsewhere in the enlarged faculty, notably in English and history, now in the School of Humanities & Cultural Interpretation. The great majority of staff now have personal research programmes in addition to their teaching and administrative duties. Rolle Faculty also gained from the merger, the in-service courses for teachers in further and higher education which the Polytechnic had been running since the early 1970s, and which had been amongst the earliest links with further education colleges in the region.

7.54 *The new lecture theatre planned for the Exmouth campus will be built on this open space between the Daw Building and the administration building.*

[Photo: A. Kennerley]

For a brief period state control of teacher education numbers was allowed to lapse. Taking advantage, Rolle managed to nearly double its numbers of education students, so as to be in a much stronger position numerically when, perhaps inevitably, controls were reintroduced with the formation of the Teacher Training Agency (TTA)(1993). This has had momentous impact and continues to exercise a tight regulation of teacher training. But the creation of the TTA brought with it a new wave of uncertainty: the possibility that all teacher training might be transferred to the schools, leaving teacher education departments out in the cold. Conscious of the threat, the University, after full consultation with the staff concerned, settled on the tactic of a restructuring of its Exeter/Exmouth faculties in 1994, which would protect the residue of teacher education work should the worst happen. There were other factors, not relevant to this discussion, which influenced the decision. Within the unified Faculty of Arts & Education there are now four departments, with staff and students sharing the Exmouth and Exeter campuses. Now the School of Humanities of Cultural Interpretation has much the same number of students as the Rolle School of Education. Moving teacher training entirely to the schools was unrealistic. Fears proved unfounded, but a positive move has been the creation of close partnerships between Rolle and the schools with which it works. The Rolle School of Education, with about 850 students, is as large as Rolle College ever was, yet manages with some 50 staff compared with the previous maximum of over 80! Furthermore, the number of students in the School of Graduate Studies is well over 1000.

The scope of work in education is broadening. In 1997/98 the intake to the B.Ed. (Primary) was set at 168 and there were 622 students in the subsequent years, representing the traditional commitment to the younger age group. The corresponding intake to the PGCE (Primary) was 68, and to the PGCE (Secondary) 40 specialising in mathematics, music and art and design. This last was a redevelopment of secondary work which had lapsed in the mid 1980s. English, Drama and Geography will be added to the list of subjects in the near future. Outside the TTA allocations is a development from 1993, the BA in Waldorf/Steiner Education having a total of 62 students, and a one year part-time course for classroom assistants taking 100 students in collaboration with local authorities. There is some £200,000 worth of educational short course provision, again a long-standing feature of work at Rolle. Educational work in the School of Graduate Studies has also seen a considerable increase under the Polytechnic/University compared with the scale of the more advanced work in educational studies as an independent college. The awards include the Certificate in Professional Studies (CPSE), a long standing Rolle course, the Certificate in Advanced Professional Studies (CAPS), the Post Graduate Diploma (Pg.Dip.Ed.) and Master of Education courses, together numbering 246 in 1997/98. Additionally there are perhaps 100 other students taking short courses or studying part-time for research masters or doctorates.[69]

Signs that earlier difficulties have been overcome are found in the favourable reports following recent OFSTED inspections, while the current shortage especially of secondary teachers means Rolle's moves in that direction are well timed. While the emphasis in this chapter has been on the Exmouth site as a teacher education establishment, it must not be forgotten that since joining with the Polytechnic in 1988, and more so since the creation of the Faculty of Arts & Education in 1994, the Arts & Design and Humanities & Cultural Interpretation departments have also functioned on the Exmouth campus as well as at Exeter. Education work is not restricted to the Rolle School. It is a significant part of the work of the Graduate School, and education staff also contribute to the work of the other departments in the Faculty. The 50 years of progression at Rolle have been full of uncertainty and incident. Though the continued use of some of the Victorian houses is a link with the early years, the institution at Exmouth has changed in almost all other respects, from a single-sex post-school establishment having some overtones of a boarding school, to a fully-fledged university departmental grouping concerned with education in all its dimensions. It has survived the vagaries of state teacher education policy through adaptation and new initiatives. Investment in the Exmouth campus continues, planning being well advanced for a new two million pound building offering performance space, a lecture theatre and flexible teaching rooms.

7.55: Development Diagram

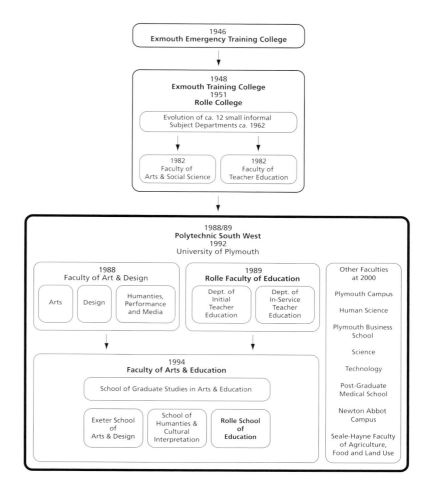

8.1 *The simplicity of the Polytechnic's early logos contrasts with the complexity of that adopted following the addition of the Exeter, Exmouth and Newton Abbot campuses in 1988/89. Plymouth Polytechnic's lower case 'pp' was soon replaced by the 'lorgnette' version, which was superseded in 1989 by Polytechnic South West's new design.*[1]

Polytechnic

CHAPTER EIGHT

The merger of the Three Towns in 1914 had led to the merger of the technical schools established by the old boroughs of Plymouth and Devonport. Although the development of the Plymouth site had effectively reduced that at Devonport to an annexe, delivering courses in an expanding college on a split location had remained problematical. Half a century later, the existence of this secondary site was to influence the location of the new College of Further Education. There was, of course, also the Council's long-designated site for Plymouth's university at Derriford, still available after the failure of the Council's 1960 bid for one of the new universities. This was part of the debate about where to develop the new colleges. However, once the London-based College of St. Mark and St. John was brought into the equation, the Derriford site must have seemed the obvious location for the college of education. It was essentially a residential establishment, whereas the largely non-residential Polytechnic and College of Further Education (CFE) needed to be close to the local transport hubs.

The changes about to take place at Plymouth were of course by no means unique. Across the country twenty-nine other new polytechnics were also making similar adjustments, often accompanied by the merger of small local authority-run colleges, such as teacher training colleges, and the shedding of less advanced work to existing or newly created FE colleges. As a result of the White Paper, *Education: A framework for Expansion* (1972), a further major restructuring of public-sector higher education took place which saw the reincarnation of many other tertiary colleges, including many former teacher education colleges which did not merge with polytechnics or did not close, as colleges of higher education.[2] How certain had Plymouth been about achieving designation as a polytechnic? The ground had long been laid through the Council's aspirations for a university, through the development of CNAA degree courses and HNDs, and through the research portfolio. But the new buildings had been funded for a local technical college, and the amount of advanced work was not necessarily impressive compared with the establishments in the larger centres of population. The intervention of persons of influence, such as David Owen, MP, certainly helped, but geography must have played a part. With a population of over a quarter of a million, Plymouth was unusual in not having an establishment exclusively concerned with higher education; it was a long distance from the nearest university at Exeter, and there was no such establishment further west.

The pace of change already seemed to be getting more rapid. Throughout the polytechnic years, hardly had one national initiative registered before another was announced. No facet of college existence remained immune. Plymouth Polytechnic was soon to gain a new master, as a result of local government reorganisation in 1974 which saw local control removed from Plymouth City Council to Devon County Council. At the same time the long established and much respected national diploma and certificate arrangements were replaced with the untried, new methodologies of the Business and Technical Education Councils, confusingly using the same award titles. Fortunately, the change from

8.2 *People alighting from the buses at the public library, could see the changing status of the College from the name on the east face of the Assembly Hall. Taken about 1970, the Plymouth coat of arm still survives, though it would soon disappear.*

[PCL-LS, donated by J.F. Hussell]

8.3 *This aerial view of the Polytechnic site, looking northwards in 1970, marks a a lull in building development following the completion of the 1960s programme.*

[UPPLY, Plymouth collection, photo: Nicholas Horne.]

working with London University to the searching approaches of the CNAA had already been started, and although there were numerous visitations to be handled, the Polytechnic soon learned to trust and value the approach of the body which now awarded the degrees taken in Plymouth. Then there was an urgent need to develop the site for its higher education function with the planning and erection of new buildings and the conversion of existing properties. Soon the Government would set about changing the basis under which public sector higher education was funded, and there would be new approaches to funding research.

Meanwhile staff had to deliver their current teaching, prepare innumerable submissions for new courses, improve their academic qualifications through advanced study and research, and live cheek-by-jowl with their former colleagues now in the CFE, but teaching in adjacent accommodation for a number of years until the new FE building was ready on the Devonport site. For many of the longer-established academic staff the changes brought about during the 1970s and 1980s constituted a culture shock of some magnitude. Some were happy with the opportunities presented for personal development related to advanced teaching and research. Others, especially some of those who had come into technical teaching on the basis of their industrial experience, found the changing environment less comfortable. Nevertheless, these were the processes which were to raise the college from a largely local institution to one of national standing which twenty years later would be an automatic choice for elevation to university status.

Creating the Polytechnic

With the Robbins Report on Higher Education (1963) fresh in the memory, it might be expected that that Report had triggered the restructuring of local authority higher education through the mutation of regional colleges into polytechnics and further education colleges. In fact, the Robbins Committee, almost entirely composed of university people, offered no clear direction for this sector, despite its clear recommendations on widening access to higher education, developing the universities, the absorption of teacher education colleges into the universities, and the creation of the CNAA.[3] Equally, it did not suggest a single system of higher education under the universities. As noted earlier, a binary policy for higher education was already evolving at the Ministry of Education/Department of Education and Science (DES) at the time the Robbins report was published, and the immediate creation of the CNAA must be seen as part of that initiative. Though actively pushed by education officials, the trend was certainly under discussion in wider educational circles. Concern about the way to divide higher education between different institutions and a desire not to spread HE courses too widely across institutions led to the emergence of the Polytechnic concept set out in the White Paper of May, 1966, *A Plan for Polytechnics and Other Colleges*.[4] Plymouth appeared in its preliminary list of establishments.

Another important part of the general context which led to the designation of Plymouth Polytechnic was the issue of the degree of self government which would be allowed. It has been shown earlier, how constrained the College at Plymouth had been through being no more than one department of the local authority and the need to refer quite minor matters to the Council's administrators and committees. The Ministry of Education had aired the problems in its circular 7/59, 'The Internal Government of Colleges', and by the mid-1960s the need for action was fully recognised. Guidance was issued in April, 1967, and the powers for setting up self-government under local authority oversight, were conferred by the Education (No. 2) Act, 1968. During the consultations, two hard-fought issues were eventually conceded by the local authorities, control of finance and the clerkship to the college governors.[5] These lay at the core of tight control, but the government of the day was determined that the Polytechnics should have a reasonable degree of freedom in the management of their own affairs. In fact greater independence was essential in the context of the prestige and status of educational institutions.

Table 8.1

Schedule to Articles of Government of Plymouth Polytechnic, 1969.

Salaries of teaching staff	Fuel, Light, Water and Cleaning Materials
Salaries and wages of non-teaching staff	Rent and Rates
Wages of Caretakers	Furniture/Fittings, Books,
Stationery/Materials,	
Purchase/Maintenance of Equipment	
National Insurance/Pensions Contributions	Postage, Telephone and General Expenses
Superannuation Charges	Central Establishment Charges
Other Employees Expenses	Debt Charges
Repairs/Maintenance of Buildings & Grounds	Revenue Contributions to Capital Outlay

Source: Plymouth Polytechnic: Instrument and Articles of Government, 1969

From the time that Plymouth appeared in the preliminary list of polytechnics, senior College of Technology staff were working with local authority officers on the innumerable aspects which had to be addressed in setting up two new establishments with revised management arrangements. A key element in the process was the drafting of the Instrument and Articles of Government which had to be accepted by the college staff and the local authority, and finally approved by the DES. Plymouth Polytechnic's document came into force on 8 September 1969, though its designation was dated from 1 January 1970.[6] The Instrument of Government set out the constitution of the Governing Body, which maintained the well-established practice of local council and university representation, but also included the Marine Biological Association and staff and student representatives. The Articles of Government set out the management and financial relationship with Plymouth City Council, the constitution of the Academic Board, staffing arrangements and made provision for a students' union. For the first time the College principal, now called Director, was to have a deputy. A schedule (Table 8.1) listed the range of administrative and financial heads which now

8.4 Dr Michael Robbins, Director of Plymouth Polytechnic, 1974-89, led the transformation from local technical college to a higher education institution of national standing on several fronts including courses, staffing, buildings, research, and the assimilation of smaller colleges.

[UPPLY, Plymouth Polytechnic Prospectus, 1983/84]

8.5 The 1970s brought the age of the 'logo' to educational establishments. That adopted at Plymouth Polytechnic was the subject of much ribald comment as these doodles from the staff magazine suggest.

[UPPLY, Spectrum, no. 11 (June, 1974)]

devolved to the Polytechnic. The Articles also specified the appointment of the Chief Administrative Officer (CAO) at the Polytechnic and that the CAO should be Clerk to the Governors. The fourteen headings in Table 8.1 provide some insight into range of management and financial structures which had to be created and overseen by the CAO. A timetable provided for the transfer of no less than twenty-four function heads from the Council Education Department to the Polytechnic administration by the end of 1971.[7] It also fell to the CAO to manage the administrative side of dividing the former College of Technology staff between the two new institutions, Plymouth Polytechnic and the College of Further Education, which was not achieved until July 1970.[8] Table 8.2 shows that the Polytechnic, concentrating on advanced work, retained 57 per cent of the teaching staff and 42 per cent of the students (FTE). The majority of the technicians would also have been retained by the Polytechnic. The 19 administrative staff in 1970 for the time being served both colleges, but are indicative of the exceptionally low base from which administrative support needed to be built up as the Polytechnic assumed responsibility. By the time the CAO had taken up his appointment in September 1970, Mr Bailey, Principal of the College of Technology, had already been appointed Director, and the heads of department and teaching staff from the former college had assumed their positions.[9] The new Deputy Director, Dr. R.F.M. Robbins, joined in May 1970.

Table 8.2

The Division of Plymouth College of Technology Staff & Students Between Plymouth Polytechnic and the College of Further Education, Plymouth, in 1970.

Department	Teaching Staff		FTE Students		Technicians		Clerical Staff	
	Poly	CFE	Poly	CFE	Poly	CFE	Poly	CFE
Civil/Mechanical Eng.	27	15	151	278	17	shared	1	
Electrical Engineering	32	15	330	211	16	shared	1	
Physics & Maths.	26	16	65	196	13	shared	0.7	
Chemistry & Biology	19		104		12		0.3	
Business/Social Sc.	32	27	272	790	2	shared	4	
Maritime Studies	19	28	428	368	4	shared	1.6	1
Architecture	9		111					
Construction Studies		23		211	8			
General Office							10.2	shared
Totals	164	124	1461	2054	72	shared	19	shared

Source, UPPLY, Governing Body papers, 1970.

As far as internal structures were concerned, it would take nearly four years before the initial period of re-adjustment could be considered complete. For the time being the academic departmental structure inherited from the College of Technology was retained, though an early adjustment in 1971 was the reorganisation of the science area into a Department of Environmental Science (chemical, biological and geo-sciences) and a Department of Mathematical and Physical Sciences. The main adjustment came in 1973/74 when the departments became Schools of the Polytechnic each with an internal sub-structure of Teaching Groups. Less formal than a large number of separate small departments, this allowed recognition to a variety of sub-specialisms which were emerging as new courses were being developed and the Polytechnic grew in size. A particular area of growth was in the social sciences, and the disciplines of psychology, sociology, politics and social administration were separated in 1974/75 from the School of Management and Business Studies, into a new School of Behavioural and Social Sciences. In the same period, the academic support services, whose development was an essential element in the continued recognition of the Polytechnic by the CNAA, were given a clear identity as Centres of the Polytechnic: Learning Resources, Welfare and Computer. The new status of research was recognised by the appointment of a Director of Research. The relationship between departments, centres and the Academic Board was put on a formal basis through the creation of a committee structure designed to facilitate the upward and downward flow of policy, decision making, information and reporting, the Academic Board having the responsibility for academic matters under the Governing Body. Course committees, examination boards, department/school and centre committees, research committees and the like, with approved constitutions, all date from these early formative years. Lines of responsibility were also set out for the growing number of administrators under the Senior Registrar, the Finance Officer and Senior Administrative Officer. Finally the Directorate was strengthened with the appointment of two Assistant Directors.[10]

The first of the Centres to be developed was Learning Resources (LRC). Indeed it was a condition of the CNAA Quinquennial Review in 1971 that the Library be rapidly brought up to university standard. However, the new academic librarian appointed in 1971 brought the latest thinking on information and educational support to the academic community. The senior staff of the LRC should also be academics, who should have a proactive role in the Polytechnic. In addition to the normal library tasks of acquiring, organising and issuing books and journals, LRC staff needed to be equipped through their education to play a major role in the selection of library stock, not least in order to achieve the rapid upgrading which was demanded.

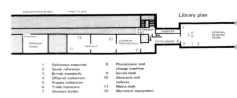

8.6 In response to the strictures of the CNAA a 'crash' programme provided a temporary expansion of the Library running almost the full length of the Engineering and Link Blocks at first floor level from 1972, pending the completion of the proposed library building.

[UPPLY, Library Guide, 1973.]

8.7 The skeleton of the new Polytechnic library was no more than a massive kit assembled on site. Note the diagonal temporary wooden shores to prevent the construction swaying .

[Photo: A. Kennerley]

8.8 This interior view of the library, for which the name Learning Resources Centre was adopted, shows the specially-designed modular 'Plymouth study carrels' a proportion of which were equipped for audio/visual media.

[UPPLY, Plymouth Polytechnic Prospectus, 1980/81]

8.9 The entrance to the Learning Resources Centre was at first floor level, where the services for readers were concentrated. Much larger and more sophisticated than previous libraries, the Academic Board required all students to take courses in library use.

[UPPLY, Learning Resources Centre Guide, 1976]

Further than this, they needed to be in regular contact with academic staff drawing their attention to new information, especially on the research front, and participating in the education of students in the use of the library as an information laboratory.[11] During the 1970s, partly owing to the absence of other suitable locations for some units, the LRC provided the base for the Polytechnic-wide provision of library instruction and study skills programmes to students, for the provision of in-service teacher education courses taken by Polytechnic staff and staff from other colleges in the region (including the schools of nursing), and for the Polytechnic's embryonic graphics, photographic and reprographic services.

A start with these developments was made in 1972 when the small College of Technology library on the first floor of the administration (link) block, was extended to run almost the full length of the south side of the Engineering Block (now the Smeaton Building) as an interim measure pending the building of the Polytechnic's new LRC building. All the initiatives noted above started in this long, thin section of accommodation. Though quadrupled in size, such was the rate of expansion of stock and services that this space was seriously overcrowded by the time the new building was ready in 1976. At the same time as building up LRC provision, work was progressing on the design of the new Centre to be located on the south side of Portland Square in a joint development with the new Student Union building. This had to provide for the broad range of services and facilities already noted, be capable of taking the heavy loadings imposed by the bookstock and be sufficiently flexible to allow for the planned expansion to 5,000 students. Designed to an exceptionally large grid of seven by ten metres, with no restrictions on loading, and with all services in the ceiling to preserve flexibility, the new structure arrived in pre-cast sections, a kind of massive, self-assembly concrete kit. Erection was not without problems owing to a spring in the rock on the north side, and the need to erect temporary shores when the structure threatened to wobble during assembly. Inside, the LRC provided an unusually high ratio of study seats to numbers of students, with a high proportion of 'Plymouth Carrels', specially designed study booths, of which a significant number were fitted to hold audio-visual equipment. Outline planning allowed for a doubling of the size of the LRC across the engineering workshops, but this was not to materialise. The provision for flexibility has allowed the interior to be remodelled on several occasions as technology has advanced and student numbers have increased threefold on the planned capacity. During the 1970s the library stock grew from some 15,000 volumes to over 110,000, while use increased from about 4,000 visits per week to 15,000. The increased use reflects the position of the library at the heart of the campus conveniently adjacent to the students' union, and the efforts made in user-education.

With an increasing proportion of students studying away from home on full-time courses at Plymouth, it was becoming much more necessary for the Polytechnic to provide structured support for the social dimension of student life. Of course traditional residential colleges had always made provision for the accommodation, catering and medical needs of students, with non-academic staff such as matrons, housekeepers and visiting practitioners providing day to day support. More intransigent difficulties mostly fell to the academic staff in a personal tutoring capacity, or even to the principal. Technical colleges had little in the way of structured welfare support so that academic staff often found themselves counselling students, visiting, and sorting out social problems on an *ad hoc* basis without any particular training. In a period when social services nationally were being established professionally and academically, it was important that the Polytechnic made proper provision through the establishment of the Welfare Centre.[12] At the heart of the Centre's staffing was the provision of personal counselling services by a team of trained counsellors who would provide the referral back up to the academic staff acting as personal tutors. These inevitably remained the initial contact for many students. Medical provision continued to be through the collaboration of local medical practices, though the Polytechnic would require its own medical suite overseen by a state registered nurse. Similarly, an accommodation service would need its own base and would replace the *ad hoc* lists of landladies held in earlier periods by those departments having a proportion of non-local students. In time this would inspect all private accommodation offered, oversee contracts and manage the Polytechnic's own limited student accommodation provision. Finally, something needed to be done about the provision of careers advice to students coming to the end of their courses. Again, this was a general development of the period. In the Polytechnic trained careers counsellors, with a careers information base, would provide general support to the *ad hoc* advice which academic staff had always provided, often through their contact with industry. A refurbished house in Rowe Street provided a central location for the Welfare Centre's services. A small physical education unit had also come into existence, to manage the Polytechnic's sports facilities at Ernesettle and the Underwater Unit at Fort Bovisand, support the student clubs and provide coaching. It remained a separate unit until 1978 when it merged with the Welfare Centre under a new name, Student Services Centre.

The third area of Polytechnic wide provision was in the new area of computing. As already noted, embryonic facilities had been provided in the 1960s by the engineering and mathematics departments, with an establishment-wide service being offered from 1968 from the latter department. In the early stages the provision of a computing service was entangled with the development of computing as a research subject and a subject in degree courses. The creation of the Computer Centre in 1973, separated the service dimension and foreshadowed the eventual separation of an academic Computing Department from the mathematics department.[13] The rapid pace of development in the world of computing is well known, and the Polytechnic's central system was replaced three times in the 1970s. Already it was providing services to users outside the Polytechnic, including local colleges, and acting as a centre for the development of applications supported by Devon County. This foreshadows the role now played by the

8.10 *The Polytechnic's first central computing facility was installed on the ground floor of the Link Block, where previously the central administration had been based. It would be moved into the general teaching Block (now the Babbage Building) at the end of the 1970s.*

[UPPLY, Plymouth Polytechnic Prospectus, 1975/76]

8.11 *These houses in Rowe Street, where the Welfare Centre had its original base in the early 1970s, are all that remain of the nineteenth century properties on the southern part of the Plymouth campus.*

[Photo: A. Kennerley]

8.12 Modular degree course structures first came to Plymouth Polytechnic in 1976 with introduction of the Combined Studies degree scheme. It soon became a seed-bed for new subjects and the dominant mode of undergraduate study, but fifteen years were to pass before the modular principle was extended to all undergraduate courses.

[UPPLY, Combined Studies course booklet, 1978]

Polytechnic as the computing centre for the south western area. With every student and member of staff in the college beginning to use computers, the Centre was increasingly under pressure to enlarge access to terminals, and increasingly heavily involved in the provision of a wide range of short courses.

Another significant initiative operating across the Polytechnic, also with roots in the School of Mathematical Sciences has been the modular Combined Studies degree scheme offering combinations in the sciences and social sciences, which was validated by the CNAA for a start in 1975-76. Eventually the modular principle would be adopted for all undergraduate courses in the establishment. The development of undergraduate courses introducing new, unusual subjects and allowing the study of established subjects in unusual combinations, was one of the marks and strengths of public sector higher education, which contrasted with the traditional single subject approaches in the universities.[14] The idea of courses assembled in standard units was being developed in the late 1960s, but the Government gave a particular thrust to the credit-based approach in *Education: a Framework for Expansion* (1972) which saw such courses as providing the flexibility increasingly demanded by students: combinations of subjects relating to future employment with the ability to carry credits earned from one establishment to another when study was interspersed with periods of work. Plymouth's scheme was not the first, so that it was able to draw on the experience for example at Oxford Polytechnic and City of London Polytechnic.[15] Despite concerns about continuity in skills development and the anticipation of problems in delivering some subjects, the unitary or modular approach took root. At Plymouth these concerns were answered by an earlier approach to what is now known as student centred learning, then called guided learning, and in preparation for the CNAA visiting panel guided learning packs for each module were hastily assembled and laid out in the Library for inspection. In fact the development of the library with its programmes for user education and study skills training was very much part of the support package for this new undergraduate scheme. One advantage of the modular approach was the opportunity to develop new subjects from a small base, as minor or major pathways. At Plymouth it was a testing ground for subjects such as oceanography, politics, sociology and transport.

With numbers taking Combined Studies (later Combined Honours) increasing each year, a separate administrative office, a kind of departmental office to which students could relate, soon became necessary. From the beginning it was obvious that in administrative terms, there would be interactions between subject departments and the Combined Studies office, and that more often than not, because Combined Studies touched almost every department, its needs must take priority over those of departments own courses. Thus it was, for example, that timetabling Combined Studies classes and rooms took priority over all other timetabling, and long and complex negotiations lasting six months or more became the order of the day. In fact the Office came to provide a valuable co-ordinating role in this and many other matters as the Scheme grew to be very much larger than any of the Polytechnic's other courses, pointing the way to standardisation across the institution of academic regulations and their interpretation.

Table 8.3

Number of Full-Time Courses Offered at Plymouth Polytechnic, 1969/70 - 1979/80.

	1970	1971	1972	1973	1974	1975	1976	1977	1978	1979	1980
Degree, PG						1	1	1	1	2	2
Degree, UG	7	9	9	9	11	11	12	12	13	15	16
HND	6	6	5	5	5	6	6	6	6	6	7
Diploma	3	3	4	4	7	7	7	7	7	7	7
Certificate	6	5	6	7	7	7	7	7	7	7	7
Totals	22	23	24	25	30	31	33	33	34	36	39

Source: UPPLY, Annual reports, 1969/70 to 1979/80. Degree includes London external courses until superseded by CNAA courses. Diploma includes Polytechnic diplomas, PG diploma and DMS. Certificate includes all professional courses.

8.13 This former board school on the site of the medieval Palace Court, was the home of the School of Architecture when it transferred from the College of Art. For the past twenty years it has been occupied by the School of Civil & Structural Engineering.

[Photo: A. Kennerley]

At Plymouth the main benefit in the wake of the 1972 White Paper was the expansion in student numbers. Although mergers were the talk of the higher education world, Plymouth was not at that time to expand through absorbing smaller colleges. The Polytechnic's relationship to all the other colleges in Devon was certainly discussed, and, in the spirit of the white paper, there was collaboration with Seale-Hayne College and the College of St. Mark and St. John. But distance or legal problems ruled out mergers.[16] So apart from the transfer of the Department of Architecture from the College of Art in 1969, the Polytechnic was unusual in having to build its numbers from the low base left after the separation of lower level work, entirely on its own efforts. While the Combined Honours scheme would become very significant, it was in the first decade only a small part of the growth achieved. Table 8.3 shows the expansion of the numbers of courses with almost the whole effort being devoted to developing undergraduate and diploma work. The numbers of full-time students had almost trebled by the end of the 1970s from the one thousand in 1969-70, as had the numbers of part-time students, so that the Polytechnic had well over 6,000 students on its books (Chart 8.1). Part-time courses demand a disproportionate amount of administrative time,

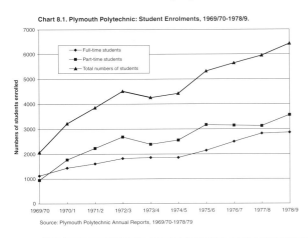

Chart 8.1. Plymouth Polytechnic: Student Enrolments, 1969/70-1978/9.

Source: Plymouth Polytechnic Annual Reports, 1969/70-1978/79

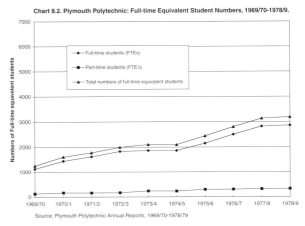

Chart 8.2. Plymouth Polytechnic: Full-time Equivalent Student Numbers, 1969/70-1978/9.

Source: Plymouth Polytechnic Annual Reports, 1969/70-1978/79

and reducing the student numbers to full-time equivalents (FTE) produces a more sober understanding of the expansion. FTE numbers (Chart 8.2) grew from about 1,200 to about 3,200 in 1978-79, and it is clear that the real expansion lay with full-time work. Research now had a much higher profile. It was under the leadership of Dr. Robbins, who succeeded Mr. Bailey as director in 1974, that the embryonic research culture was extended across the Polytechnic. Crucial in this initiative was the support of Devon County Council, which became the Polytechnic's education authority following the local government re-organisation of 1974. It was able to devise a formula for funding FE students which allowed the support of this development, such that research grew faster at Plymouth Polytechnic than at many other polytechnics. An early benefit lay in the relationship with the CNAA, but the development of a strong research base during the 1970s and 1980s, together with a growing research reputation nationally and internationally, would ultimately have implications for the achievement of university status and for major new subject initiatives, most notably the recent allocation of medical school.

Table 8.4

Research at Plymouth Polytechnic, 1973/4 - 1979/80.

	1973-4	1975-6	1976-7	1979 & 80*
Academic journal papers	35	32	40	88
Conference papers	28	26	32	71
Reports	3	5	3	14
Chapters in books	5	4	7	20
Books	2	4	2	11
Articles, etc	15	10	7	58
Special lectures	25	39	36	13
Research projects in progress	108	161	310	n/a
New research grants (£)	22,475	145,520	96,380	445,342
Research staff			36	48

Source, UPPLY, Annual reports. * Two years, Plymouth Polytechnic, Quinquennial Review for CNAA, 1981.

Significant though students were as the prime generator the Polytechnic's funding, there were other important aspects of its the work. Table 8.4 provides an indication of the growth in research activity which was particularly marked in the later years of the 1970s. The expansion is seen in the numbers of projects, amount of research grants, numbers of research staff, delivery of conference papers and numbers of research publications. The Polytechnic was making its mark on the national and international stages, through service on national and international bodies, and overseas collaboration. Also, towards the end of the decade, the Polytechnic's policy of encouraging staff to work for research qualifications through its Fellowship scheme, was bearing fruit in the rise of the numbers of staff who were research active. Special recognition was given to leading researchers through the creation of the readership grade, with seven readers in post by 1980. The structures for the encouragement and oversight of all this activity, led by the Research Co-ordinator, the Research Committee and Research Degrees Committee, involved in approving projects, training, submissions and examination arrangements, had the approval of the CNAA. The science departments, with their lengthy experience, remained

8.14 After the College of St Mark and St John had moved from London to Plymouth to occupy Plymouth's 'university' site, it collaborated with the Polytechnic in ther development of degree courses in the humanities and social policy. [Plymouth Polytechnic Prospectus, 1979/80]

amongst the most research-active areas, while the social sciences were making rapid progress in this period. But all areas were advancing their research and consultancy portfolios.[17]

A college is its staff, and the kind of progress indicated in the development of research and courses, and of student numbers, could not have been achieved without building up the staff by appointing people with the appropriate backgrounds, to teach the new subjects on offer and with established research portfolios. In the process the use of part-time staff, a significant element before 1970, was considerably reduced, as the emphasis turned to full-time work. As already noted, part of this growth was in professionally qualified staff to develop the Polytechnic's support services, who also contributed academically to their own disciplines.

Vol. 6. No. 3. Date: Monday 23rd January 1984   COPYDATE for the next edition of P(15th February for publication on 2(1984.

8.15 The staff magazine, Spectrum, died in the late 1970s, and was succeeded in the 1980s by this publication which was edited by the Polytechnic's Publicity Officer.

[UPPLY, Plymouth collection]

Table 8.5

Plymouth Polytechnic Staffing, 1977-9.

	1977	1978	1979
Directorate	3	3	3
Heads	12	12	13
Principal Lecturers	45	49	57
Senior Lecturers	162	178	188
Lecturers	88	91	79
Research	37	48	49
Total Academic	346	380	387
Technician	113	124	137
Administrative (P)	37	38	42
Administrative (C)	80	99	105
Manual	37	78	80
Total Non-Academic	267	339	364
Total Staff	650	751	751

Source: UPPLY, Annual Reports, 1971/72 to 1978-79. Heads includes heads of departments and centres, and the Research Co-ordinator. Lecturers includes centre staff on lecturing grades. Administrative staff are separated as professional or clerical, the latter including various other grades. Manual staff includes, catering, ground and caretaking staff.

By 1979-80, academic staff had increased from 164 to 387 (236%), FTE student numbers from 1461 to 3402 (233%) technician staff from about 47 to 137 (291%), and administrative staff from about 10 to 147 (1470%) (Table 8.5). With significant numbers in the various categories, the Polytechnic was now much more involved in employment and personnel matters than its predecessor establishment had been. Each group of staff had an identity, and being unionised, could make representation on personnel matters, such as conditions of service and salaries or wages. The union groups at the Polytechnic included the Association of Teachers in Technical Institutions (ATTI) or the new Association of Polytechnic Teachers (APT) (academic staff), National and Local Government Officers (NALGO) (administrative staff) and Association of Scientific, Technical and Managerial Staff (ASTMS) (technician staff). Teaching salaries were regulated by the national Burnham Committee settlements, but technician and administrative staff conditions were still related to local authority approaches. It took a long time for a satisfactory structure for technicians to be worked out. In 1973, the salary grades were well below those prevailing in higher education establishments

8.16 *The growing importance of the Student's Union meant that it outgrew its earlier accommodation in the Link Block and the Science Block. When the Queen Anne's Terrace properties were relinquished as halls of residence for Merchant Navy cadets, number 6 was allocated to the SU as its headquarters and club facility until its new building adjacent to the Learning Resources Centre was ready.*

[Photo: A. Kennerley]

elsewhere, and 28 per cent of the posts in the Polytechnic were vacant.[18] Factors such as these and the changes taking place as the college underwent its metamorphosis, pushed staff morale to an unusual low. The Academic Staff Association (ASA) was formed to promote staff interests in the life of the college, as distinct from union concerns. There was a staff social committee organising events across the establishment and for a time travel and wine clubs flourished. The ASA was also involved in founding a magazine for staff, called *Spectrum*, independently edited and produced by a staff team. This was perhaps the most successful approach to keeping staff informed on developments and issues, and provided an outlet for staff opinion. After twenty-four issues in four years, this lapsed, to be replaced in time by *Polynews*, produced by the corporate information unit as a house publication, thereby losing some of the vibrancy which *Spectrum* had achieved.

Spectrum certainly had ample solid content, for example explaining new structures as they were introduced, reporting on Governors' meetings and keeping staff up to date with the building programmes. But there was also humour. It was not afraid to criticise or poke fun. Its cartoons sometimes came close to the mark. Educational technology, a child of the times, was depicted in a cauldron as a witches' brew fuelled by government finance. Peter Knight (now vice-chancellor of the University of Central England) frequently contributed on union matters, but also 'had a go' at the complex language used in Polytechnic documents in an article on the Fog Index. In a comparison with the *Sun* newspaper (fog index 6 to 8) and *The Times* (12 to 16), texts from the Directorate scored 14 to 17, degree submissions, 13 to 15, but articles on educational technology peaked at 16 to 20. And there was poetry, with Peter Bedford a frequent contributor - he clearly had a love/hate relationship with the computer:[19]

COUNTY OF DEVON
PLYMOUTH POLYTECHNIC

hese buildings were opened on 30th June 1976 by
IS ROYAL HIGHNESS THE PRINCE PHILIP
Duke of Edinburgh, K.G., K.T.
The Lord High Steward of Plymouth

8.17, 8.18 *The Student Union 'patio' had to be crossed to enter both the SU (on the right) and the Learning Resources Centre (ahead). The arrangement created a kind of one-stop student facility. It would be some years before the atrium on the left giving daylight to the student communal rooms below, would be covered with a glazed pyramid. The official opening of the pair of buildings was performed by the Duke of Edinburgh making his second visit to the Plymouth campus.*

[UPPLY, Plymouth collection, LRC opening brochure, 1976; photo: David Griffiths]

This Fortran Through My Mind

I couldnt	I'm sposta	Inscruta	Mecha
Refuta	Resista	Ble ora	Nical Budda
Computa,	Riposta,	Cle's gotta	I'd luvta
Its data's	But it makes ya	Weak spot, a	Unplugya
A fait a	Feel da	Perture in sa	Coup da
CCompli!	Trop!	Voir faire!	Grace!

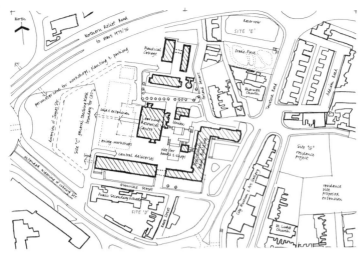

8.19 This map of the Polytechnic site in the mid-1970s shows the proposed northern relief road, which constrained site planning and development for many years. Note the range of sites which were proposed for future development.

[UPPLY, Plymouth collection, plan drawn by David Booth]

With the formation of the Polytechnic, the Student's Union (SU), growing in stature, was soon turning out a news sheet, *Extension*. Issued each week, it must have occupied much of the spare time of its student editors, as at that time the SU had no paid employees, except the sabbatical presidency, which was approved by the Governors in 1971. By 1975 *Extension* had become *Fly*, when the first SU Information and Communications Officer (a sabbatical post from September 1975) considered it the most effective and successful medium of communication amongst Polytechnic students.[20] Still under that title today, it has been an unusually long-lived student publication, though the content of the 1970s might be found heavy going compared with today's approach. Then the SU was the leading member of the Plymouth Area Students Association, and *Extension* carried pieces about the embryonic CFE union, which still worked out of 6 Queen Anne Terrace, and the problem of financing it when membership was not compulsory, the Art College, then in numerous annexes, the status of the Polytechnic compared with the universities, weekend access to watersports equipment because it had to be supervised by Polytechnic staff who were not paid for weekend work, and the state of student grants (there was a protest march in February 1973).[21]

At least the SU had soon acquired a home of its own, 6 Queen Anne Terrace, which was adapted to provide a kitchen, licensed bar, lounge and common room, with administrative accommodation upstairs. Initially it was manned on a voluntary basis. Before the responsibility of managing its own property had sunk in, on at least one occasion the building was left unattended and unsecured overnight. The appointment of a full-time manager provided the necessary continuity, and it was from this base that the SU developed its range of activities and services in anticipation of its purpose-built club facility, which opened adjacent to the new Library, in 1976. This provided administrative offices, refectory and bar, amenity areas, shop, launderette, travel agency, and insurance office. By the end of the 1970s the SU was also managing facilities in the Hoe Centre, and employing eleven members of staff. Apart from the club facility, much of SU income

MISS WESTON

8.20 8.21 Students staying at the Devonport Hall of Residence often used the old Navy slang for their accommodation, 'Aggies', that is Dame Agnes Weston, founder of the Royal Sailor's Rest (temperance hostel/club facility). The Polytechnic leased most of this post-war building in 1973. This drawing shows Miss Weston in 1879 at the age of 39 during the early years of her charitable work with the Royal Navy.

[Photo: A. Kennerley; PCL-LS, Western Figaro (22 May 1879), 1.]

8.22 In this aerial view of the Plymouth site Portland Square has more or less disappeared under the LRC/SU buildings and at the top of the picture the site has been cleared for the General Teaching Block (Babbage Building).

[UPPLY, Plymouth collection]

was devoted to supporting the sixty or so clubs it recognised. Of these seven were for group sports, 27 for solo sports and 46 for non-sporting interests.[22] One of the most valuable of the groups has been Nightline, the telephone counselling service manned by students (after training) for students.

Writing in his Annual Report in 1976, the Director, Dr. Robbins noted the great difference which Student's Union and Library buildings had made to the Polytechnic, providing a focus for the community of students and staff engaged in a common enterprise. The buildings had been opened by the Duke of Edinburgh in July when most students had gone away for the summer vacation, so he did not see the high level of activity which would have been evident had the opening been in the autumn. The Polytechnic's building programme had not progressed as rapidly as had been planned, largely owing to the Government's financial cut-backs. Indeed under the system then operating, it was the fate of almost all new buildings to have their start dates postponed, after which it was frequently two years before a building was ready for use. The SU/LRC complex had been so delayed, as had the General Teaching Block (GTB, now the Babbage Building). A critical disappointment was the delay in starting the student residences at Gilwell Street, given that the Polytechnic was particularly poorly endowed with student accommodation. That situation was not eased until the first phase of the Gilwell complex opened in 1979-80, and the former NAAFI club, which the Polytechnic had purchased, had been converted, to provide study bedrooms and teaching accommodation. Still with only 60 student study-bedrooms in 1979, the accommodation facility at the Royal Sailors' Rest in Devonport, no longer needed for naval personnel, was acquired as student residences. Though named the Devonport Hall of Residence by the Polytechnic, generations of students have known it as 'Aggie Weston's', the term the naval ratings had used in recognition of the founder of the Royal Sailors' Rest, Dame Agnes Weston (1840-1918). The GTB had been started, but in 1976 the contractor went into receivership, so that completion was further delayed. Its completion in the 1978/79 session, triggered off a major round of departmental migration. Designed like the library, as a climate controlled building, it was to house the

Computer Centre as well as provide large lecture theatres, a variety of other educational accommodation, a suite of committee rooms and a refectory. Teaching staff were less than happy with the nature of the staff office accommodation. In the business world open plan offices with personal areas separated only by partitions were all the rage, and the interior designers went to some trouble to convince academic staff that this would be right for them. The arguments were exercised in *Spectrum* for a year or more. Eventually, staff moved into the open plan areas, but the aversion remained. It was not all that long before, through minor adaptations, all academic staff accommodation had reverted to the traditional enclosed offices.

The position of the GTB was influenced by the long standing plan to drive the northern relief road in a great loop from the Charles Church roundabout, crossing Tavistock Road in the vicinity of Drake's Place Reservoir, where a roundabout was envisaged, and curving across Portland Villas to join the North Cross roundabout. The road would have constrained the size of the main Polytechnic site, but offered the possibility of closing North Hill to through traffic and uniting with it the area to the east of Tavistock Road, containing the Museum and Public Library, as the City's cultural and educational zone.[23] The prospect of this road continued to influence planning into the 1990s, but the idea has apparently now been abandoned. Meanwhile developments at the CFE, whose new main building at King's Road, Devonport, was occupied in 1974, removed some of the pressure on accommodation at the Polytechnic site. However, the CFE Maritime Studies department, continued to use the 'nautical college' buildings until it was re-absorbed by the Polytechnic in 1984. The merger of the College of Domestic Science with the CFE, released the area between Portland Square and Sherwell Church to the Polytechnic, for which additional communal facilities were planned, including shops, a swimming pool and student accommodation.[24] The ideas got no further than the drawing board, though the squash courts were eventually built there. In 2000 it was designated for new teaching accommodation and a proper main entrance to the University. In the 1950s a swimming pool had been planned for the site where the library was built, while the allocation of the reservoir site to the education zone had long conjured up ideas of its use for swimming.

Although growing rapidly in stature, developments at the Polytechnic, as just noted, continued to be influenced by the existence of other tertiary colleges in Devon and Cornwall. In public sector higher education sector duplication needed to be avoided, and in 1976 the Directorate of the Polytechnic proposed a South West Higher Education Advisory Council, to include Plymouth Polytechnic, College of St. Mark and St. John (CMJ), Dartington of the Polytechnic College of Arts, Seale-Hayne College, Rolle College, Exeter College of Art, Plymouth College of Art and Cornwall Technical College.[25] It would probably have overlapped with the South West Regional Advisory Council which regulated tertiary provision at all levels in the six south western counties. Though nothing came of the Plymouth proposal, it foreshadowed developments at the end of the 1980s when three of

8.23 The Rumleigh Experimental Station in the Tamar Valley, was acquired in 1971 as an environmental research laboratory for long-term studies on glasshouse and field crops, and related topics.

[UPPLY, Plymouth Polytechnic Prospectus, 1980/1]

8.24.8.25 When the NAAFI club just below Plymouth Hoe, came on the market in the early 1970s, it was purchased for the Polytechnic to ease its pressing teaching and student accommodation problems. The educational television studio was removed from the Science block and installed there. The main occupant for many years has been the School of Architecture. The interior view shows the huge lounge area before it was broken up to create smaller teaching and office spaces.

[UPPLY, Plymouth collection]

those colleges merged with the Polytechnic and others were brought into a closer relationship through partnership agreements and the validation of courses by the Polytechnic.

However links with CMJ (1840) were not destined to progress very far. Preceded by an outpost in 1969, the college had migrated from London owing to its site there being requisitioned for a major road scheme. Its compensation enabled it to build a new college on Plymouth's 'university' site at Derriford into which it moved in 1973. At the same time the Polytechnic worked out an agreement with CMJ, which respected each establishment's independence and separate identity, but committed them to work together in collaborative projects. Oversight would be vested in a joint council. However the problem of the single, overall control of the joint ventures was never really overcome. The main product was the proposal and validation of two CNAA degrees to be offered jointly at each establishment, the BA in Humanities and the BA in Social Policy and Administration. There was some exchange of teaching, but effectively the former was mainly provided by the College and the latter by the Polytechnic. The experiment was relatively short lived, collaboration having effectively broken down by 1977, owing to different management approaches, differing aspirations, and the differing legal status. The College soon went its own way as a free standing college of higher education validated by the University of Exeter.[26]

The Departments and Schools in the 1970s

Although staff allegiances to subject areas, facilities and departments tend to be strong, and structural change can be severely unsettling, there is no standard way of subdividing areas of knowledge and there can be no exclusivity.[27] To a greater or lesser extent subject areas are dependent on each other and this was particularly so for the new ways of grouping subjects which were a feature of polytechnic courses. Industry-related subject areas such as Maritime Studies ranged exceptionally widely in their subject coverage, but breadth was also a feature of new areas such as environmental sciences. Viewed from another direction, there was core subject teaching, such as mathematics and computing, which was needed in almost all subject areas throughout the Polytechnic. Inevitably, then, departmental groupings

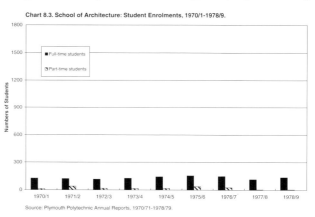

Chart 8.3. School of Architecture: Student Enrolments, 1970/1-1978/9.

Source: Plymouth Polytechnic Annual Reports, 1970/71-1978/79.

are always in tension with each other, and from time to time, owing to changes in scale, popularity, demand or policy, subject areas wax or wane, and regrouping becomes necessary. Despite being a 'polytechnic', that is concerned with 'many arts', there were major areas of knowledge missing from its portfolio, notably the liberal arts and humanities, which was one of the reasons why being involved with CMJ had some attraction. Plymouth Polytechnic's subject scope had historical roots, but it adopted a deliberate policy of playing to its strengths in the sciences, technology and social sciences.[28] Student enrolment data for Maritime Studies, the largest department in 1970, is included at Chart 8.9.

8.26 Third year architecture students in their studio in the late 1970s.

[Plymouth Polytechnic Prospectus, 1978/79]

The School of Architecture, straddling technology and the liberal arts, was absorbed from the College of Art in 1969 as the one advanced subject offered in Plymouth which was not already fully within the College of Technology. Throughout much of the 1970s, as an inheritance of its earlier existence, the School was located, variously, in accommodation at 22 Portland Square, Palace Court, Virginia House and Martin's Gate, being brought together at the end of the decade in the Hoe Centre as part of the general relocation of departments following the completion of the GTB. Its courses have long been tightly regulated by the Royal Institute of British Architects (RIBA), and although its Diploma in Architecture was approved in 1970, the RIBA inspection in 1971, effectively marked it for closure with the four other 'listed' schools of architecture, unless it could achieve accreditation of a first degree course by 1974. Enhancing the staff and restructuring its courses achieved this essential recognition. Its degree course was validated from 1978 and recognised by RIBA for exemption purposes. Always closely related to the local architectural profession, and with several staff engaged in research or practising as architects, from the mid-1970s the School has sought to function as a regional centre for the profession. Chart 8.3 shows that Architecture student numbers were maintained at a little under 150 throughout the 1970s.

8.27 Student Practical work in the School of Engineering Science assessing the performance characteristics and energy balance of a hot air balloon.

[Plymouth Polytechnic Prospectus, 1974/75]

The long established subjects of civil and mechanical engineering had been grouped together as the School of Engineering Science in the restructuring of 1973/4, and Chart 8.4 shows a doubling of full-time student numbers during the 1970s, while part-time numbers fell in the middle years

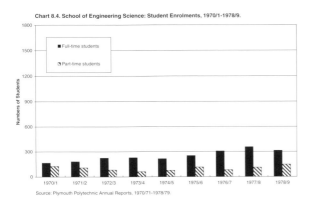

Chart 8.4. School of Engineering Science: Student Enrolments, 1970/1-1978/9.

Source: Plymouth Polytechnic Annual Reports, 1970/71-1978/79.

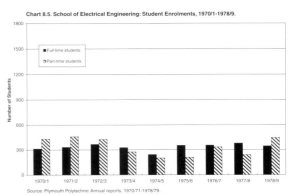

Chart 8.5. School of Electrical Engineering: Student Enrolments, 1970/1-1978/9.

Source: Plymouth Polytechnic Annual reports, 1970/71-1978/79.

8.28 Field work played a big part in student course work in the School of Environmental Sciences. Here a group are making stratigraphical investigations.

[Plymouth Polytechnic Prospectus, 1974/75]

but had recovered by the end of the decade. Students enrolled for London external degrees had completed their courses by the mid-1970s, having been replaced by students taking the CNAA- validated degrees in civil or mechanical engineering. Mechanical engineering continued to occupy the Engineering and Workshop Blocks, but at the end of the decade civil engineering teaching moved into Palace Court which had been vacated by Architecture. The staff development programme resulted in fourteen staff being awarded doctorates, and a feature of the period was the provision of short courses for industry and the growth in consultancy. A particular success was the Plymouth Energy Conservation Unit which achieved an international reputation. Research also made significant progress with the formation of six research groups ranging from composite materials to road surface wear characteristics, and some sizeable research grants were acquired. A feature of these developments was the establishment or upgrading of the suite of specialised laboratories including soil mechanics and advanced machine tools. Another successful area, schools liaison, helped to publicise the merits of engineering careers to school leavers, and the School of Engineering Science was able to boast a very high employment rate amongst its graduates.

A similarly successful employment rate was achieved in electrical, electronic and communication engineering, the subjects encompassed by the School of Electrical Engineering. The combined full-time student numbers (Chart 8.5) averaged between 300 and 400 for most of the decade, though there was a significant drop in 1974/5. Part-time numbers also fell in the middle years but had recovered by the end of the decade. The work in communication engineering was based around the degree, which was a new departure in 1970, but the Marine Electronics Diploma remained significant. In electrical and electronic engineering, the HND/College Diploma course was well established and students successfully found sandwich placements. An interesting development at the end of the decade was the degree course in Scientific and Technical Graphics. Research was developed in five main communication engineering areas, including signal processing and computer-based systems for interactive learning, while in electrical and electronic engineering, micro magnetics and electrical switch contact phenomena were the leading topics. Consultancy continued to be a significant element maintaining contact with industry, while large numbers of short courses were run for the television industry, associated with the introduction of colour television. The television studio was also involved heavily in short course work, for example for police forces, and when the Polytechnic acquired the Hoe Centre, the opportunity was taken to relocate the studios from the Science Block, and, of course, to upgrade this facility.

The School of Environmental Sciences was another department with a facility much in demand and highly rated by organisations outside the Polytechnic. The Electron Microscopy Unit, in its own building immediately north of the workshop block, undertook work on behalf of industry, the health service and government departments, and was, of course, a valuable facility for the department's own research programmes. Having inherited the longest research tradition in the Polytechnic (in chemistry and biology), its research activities, covering environmental science, ecology, chemistry, biology, geography and geology, was of a significant scale leading to nearly 500 research publications in the decade since 1970. There was success in gaining research studentships and fellowships, and government grants for projects carried out at the Polytechnic, with results presented at innumerable conferences throughout the world. As well as developing the Schools's laboratories, mostly contained in the Science block (now the Davy Building), the eleven acre Environmental Experimental Station at Rumleigh in the Tamar valley was acquired in 1971. Here long-term interdisciplinary studies on glasshouse and field crops, pest control, bee diseases, and related topics were undertaken. Allied to the research, of course, were a significant number of research students working for masters and doctoral degrees. Chart 8.6 shows how undergraduate teaching has expanded during the first decade of the Polytechnic, with full-time student numbers doubling from below 300 to 600. Building on the comparatively small numbers taking science subjects (including geography) in the old London external degrees, the CNAA courses in Biological Sciences (1971), Environmental Science (1973) and Geography (1974) proved very attractive to students, while the HND in Applied Biology had no difficulty in sustaining its high level of recruitment. The School was a significant contributor to the Combined Studies scheme, with pathways in chemistry, geology, biology, and geography. It also led the way with the Polytechnic's first taught master's course in Applied Fish Biology, and in collaborative undergraduate provision with Seale Hayne College, a CNAA degree in Agriculture.

Compared with the other schools in the 1970s, Mathematical Sciences appears to have very few students (Chart 8.7). The degree in Physical Sciences was not successful and was discontinued in 1976, and the new HND in Computer Studies was still being built up. Its part-time courses, as elsewhere, did not lead to large numbers in FTE terms. But allocating students to the department owning the course inevitably leaves important service departments with unrepresentative statistics. In the Combined Studies scheme it offered pathways in mathematics and statistics and later computing and operational research, but, as previously noted, it provided

8.29 The advent of CNAA degree courses meant that the Polytechnic could run its own degree awards ceremonies, which soon demanded the largest public hall available. In the 1970s and 1980s this was Plymouth Guildhall. This picture shows a ceremony in 1982.

[UPPLY, Plymouth collection]

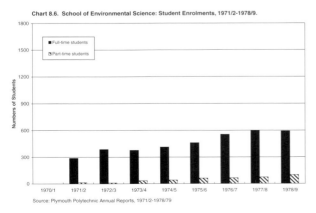

Chart 8.6. School of Environmental Science: Student Enrolments, 1971/2-1978/9.

Source: Plymouth Polytechnic Annual Reports, 1971/2-1978/79.

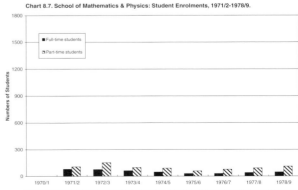

Chart 8.7. School of Mathematics & Physics: Student Enrolments, 1971/2-1978/9.

Source: Plymouth Polytechnic Annual Reports. 1971/2-1978/79. Omits mathematical service teaching to other departments.

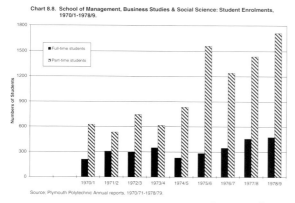

Chart 8.8. School of Management, Business Studies & Social Science: Student Enrolments, 1970/1-1978/9.

Source: Plymouth Polytechnic Annual reports, 1970/71-1978/79.

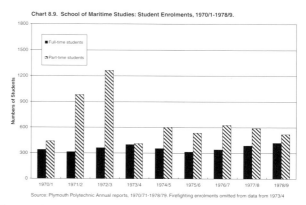

Chart 8.9. School of Maritime Studies: Student Enrolments, 1970/1-1978/9.

Source: Plymouth Polytechnic Annual reports, 1970/71-1978/79. Firefighting enrolments omitted from data from 1973/4

classes at first and second year level in mathematics and statistics in almost every course in the Polytechnic, a very significant commitment. The School's research expanded from work based in physics in 1970, most notably in rheology for which it gained one of the first readership appointments, and it has achieved a number of research grants and studentships.

Chart 8.8 shows the student data for Management, Business Studies and Social Science. Full-time numbers have doubled over the decade from under 200 to about 400. This success was shared equally between the business courses, the BA degree (1973), HND, accountancy and DMS, and the Social Science courses, the degrees in Psychology and in Social Policy and Administration, together with the professional courses for social workers and health visitors. But the trebling of part-time numbers was almost entirely attributable to the large number of part-time and short courses arranged for the business world. Management and Business staff were also involved in the undergraduate partnerships, humanities with CMJ and agriculture with Seale-Hayne College, and were also responsible for delivering the liberal or general studies and management elements which were part of technology courses offered elsewhere in the Polytechnic. The language unit also found a home with the management staff, language being seen as an important attribute for graduates from business and other courses from which students passed into management positions in industry. Research in the business area began to make progress in the 1970s, but there was significant activity in consultancy and in providing business and economic overview reports for industry.

So rapid was the development of Social Science subjects from the late 1960s, that these were separated from Business in 1974-75 to form the School of Behavioural and Social Science. The degrees in Psychology (1973) and Social Policy and Administration (1976) have already been noted, but the School also contributed pathways in politics, sociology and psychology to the Combined Studies scheme and classes on social topics to other courses across the Polytechnic. Staff moved rapidly into research activity and in the second half of the decade acquired a significant number of research grants and studentships. Consultancy also developed rapidly with projects in most areas of the caring services.

Consolidation and Maturity: the 1980s

A strong identity and the much improved levels of self management did not mean that the Polytechnic was free of external controls. Short of complete independence as a private institution, it was bound to remain subject to the twists and turns of Government policy, the bulk of its finance being received from central sources, while the local authority, Devon, through which its income was channelled, still played a significant part in financial oversight and broad policy. In the 1970s, the control, management and funding of public sector higher education had never been satisfactorily worked out. The role and status of local authorities had become blurred, and their autonomy had been threatened. The expansion promoted in 1972 had benefited Plymouth, but it was not very long before the politicians became concerned about the uncontrolled rise in expenditure, especially in the wake of the oil crisis of the mid-1970s. As the pooling system for financing the sector also dictated local authority expenditure, the establishments in public sector higher education naturally felt that they were under attack. All the parties, the local authorities, the institutions, lecturing staff, through their national associations and committees, the DES and the Government, became locked in debate as various ways forward were discussed and found wanting. The 'capping' of the advanced further education (AFE) pool under the Education Act 1980, ensured that the 1980s would be a period of financial constraint, with efficiency, through the allocation and use of resources, as the bye word. The government of the day forced through the creation of the National Advisory Body for Local Authority Higher Education (NAB, 1982), to advise on the apportionment of the AFE pool and on approval of courses, a structure which, for the time being, sustained the local authority interest in higher education.[29]

The changes in the regulatory and financial framework controlling higher education from the mid-1970s have been labelled an attack by some commentators, while others have identified a long drawn out strategy, masterminded by the DES from the early 1960s, to bring all higher education, the universities as well as public sector, fully under its control.[30] The aim, it is argued, was to replace the myriad of indirect structures, such as capital projects and course approval, through which the state was forced to exercise such control as it could achieve, by simple direct regulation of a single higher education system of about one hundred institutions. Individual establishments had no say in the drawn out play. There were two fronts. The creation of the polytechnics, increasingly self managing and free of local authority control, and the break up of the teacher education, were tactics in wresting control of public sector higher education from the local authorities. The breakdown of the independence of the universities was achieved through the transfer of the University Grants Committee (UGC) from the Treasury to the DES, by undermining its authority and turning it into an agent for the state management of the universities. Through the 1980s, the management of the two sectors by the state was brought closer together, culminating in the unifying Higher Education Funding Councils, for England (HEFCE), Scotland (HEFCS) and Wales (HEFCW), from 1993.[31]

8.30 With growing numbers of graduates several ceremonies soon became necessary. In the 1980s, the musical life of the college was vibrant, and joint student/staff ensembles were able to provide live music during the ceremonies.

[UPPLY. Plymouth collection]

The NAB, which lasted until 1988, as a non-statutory body, had no powers of its own, so its recommendations had to be applied through the existing legislative framework. Its planning exercises produced a succession of funding formulae, in which unit costs featured significantly. For the quality dimension it attempted to draw on the CNAA and HMI. Overall, the NAB processes were clumsy and soon a more straight forward mechanism was being sought. Having signalled the new direction in a Green Paper in 1985 and a White Paper in 1987, the establishment of the Polytechnics and Colleges Funding Council (PCFC) in November 1988, was built in to the Education Reform Act earlier that year.[32] Simultaneously, the Act replaced the UGC with the parallel Universities Funding Council (UFC),[33] and freed the polytechnics from local authority control, by turning them into 'independent' higher education corporations funded by the state. It was against this national background that the mergers of Seale-Hayne College, Rolle College and Exeter College of Art and Design with Plymouth Polytechnic, were being negotiated from 1984.

Throughout the time the development of national policy was being worked through, Plymouth Polytechnic was heavily involved in establishing itself as an institution of academic stature, largely through its interaction with the CNAA. At the start of the 1980s, the CNAA policy of 'Partnership in Validation', set out in 1975, was becoming effective in the Polytechnic. Its internal validation and course review arrangements had been approved and CNAA boards were now granting indefinite approval to its courses. By 1985 the internal arrangements had been fully elaborated and almost all courses were validated under delegated authority. The Research Degrees Committee was also recognised for registration of candidates for M.Phil. degrees. Here also progress was such by the middle of the 1980s that the Committee had achieved full delegated powers. Needless to say, the CNAA institutional reviews of 1981 and 1986 had been highly satisfactory, and significant stages on the path towards approving courses and making awards in the Polytechnic's own name.[34] In 1986 Plymouth Polytechnic became one of only ten institutions at that time to achieve fully delegated powers from the CNAA. The accreditation was formalised by the CNAA at a ceremony in April 1988.

Early in the 1980s, the Polytechnic had managed to minimise the effect of the financial constraints imposed in the wake of the creation of the NAB. In 1982/83 a formula based on staff/student ratios (SSR) was adopted for allocating state funding. As Plymouth's SSR had increased significantly during the 1970s, it emerged with the minimum possible cut in the allocation from the pool of only two per cent, marking the Polytechnic as one of the three establishments with the lowest unit costs. But the situation with respect to improving the site and facilities was less promising as a serious shortfall in the funding of capital projects seemed likely. Then the NAB sustained the downward pressure on costs, using a formula for allocating target student numbers by subject area to each institution to which pool funding was related. Although there was an apparent increase for Plymouth, other factors, such as inflation and cuts in local authority contributions, left the Polytechnic with no room for improvements or manoeuvre in the middle years of the decade.

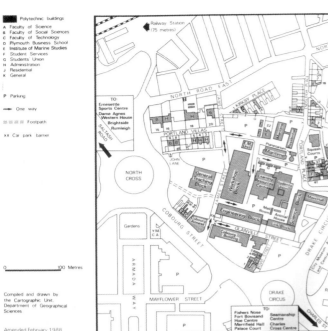

8.31 The site map of 1988, shows how the
Polytechnic was gradually acquiring
properties in the streets within the Coburg
Street/ North Road/North Hill educational
zone, and also the extension eastwards behind
the public library/museum.

[UPPLY, Cartographic Unit, Department of
Geographical Sciences]

The pressure on finances was sustained under the successor to the NAB, the Polytechnics and Colleges Funding Council (PCFC). This was a much tighter, statutory organisation with oversight of many fewer establishments compared with NAB as those predominantly of a further education nature remained under the local authorities. The others, including Plymouth Polytechnic, had become independent higher education corporations as a result of the Education Reform Act, 1988. PCFC required establishments to establish their own internal financial audit mechanisms and to submit financial reports. It set about devising new formulae for the distribution of state funds which would keep the pressure on the already lean ones, such as Polytechnic South West (PSW, the title of the newly expanded college from 1989), as well as force down the unit costs of more expensive colleges. The 'core plus margin' approach was applied for 1990/91: establishments received 95 per cent of their previous year's funding to enrol 95 per cent of their previous year's numbers of students, and were required to bid for the remaining numbers and for their finance, across the range of programme areas.[35] Getting this latter element wrong carried significant penalties for funding in future years, and created considerable local stresses as the Polytechnic teased out the tactics required.

Funding and CNAA oversight were not the only measures of the quality of the work going on at Plymouth Polytechnic/PSW. Although the methodologies of Her Majesty's Inspectorate had changed in the 1980s, the Polytechnic nevertheless continued to undergo subject and institutional inspections. The most wide ranging occurred in 1987-88, at the time of the mergers and change in the Polytechnic's status, but there had been others earlier in the decade concerned with applied environmental science, part-

8.32, 8.33 With the expansion of the
Polytechnic in 1988/89 to become Polytechnic
South West, the house magazine was renamed
and issued in a large A3 format. The new logo,
designed to commission, now appeared on all
publications, note paper and and notices. Here
it was used on the dinner menu marking the
retirement of the director, Dr. Robbins.

[UPPLY, Plymouth collection]

time higher education and research in science.[36] In 1987-88 the HMIs observed 23 courses and examined a range of institutional issues including staff development, quality control research, accommodation, administrative support, learning resources and student support. Their report gave just the right kind of endorsement as the Polytechnic assumed its new status. Generally complimentary in tone, it identified a few issues which were already receiving attention:

"None of these issues stems from fundamental weakness. Rather, they are symptomatic of an institution which has been keen to promote growth and excellence.... The Polytechnic has been effectively managed. It is generally in good shape to face the challenges that will arise as a consequence of its transition to corporate status in 1989."

Weaknesses included the absence of a standard tutoring system across the establishment, a small amount of teaching, a shortage of administrative and clerical support, outdated equipment, inadequate staff accommodation, a lack of tutorial rooms, and an undue emphasis on statistics in the review process. However, in contrast, the list of areas of good practice was lengthy.

That there should be such a favourable report at the end of the 1980s, despite the pressure for ever greater efficiency, owes something to the internal structures which had been put in place in the 1970s and to their refinement from 1980. One important change, not yet noted, took place in 1980, the adoption of a faculty organisation. Although not the only structure under which academic establishments could be arranged, it was by far the most common, and carried with it the overtones of maturity. The implications for almost all sections of the Polytechnic were significant, and the debate was lengthy and by no means easy. What were to be the new subject groupings? Who would become the new heads of department and the deans of faculty? What would be the relationship to the central administration? To what extent would central functions and powers be devolved to faculties? How were the faculty offices to be staffed? These were only some of the questions. In the event there were to be five faculties representative of the strengths of the Polytechnic, and many of the teaching groups were to survive as departments. However, four of the previous schools were brought under the umbrella of the Faculty of Technology which emerged with five

8.34 The Plymouth site has never provided students with a proper range of recreation facilities. The planned swimming bath, gymnasium and exercise hall had to make way for the library and students' union buildings. Apart from a small gymnasium created in the hall of the former Public Secondary School (now the Scott Building), the squash courts photographed whilst being built in 1987, have been the only on-site facility.

[Photo: A. Kennerley]

departments. Three schools emerged as faculties, with some minor regrouping of teaching groups into departments, while the management and business subject grouping opted for the title Plymouth Business School and an internal non-departmental matrix structure. The functions previously carried out by School administrations transferred to the faculty offices, while departmental offices were allocated minimal clerical support. Much of the common administration was to remain centralised into the 1990s. The Combined Studies scheme, spanning all faculties, soon gained its own pseudo-faculty status, a condition of the 1981 CNAA Quinquennial Review, and one or two other new central units came into existence as the Polytechnic assumed more responsibility. The relationship between faculties and the centre was settled by appointing all deans as assistant directors and incorporating them in the executive team.

The expansion of the Polytechnic, in the making through much of the 1980s, eventually tied in with Education Reform Act, 1988, and the final element, the merger with Seale-Hayne College was delayed until the Polytechnic had been designated a higher education corporation, independent of the local authority. In its fifteen years under Devon County Council, the relationship had generally been positive, the Council giving steady support within the constraints with which it was burdened, and nurturing its most significant higher education establishment to its maturity in the 1980s. From the Polytechnic's perspective perhaps Devon's most significant contribution was its brokerage of the unification of the four establishments. The Polytechnic acquired three new faculties, Arts and Design, Education and Agriculture, Food and Land Use and eight new departments. Most of the subject areas were new and greatly broadened the Polytechnic's subject scope. Overlap in the humanities and performance arts between the Exmouth and Exeter campuses, led to those staff and students at Rolle joining a department in the Faculty of Arts and Design, while Plymouth's activity in education, developed in the Learning Resources Centre, now came under the Faculty of Education. Apart from some restructuring within the existing faculties on the Plymouth campus, in response to changes in subject emphasis, the only other change during the polytechnic years at faculty level came in 1991, when the Institute of Marine Studies lost its faculty status, in the wake of the demise of professional courses for Merchant Navy, becoming a very large department in the Faculty of Science.

The mergers had great impact on the administration and central services. A review of the three service centres: learning resources, student services and computing, undertaken in 1987 with mergers pending, led to the creation of an umbrella organisation, Academic Services, with its own Assistant Director to provide a link at the highest management level. Below this, the former heads of centres became heads of services: library, student and computer. It was into this structure that the equivalent services in the new faculties were absorbed. Similarly, their administrative structures had also to be aligned with the arrangements prevailing at Plymouth. The transfer of functions and responsibility took place to a carefully planned timetable. Although of

8.35 Even in the late 1980s, the Polytechnic South West Students' Union felt the need for a coat of arms to use as a blazer badge and this design was created. Using the same motto adopted in the 1940s provided a link with the Students' union of forty years earlier.

[UPPLY, Plymouth SU collection]

8.36 On 19 December 1983, a violent storm caused the collapse of the cladding of the south wall of the Science Block. Some 30 tons of brickwork fell onto the Link Block. Fortunately, it being a weekend in the Polytechnic vacation, there were no casualties.

[UPPLY, Media Services]

8.37 The last of the 1970s building developments, the General Teaching Block accommodated the Polytechnic's growing computing facility in its basement. This relationship was symbolised by the design of the building's cladding, which drew its inspiration from the computer punch cards then in use. It is now called the Babbage Building after the father of the computer Charles Babbage (1791-1871).

[UPPLY, Marketing Dept.]

necessity the individual units comprising the management structure had grown in size, the broad shape of the post-merger structure of PSW remained substantially that adopted at the start of the 1980s.

The absorption of three colleges greatly increased the Polytechnic's estate, in area of land owned and number of properties. But even before 1988, estate management at Plymouth had become a substantial operation, which involved juggling routine maintenance and the updating or conversion of existing properties with the planning or adaptation of new buildings, all within the prevailing financial situation. Indeed, the constraints of the 1980s meant that a number of proposals were delayed or never materialised. However, the desperate need in Plymouth in the context of rapidly expanding numbers of students did lead to a number of significant building developments. Early in the decade the second phase of the Gilwell student residences complex was completed, and there was some relief for the shortage of staff, teaching and administrative space through the acquisition and conversion of private houses, particularly in Portland Villas and Endsleigh Place. In the mid-1980s, the Public Secondary School (now the Scott Building) and Plymouth's former education offices (now the Reynolds Building) were acquired. Neither was ideal for higher education usage, but the former was converted to create the larger lecture theatres and larger class rooms now required for the larger undergraduate class sizes. The Polytechnic also gained the maritime halls of residence, Merrifield in Greenbank and the ten story block on Portland Square (now Mary Newman Hall), both of which needed updating to meet the modern standards for student residences. At the end of the decade more residences in Gibbon Street were being planned: Robbins, which would include a modern large lecture theatre and conference suite, while the terrace of houses there also became student residences. The most prestigious development in teaching accommodation was undertaken at Plantation House where rebuilding produced a modern block (Cookworthy) for the Plymouth Business School.

Despite the proliferation of Polytechnic buildings in various locations, it seems that throughout the 1950s, 1960s and 1970s, no thought was given to how the buildings and sites were to be known. The architects of the major buildings allocated them working titles, which tended to stick after they were finished: Engineering Block, Science Block, Link Block, General Teaching Block, and for the Maritime suite, Residential Block, Communal Block, Teaching Block. Private houses have continued to be known by their street name and house numbers or former names. Some have acquired nicknames, such as the White House. Clearly such casual usage could be unsatisfactory. The first attempt to name the major buildings was made in 1985, but allowed to lapse. Finally in 1991, in anticipation of hosting the annual meeting of the British Association for the Advancement of Science (BAAS), the main buildings were allocated the names of famous people, scientists, technologists, artists, explorers, politicians, educationalists, having Plymouth, Devon or Cornwall associations hence: Astor (now Mary Newman Hall of Residence),

Babbage, Brunel, Cookworthy, Davy, Fitzroy, Hawkins, Isaac Foot, Robbins, Scott, Smeaton. Some confirmed previous associations or locations: Merrifield, Agnes Weston (now Devonport Hall of Residence), Gillwell, Hoe Centre, Palace Court, Sherwell. It did not prove easy to identify a suitably famous woman. Lady Astor (the first woman MP) seemed an obvious solution. Astor Hall, the name of the first 'university' hall of residence in 1929, had been named jointly after Lord and Lady Astor. But the building and its name were still in use in Stoke (as a centre for the disabled) and the use of the same by the Polytechnic led to postal confusion and a change to Mary Newman (Francis Drake's first wife). In the 1990s, however, Barbara Hepworth's name was attached to the new administration building.

Students are hardly aware of all the policy making, administration, politics, management structures and so on, which comprise the operational setting of the college they attend, but they do remember buildings and learning conditions, their teaching staff, course features, student life and anything that affects their finances. Throughout the 1980s, the student body at Plymouth had the use of a central, modern Student's Union, other Polytechnic rooms for recreational use, a much improved off-site sports facility at Ernesettle, the underwater facility at Fort Bovisand, and the watersports centre at Coxside. The completion of the squash courts on the east side of Portland Square and the inclusion of a gymnasium in the remodelled Public Secondary School, provided some convenient on-site facilities. The general pattern of SU activity was well established, with continuity provided particularly by the great majority of students following three year full-time courses, and a number of student sabbatical officials. Their social needs were well supported by the Polytechnic's accommodation, welfare and recreational services. But all this did not prevent a violent reaction to the Government's first inroads on student finance, following the early NAB financial exercises in 1982/83. Events in Plymouth were part of a nationally orchestrated reaction by the National Union of Students. The occupation of Directorate offices, 18 Portland Villas, in February 1983, caused severe disruption to Polytechnic business for a week or so, though without significant damage. In the letter to the Director, national demands were mixed with local aspirations, and the tone was somewhat aggressive. The students called for a public statement of opposition to the cuts in student grants, the removal of the deadline on payment of tuition fees, the establishment of childcare facilities, better access for disabled students, improved campus lighting, better consultation with students in decision making, and the restitution of the block grant to the SU which had suffered a 21 percent cut since 1980. The affair was settled with the students quietly vacating the offices, and those matters which the Polytechnic was able to handle, such as access and lighting, were addressed. Play group provision was finally made in 1989.

Students, backed by Polytechnic staff, were very active in the British Polytechnic Sports Association (BPSA), both as participants in its competitions and through active involvement at the organisational level.

3.38 Several large communications research contracts were won by the Polytechnic, and managed by the centres. One of the earliest was the PACNET project (1984), the Plymouth Audio-Conferencing Network, for £250,000 sponsored by and industrial group including British Telecom, was concerned with the provision of education, training and small business advice. This picture shows an audio conference in progress. The special loudspeaker/microphone linked to the telephone system, is on the table in the centre of the group.

[UPPLY, Plymouth collection]

8.39, 8.40 This sculpture by Ron Mansfield of Dartington College of Arts, has been a talking point at the entrance to the library ever since it was installed in 1984.

[UPPLY, Media Services; A. Kennerley]

For much of the 1980s Plymouth students served on BPSA committees, and at various times students held office as Vice Chairmen/Vice President or Chairman/President. Recreation staff provided continuity at various levels, notably Brian Mawe, who served as staff officer and organised annual sailing and badminton competitions, and Winni Coles who organised events for ladies hockey and ladies badminton. Plymouth students, in teams or individual sports, were champions or runners up at various times in cross country, association football, rugby union, canoeing, cricket, fencing, golf, netball, and riding. Between 1985 and 1989 Plymouth dominated the skiing events.[37]

Although there are numerous past students of all ages to be found in Plymouth, Devon and Cornwall, as well as across Britain and overseas, the Polytechnic and its predecessor colleges had no strong tradition of contact with former students. As subject level some groupings had emerged in the 1970s, notably PYNDA, the Plymouth Nautical Degree Association, which played a useful role in employment opportunities for Plymouth graduates. Rolle College had a former students organisation in the 1960s and 1970s which had subsequently lapsed. In contrast Seale-Hayne brought with it in 1989 a vibrant, long standing Old Sealehaynian Association, whose members over the years had made significant contributions to the College. It was against this background, that the Polytechnic in 1990 set up its alumni organisation to foster links through a register and the publication of a magazine, *In Touch*, recognising the potential value of long-term external links in the increasingly competitive world of higher education.

Table 8.6

Polytechnic Staffing, 1981-1990.

	1981	1984	1987	1990
Directorate	3	3	3	4
Deans of faculty	5	5	5	8
Heads of centre,etc	3	3	4	2
Heads of department	17	12	18	24
Readers/professors	9	11	11	20
Principal lecturers	57	66	66	93
Senior lecturers	222	244	260	306
Lecturers	55	55	54	69
Research	48	45	45	64
Total academic	19	444	466	600
Technician	154	156	154	215
Administrative (P)	35	78	162	) 290
Administrative (C)	66	87	45	)
Manual	118	127	148	209
Total Non-academic	373	448	510	714
Total staff	792	892	976	1304

Source: UPPLY, Annual Reports, 1980/81 to 1990-91. Heads includes heads of departments and centres, and the Research Co-ordinator. Lecturers includes centre staff on lecturing grades. Administrative staff are separated as professional or clerical, the latter including various other grades. Manual staff includes, catering, ground and caretaking staff.

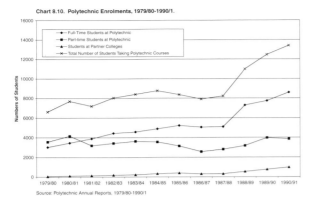

Chart 8.10. Polytechnic Enrolments, 1979/80-1990/1.

Source: Polytechnic Annual Reports, 1979/80-1990/1

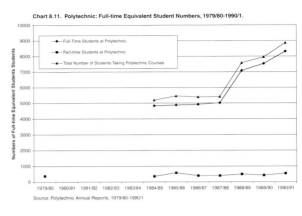

Chart 8.11. Polytechnic: Full-time Equivalent Student Numbers, 1979/80-1990/1.

Source: Polytechnic Annual Reports, 1979/80-1990/1

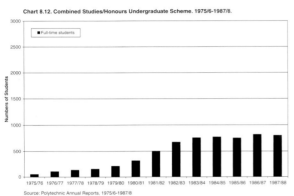

Chart 8.12. Combined Studies/Honours Undergraduate Scheme. 1975/6-1987/8.

Source: Polytechnic Annual Reports, 1975/6-1987/8

By the end of the 1980s size of the student body was showing significant increases, partly in the context of funding mechanisms, partly owing to absorption of the three colleges, partly because of the development of improved access arrangements, and partly through the growing numbers of franchise courses in partner colleges with their potential for feeding students into the Polytechnic. Between 1980 and 1991 numbers of students at the Polytechnic increased more than three times, part-time as well as full-time, and almost four times if students taking Polytechnic courses in partner colleges are included. In comparison with other Polytechnics, that based at Plymouth was climbing from being one of the smallest to becoming one of the larger establishments (Charts 8.10 and 8.11). Throughout this period, the Combined Honours scheme was more than growing in proportion, becoming such a significant vehicle that its numbers ceased to be counted separately, but were allocated proportionately to the numbers of particular faculties (Chart 8.12). Indeed, the modular methodology was increasingly being applied to existing courses as they came up for revalidation, as well as to new courses.

Naturally, the numbers of Polytechnic employees had to increase to cope with the greatly increased and more diverse workload. However, the rate of increase in numbers of academic staff lagged behind that of the student body, 211 per cent compared with 266 per cent. The numbers of administrative staff trebled, as did manual staff employees, though the growth in technician numbers was rather less marked. By 1991 PSW had about 2000 staff names on its books. However, Academic staff not only found themselves teaching much larger classes, with the attendant growth in assessment, and having to adapt to modular structures, they were also faced with new contracts in which the leave arrangements linked to the term system, of the local authority period, gave way to university arrangements and included an expectation in research as well as administrative duties and teaching. The quality of all these spheres of activity, teaching, administration and research, was increasingly under internal and external scrutiny. Academic staff were used to the work of the CNAA and of the HMIs, but from 1990 a system of annual teaching staff appraisal, emulating practices long established in the forces and in industry, was yet another dimension of the changing culture to which they had to adapt. In addition arrangements for the regular mutual observation of teaching and the external evaluation of research activity were on the agenda.

The 1980s produced a series of initiatives which reflected the Polytechnic's growing stature in research, development and consultancy. Following the establishment of the Research Committee, an early move was the appointment of the first group of readers, usually with the task of leading the development of research in their subject areas. In 1981 the first professorships were announced. These were awarded to a few existing staff having established and substantial records in personal research and publishing, supervising research students and gaining research grants. The ability to offer a professorial grading was also significant in making new

8.41 The Polytechnic is visible from many locations in the city centre of Plymouth. The Science Block (Davy Building) is seen here bearing the Polytechnic South West logo.

[UPPLY, Plymouth collection]

senior appointments and attracting to the Polytechnic new staff having substantial research experience and portfolios. As the number and variety of research and consultancy projects increased, the need for a satisfactory way of relating to the industrial and commercial world was becoming more marked. Receiving income had long been a problem under local authority administrations, in educational terms geared only to expenditure, where in the worst scenario, monies earned by educational establishments simply disappeared into council coffers with no benefit accruing to the college. Before the polytechnic era this had certainly inhibited research and stifled entrepreneurial initiatives. So in 1983 Plymouth Polytechnic set up its own company, Polytechnic Enterprises Plymouth Limited (PEP) to serve as the much needed interface, by overseeing the administrative, contractual and financial dimensions and advising academic staff in the formative stages of research and consultative initiatives.

Table 8.7 provides an indication of the changing scale of research activity in its various dimension from financial awards and research students to outcomes in terms of reports and numbers of publications, which place PSW near the top of public sector establishments and ahead of some long established universities. By no means all the activity has been at the high science and technology ends of the spectrum, significant though that has been. There have been many projects concerned with industrial applications and with society in general. Amongst these have been a number having an educational dimension. For example, a series of large awards from industry and the state have established Plymouth as a leader in distance learning through teleconferencing, and the use of satellites for broadcasting educational material with an interactive dimension. The Polytechnic was also heavily involved in government initiatives such as the PICKUP project for updating industrial skills and the Enterprise in Higher Education scheme for enhancing links between higher education and employers.

8.42, 8.43 During the 1980s large communications discs appeared on the roof of the Engineering Block and in the Polytechnic grounds marking the development of major research projects using the new dimension for communications.

[UPPLY, Plymouth Polytechnic Prospectus, 1989/90] [add picture of satellite discs]

Table 8.7
Polytechnic Research, 1981 - 1990.

	1981	*1984*	*1987*	*1990*
Refereed publications	137	169	257	301
Conference papers	11	36	275	329
Reports			66	148
Books/chapters	11	24	39	42
Articles/other output	21	50	21	
Special lectures	132	233		
Research income (£)		537,656	1,258,726	3,484,223

Source, UPPLY, Annual reports.

The Plymouth faculties in the 1980s

In its original university usage, the term 'faculty', deriving from the four faculties of the medieval world, theology, law, medicine, arts, simply referred to groups of members of learned professions, such as academics, concerned with a particular subject. Faculty was simply a university term for a department.[38] More recently, however, it has acquired a supra-departmental usage, as an overarching structure for a number of departments whose subjects have some form of relationship with each other. In essence a faculty is a layer of administration and management in a large educational organisation, which at one end of the scale of devolution of functions from central management, may be close to being a separate establishment. Given the tendency of academics in a subject area to sub-divide when numbers grow beyond about twelve, it was inevitable that the expanding Polytechnic would regroup, and hardly surprising that it would adopt the more recent idea of a faculty structure. Faculties for Technology, Science, Business and Social Science, had become conventional in the twentieth century, but that for Maritime Studies (discussed in Chapter 4), with its interdisciplinary focus, was novel. However it represented the kind of subject grouping found in the three additional faculties (1988/89), Art & Design, Education, and particularly Agriculture (discussed in Chapters 5, 7 and 6), despite the apparently simple approach of converting each college to a faculty. Student enrolment data for these four faculties is given here to facilitate comparisons (Charts 8.13 & 8.14)

The Faculty of Technology emerged with the most departments and the largest number of students in 1980 (Chart 8.15), all touching technology, but ranging in scope from the applied art of the School of Architecture to the pure science of the Department of Mathematics, Statistics and Computing. Indeed the latter might well have been in the Science Faculty but for its involvement in computing. The Department of Computing was separated from Mathematics and Statistics in 1986. Four departments had emerged from the two 1970s engineering schools, Civil Engineering, Mechanical Engineering, Electrical and Electronic Engineering and Communication Engineering. During the 1980s, hardly a year was to pass without a new course being introduced, including BSc degrees in Electrical and Electronic Engineering, Computing and Informatics, a BA in Applicable Mathematics, and HND in Civil Engineering, a BEng in Engineering Systems. Access was given attention through engineering foundation courses including extended engineering and extended science courses in collaboration with partner colleges. Some of this development was funded through a major grant from

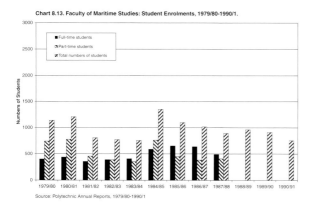

Chart 8.13. Faculty of Maritime Studies: Student Enrolments, 1979/80-1990/1.

Source: Polytechnic Annual Reports, 1979/80-1990/1

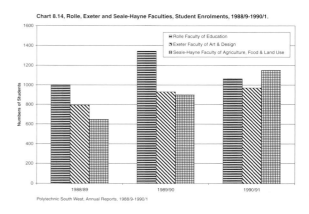

Chart 8.14, Rolle, Exeter and Seale-Hayne Faculties, Student Enrolments, 1988/9-1990/1.

Polytechnic South West, Annual Reports, 1988/9-1990/1

Chart 8.15. Faculty of Technology: Student Enrolments, 1979/80-1990/1.

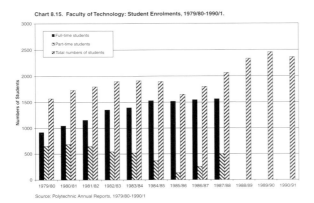

Source: Polytechnic Annual Reports, 1979/80-1990/1

Chart 8.16. Faculty of Science: Student Enrolments, 1979/80-1990/1.

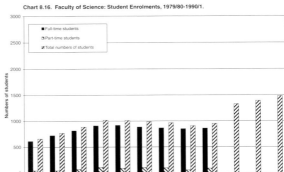

Source: Polytechnic Annual Reports, 1979/80-1990/1

8.44 Students engaged in production study using a capstan lathe in the Mechanical Engineering Workshop.

[UPPLY, Plymouth Polytechnic Prospectus, 1987/88]

the 'Switch Initiative' for new engineering courses. Amongst the products of links with industry was the Plessey Chair of Electronic Engineering, and a series of professional accreditation visits in Architecture, Civil Engineering and Mechanical Engineering. Research groups created in this period included the Industrial Statistics Group, the Centre for Teaching Mechanics, The Centre for Research in Information Storing Technology and the Engineering Design Centre. Strong links with schools were promoted through competitions for teams of youngsters to build mechanical structures for testing to destruction. Amongst major research projects were those in mobile communications, super computers, a device for measuring waves in the context of coastal protection, assessment of the effect of concrete cancer, a mini compass, and computer controlled unmanned ships.[39]

Compared with Technology, the Faculty of Science largely emerged from the School of Environmental Science, with three departments, Environmental Sciences (including geology, chemistry, physics and environmental science), Biological Sciences and Geographical Sciences. The Department of Geological Sciences was separated in 1985, in a

8.45, 8.46 Students at work in the Microbiology Laboratory and at the electron microscope in the 1980s.

[UPPLY, Plymouth Polytechnic Prospectus, 1985/86]

8.47 A Psychology lecture in the Babbage Building in the 1980s.

[UPPLY, Plymouth Polytechnic Prospectus, 1981/82]

8.48 Electoral research and opinion polls carried out by the Polytechnic were in demand nationwide in the 1980s, as they are in the University of Plymouth today.

[UPPLY, Plymouth Polytechnic Prospectus 1989/90]

reorganisation of Environmental Sciences, in recognition of the newly validated degree in Applied Geology and the strong research portfolio. At the beginning of the 1990s the Faculty was further expanded by the incorporation of the Institute of Marine Studies as a department. Chart 8.16 shows the expansion of student numbers in the Faculty, excluding maritime students. As well as its established single honours courses the Faculty was a significant contributor to Combined Honours scheme. The geology degree had already been developed through the scheme and in 1990 a degree in Applied Chemistry emerged from particular combinations of Chemistry modules. Each of the departments had high levels of staff involvement in research, maintaining the established tradition for scientific research and ensuring that the Faculty was a leader in the Polytechnic. In 1986 Biological Sciences was one of only five departments in the country to be recognised by NAB for research and teaching in biotechnology. This Department was also particularly strong in fish biology research, which led to the establishment of a Fish Nutrition Unit. Research in Chemistry received a particular accolade through the award of the Silver Medal of the Royal Society of Chemistry to Professor Ebdon. Other projects in the Faculty included remote sensing as a research tool, studies of the sandstone cliffs at the onshore oil field at Wych Farm in Dorset, global warming studies and studies of the economic effects

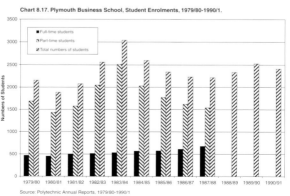

Chart 8.17. Plymouth Business School, Student Enrolments, 1979/80-1990/1.

Source: Polytechnic Annual Reports, 1979/80-1990/1

of the Channel Tunnel. The electronmicroscopy unit maintained its services to local organisations and other sections of the Polytechnic, and in 1991 installed a new one million pound unit. The discovery by the geologists of a mini-dinosaur in 1991, caught the attention of the media.

In adopting the title 'Plymouth Business School' (PBS) for the management and business faculty, the Polytechnic was following the practice for naming such departments in other parts of the country. With strong links to local commerce and industry, PBS continued its policy of serving the community through offering a large number of short and part-time courses suited to the professional development which was required. It also found itself with subject areas which were particularly attractive to students. In addition to its large HND course in Business Studies (and related courses in partner colleges), PBS soon introduced BA degrees in Business Studies and in Accounting, and from 1987 offered the Master in Business Administration (MBA) course. In 1988 its BA in Marketing was probably the first such course in the country, and it also offered a BA in International Business from that year. Chart 8.17 graphs the changes in student numbers studying at PBS. The creation of the South West Economy Unit in 1987, and the production of a series of reports has kept the public eye.

The Faculty of Social Science (retitled Human Sciences in 1989) was formed with three departments in 1980, Psychology, Social and Political Studies, and Social Work. Its undergraduate and professional courses were well established and it made a considerable input to the Combined Honours scheme. In 1989 this portfolio was expanded through the introduction of the BA in Social and Organisational Studies (Police). At masters level, the MSc in Clinical Psychology was offered from 1981, and an MA in Policy and Organisational Studies from 1989. The approval in 1986 of the Doctor of Clinical Psychology as a taught doctorate was an unusual development. The widening range of teaching activity is reflected in the data on student numbers shown in Chart 8.18. In 1986, along with other areas of the Polytechnic, it looked as though financial cuts of 30% recommended by NAB would completely undermine the work of the Faculty, but the strong links it had with outside organisations, which included provision in

Chart 8.18. Faculty of Social/Human Science, Student Enrolments, 1979/80-1990/1.

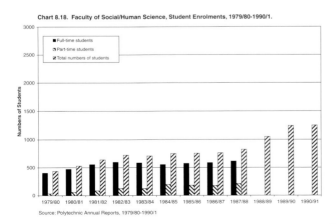

Source: Polytechnic Annual Reports, 1979/80-1990/1

association with the local schools of nursing, and the expressions of support received played a part in averting that disaster. A high level of research and consultancy was well established in the Faculty. Research projects included leisure for disabled people, stress disorders including the impact of disasters, the risk of heart disease, the well-being of long-distance patients, bereavement counselling. The Local Government Chronicle Election Centre with its detailed database of local election results was a development of 1990, and part of the high profile of the politics staff in providing data and commentary to the media. In 1988 the Agewell Roadshow was doing the rounds advocating health lifestyles.

Staff in all faculties were involved in enhancing the public image of the Polytechnic through public appearances, the participation in and organisation of conferences and through service on national and international bodies. By the end of the 1980s Plymouth was on the map as a conference venue. One of the last events before designation as a university, was the hosting of the BAAS meeting in the summer of 1991, the first time it had been entirely hosted by a Polytechnic. Needless to say staff from all areas were involved in giving demonstrations and hosting sections, and they provided a significant number of the academic lectures.

8.49 Development Diagram

1. In 1898, those ancient inspirers of study, thought and creativity, the Muses, the goddess daughters of Zeus and Mnemosyne, were called up to portray likenesses of the main subject areas addressed in Devonport's new Science, Art and Technical Schools building. The four main panels depict Art, Science, Mechanical Engineering and Naval Architecture.
[Photo: UPPLY, Media Production Services]

II. This visual representation of enlightenment through study emphasises the values of scholarship, quality, people, community, accessibility and effectiveness. It was installed in a new window opening in the University of Plymouth's Sherwell Centre in 1994.
[Photo: UPPLY, Media Production Services]

III. The rapid changes in local public sector higher education between 1988 and 1992 were reflected in the changing signs which adorned the buildings.
[Photos: UPPLY, Marketing Department (PP & PSW); A. Kennerley (UoP)]

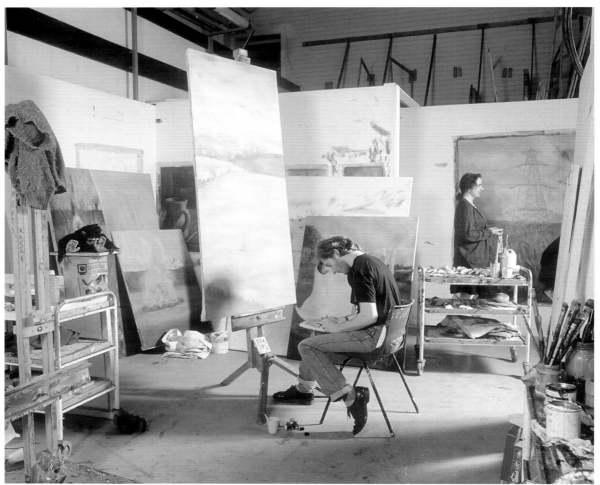

IV *After over one hundred years residence behind the gothic splendour of the much extended Albert Memorial building in the centre of Exeter, Exeter College of Art and Design (now part of the Faculty of Arts and Education) moved out to the Earl Richards Road North suburban site in the 1970s. This became the University of Plymouth's Exeter Campus in 1988. In both locations the real colour lay inside, particularly in student work produced in the art studios.*
[Photos: A. Kennerley (Albert Memorial building); UPPLY, Marketing Department.]

V. The ivy which has grown across the north block of the Seale-Hayne Agricultural College quadrangle presents a dramatic image from the archway in the south block. The quad provides a fine location for special student social events at Seale-Hayne Faculty while the bar of the student's union offers a regular meeting point.
[Photos: UPPLY, Marketing Department]

VI. On the Exmouth Campus, now occupied by the Faculty of Arts and Education, the buildings are mostly those erected in the 1950s and 1960s for Rolle College, named here over the main entrance to the Daw Building. Music education was one of the strengths of the former college which merged in 1988. The summer display of flowers before the administration building will be seen no more as the space is now occupied by the new lecture theatre.
[Photos: UPPLY, Media Production Services]

VII. At Plymouth , the student union patio, with the Library adjacent, is at the heart of the campus and a hive of activity in term time. The Babbage and Davy Buildings, resplendent in their new, sleek cladding, stand out when viewed from the city centre to the south.
[Photos: UPPLY, Marketing Department and Media Production Services]

VIII. In this aerial view taken in the summer of 2000, the Plymouth Campus is outlined in red. The original site is towards the top left of the picture and the student village developed in the 1990s is towards the bottom right. [Photo: Western Morning News.]

9.1 *The University of Plymouth logo continued the circular theme established in the previous PSW logo. The three bands represent the south west peninsula and the three counties of Cornwall, Devon and Somerset.* [1]

University

CHAPTER NINE

By the end of the 1980s the Polytechnic had progressed to such an extent that it was a university in everything but name. It was a corporate entity managing its own affairs and independent of local control and with delegated authority in academic matters. A sizeable student body had been built up and, across its four campuses, it had substantial physical assets and a reasonably wide subject base working almost entirely at advanced levels. Nor was Polytechnic South West standing still. It was already overseeing advanced work in local further education colleges and its portfolio of links with higher education institutions overseas was growing. Like the other polytechnics, PSW took every opportunity of drawing its achievements to the attention of education ministers and officials, and to agencies such as the PCFC. Yet despite all that had been achieved, the Government decision to grant university status so soon after allowing corporate status came as something of a surprise. Although no longer closely involved on a day to day basis with higher education, the City of Plymouth could at last take pride in the identity of a university city after some seventy years of disappointment.

9.2 This 1992 application reply card acknowledges the change of status, provides a visual explanation of the University of Plymouth logo and emphasises the four principal locations at which students could study.

[UPPLY, Plymouth collection]

Being allowed to call itself University of Plymouth was, of course, important for the establishment's external image and internal self-esteem, but it by no means signified any relaxation in the relentless downward pressure on unit costs exerted through the funding council mechanism, or on the pace of change affecting British higher education. Student numbers continued to grow for some years. The 1990s saw the withdrawal of much of the state funding for students, a revised approach to the distribution of finance for research, and a complete re-organisation of the oversight of standards and quality. Nevertheless the University found ways of improving its range of educational and residential accommodation, areas of marked weakness at the end of the 1980s, and it achieved some significant successes through the development of its partnership network and the incorporation of nurse education. Towards the end of the century, the cumulative effect of government policy, would lead to an era of further retrenchment.

9.3 9.4 The recognition of the University of Plymouth was a matter for celebration on 18 June 1992, after 70 years of disappointment from the time the idea was first explored.

[UPPLY, Plymouth collection]

The decision to allow the Polytechnics "...if they wish, to adopt a university name or to include it in their titles...", was announced in the white paper, *Higher Education: a New Framework*, in May 1991, though legislation would be required.[2] The guidelines demanded full consultation with staff, local authorities, industry, and higher education establishments in the region, to avoid duplication or similarities in titles, and names which were offensive or misleading. Proposals would be subject to Privy Council approval. Once the news had spread amongst PSW staff, the collective brain power set about the task of choosing a name. Plymouth had not long before gone through a similar exercise, and attempting to cater for the sensitivities of the merging colleges, had settled on Polytechnic South West. Even in the short period since 1989, this had hardly proved to be a memorable title, and it was generally thought that its lack of geographical precision had led to some loss of student applications as well as of public image. The staff consultation exercise produced over sixty suggestions and over six hundred responses. Seventy per cent of staff, favouring the association with a town or city,

9.5 *Professor R.J. Bull, from 1984 Deputy Director of Plymouth Polytechnic, from 1989 Director of Polytechnic South West, and from 1992 the University of Plymouth's first Vice Chancellor, has been at the heart of the momentous changes to higher education in Plymouth for over fifteen years.*

[UPPLY, Plymouth collection]

9.6 *Mr Alan Macfarlane, wearing the robes of the Chairman of the Governors of the University of Plymouth.*

[UPPLY, Plymouth collection].

nominated either University of Plymouth or Plymouth University. Some of the other suggestions were untenable in the context of other establishments as far east as Bristol, though senior management must have been concerned about the two confused staff who offered 'University of Portsmouth'. The tendency of those whose geography is weak to hear Plymouth but think Portsmouth is longstanding. So it was that following the passage of the Further and Higher Education Act, 1992, the PSW applied to the Privy Council for its name to be changed to University of Plymouth. Also as a result of the Act, it acquired the power to award degrees.[3] The process adopted by the Government was very different from that used in earlier rounds of university creation, while the period of recognised gestation at the end of which the Polytechnic acquired the designation, twenty-two years, compares favourably with the thirty-three years taken by the University of Exeter from the time it was funded by the UGC, whose criteria were rather different from those prevalent in 1992.[4]

Building a Corporate University in the 1990s

From the University's perspective the Further and Higher Education Act provided the keystone for a revised management structure, which was substantially in place as an outcome of the Education Reform Act (1988), and the mergers of 1988/89. The original preparatory work for incorporating the three colleges as faculties of the Polytechnic had been undertaken in the context of continuing oversight and support from the local authority, Devon County Council. Although much of the day to day management had long been the responsibility of the Polytechnic there were still some elements, notably in the financial area, which were conditioned by local authority processes. The comparatively short period between the white paper *Higher Education: Meeting the Challenge* in 1987, which announced the intention to establish the polytechnics as higher education corporations, and the Education Reform Act in 1988, which brought them into existence, demanded the rapid introduction of revised management and financial arrangements appropriate for the running of a large business:

"In 1989, the vocabulary of the then polytechnics underwent a remarkable transformation. In Plymouth, students became 'clients' or 'customers', heads of department 'managers'; the language of finance - cash flow, profit centres, full cost pricing, liquidity ratios - became commonplace....Up to 1989, the Polytechnic's financial systems...had been maintained by the LEA. Problems of budgets, deficits (overspends), cash flow and asset management were almost beyond the institution's experience."[5]

One casualty of the management changes was the post of Chief Administrative Officer, a key appointment in 1970 and a member of the directorate team, who for twenty years had had overall responsibility for all non-academic staff and their functions, including finance, registry, personnel, sites and buildings, secretariat and technical services. Now under the Vice-Chancellor, functions relating to the academic dimension, registry, library, computing, welfare, registry, partnerships, and so on became the responsibility of the Deputy Vice Chancellor (Academic); finance and estates came under the Deputy (Resources); and the remaining functions, secretariat, personnel administration, health and safety, under the Deputy (Secretariat). As already noted the deans of faculty, managing devolved budgets, now share in the day to day management of the University as members of the Senior Management Executive, under the chairmanship of the Chief Executive of the new higher education corporation, Professor R.J. Bull, Director of PSW from 1989, and Vice-Chancellor of the University from 1992. Although the Governors adopted the traditional title used by universities for their chief executives, as yet the titular position of Chancellor has not been used. Fiscal acumen and skilled management abilities were to prove of vital importance in seeing the University of Plymouth make a successful transition in a period of rapid change and financial constraint.

Plymouth had become experienced at adapting rapidly to new state-imposed financial situations, one advantage that it had over the old universities which had suddenly to get used to the very different *dicta* of the Universities Funding Council, following the abolition of the UGC. The 1992 act levelled old and new universities by placing them in the same funding regime under HEFCE. But there was to be no stability in the funding mechanisms these agencies imposed. In the drive to reduce the unit of funding per student, competitive price bidding under PCFC had had the effect of causing a rapid expansion in student numbers without additional resources. For 1993/94, HEFCE introduced a method by which required efficiency gains were inversely related to the average unit of council funding per registered student. The penal element in these funding council methodologies, could cost the University dearly. Student withdrawals in 1993/94 cost £660,000, which had to be absorbed in the faculty budgets. The methodology changed again in 1994/5 in order to eliminate fee only growth. Now award bearing student numbers (MASNs) were imposed with penalties if the target numbers were not almost exactly met. Achieving such tight requirements required a tricky management balancing act, but the pressures on institutions were compounded by drastically reducing the tuition fees paid for students and demanding increased accountability through financial monitoring by the funding agencies. Such demands inevitably increased the numbers of administrative staff needed to gather the data.

Despite the difficult funding context, the University has through the 1990s been able to create a financial cushion by steadily building up its reserves. In 1989 these stood at only £200,000, and a deficit was forecast for 1991/2. But the unexpected expansion in student numbers helped turn this into a surplus, and most years since then the University has been able to add in excess of £2 million to reserves, so that by 1996/97 they stood at £22.5 million. As security against unexpected setbacks such sums are a vital element in financial management, but they can also be used as collateral for improvements in University facilities, and that is one way in which a number of conversions or new buildings have been undertaken. Already a major force in the local economy, the University had a turnover in 1993/94 of £68 million, which had increased to £90.8 million in 1996/97. By then it was estimated that the spend in the region was £109 million and that some 5,000 local jobs depended on the University, which had relations with some 2,000 businesses.

9.7 Under the CNAA the Polytechnic had been able to make recommendations for honorary awards. Now as a University it was able to do so in its own right. Here politicians with Plymouth connections have been honoured, Michael Foot, Janet Fookes and David Owen.

[UPPLY, Plymouth collection].

9.8 Since the opening of Plymouth Pavilions, the University's numerous award ceremonies for Plymouth based students have been held there, as it provided the largest location in Plymouth. A complete range of academic gowns and hoods had to be designed and manufactured ready for the 1993 ceremonies incorporating the University's adoptive colour of terracotta.

[UPPLY, Plymouth collection].

9.9, 9.10 In 1993 a permanent link with the old Hoe Grammar School was established when the surviving old boys, the Old Drakonians, presented the University with a ceremonial Mace. Now paraded at all degree award ceremonies, the Mace was designed and made at the University's School of Arts and Design in Exeter, by David Hawkins and Brian Adams, with the assistance of a team of five other members of the department.

[UPPLY, Plymouth collection]

Finance was not the only area in which Government policy prompted the development of special administrative units to co-ordinate the most effective responses from the University. High on the list has been the whole area of standards and quality, which had acquired a special emphasis from the 1980s. Unlike the old universities the former polytechnics were well accustomed to evaluation by external agencies, notably the HMIs who looked at the delivery and product of courses, the CNAA and BTEC who assessed the fitness of the establishment to deliver courses and made the awards, and the learned institutions which accredited courses for professional purposes. In addition there were the internal systems of validation and the external examiner system. The 1992 Act removed the need for the CNAA, and it was dissolved in 1993.[6] Her Majesty's Inspectorate was also disbanded (1991), though for schools and departments of education, the OFSTED methodology was substituted. So the Act provided for the HEFCE to assume responsibility for quality assessment. Meanwhile the institutions had established the Higher Education Quality Council (HEQC) to handle quality assurance. The methods adopted were controversial, but there was a considerable element of peer assessment. As with other universities, staff from Plymouth underwent special training before joining visiting teams which assessed courses in other establishments. During the 1990s the approaches were changed three times, but overall Plymouth achieved excellent awards (or equivalent) in a wide range of subject areas.

At the subject level, the processes involved much more than staff had been used to during HMI visits. A particular dimension was the paper trail in which the handling of particular issues was traced through all their stages. A breakdown in the record could lead to the loss of a grade, even though the staff knew that an issue had been managed correctly. The culture this demanded was alien to many staff. So the Quality Evaluation and Enhancement Unit (QEEU) was formed in 1993 to coordinate experience, and train and advise staff teams. In 1997 the quality activities of HEFCE and HEQC were brought together in a joint body, the Quality Assurance Agency (QAA), which thus became responsible for all the quality dimensions, audit, assurance and assessment. This is currently addressing the validity of academic programmes through the definition of benchmarks. The internal quality processes were augmented by the introduction of the student compact (subsequently charter), the annual student questionnaire and student review of module delivery. It has not proved easy getting the questions and methodology in the last two right, as these processes touch lecturer sensitivities. This was yet another aspect of the changed status of higher education institutions to which staff have had to adapt in recent years.

One significant outcome of the changed culture has been the much greater recognition given to the educational dimension than had been in the past. It has never been easy to pin down the professional element amongst university academic staff.[7] The educational dimension of being a lecturer had long been swamped in universities by the subject, research and publication dimensions, and in technical colleges by the subject and industry dimension.

These were the criteria for making appointments. There was no teacher training requirement. Gradually from the 1970s the Polytechnic offered the opportunity of in-service training, though its part-time courses were mostly populated by further education college staff. On this was built the new staff induction course which has gradually become an increasingly substantial programme and can now lead to recognition by the Staff Education and Development Association (SEDA) for Accreditation as a Teacher in Higher Education. This in turn offers one route to membership of the Institute of Learning and Teaching (1999), membership of which has the support of the University. More recently, the University has established advanced educational grades to match the advanced research grades of reader and professor: teaching fellow and professor. Achieved through submission of portfolio, in the British context these are still too new to have gained the general approbation accorded to the research grades, though it might be noted that in some societies the word professor actually means teacher.

The higher profile accorded to teaching quality coincided with concerns about the negative impact of handling ever increasing class sizes. How could a satisfactory student learning experience be sustained without significant increases in numbers of academic staff? Traditional small group sessions, tutorials and practicals including field work were in danger of being squeezed out. Internally, a staff development manager was appointed to promote the sharing of good educational practice, and new phrases were added to the staff vocabulary, 'away days' and 'student centred learning' (SCL). Full advantage was taken of external funding initiatives, such as Enterprise in Higher Education (EHE) and more recently Science Education Enhancement and Development (SEED), through which staff could bid to undertake projects to test out solutions to educational problems and to provide links with industry. The industrial management technique of annual staff appraisal, introduced in 1992, as well as offering a structure allowing staff to evaluate career development, encouraged staff to participate in staff development events. Regular peer teaching observation, another novelty in the 1990s, attempted to provide a non-threatening means of improving performance in the classroom. With the SSR now approaching 1:20, which for some staff meant many class sizes in excess of 100, in some cases even with third year students, the cumulative effect of rapid change with a variety of additional demands, undoubtedly increased levels of stress amongst staff. The establishment of the Occupational Health and Safety Centre in 1993 was a recognition that staff as well as students, sometimes need specialist counselling support.

The change, in a decade of change, which perhaps added more to work loads than was appreciated at the time, was the decision to adopt a semester structure for the academic year from 1993. Long in use on the continent and in America, this was an alien arrangement in Britain. Although widely debated in committees and other events, the idea would certainly have been voted down had it been put to a ballot of staff. They could see a doubling of the assessment and administrative work load, the fragmentation of the learning cycle, reduced student motivation and no particular educational

9.11 As well as the University logo, the Mace is engraved with the coats of arms of the City of Plymouth and the Counties of Devon and Cornwall. The base engravings shown here, represent the various faculties of the University.

[UPPLY, Plymouth collection].

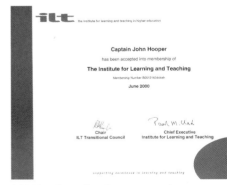

9.12 The advent of quality assurance has placed much more emphasis in higher education on the abilities of lecturers as teachers. The University has run its own staff training schemes for many years. Staff are able to study education to a high level, and may be admitted to membership of the Institute of Teaching and Learning.

[UPPLY, Plymouth collection; John Hooper].

9.13, 9.14, In 1996, the Tor and South West
College of Health was incorporated in the
University as the Institute of Health Studies.
In Plymouth it was allocated the Reynolds
Building as its base.

[UPPLY, Plymouth collection; A. Kennerley].

9.15, 9.16, 9.17 At Taunton the Institute of
Health Studies has accommodation at
Somerset College of Arts and Technology; at
Pool in Cornwall it occupies the Penhaligon
Building; at the University's Exeter campus it
is based in the Veysey Building.

[UPPLY, IHS]

benefit. It was, however, a period in which state pressure for the more
efficient use of educational resources caused institutions to look to the
possibility of attracting students from abroad for short periods, so that it
seemed sensible to be able to offer the semester period of study. In fact a
significant proportion of universities made the change more or less at the
same time, which led staff to suspect a hidden agenda leading to the
introduction of a four term or three semester year. Particularly worrying has
been the long dead period in the middle of the academic year, which many
students have treated as an extended Christmas break. Only seven years on,
some universities are reverting to terms, though in a recent ballot of
University of Plymouth staff, opinion divided roughly equally between
reverting or staying with some form of semester structure.

Although the change to semesters was phased, every course in the
University had to be completely redesigned and at the same time structured
in standard units or modules. It was not simply course structures and the
timetabling of staff, students and teaching accommodation which were
affected. The academic regulations had to be rewritten, and staff had to adjust
their understanding of the regulations as well as their teaching cultures in
relation to the shorter time-frame allowed in semesters. With modularity
came the pressure to widen subject combinations, providing the valuable
opportunity to many more students of having experience of two distinct
subjects. Time tabling inevitably became more complex, though through the
arbitration of the Combined Honours Office, this was achieved successfully
using manual approaches and the central allocation of non-specialist
teaching rooms. This had been introduced in an attempt to make the best use
of the space available. In 1997, however, with the manual approach to room
allocation near collapse, a commercial time tabling computer package was
purchased and introduced in the hope of easing the process on the Plymouth
campus. Unfortunately, this aspiration proved unfounded in the short term.
The chaos which ensued in its first year of operation was overcome through
the intervention of staff experienced in the nuances of time tabling. At that
time there were some 5,000 modules on offer to about 12,000 students so by
rationalising student choice, reducing the number of modules on offer and

9.18 In 1994, The University of Plymouth's success in making higher education widely accessible in the south west region, through its extensive partnership network, was recognised through the award of The Queen's Anniversary Prize for Higher and Further Education.

[UPPLY, Plymouth Collection]

the number of pathway combinations, and through the more systematic and standardised collection of data, time tabling problems were brought under control. It is difficult to avoid the conclusion that at Plymouth as, perhaps, at many other universities, the desire to provide greater student choice coupled with the understandable wish of academic staff to promote their particular specialisations, had led to nearly unmanageable course structures.

Although staff workloads undoubtedly increased in the 1990s, between 1992 and 1997 sufficient additional staff were engaged to maintain the academic staff/student ratio at about 1:17 and the support staff/student ratio at about 1:11. The reduction caused by the incorporation of nurse education staff in 1995.6 was soon 'corrected' through rationalisation. Over the past five years increasing student numbers, especially in the part-time/short course sector, and the continued pressure on finances, has raised the academic staff student ratio to about 1:17.5 and that of support staff to about 1:14. The ratio between support staff (administrative. Clerical, technical, manual) and academic staff remained constant at about 1:1.5. Much of the support staff growth was in faculty offices as increasing amounts of administration were devolved from the centre. But there was also growth in the number of administrative units engaged in specific tasks, often associated with the demands of Government and the Funding Council. With so many changes, flexibility in staffing was increasingly important, and in the latter part of the 1990s approaching a fifth of positions were of a temporary nature.

9.19, 9.20, 9.21 The Cookworthy Building, for the Plymouth Business School, was completed in 1994. On the fifth floor its Conference Room offers spectacular views of Sutton Harbour and Plymouth Sound.

[UPPLY, Plymouth collection; photos: A. Kennerley]

Since the Polytechnic days, the scale of the University of Plymouth's activities has increased considerably, in Plymouth and in the South West region at its other campuses and at partner establishments. In terms of numbers of students, regardless of which measure is taken, the scale has nearly doubled. Charts 9.1 and 9.2 break down the registration data since 1991/92. On the University's campuses full-time students, the core of its work, now exceed thirteen thousand, while the numbers studying part-time and taking short courses has grown in recent years to nearly nine thousand. Partnership student numbers rose to exceed three thousand. Thus the overall head count reached twenty-five thousand students. Whether this level can be sustained in the present climate, which is throwing much of the cost of higher education on to the individual student, remains an open question. With less than half its students coming from homes within convenient commuting distance in Plymouth, Devon or Cornwall, there is concern that those coming from further afield may in future be tempted to study at establishments nearer to their homes.

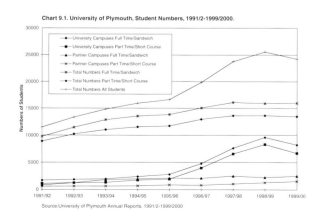

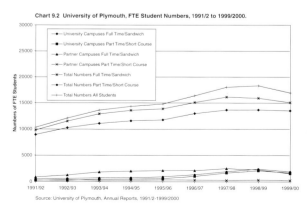

A major development in the 1990s has been the expansion of partnerships with other colleges in the region, in which the University validates the delivery of courses of higher education in local establishments, at the end of which University of Plymouth awards are granted. All such colleges in Devon, Cornwall, Somerset and Jersey now participate in the arrangements, which also embrace naval education and training establishments thus giving external recognition to the quality of naval training. To facilitate these developments, the University early in the 1990s decided to phase out its own BTEC/EDEXEL HND and HNC courses and to encourage partner colleges to develop their own range of courses for those awards. Since then some of the better developed colleges have had degree awards approved, thus bringing most aspects of higher education within reach of potential students who for personal reasons were not able to travel to Plymouth for their advanced study. This has added significantly to the already large amount of validation work co-ordinated by the University's Validation Office and to the work load of academic staff who undertake the evaluation of partner establishments and maintain the ongoing contact to ensure that the University's standards are being upheld. It was for this "exceptional work of the highest standard", that the University of Plymouth was awarded a Queen's Anniversary Prize for Further and Higher Education, in 1994.[8]

The flow of new courses (programmes in the jargon of the period) throughout the 1990s has been substantial. By 1993 there were already 38 access courses in operation across the region and in September 1992 some twenty new courses started at partner colleges, and a similar number in September 1993, a pattern which has been sustained. A particular issue which has had more focus as the decade progressed has been that of 'articulation', the arrangements, or educational ladder, through which successful students at partner colleges could progress to degree studies at one of the University campuses. With the development of new courses at the University itself, and the re-validation of existing courses, it is hardly surprising that in excess of seventy validation events became a typical annual work load. The incorporation of the Tor and South West College of Health in January 1996, as the Institute of Health Studies (now part of the Faculty of Human Sciences,) added another batch of courses as well as some 1300 FTE students, a move that would be significant in the context of events in 2000. Plymouth had long had links with local nurse education, from the days of the separate schools of nursing, and of course in connection with social work and health visiting. With sub-degree courses now largely based in partner colleges, the University has concentrated course development at undergraduate and postgraduate levels on courses having stronger relevance to future employment. The growing numbers of taught masters courses, often with a part-time study facility, also recognises a trend in that direction as well as the tendency of industry and graduates to look for an element of more focused study after industrial experience.

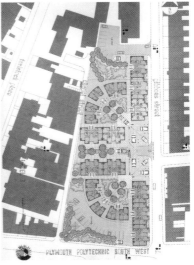

9.22, 9.23, 9.24 1994 saw the completion of the first of four major building developments on the Plymouth campus in the middle 1990s. The Robbins complex, named to recognise the contribution of Dr. Robbins, Polytechnic Director in its formative years, provides student accommodation of unusually high standard and incorporates a conference centre which has seen heavy use since it opened.

[UPPLY, Plymouth collection]

Some indication of the changed higher educational climate in the 1990s has already been conveyed. An aspect not so far addressed has been the

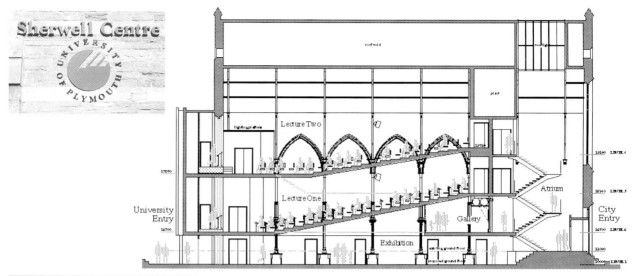

Recital to celebrate the opening
of the Sherwell Centre

University of Plymouth

JOHN LILL

Tuesday 27 June 1995 - 6.30pm
Opening ceremony - 6.45pm
The recital will be followed by a buffet supper in the
Robbins Conference Centre

seat O 14

*9.25, 9.26, 9.27, 9.28 One of the most
dramatic building developments of the 1990s
was the conversion of Sherwell Church to
provide two large lecture theatres and an
exhibition facility. This elevation shows how it
was achieved. The internationally renowned
concert pianist, John Lill, gave the inaugural
performance in 1995.*

[UPPLY, Plymouth collection; photos: A. Kennerley]

heightened role played by the professional institutions in the content and nature of courses related to particular industries and fields of employment. Professional accreditation, which has a long history, provided partial exemption from the requirements laid down by professional bodies, for full member status. The importance of the relevant bodies, for example in pharmacy and architectural education, has already been noted. A wide range of courses at the University of Plymouth are granted such exemptions, but, as part of their roles in controlling entrance to particular professions, these bodies have been very active in recent years, most notably with technological subjects, in setting new standards and evaluating academic courses, in some areas substantially influencing the nature of the courses offered. For University staff responsible for accredited courses, the recognition is important both as a marketing feature and as a form of wider recognition for their department's academic achievement, in research and consultancy as well as in course delivery.

Table 9.1
Research Students, Awards and Income, 1991/2 to 1999/2000

	Students	*Degrees Awarded*	*Income £ million*
1991/92	263	35	4.4
1992/93	367	37	5.2
1993/94	460	42	6.0
1994/95	523	49	6.0
1995/96	570	64	7.2
1996/97	550	73	6.3
1997/98	555	78	8.4
1998/99	529	68	8.5
1999/00	468	65	9.4

Source: University of Plymouth, Annual Research Reports and Annual Reviews.

An important underpinning to a successful accreditation visit is the nature and extent of research and consultancy in a subject area. As a

Polytechnic, Plymouth had risen to be one of the leading public sector higher education institutions for its research activity, and in the 1990s this position was more than sustained amongst the new universities. Its research income has trebled to over twelve million pounds annually, research student numbers have doubled to over 500 and the number of research degrees awarded annually has also doubled to some seventy (Table 9.2). For many research active staff the 1990s have been dominated by the three Research Assessment Exercises (RAE) in 1991, 1996 and 2001, in which the research activity (especially publications) of subject teams is graded by a national panel. This provides the basis for future research funding by HEFCE. Changes to the criteria for assessment, seen as favouring the long-established research universities, have meant that despite a greatly increased level of research activity at the University, Plymouth's bids in a larger number of subject areas, actually generated less research funding through this mechanism in 1996 than had resulted from the previous exercise. Since 1992, the number of research outputs (articles in journals, conference papers, books, reports, etc.) annually has increased from about 1200 to over 1800 in 1999.[9] In the broad area of interaction with industry, the University's company, PEP, has been converted to a technology transfer company and doubled its turnover to some two million pounds. There has also been a significant expansion of the Teaching Company Scheme, which places graduates with industrial companies to assist the upgrading of management processes. In addition the University has joined with Plymouth City Council and Devon and Cornwall TEC, in promoting the Tamar Science Park, where the first building opened in 1998, the Innovation and Technology Transfer Centre.

Such have been the changes in the physical entity of the establishment since the mergers of the late 1980s that thinking of the University as that group of educational buildings on the northern edge of Plymouth City centre in the triangle bounded by Tavistock Road, Coburg Street and North Road, seriously under-represents the magnitude and extent of its presence in the

University of Plymouth

HEPWORTH HOUSE

Formal Opening
and
Unveiling of Sculpture
by
Sir Alan Bowness, CBE

Tuesday 7 November 1995

9.29, 9.30, 9.31 Hepworth House, named for Barbara Hepworth, the sculptor who worked in St. Ives, was an unusual conversion of a row of late nineteenth century houses. The façade on North Road has been preserved, but the entrance is now on the south side. This Hepworth sculpture, The Three Forms, may be seen in the foyer. Many of the University's central administrative staff work from this building.

[UPPLY, Plymouth collection; photos: A. Kennerley]

9.32, 9.33, 9.34, 9.35 Toward the end of the 1990s the condition of the 1960s and 1970s buildings was such that major renovations to the external cladding had to be undertaken. The external appearance of the Babbage, Smeaton and Davy buildings was radically altered in the process.

[Photos: A. Kennerley]

South West of England. As has already been shown, for a century or more it has always been the case that higher education under the auspices of the central establishment was to be found in a variety of locations in the Plymouth area. Now the University estate includes buildings on its four campuses at Plymouth, Newton Abbot, Exeter and Exmouth, and the buildings of the Institute of Health Studies in Cornwall and Somerset, a span of some 150 miles. Invariably, the extent and condition of the spaces in which staff and students must work lags behind the ideal, and despite new developments, Plymouth must still be classed among those universities whose facilities need improving. In recent years it has been successful at every round in competition against other establishments, for funding of Council 'poor estates' works. Indeed, because buildings do not last for ever, the University has had to undertake major programmes of renovation at the same time as trying to extend its range of modern buildings.

At each of the University's campuses, buildings erected in the 1960s in the great expansion of technological education of the period, are now about thirty to forty years old, and some have needed major structural work during the 1990s. Most noticeable have been the recladding of the Babbage building, which suffered from concrete cancer, completed in 1995, and the recladding of the Smeaton, Link and Davy buildings, completed in 1999. Even with buildings whose main structure is in good order, it is probably the case that major internal re-organisation takes place at intervals of less than ten years, owing to the changing needs of education. Nevertheless, there are lecture theatres, for example in the Davy Building which survive, in their original condition after forty years, and it is possible to find rooms in other buildings which have not been redecorated in thirty years. Old smaller buildings, often private houses, continue to be acquired and renovated for short-term use within the general areas of the main campuses as part of the policy of completing acquisitions within the educational zones, in anticipation of redevelopment at some time in the future.

Particularly at Plymouth, there have, however, in recent years been some significant building developments, in the early 1990s under the Hunter scheme for the regeneration of educational facilities, under the HEFCE Poor Estates programme and, most recently, under the National University Partnerships Programme organised by Jarvis, plc, with the support of financial houses. On the student accommodation front, the Robbins complex of 430 study bedrooms incorporating the University's conference suite, started in 1992, was occupied in 1994. The Radnor accommodation scheme was completed in 1999 adding a futher 400 study bedrooms, and a further scheme to complete the University village in the areas east of Plymouth's Museum and Public Library, will be ready later in 2000. A hotel at Exeter provided 100 beds, and a new development will provide a further 100 beds in 2000. And at Newton Abbot, the Frank Parkinson Building was refurbished. The most dramatic development in teaching accommodation has been the conversion of Sherwell United Reform Church to provide two, 250 seat lecture theatres, and the University's cultural centre for concerts and

exhibitions. The other major development at Plymouth was the Cookworthy Building completed in 1994, and occupied by the Business School. In Somerset and at Cornwall College (the Penhaligon Building, 1997) there were buildings for the Institute of Health Studies, which found its Exeter base in the new library building (1997) on the Exeter campus. At Plymouth, the Reynolds building was adapted for its use. Soon there will be a new lecture theatre at Exmouth and three new educational blocks on the Plymouth campus. The major disappointment in this period was the failure to acquire the site of the former Royal Engineering College at Manadon in Plymouth, which had been closed in 1995. The location offered student accommodation teaching and support facilities, such as a library, and it seemed appropriate to move the Faculty of Technology there. However, converting all this to suit the University's needs would not have been cheap. In the end, with the Government departments concerned pursuing different agenda, acquiring Manadon became too expensive for the University. It has been demolished to make way for a housing development. Perhaps from the student viewpoint, studying and living at Manadon away from the main student union in the centre of Plymouth might not have been so attractive.

9.36, 9.37 Amongst student sporting successes has been the University's student sailing teams, which have been highly placed in national and international student yachting events over a number of years.

[UPPLY, Plymouth collection]

For a significant proportion of students in the 1990s, time at university has been dominated by the struggle to limit indebtedness, the removal of maintenance grants and in some situations the need to contribute to tuition fees exacerbating the situation. Parental support, where offered, often fails to fill the gap Student loans are leading in some cases to large debts exceeding £10,000. Part-time work, by no means plentiful in the south west, frequently conflicts with the demands of study. Some of the more severe cases have been helped through the University's hardship fund which in 1993 supported 887 students to the extent of £263,000. As the decade has progressed the need has increased. Amongst attempts to draw public attention to the situation was that at the Exmouth campus in 1996 in which a mock student evacuation was staged as a protest against the funding cuts. Other factors impeding a focus on study include the situation of students having family responsibilities, a growing number, for whom timetabled classes and coursework deadlines can conflict with the daily cycle of family life. It is with these kinds of circumstances that both the University and Student Union's welfare unit are concerned day by day.

9.38 Throughout the 1990s Freshlings Nursery has provided a haven for the young children of members of the University.

[Photo: D. Griffiths]

The Union facilities on each of the four campuses remain the focus for student social life, and despite the difficulties experienced by some students, many are able to participate fully in club and society activities, which remain every bit as extensive as they were in the 1980s. In general the buildings occupied are the same as in that period, despite the great expansion in numbers and so the facilities are very heavily used. The one noticeable addition on the Plymouth campus, has been the erection of a wooden chalet-type bar on the patio roof area not too far from the entrance to the library, at which students weary of their books may be seen taking 'time out'. On a wider stage, University of Plymouth students have enjoyed some success at national and international sporting events. Notable have been the yachting teams which in 1995 came second in the World Student Yachting Cup, held in Finland with eighteen teams competing. That same year Plymouth also hosted the British Universities Sports Association (BUSA) National Dinghy Championships. The following year the Plymouth team won the BUSA National Yachting Championships held at Portsmouth. In 1997 Karen Friend was a member of the BUSA gymnastics team at the World University Games in Sicily. Students have also enjoyed success in national events arising out of their studies. In 1994 two final year law students won the National Client Interviewing Competition, and in 1999, Flo Whitcombe, who studied at Exmouth, won one of the first National Teaching Awards. In 1999, a publishing student won the Paul Hamlyn Foundation publishing award for the best dissertation on publishing and Janet Beale (Agriculture) reached the finals of the Pinnacle Awards for Excellence in Business Management.

Faculty development at Plymouth in the 1990s

Attention has already been drawn to increasing scale, diversity and rate of change of educational activity at the University of Plymouth during the 1990s. No section of the establishment has remained untouched by these processes. Most noticeable in recent years has been the devolution of management and administrative functions (within specified limits). Indeed, by the end of the twentieth century five faculties each had larger student numbers than had Plymouth Polytechnic as a whole in the early 1970s. In relationships between faculties and the central management of the University, it is tempting to find parallels with the relationships thirty years ago between the Polytechnic and the local authority which had just been persuaded to devolve a whole range of functions to the establishment. Is it too far fetched to extend the model, particularly with reference to Devon County Council after 1974 responsible for colleges at Exmouth, Exeter and Plymouth and elsewhere? Given the University's regional responsibilities at an academic level at least, it is already functioning as a kind of regional educational authority. With devolved responsibilities, for example budgets, student administration, academic validation and quality, aspects of staffing, faculty offices are now significant administrative units, and faculties are increasingly evolving sub-units for handling particular tasks.[10]

The academic staff have remained grouped by subject interest and course delivery in departments, but for research, consultancy and other relationships, numerous recognised and informal groupings, some crossing departmental and faculty boundaries, have been created particularly in recent years. Similarly, there have been increasing numbers of new course developments, taking advantage of modular structures, which cross departmental and faculty boundaries, some at undergraduate level, but particularly at post-graduate level. Invariably these have been designed to serve the needs of particular industries and professions. A major change at undergraduate level was the closure of the Combined Studies office in 1994, responsibility for students taking combinations of pathways being devolved to the faculties. Where strong sub-modular schemes had been developed, this was a logical evolution and transition was seamless. But where the strength lay in the single honours culture closely related to departments, the change was less satisfactory, particularly for students taking pathways in different faculties where differing patterns of administration prevailed. This has resulted in some curtailment of the numbers of students attempting courses combining differing disciplines. Charts 9.3 and 9.4 giving student enrolment data for the Seale-Hayne and Arts and Education faculties (chapters 5, 6 and 7), are included here.

9.39 Amongst the innovative research projects in the Faculty of Science has been the computer modelling of the simple sponge. The modelling and analytical software is used to formulate new absorbent materials.

[UPPLY, Marketing Dept.]

By 1992, owing to the incorporation of the Institute of Marine Studies, it was the Faculty of Science which had the largest student body, some 2,500 students, a number which had increased to over 3,000 by the end of the decade (Chart 9.5). The bulk of scientific teaching was at undergraduate level in the well-established subject areas of biology, chemistry, geology, geography, and the environment. The development of the Earth Sciences degree in 1992 provided a structured approach to natural combinations between geography and geology. In 1994 the Faculty assumed responsibility for the new BA in European Studies, though the only subject it contributed was geography, the other content, which included languages, being provided by the Business School and Human Sciences. Student demand for a course in Marine Biology was satisfied in 1995 by the incorporation of a new course in the Department of Biological Sciences, which the following year

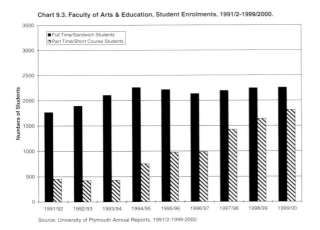

Chart 9.3. Faculty of Arts & Education, Student Enrolments, 1991/2-1999/2000.

Source: University of Plymouth Annual Reports, 1991/2-1999-2000

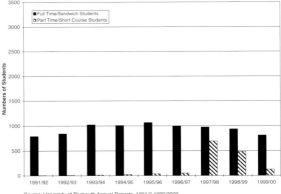

Chart 9.4. Seale-Hayne Faculty of Agriculture, Food & Land Use, Student Enrolments, 1991/2-1999/2000.

Source: University of Plymouth Annual Reports, 1991/2-1999/2000

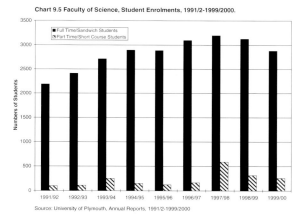

Chart 9.5 Faculty of Science, Student Enrolments, 1991/2-1999/2000.

Source: University of Plymouth, Annual Reports, 1991/2-1999/2000

restructured its courses as a modular scheme with eight undergraduate award titles to cater for over 500 biology students. At taught masters level the MSc in Applied Marine Science drew all the departments together in the delivery of the first modular course at that level. The Faculty did particularly well in teaching quality assessment, achieving excellent grades in geology, geography, environmental policies and oceanography in 1994/5.

Behind this advanced teaching lay the exceptionally strong research culture in the Faculty. Its Analytical Chemistry Research Unit enjoyed a world reputation for the analysis of environmental samples, such as those from the Wheale Jane pollution incident in Cornwall. It was recognised by the EC Bureau of Community Defence, and its work had led to the banning of tributyl tin from boat anti-fouling paints. In 1994 the University recognised the Plymouth Environmental Research Centre (PERC) which received a 'Realising Our Potential' award for research in chemicals in sediments. Within two years PERC was the largest environmental research centre in Britain with some fifty scientists and 150 associates, with staff functioning internationally as advisers and involvement in research programmes. Much of its work has industrial applications such as calculating the fluid absorbtion properties of porous materials. The status of Geographical Sciences has been marked recently by its establishment of the

9.40 Following the university's investment in the Tamar Science Park close to Derriford Hospital, The Post-Graduate Medical School was able to occupy these new premises in 1998.

[UPPLY, Plymouth collection]

SEED programme, concerned with good practice in science teaching, and the basing of the National Study Centre for Geography, Earth and Environmental Sciences in the Faculty. This is a particularly significant development. Geography was one of four subject areas in the Faculty to achieve the highest ratings in external teaching quality assessment.

A similar range of research success has been achieved in the Faculty of Technology. In 1991 it was distinguished as one of only six National Design Centres by the Science and Engineering Research Council (SERC). Then in 1993 Sony Research Centre in Japan endowed the Sony Chair in Electronic Information Engineering. The associated Centre for Information Storage Technology Research Council gained over one million pounds in research funding in 1999. Another achievement was the successful bid to establish a Telematics Network for the South West whose purpose was to bring together computing with communications. In 1992 the School of Architecture became the home of the Regional Centre for Architectural Conservation with a research programme on earth buildings including the properties of cob, and a programme of short courses in aspects of conservation. Other research in the Faculty has included super springs for the automotive industry and mathematics education for children. Out of the latter has come a card game to make learning mathematical tables fun. An important element in promoting engineering in schools has been the annual competition for school teams to design and construct a model structure, such as an oil rig for testing to destruction, run by Civil Engineering staff.

In recent years some of the engineering courses in the Faculty of Technology have shared in the national difficulties in recruiting undergraduates to their courses, while at the same time the engineering institutions have been raising the entry standard which they required if accreditation of undergraduate courses were to retain their accreditation. These trends and the need to make courses as relevant and as interesting as possible have led to a range of new and restructured courses, and the

9.41, 9.42 A student success in the Faculty of Technology was the design for a racing bicycle frame adopted by the Greek National Team, and raced in the World Cycling Championships.

[UPPLY, Marketing Dept.]

consolidation of technology in the University by moving Marine Technology courses, students and staff out of the Institute of Marine Studies in 1998 to a new Department of Mechanical and Marine Engineering. The Faculty already had a large portfolio of BA, BEng, MEng, and BSc, MSc and HND courses in 1992. These underwent a major restructuring in 1998, but meanwhile between 1993 and 1996 a range of new courses had been added, including Media Lab Arts, Robotics and Automated Systems, Computing Systems and Networking, Architectural Studies (design environment), Building and Surveying. Also towards the end of the 1990s came a string of taught masters courses including Architectural Conservation, Computational Intelligence, Data Storage Systems, Communication and Signal Processing. A notable student success was the carbon fibre framed bicycle which was ridden at the Olympic Games at Atlanta. In 1998 Civil Engineering topped the national league table for external teaching quality assessment, while Mathematics and Statistics received a high rating. Chart 9.6 shows the trend in student numbers, with a significant increase in part-time and short course students.

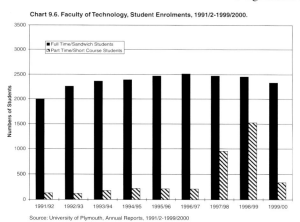

Chart 9.6. Faculty of Technology, Student Enrolments, 1991/2-1999/2000.

Source: University of Plymouth, Annual Reports, 1991/2-1999/2000

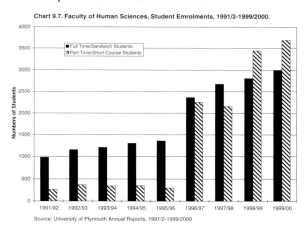

Chart 9.7. Faculty of Human Sciences, Student Emrolments, 1991/2-1999/2000.

Source: University of Plymouth Annual Reports, 1991/2-1999/2000

9.43 These publications are a small proportion of the research output of the Faculty of Human Sciences in the 1990s. They represent only one of the principal subject areas of the Faculty.

[UPPLY, Marketing Dept.]

In the mid-1990s student numbers in the Faculty of Human Sciences were increased at a stroke by the incorporation of nurse education to form a new multi-site department, the Institute of Health Studies. But expansion in other areas also led to the restructuring of the Department of Applied Social Science in 1995 which broke into three departments, Politics, Social Policy and Social Work, and Sociology. Chart 9.7 shows the trend of student numbers in the Faculty, and particularly the leap in part-time and short course numbers in 1996 owing to the inclusion of nurse education. As in other faculties, course development was a major activity during the 1990s. The demise of the central Combined Honours management led to the creation of the Social Science undergraduate scheme in 1993, though the modular approach had already led to the design of a degree in Sociology in 1992. To these were added a range of degrees including European Society and Policy (1995), Community Work and Social Policy, and International Relations (1999), and the Dip.HE in Nursing (1998). For post-graduate students the Faculty offered masters degrees in Policy and Organisation Studies (1994), Women's Studies (1994) and Health Care and Practice

(1998) and Psychological Research Methods (1998). The introduction of the taught doctorate in Clinical Psychology in 1995 broke new ground in the University. As with the Faculties, Human Sciences subjects scored particularly well in teaching quality assessment, sociology in 1995/6 and psychology in 1998/9 and nursing in 1999.

Such developments were based on the Faculty's well established research profile, which was further consolidated by the designation of new research groups, in 1994, the Community Research Centre, the Health Research Centre and the Human Assessment Centre, the Quality of Life Research Centre (1995), the Centre for Research into the Social Impact of Gambling (1997), and in 1998 the Macmillan Education Unit. The titles of the Faculty's centres indicate the wide scope of its research commitments. Underlying their designation has been the acquisition of many large research grants. Projects have included the integration of the sea service (Royal Navy), equal opportunities policy in nursing, computer-based cognitive abilities testing (Army), computer-based assessment (Navy), the psychological benefits of cosmetic surgery. With an extensive external reputation, it is not surprising to find staff elected to senior positions in professional bodies, such as British Psychological Society, and the British Sociological Association.

The University of Plymouth Business School has also evolved a number of research units during the 1990s, in addition to its well established South West Economic Research Centre. The Management Research Unit has carried forward the School's on-going concern for researching and supporting small to medium-sized enterprises (SMEs), while the Teaching Company Centre is now one of the largest such organisations in Britain. More recently the Global Organisational Learning and Development Group has been involved with projects on learning networks and problem solving in small firms. Other projects over this period have included the impact of IT in health care management, computer aided visioning, retail marketing and

9.44, 9.45 The University of Plymouth Teaching Company Centre has been an outstanding success in linking the university world with industry and business. It places graduates with companies on two year jointly funded projects, keeping a close watch on progress.

[UPPLY, Marketing Dept.]

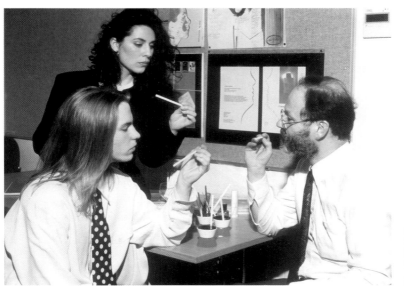

9.46 Amongst the numerous initiatives of the Plymouth Business School has been the honours degree in the Business of Perfumery, which has attracted much public attention.

[UPPLY, Marketing Dept.]

9.47, 9.48, 9.49 Former Plymouth students are to be found all over the world, but they are helped in maintaining links with the University and with each other through the University of Plymouth Graduates Association and its magazine In Touch, as well as through local graduate groups such as that in Malasia.

[UPPLY, Plymouth collection]

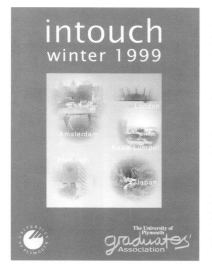

advertising, new graduate abilities in growth enterprises, stochastic financial modelling and entrepreneurial marketing. Amongst major grants for research projects has been EU funding for projects on employment law, the management of science and teaching quality.

The international dimension to the Business School's research and consultancy, is mirrored in its student body through its major involvement in international student exchange, and its membership for Business Administration of the inner circle of the EUs credit transfer system. The portfolio of undergraduate courses was extended by degrees in European Studies (1994), the Business of Perfumery (1994) and Sports Management (1999), and new masters courses in the Management of Human Resources, the Management of Health Care and the Management of Technology were introduced in 1995. Having its own building, Cookworthy, has been particularly advantageous in providing a clear focus for both business staff and business students. The expansion in student numbers is shown in Chart 9.8.

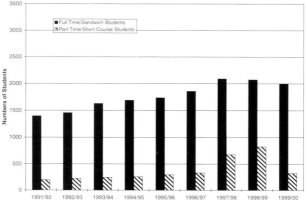

Chart 9.8. Plymouth Business School, Student Enrolments, 1991/2-1999/2000.

Source:University of Plymouth Annual Reports, 1991/2-1999/2000

The most recent addition to the University's faculty structure has been the Plymouth Postgraduate Medical School (1991), "...first and foremost a research driven academic development which seeks to attract progressively better personnel for the provision of health care in the south-west peninsula."[11] For much of the 1990s the School was based at Plymouth's Derriford Hospital, where its staff continue their work in clinical practice. Pending the erection of their own premises, a research laboratory was fitted out in the Davy Building on the University campus. In January 1999, the School's administration, its research laboratories and specialisms in primary health care and molecular medicine moved into a new building on the University sponsored Tamar Science Park. Including support staff, the School's full time staff has grown to over fifty, and in addition there are some forty honorary and visiting research staff. Research specialisms, in addition to those already noted, include general practice, perinatal research, rheumatology, rehabilitation medicine, surgery, medical physics and biomedical engineering. There are strong links with the Nuffield hospital in Plymouth, Trelisk Hospital in Cornwall and Torbay Hospital in South Devon. A wide range of collaborative research, with other University faculties, the hospitals, pharmaceutical companies and researchers overseas, has been developed and major grants have been received, for example, from the Medical Research Council and the European Commission.

9.50 The University's student village in the area east of the City Museum and Public Library, now extends to Radnor Street with the completion of the Radnor group of student residences. It includes a large student café.

[Photo: A.Kennerley]

For the University, the twentieth century has been rounded off in a most satisfactory manner with the announcement by the Government in July 2000 of the foundation of the Peninsula Medical School. The success of the joint bid from the University of Plymouth, University of Exeter and Health Trusts in the South West, owes much to the establishment of post-graduate medical schools in both universities, to Plymouth's experience with its Institute of Health Studies and its partnership network, and to the proven research strengths and potential of both universities. This major investment must be ready to receive its first undergraduate medical students in 2002. The impact will be huge and it is anticipated that it will lead to an expansion of science at the University.

That the University has such a catalogue of achievement is attributable to the efforts of the large number of people who have over time made up the establishment's staff team. The present position rests on foundations built up over the past quarter of a century under the leadership of Michael Robbins, with his particular contribution in promoting research and seeing through the integration of Exeter College of Art and Design, Rolle College and Seale-Hayne Agricultural College, and John Bull whose financial expertise allied to his management abilities have been of vital importance in the implementation of the 1988 Education Reform Act and the 1992 Further and Higher Education Act. In this time of rapid change in the world of education he has had the vision and determination to persuade nearly every HE institution in Devon, Cornwall and parts of Somerset to link with Plymouth to form the first regional University, an achievement recognised by the Queen's Award in 1994. It must not be forgotten that behind the higher education corporation's senior management is the Board of Governers whose advice and support under the chairmanship successively of Alan Macfarlane and Victor Parsons has been invaluable during this period of University development and transformation.

9.51: Development Diagram

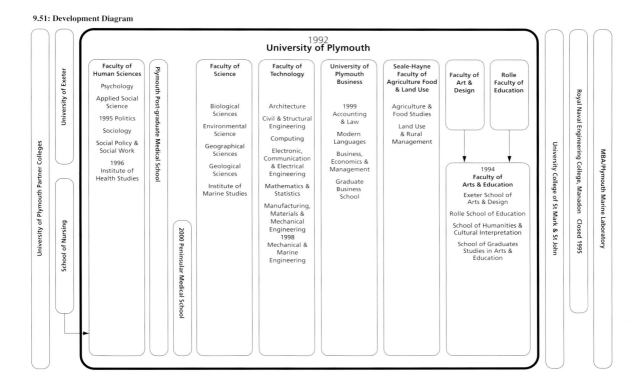

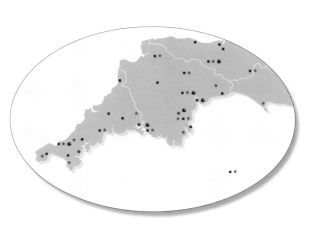

Epilogue

CHAPTER TEN

From its roots in self-help, adult and technical education, higher education in Plymouth has progressed along a complex, even unpredictable path to its current status having local, regional, national and international dimensions. Change has often been on the agenda but it has only been in the later decades of the twentieth century that the pace has advanced increasingly quickly within an ever more rapidly evolving regulatory context. Except in minor ways, local provision has largely danced to the erratic tune of government departments: Department of Science and Art, the Board of Education, Ministry of Education, Department of Education and Science, Department for Education and Employment, while some sections of the present University have been beholden to the Board of Trade (and successors), Board/Ministry of Agriculture, Fisheries and Food, and even to the Admiralty. Locally, for a century, this has been tempered by the lead of the local authorities, particularly Plymouth City Council and Devon County Council, to a lesser extent Cornwall County Council and Exeter City Council.

Dominated by its single, well developed industry, the area formerly known as the 'Three Towns'(modern Plymouth) might be compared with one of the northern industrial towns similarly dependent upon a key industry, and we might look for the kind of investment in local higher education through which successful industrialists provided the foundation of some of the northern universities. A number of the 'civic universities' were being given this kind of initial support in the later decades of the nineteenth century and the early years of the twentieth. It was not unusual for the early subject development to reflect the needs of the local industry, though industrialists gave ready support to a diverse range of subjects.[1] Had all that comprised the naval presence in the Three Towns in that period been a commercial enterprise built up by a civilian industrialist, the endowment of a local university college would surely have contained provision for quite a wide range of subjects. Clearly, given the design and manufacturing needs of that advanced industrial complex, the naval dockyard, naval architecture, mechanical engineering, physics, mathematics and chemistry would have been high on the list of subjects. As a major, world-wide operator of ships, navigation, oceanography, meteorology (also based in physics and mathematics) would certainly have been included. The fleet's supply needs had produced that most important food preservation establishment, the Royal William Yard, so that food science would have been a research subject. The scale of naval training built up to support the manning of the ships, would have called into being a department of teacher education. With one of the largest hospitals in Europe from the 1760s, the higher training of medical people would have been a priority leading to the early establishment of a medical school.

In the context of this scenario, Plymouth was unfortunate in its industry. True, it was a national concern with significant 'factories' in other locations, but it was a state enterprise and there was no local benevolent industrialist to pump-prime a university college. The Naval Dockyard certainly made Devonport and was long the dominant influence in the local economy, engendering business opportunities and dominating direct and indirect employment. But unlike many of the industrialists elsewhere, the naval presence made little contribution to local leadership. The Admiralty did flood the area with its own training establishments including the 'dockyard tech' (very early example), several rating's training units and its engineering college. But these were not for the wider educational benefit of the locality, though the first, particularly, interacted with the local technical college.

It took a public subscription to get the latter started, and there never were any major endowments. Ambition there was to achieve the elevation observed elsewhere, but in the context of the attitudes of those who regulated university funding, the drawn out flirtation with the University College at Exeter was always doomed to failure. Yet the substantive areas of the present University were evident, at least in the thinking, in the early decades of the twentieth century. The technologies and sciences were the earliest strengths of the embryonic technical college, to which were added business subjects.

Early pronouncements anticipated a medical school, and there were worked out plans for behavioural and social sciences in the 1930s. Maritime subjects were present from the 1860s, and east of Plymouth art and design from the 1850s, agriculture from the early twentieth century and education from the 1940s. Had Plymouth been a northern city it might have founded its own teacher training college. Instead the college that came to Plymouth, St. Mark and St. John, did so through circumstances which had to do with London rather than Plymouth, while Plymouth's earliest undergraduates, at Western College, looked neither to Plymouth nor the state. Higher educational developments at Plymouth then, have depended almost entirely on the evolution of national educational policy from the mid-nineteenth century, and the pattern is mirrored in many another larger town and city across the country.

Policy is influenced by attitudes, and it has recently been argued by Sanderson, that those attitudes, endemic in the nineteenth century, to "...liberal education with its emphasis on gentlemanly values and the cultivation of the mind for its own sake...conferred [a second rate status] on vocational, practical, technical and commercial training for earning a living...". They have a persistent influence in Britain up to the present day.[2] He continues:

"This in turn shaped many of the attitudes and curricula of the public schools. We see in it the slow growth of the JTSs [Junior Technical Schools] and the eventual demise of the Secondary Technical Schools... It is still reflected in the recurrent complaints of British engineers that they are undervalued. More recently it shaped the formation of the new universities in the 1960s and the forsaking of their noble Victorian roots by many of the technological and polytechnic universities as they converged on the old liberal arts ideal...We were unusual in abandoning the stream of technical education for school going teenagers..."

The arguments that the nature of tertiary education available in the latter part of the nineteenth century and the early part of the twentieth century was appropriate for those times, have been made in Chapter One. Even so, the separation of education from training through the attitude that industry must fund its own training and that the state should only concern itself with some pure ideal of education, was then prevalent, and is still with us today. Yet as Sanderson goes on to point out, whatever the period, employers in Britain have, in general shown little interest in education and training. He cites the failure of successive training initiatives from the 1960s onwards, the continuing complaints about skill shortages and unsatisfactory recruits and the conflicting advice from employers about what they want from educational establishments.[3] Yet government rhetoric of the late 1990s insists that higher education as well as further education must be clearly relevant to future vocational employment.

Inevitably, much has been written here about the relationship of the central education authority to local tertiary education provision, since the 1850s. Aldrich has recently endorsed Bishop's opinion of central oversight in the nineteenth century, as being equally applicable throughout the twentieth: 'slow, tortuous, makeshift, muddled, unplanned, disjointed'.[4] The list of partially or unfulfilled education and training initiatives is embarrassing. The persistent low status of the education board, ministry, department, of its minister and senior officials, in the hierarchy of government departments has been a key factor, witnessed by an average of a new minister almost every two years since 1900. However, both Sanderson and Aldrich suggest that there is some promise for the future, through the creation in place of the DES of the more substantial Department for Education and Employment (1995), the recognition of teachers for teaching awards, the possibility of charging fees at universities, and student demand for vocationally-oriented education. Further, although the Education Reform Act, 1988, weakened the local authorities, the local dimension has in the 1990s been bolstered through a range of local initiatives and agencies, such as the Training and Enterprise Councils (TECs), though the TEC's have now been abandoned for a new structure.

Given this broad context, how well does Plymouth stand up? The strong technological, scientific and vocational dimension to the work of its technical college has been demonstrated. This carried through into its Polytechnic and its firm policy decision to develop as an establishment devoted to the sciences and technologies, though balanced by the maritime, business and human science areas, all of which had strong vocational emphases. After 1970 partly owing to mergers with small local vocational colleges, less advanced vocational education was concentrated at the new College of Further Education, and at the College of Art. The liberal arts were not developed on the Plymouth campus. Plymouth did establish two highly-regarded junior technical schools whose purpose was to prepare youngsters for a technical education leading to vocational employment, and after World War II it did have one secondary technical school, but it did not create a city technology college for secondary school pupils. So this form of feed was lost in the latter half of the twentieth century. The weakness of sustaining a strong vocational orientation in an establishment of higher education is that the institution's own stability is threatened when particular industries suffer decline. This has already been touched on with reference to the maritime, engineering, and agricultural industries, while external policy decisions can distort other areas of vocational education, as in the cases of pharmacy and teacher education. The ability to adapt has been important in the rise to University status, and will remain so in the future.

What does the twenty-first century hold for the University of Plymouth? From the deliberations of one group that looked at the future of higher education as a world phenomenon, it seems clear that it will be essential that Plymouth keeps in close touch with trends and developments well beyond the insularity of the South West and of the British Isles.[5] The arguments range from the complete disappearance of universities, to the emergence of super-complex organisations functioning on a global scale. The ability of the campus-based university to survive the impending changes is questioned, and it is argued that universities will be forced to change their structures and *modus operandi* radically, such that, though using that name, they will in fact be vastly different institutions. Only in the twentieth century have universities become the repositories and principal creators of almost all knowledge. Modern information technology and communications already enable those seeking knowledge to by-pass the campus university, and in the ultimate conclusion could render the university, as currently understood, unnecessary. It seems certain that with students as consumers in an educational global market, it will be students who will drive the character of universities where they survive. Take up of higher education opportunities on a world basis is predicted to grow to 50 to 70 per cent of the world population, and many universities are already operating as semi-global establishments in structures that are increasingly complex. Even if the campus survives personal contact between tutor and student will reduce to a small proportion of learning time as information technology becomes more and more dominant as the medium of education. Even the position of research in universities is questioned. This has become the dominant pattern in Britain, but it is not the case in some other countries, where scholarship in support of higher education teaching does not need to be research-based. The pressures in the direction of applying knowledge to the solution of specialist problems will lead to a regrouping of subjects, application centred, trans-disciplinary, heterogeneous, reflexive.

With its multi-campus core and its regional linkages, the University of Plymouth is already on the road to supercomplexity and it has a range of overseas connections which hint at globalisation. Further, it already has knowledge groupings such as agriculture or maritime, which can be seen as a regrouping of traditional subjects. The reconfiguration of its information systems and the experimentation with electronic delivery, through the internet and via satellite overseas is preparing the way for the new learning environment. How well future incoming students will be prepared for this brave new world must however remain open to question. The training they receive in preparation for higher education as well as initial preparation for future vocational employment will need to be much more thorough than at present. Certainly many of today's students lack these skills on entry and are ill-equipped in terms of personal motivation to pursue to completion what may be much nearer to self guided programmes of study. At present they need the discipline of class-based teaching and high levels of contact with academic staff.

It seems unlikely that the more extreme of the future scenarios explored above will materialise in the coming decades. The speculation may be premature. Traditional approaches to the delivery of higher education have been remarkably durable despite the series of explorations of alternative approaches to learning which have come and gone. Students remain comfortable with traditional timetables and high levels of contact with staff. In the immediate future the University of Plymouth is continuing to invest in its campuses, with recent approvals for a lecture theatre complex at Exmouth and three new teaching blocks at Plymouth. Its role as a leading educational establishment in the south west region is established, and set to grow in collaboration with, amongst others, the University of Exeter, though as a major partner compared with the satellite relationship of the 1930s. As the map included in Chapter One shows, its partnership connections across the region are far reaching, and a new area of collaboration for a university campus in Cornwall, still being worked out, will take this one step further. The University of Plymouth is already evolving as a 'dispersed university' working in collaboration with partner colleges and drawing on its involvement with distance learning, so that it will be able to function in a future changed world of higher education while sustaining the current approaches for the immediate future.

Appendix 1

Appendix 1: Personalities
Chapters Two and Three
Heads of Technical Schools/Colleges in Devonport/Plymouth

1893-1895	Mr. R. Elliot Steel, MA, Headmaster, Plymouth Science & Technical Schools
1895-1898	Dr. J.T. Dunn, DSc, Head Master, Plymouth Science & Technical Schools
1898-1916	Mr. J. Burns Brown, BSc, Headmaster, Plymouth Science & Technical Schools
1908-1910	W. Mansergh Varley, MA, D.Sc., Principal, Devonport Science & Technical Schools
1910-1916	Mr. W.S. Templeton, MA, BSc, AMInstEE, Principal, Devonport Technical School
1916-1933	Mr. W.S. Templeton, MA, BSc, AMInstEE, Principal PDTC
1934-1946	Mr. A.R. Boeree, MA, BSc, FIC, Principal, PDTC
1947-1959	Dr. John Graymore, MSc, PhD, FRIC, Principal, PDTC
1959-1974	Mr. E. Bailey, BSc, FRIC, AMIChemE,, Principal, PDTC/PCoT
1957-1969	Mr. P.S. Bebbington, B.Comm, M.Comm, MBIM, Vice Principal, PDTC/ PCoT

Chapter Four
Heads of Plymouth School of Navigation, etc.

1862-1891	Dr. John Merrifield, PhD, FRMS, FRAS, Headmaster
1891-1919	Mr. Charles Morris, FRMS, Headmaster
1919-1933	Mr. W.J. Liddicoat, Headmaster
1933-1934	Lt. Cdr. E.E. Frost-Smith, RNR, Lecturer-in-Charge
1934-1944	Mr. H. Keast, Lecturer-in-Charge
1944-1954	Capt. F.W. Johnson, Master Mariner, FRMetS, MRIN, Lecturer-in-Charge
1954-1958	Capt. F.W. Johnson, Master Mariner, FRMetS, MRIN, Head of Department
1958-1973	Capt. G.R. Hughes, MBE, Extra Master, FNI, Head of Department [PCoT/Polytechnic]
1970-1983	Capt. T.G. Nelson, Extra Master, Head of Department, [Plymouth CFE]
1973-1980	Dr. D.H. Moreby, Extra Master, FNI, Head of Department, [Polytechnic]
1983-1984	Mr. J.E. Forshaw, BSc, MSc, FRMetS, MNI, Head of Department, [Plymouth CFE]
1980-1986	Prof. D.H. Moreby, Extra Master, PhD, FNI, Dean of Faculty of Maritime Studies
1986-1991	Prof. K.R. Dyer, BSc, MSc, PhD, FGS, Dean of Faculty [Institute of Marine Studies]

Chapter Five
Heads of Exeter School of Art, etc.

1854-1861	Mr. M. Wigzell, Headmaster
1861-1899	Mr. J. Birkmyer, AMC, Headmaster
1899-1913	Mr. J. Shapland, AMC, Headmaster
1913-1939	Mr. W. Burman-Morrall, AMC, Principal
1940-1957	Mr. W. Green, ARCA, Principal
1958-1985	Mr. C. Fishwick, ATD, MA, Principal, Exeter College of Art & Design
1963-1966	Mr. W. Ruscoe, ATD, Vice Principal, Exeter College of Art & Design
1966-1987	Dr. A. Goodwin, ATD, Vice Principal, Exeter College of Art & Design
1985-1989	Prof. D. Jeremiah, BA, PhD, DipEd, Principal, Exeter College of Art & Design
1987-1988	Mr. D. Sample, BSc, MSc, MA, Vice Principal, Exeter College of Art & Design
1989-1994	Prof. D. Jeremiah, BA, PhD, DipEd, Dean, Faculty of Arts & Design
1994 onwards	Prof. M.J.B. Newby, BA, MA, Dean, Faculty of Arts & Education

Chapter Six
Principals of Seale-Hayne Agricultural College, etc.

1910-1919	Mr. B.N. Wale, BSc, Dip Agric, MRAS, FHAS, Principal
1919-1933	Lt. Col. D.R. Edwardes-Ker, OBE, MA, BSc, Principal

1933-1943   Mr. W. Henderson Hogg, BSc, Principal
1943-1948   Professor A.W. Ling, MSc, NDA, Dip Agric, Principal
1948-1971   Professor H.I. Moore, CBE, MSc, PhD, NDA, Dip Agric, Principal
1964-1988   Mr. R.J. Halley, MSc, MA, Deputy Principal
1971-1988   Prof. D.J. Dowrick, PhD, Principal
1988-1989   Prof. F. Harper, BSc, PhD, ARAgS, Principal.
1989-1997   Prof. F. Harper, BSc., Ph.D, ARAgS, Dean of Seale-Hayne Faculty
1997-1998   Prof. R.P. Blackshaw, BSc, PhD, Acting Dean of Seale-Hayne Faculty
1998 onwards Mrs C. Broom, MSc, BSc, FRGS, FRSA, Dean of Seale-Hayne Faculty

Chapter Seven
Principals of Exmouth Training College, etc.

1946-1948   Mr. W.F. Morris, BA, Principal, Exmouth [Emergency] Training College
1948-1959   Miss G.M. Croft, OBE, BA, Principal, Exmouth Training College/Rolle College
1948-1953   Miss I.M. Cooper, BA, Vice Principal, Exmouth Training College/Rolle College
1954-1962   Miss E.M. Richardson BSc, Vice Principal, Rolle College
1959-1972   Miss D.E.L. Spicer, MA, BComm, Principal, Rolle College
1962-1965   Miss I.K. Sharpe BA, Deputy Principal, Rolle College
1965-1972   Mr. J.R. Williams, MA, Deputy Principal, Rolle College
1972-1981   Mr. F.C.A. Cammaerts, MA, Principal, Rolle College
1972-1988   Mr F. Aldred, MA, Deputy Principal, Rolle College
1981-1988   Dr. M. Preston, MEd, Principal, Rolle College
1988-1989   Mr. R.M. Owen, MEd, Acting Dean, Rolle Faculty of Education
1989-1994   Prof. M. J.B. Newby, BA, MA, Dean, Rolle Faculty of Education
1994 onwards Prof. M. J.B. Newby, BA, MA, Dean, Faculty of Arts & Education

Chapter Eight
Directorate of Plymouth Polytechnic/Polytechnic South West

1970-1974   Mr. E. Bailey, BSc, FRIC, AMIChemE, Director
1970-1974   Dr. R.F.M. Robbins, BSc, PhD, FRIC, Deputy Director
1974-1989   Dr. R.F.M. Robbins, BSc, PhD, FRIC, Director
1974-1977   Mr. R. Carus, MA, MBIM, Deputy Director
1974-1984   Dr. I.C. Cannon, BSc, PhD, Assitant/Deputy Director (Academic)
1974-1981   Capt. G.R. Hughes, MBE, FRIN, MCInstT, FNI, Extra Master, Assistant/Deputy Director (Resources)
1981-1984   Dr. C. Booth, MA, MA, PhD, Deputy Director (Resources)
1984-1989   Mr. R.J. Bull, BSc, FCCA, Deputy Director (Academic)
1984-1992   Dr. C.M. Gillett, BSc, PhD, MInstP, CEng, MIEE, Deputy Director (Resources)
1988-1990   Prof. G.J. Dowrick, BSc, PhD, CBiol, FBiol, Polytechnic Secretary
1990-1992   Dr. R.M. Thorpe, BSc(Econ), PhD, Deputy Director, (Corporate Services)
1989-1992   Mr. R.J. Bull, BSc, FCCA, Director
1989-1992   Prof. L. Ebdon, BSc, PhD, ARCS, DIC, MIWEM, CChem, FRSC, Deputy Director (Academic)

Heads of Schools/Deans of Faculties, Plymouth Polytechnic/Polytechnic South West (Plymouth campus)

1947-1976   Mr. P.S. Bebbington, BCom, MCom, MBIM, Head of Management & Business Studies
1960-1980   Mr. B.R. Webster, BSc(Eng), FIEE, FIERE, Head of Electrical Engineering
1966-1981   D.R.S. Rabley, BSc(Eng), CEng, FIMechE, MIMarE, MIProdE, MBIM, Head of Civil & Mechanical Engineering
1969-1975   Mr. R. Hardy, DA, ARIBA, Head of Architecture
1972-1980   Dr. L.A.F. Heath, BSc, PhD, MIBiol, Head of Environmental Science
1972-1980   Dr. C.M. Gillett, BSc, PhD, MInstP, CEng, MIEE, Head of Mathematics & Physics
1975-1981   Mr. T.R. Mattoff, RIBA, Head of Architecture
1975-1978   Mr. A.J. Nisbett, BA, MSc (Econ), Head of Behavoural & Social Science
1977-1980   Mr. G. Payne, BA(Econ), MA, Head of Behavoural & Social Science
1980-1992   Prof. K.C.C. Bancroft, BSc, PhD, C.Chem, FRIC, MIEnvSc, Dean of Science
1980-1984   C.M. Gillett, BSc, PhD, MInstP, CEng, MIEE, Dean of Technology

1980-1992   Prof. G. Payne, BA(Econ), MA, PhD, Dean of Social Science
1980-1983   Mr S.H. Starks, MSc, CertEd, Dean of Plymouth Business School
1983-1985   Mr. D.T. King. BSc (Econ), MSc, FBIM, Acting Dean of Plymouth Business School
1884-1991   Prof. D.W. Cowell, BA, MSc, PhD, MIM, Dean of Plymouth Business School
1984-1989   Prof. D.E. Fussey, MA, PhD, CEng, FIMechE, FInstE, Dean of Technology
1989-1992   Prof. R.J. Cope, DSc, PhD, BSc, CEng, FICE, FIStructE, Dean of Technology

Chapter Nine
Vice Chancellery, University of Plymouth

1992 onwards Prof. R.J. Bull, BSc, FCCA, Vice Chancellor
1992-1995   Dr. C.M. Gillett, BSc, PhD, MInstP, CEng, MIEE, Deputy Vice Chancellor (Resources)
1992-1997   Dr. R.M. Thorpe, BSc(Econ), PhD, Deputy Vice Chancellor (Secretariat)
1992 onwards Prof. L. Ebdon, BSc, PhD, ARCS, DIC, MIWEM, CChem, FRSC, Deputy Vice Chancellor (Academic Development)
1996-1999   Prof. N. Reid, BSc, MSc, DPhil, FSS, FRSA, Deputy Vice Chancellor (Resources)
1999 onwards Prof. N. Reid, BSc, MSc, DPhil, FSS, FRSA, Deputy Vice Chancellor (Corporate Development)
2000 onwards Prof. P.D. Evans, BSc, PhD, FIEE, CEng, Deputy Vice Chancellor (Resources Development)

Deans of Faculty, University of Plymouth, Plymouth campus

1991-1994   Prof. K.Rosen, Dean, Plymouth Post-Graduate Medical School
1992-1997   Prof. G. Payne, BA(Econ), MA, PhD, Dean of Human Sciences
1992-1996   Prof. K.C.C. Bancroft, BSc, PhD, C.Chem, FRIC, MIEnvSc, Dean of Science
1992-1995   Mr. D.T. King. BSc (Econ), MSc, FBIM, Dean of Plymouth Business School
1992 onwards Prof. R.J. Cope, DSc, PhD, BSc, CEng, FICE, FIStructE, Dean of Technology
1994-1996   Mr. Ellis Strachan, MB, CHB, FRCS (Edin), Acting Dean of Plymouth Post-Graduate Medical School
1995-1997   Prof. P. Jones, Dean of Plymouth Business School
1996-2000   Dr. P. O'Neill, BSc, MSc, PhD, CChem, MIEnvSc, MRSC, FRGS, Dean of Science
1996-1997   Prof. K. Rogers, Dean of Plymouth Post-Graduate Medical School
1997-1998   Mr A.N. Lee, BSc, MSc, Acting Dean of Human Sciences
1997-1999   Mr S Rainbow, BA, MSc, DipM, GInstM, MBBGS, Acting Dean of Plymouth Business School
1997 onwards Prof. J.R. Sneyd, BA, MA, FRCA, MB,BChir, MD, Dean of Plymouth Post-Graduate Medical School
1998 onwards Prof. M. Beveridge, BA, PhD, CPsychol, Dean of Human Sciences
1999 onwards Prof. C. Greensted, BSc, MSc, FRSA, Dean of Plymouth Business School
2000 onwards Prof. A.M.Y. Blacksell, MA, DPhil, FRGS, Dean of Science
2000 onwards Prof. J. Tooke, Dean of Peninsula Medical School

Appendix 2

Appendix 2 Buildings

In general dates are those of occupation or acquisition. Numerous minor buildings, particularly on the Plymouth campus, are omitted from this listing. The University also owns properties at other locations in the south west counties.

Chapters Two and Three

1892-1966	Plymouth Science Art & Technical Schools, extended 1897, demolished 1966.
1898-1970	Devonport Science Art and Technical Schools; 1970 to Plymouth CFE.
1954 onwards	Engineering Block, Glanville St, named *Smeaton Building*, 1991.
1960 onwards	Workshop Block, named *Brunel Building* 1991.
1960 onwards	Science Block, named *Davy Building* 1991.
1961 onwards	Nucleonics Laboratory.
1961-1970	North Road Annexe (former School). 1970 to Plymouth CFE.
1962 onwards	Administration (Link) Block.
1963 onwards	Playing Fields at Ernesettle.
1965-1970	Workshop at North Road Annexe; 1970 to Plymouth CFE.
1966 onwards	Assembly (Main) Hall .
1966 onwards	Recreation Hall at Ernesettle playing fields.
1966 onwards	Pavilion at Ernesettle playing fileds.
1968 onwards	Pavilion extension at Ernesettle playing fields.

Chapter Four

1862-1922	13½ Gascoyne Place, Plymouth, now private lodgings.
1922-1932	Junior Technical School building, Durnford Street, now residential flats.
1932-1945	Plymouth Technical College Building, Tavistock Road, since demolished.
1945-1954	Stoke Military Hospital, now Devonport High School.
1950-1967	Seamanship Centre, Mutton Cove, use reverted to local boatmen.
1954-1970	Glanville Street engineering building, now Smeaton Building.
1955-1990	Radar School, Fishers' Nose, Hoe, now Dutton's Café.
1958-1982	*Merrifield Hall*, (Merchant Navy cadet hall of residence), now a University hall.
1960-1967	North Road School building (MN cadets), now a Plymouth CFE building.
1961-1970	*Plymleigh House* (MN cadet hall of residence), since demolished.
1962 onwards	22 Portland Square (MN cadet hall of residence), now maritime teaching .
1964-1980	Training Ketch, *Tectona*, sold to France.
1966-1970	6 Queen Anne's Terrace (MN cadet hall of residence), now staff offices.
1966-1970	18 Queen Anne's Terrace (MN cadet hall of residence), now staff offices.
1966-1982	*Standard House* (MN cadet hall of residence), now private student lodgings.
1967-1970	*Grimstone House*, Houndiscombe Road (MN cadet hall of residence).
1967-1970	Former Notre Dame school, Wyndham Street (MN cadets), since demolished.
1967-1987	Seamanship Centre, Coxside, now University water sports centre.
1970-1992	Residential Nautical College (MN cadet hall of residence), now *Mary Newman Hall*.
1970-1992	Residential Nautical College (communal block), now *Isaac Foot Building*.
1970 onwards	Nautical College teaching building, named *Fitzroy Building*, 1991.
1970 onwards	*William Day Planetarium*.
1977 onwards	4 Endsleigh Place (staff offices).
1978 onwards	18 Endsleigh Place (staff offices).

Chapter Five

1854-1868	Rooms over entrance to Lower Market, Fore Street.
1868-1959	Royal Albert Memorial Museum, Queen Street, upper north wing & elsewhere.
1954-1960	Premises at Burnthouse Lane: printing.
1959-1984	York Wing, Royal Albert Memorial Museum, Queen Street.

1960-1984   The Mint and other premises, Bartholomew Street: printing & print making.
1960-1963   22, Queen Street: painting , decorating (from huts in Rougemont Park)(to CFE).
1962-1986   21-22, Gandy Street: Art history, printing, technicians workshop.
1965-1968   Former school for blind, St. David's Hill: painting, foundation (dates approx).
1965-1986   Exe Gallery, Gandy Street. Opened 28 January, 1965.
1967-1978   Former hospital premises, Paul Street: students' common room (dates approx).
1968 onwards former British Restaurant, opposite Paul Street: fine art (date approx).
1968-1981   22, Queen Street, 229, High Street: additional accomodation.
1973 onwards Earl Richards Road North: new main campus; *Towne Building* named in 1997.
1978 onwards 26, Queen Street: photography.
1981-1983   71, Holloway Street: studios for fine art (dates approx).
1984 onwards Earl Richards Road North. Phase 2.
1993 onwards 74, Queen Street. Media course.
1997 onwards *Veysey Building*: Library & Institute of Health Studies.

Chapter Six
1907 onwards Howton Farm purchased [230 acres]
1912 onwards Seale Hayne College: Foundation stone laid 28 November 1912
1916 onwards Seale Hayne College: South side completed.
1943 onwards *Daracombe*: women's accommodation
1951 onwards Four staff houses
1951 onwards Sports pavilion: donated by Old Sealehaynians
1954 onwards Great Hall
1955 onwards National Institute of Agricultural Botany Building.
1958 onwards *Frank Parkinson Building*: centre block, student accommodation
1962 onwards *Lambert Building*: opened on 50th anniversary of foundation stone laying.
1965 onwards Parkinson wings: East and West wings, student accommodation
1966 onwards College Chapel: donated by Old Sealehaynians
1968 onwards *Thompson Building*: School of Animal Health
1969 onwards *Moore Building*: Students' Union
1971 onwards *Hayter-Haynes Building*: machinery management
1972 onwards *Devon Building*: Library and classrooms
1974 onwards Sports Hall
1977 onwards *Hosking House*: student accommodation block at Daracombe
1979 onwards Squash Courts
1981 onwards Science Block
1982 onwards Refectory
1986 onwards Food Technology Laboratory extension

Chapter Seven
1946-1960   *Fairfield/Southlands:* previously Southlands School; demolished
1946-1957   *Brockhurst:* hall of residence; demolished *ca.*1957. Daw Building on site.
1946-1962   *Coonoor Lodge:* hall of residence; purchased 1950; sold *ca* 1962; building still exists.
1946 onwards *Eldin:* hall of residence; now the Student Union Building
1946-1962   *Ryll Court:* hall of residence; sold *ca* 1962.
1946 na   *Devonia:* hall of residence; disposal [disposal information not located]
1946 na   *Welbeck:* hall of residence; disposal [disposal information not located]
1946-1996   *Ferniehurst:* hall of residence; purchased 1950; sold 1996, now demolished.
1947 onwards *St Hilarian:* hall of residence; purchased 1950; still in use.
1950 onwards *Seacroft:* hall of residence; 1998 administration.
1950 onwards *Seacroft Lodge:* hall of residence; still in use.
1951 onwards *Dunisnane:* hall of residence; still in use.
1951 onwards *Hasledene:* hall of residence; still in use.
1953 onwards *Langstone:* hall of residence; sick bay & Principal's flat; teaching space.
1955 onwards Playing fields: land at *Kingsdon* acquired following public enquiry.

1957 na   *Kingsthorpe:* hall of residence; subsequently sold and demolished [date of disposal not located].
1959 onwards *Daw Building:* official opening, named for Sir John Daw, Chairman Devon CC
1959-1960   *Carlton Hill:* hall of residence. Burnt down in 1960, no casualties.
1962 onwards *Courtney, Fulford* study blocks in *Seacroft* grounds named after Devon families.
1962 onwards *Clinton, Gifford* study blocks in *Dunisnane* grounds named after Devon families.
1962 onwards *Cary, Edgcumbe, Fortescue, Grenville Peverell, Russell, Tracy* study blocks at *Hasledene*
1962 onwards Pavilion at playing fields.
1963 onwards Administration block includes, gymnasium, main hall, refectory, art block, etc.
1965 onwards *Tamar:* Deputy Principal's house; 19 ?: hall of residence.
1965 onwards *Carlton Close:* hall of residence; former hotel.
1966 onwards *Midway/Wandale:* Principal's house; name changed 1980s; now education research base.
1966 onwards *St Olans:* hall of residence;
1967 onwards *Seymour:* originally named *Gay Holme*, teaching accommodation.
1978-1980   *Kempston:* hall of residence; demolished. Cheshire Home on site.
1978 onwards *Kempston Lodge:* hall of residence; still in use.
1979 onwards Spicer Memorial Garden: created (east of Daw Building)
1979 onwards *Spicer Building:* teaching accommodation, named for Principal Spicer.
1979 onwards *Stork Building:* teaching accommodation, named for Mr J.W. Stork, Governing Body chairman.
1995 onwards *Kimsbur:* Graduate School

Chapter Eight
1970 onwards *Hoe Centre*, former NAAFI club: Architecture and student accommodation
1973-1992   Rumleigh Environmental Experimental Station, Bere Ferris
1973 onwards *Palace Court* (Palace Street): civil engineering
1976 onwards Learning Resources Centre, now Library
1976 onwards Student Union Building
1977 onwards *Brightside:* hall of residence.
1977 onwards *Gilwell:* hall of residence (Gibbon Street), phase 1.
1978-1999   Terrace of properties in Gibbon Street for student accommodation, demolished 1999.
1978-2000   Terrace of houses on east side of Portland Square: staff offices.
1979 onwards General Teaching Block, named *Babbage Building* 1991, reclad1998.
1979 onwards *Gilwell:* hall of residence (Gibbon Street), phase 2.
1983 onwards *Devonport Hall of Residence* leased from Agnes Weston Royal Sailors' Rest
1984 onwards Former education offices named *Reynolds Building* 1991
1985 onwards Former Public Secondary School, named *Scott Building* 1991
1985 onwards *Charles Cross Centre* (off Regent Street): leased
1989 onwards Security Lodge.

Chapter Nine
1992 onwards *Pitts Memorial Hall*, now the gymnasium.
1993 onwards *Cookworthy Building*, Hampton Street: Plymouth Business School
1993 onwards *Hepworth House:* conversion of 81-93 North Road East
1994 onwards *Robbins:* hall of residence and conference centre
1995 onwards *Buckland House:* leased.
1995 onwards *Sherwell Centre*, leased. Church converted to lecture theatres and exhibition centre.
1997 onwards Moneycentre: two floors leased

Notes and References

Additional abbreviations used in references:

BPP,
British Parliamentary Papers

HESC
Higher Education Sub-Committee

DCC
Devon County Council

DfEE
Department for Education & Employment

DRO
Devon Record Office

PCL-LS
Plymouth Central Library - Local Studies

PDSH
Plymouth, Devonport & Stonehouse Herald

PDTC
Plymouth and Devonport Technical College

PRO
Public Record Office

PWDRO
Plymouth & West Devon Record Office

Rep.Trans. Devonshire Assoc.
Reports & Transactions of the Devonshire Association

SHFECM
Seale-Hayne Finance & Emergency Committee Minutes

SHGM
Seale-Hayne Governors' Minutes

UPEXE
University of Plymouth, Exeter Campus

UPEXM
University of Plymouth, Exmouth Campus

UPNAB
University of Plymouth Newton Abbot Campus

UPPLY
University of Plymouth, Plymouth Campus

WCSL
West Country Studies Library

NOTES AND REFERENCES CHAPTER 1

1. There is a large literature on the history of education. The following works have been consulted in drafting this brief overview: W.H.G. Armytage, *Four Hundred Years of English Education* (Cambridge, University Press, 1964); A.S. Bishop, *The Rise of a Central Authority for English Education* (Cambridge, University Press, 1971); H.C. Dent, *The Educational System of England and Wales* (London, University of London Press, 1961); John Lawson and Harold Silver, *A Social History of Education in England* (London, Methuen, 1973).

2. In addition to the works previously cited, the following studies have been consulted in preparing this section: B.W. Clapp, *The University of Exeter: a History* (Exeter, University of Exeter, 1982); A.B. Cobban, *The Medieval Universities: Their Development and Organization* (London Methuen, 1975); Michael Sanderson, *The Universities and British Industry, 1850-1970* (London, Routledge and Kegan Paul, 1972); Paul R. Sharp, *The Creation of the Local Authority Sector of Higher Education* (London, Falmer Press, 1987).

3. Public Record Office (PRO), London, ED 166/284-293, University of Southampton School of Navigation files.

4. Negley Harte, *The University of London, 1836-1986: an Illustrated History* (London, Athlone Press, 1986), *passim.*

5. For more detailed treatments of the discussion which follows see Sidney Pollard, *Britain's Prime and Britain's Decline: the British Economy, 1870-1914* (London, Arnold, 1989), especially chapter 3, W.B. Stephens, *Education in Britain 1750-1914* (Basingstoke, Macmillan, 1998), chapter 7, and D. Edgerton, *Science, Technology and the British 'Decline', 1870-1970* (Cambridge, Cambridge University Press, 1996). The author is particularly indebted to Bill Stephens for his advice on this chapter. For a study on technical education at school levels, see Michael Sanderson, *The Missing Stratum: Technical School Education in England, 1900-1990* (London, Routledge 1994)

6. In addition to the works noted above, the following books have been consulted in drafting this section: Roger Fieldhouse, *et al.*, *A History of Modern British Adult Education* (Leicester, National Institute of Adult Continuing Education, 1996); Thomas Kelly, *A History of Adult Education in Great Britain* (Liverpool, Liverpool University Press, 1962); W.B. Stephens, *Education, Literacy and Society, 1830-1870: the Geography of Diversity in Provincial England* (Manchester: Manchester University Press, 1987).

7. In addition to works noted above the following have also been consulted in drafting this section: Michael Argles, *South Kensington*

to *Robbins: an Account of English Technical and Scientific Education Since 1851* (London, Longmans, 1964); R.J. Montgomery, *Examinations: an Account of their Evolution as Administrative Devices in England* (London, Longmans, 1965); Gordon W. Roderick and Michael D, Stephens, *Scientific and Technical Education in Nineteenth Century England* (Newton Abbot, David and Charles, 1972)

8. Rhodri Phillips, 'Growth and Diversity: a New Era in Colleges and Universities', in Susan Weil (ed), *Introducing Change from the Top in Universities and Colleges: Ten Personal Accounts* (London, Kogan Page, 1994), 169-182.

NOTES AND REFERENCES CHAPTER 2

1. The device, combining the crests of the Plymouth, Devonport and Stonehouse, was used on the title page of the *Three Towns' Almanac*, published from 1861. Motto translations: Plymouth - *Turris fortissima est nomen Jehova* - The strongest tower is the name of God (from Proverbs, 18:10); Stonehouse - *Au plaisir fort de Dieu* - At the mighty will of God (Mount Edgcumbe family motto); Devonport - *Prorsum semper honeste* - Forwards always honourably.

2. C.W. Bracken, *A History of Plymouth and Her Neighbours* (Plymouth, Underhill, 1931; Wakefield, S.R. Publishers, 1970), 52.

3. *ibid,* 182.

4. R.N. Worth, *The History of the Town and Borough of Devonport* (Plymouth, W. Brendon, 1870), 36.

5. Bracken, *op.cit.,* 160.

6. E. Chandler Cook, 'The Growth of Education in Plymouth,' *The Book of Plymouth: Souvenir of the National Union of Teachers Conference, 1910* (London, T.C. & E.C. Jack, 1910), 51-73.

7. Mark Brayshay, 'Plymouth's Past: So Worthy and Peerless a Western Port', in Brian Chalkley, *et al.* (eds), *Plymouth: Maritime City in Transition* (Newton Abbot, David and Charles, 1991), 38-61.

8. W.H. Crang, 'Educational Facilities of Devonport', in *The Book of Plymouth, op.cit.,* 73-78

9. R.N. Worth, *The History of Plymouth from the Earliest Period to the Present Time* (Plymouth, Brendon, 2nd ed, 1873), 356.

10. Plymouth Education Authority, *Plymouth Education Directory, 1907-8,* Table XXI.

11. M.I. Lattimore, The History of Libraries in Plymouth to 1914: a Study of Library Development in the Three Towns of Plymouth, Devonport and Stonehouse Amlgamated into Plymouth in 1914, unpublished PhD thesis (University of London, 1982).

12.Thomas Kelly, *A History of Adult Education in Britain* (Liverpool, Liverpool University Press, 1962), 173-180.

13. Lattimore, *op.cit.,* 242-246.

14. Lattimore, 247-252.

15. Lattimore, 120-134, 154,

16. Lattimore, 189, 195, 215.

17. Lattimore, 146, 415, 426-429.

18. Lattimore, 257, 285, 369, 400.

19.The Opening of the New Museum, *Transactions of the Plymouth Institution*, 8 (1883), 270-277.

20. J.W. Hudson, *The History of Adult Education in Which is Comprised a Full and Complete History of the Mechanics' and Literary Institutions, Athenaeum, Philosophical, Mental and Christian Improvement Societies, Literary Unions, Schools of Design, etc., of Great Britain, Ireland America, etc, etc.* (London, Longman, Brown, Green and Longmans, 1851), 152

21. *PDSH*, Saturday, 12 March 1859, 5a, reported a lecture on computation at the Working Men's Mutual Instruction Society.

22. C.A. Lewis, The Education of the Adult in Plymouth, 1808-1941, unpublished PhD thesis (University of Exeter, 1982), 161-167.

23. Lewis, 118-119, 125-127.

24. The Handbook Committee, *Plymouth: a Handbook of the Forty-Second Annual Co-operative Congress* (Manchester, Co-operative Wholesale Society, 1910), 175-7.

25. Bracken, *op.cit.,* 264. Worth, *...Devonport...*, *op.cit*, 75, Worth, *...Plymouth...*, *op.cit.*, 330.

26. Hudson, *op.cit.,* 153; Lewis, *op.cit.*, 1982., 61.

27. Lewis, *op.cit.*, 67-71.

28. *PDSH,* (8 January 1859), 5.

29. Lewis, *op.cit.*, 77-82.

30. Bracken, *op.cit,* 264.

31. Dock Literary and Philosophical Society (instituted 1808), *Rules and Regulations, 1816.* This printed booklet in the Local History Library of Plymouth Central Library, includes a membership list and library catalogue.

32. Lewis, *op.cit.*, 19-21.

33. Bracken, *op.cit,* 262.

34. G.W. Roderick and M.D. Stephens, 'The Role of Nineteenth-Century Provincial Literary and Philosophical Societies in Fostering Adult Education', *Journal of Education History and Administration,* 5:1 (January, 1973), 28-33. This paper uses the Plymouth Institution as one of its examples.

35. Lewis, *op.cit.*, 28.

36. Lewis, 29-30.

37. Lewis, 28.

38. *Annual Reports of the Committee of Western [Academy] College, 1837-1860,* a bound set in the Local History Library of Plymouth Central Library.

39. The author is indebted to Chris Robinson for basic information about Western College.

40. Arnold W. Sims, *The Western College, Bristol: an Outline History* (Bristol, Western College, 1952). A copy held in Bristol Public Library.

41. Bristol Public Library, Western College, *Annual Reports*, 1899-1916.

42. A.J. Southward and E.K Roberts, 'The Marine Biological Association of the United Kingdom, 1884-1984, One Hundred Years of Research', *Reports and Transactions of the Devonshire Association*, 116 (1984) 155-199.

43. *Western Daily Mercury*, 11 April 1885.

44. For an early description of the MBA laboratory see William Crossing, 'A Visit to the Marine Laboratory on Plymouth Hoe', *Doidge's Western Counties Illustrated Annual* (Plymouth, Doidge, 1900), 249-264.

45. Lewis, *op.cit.*, 229-250.

46. Peter Kemp (ed), *The Oxford Companion to Ships and the Sea* (London, Oxford University Press, 1976), 414; Andy Endacott, *Naval Heritage in the West 1* (Plymouth, Endacott, 1986); Conrad Dixon, *Ships of the Victorian Navy* (Southampton, Ashford, 1987). The sources differ on the date the *Implacable* became a training ship.

47. Lewis, 169-171.

48. *ibid*, 169; Terry J. Bickford, 'Royal Dockyard School', in Alston Kennerley (ed) *Notes on the History of Post-School Education in the Three Towns, 1825-1975* (Plymouth, Plymouth Polytechnic, 1976), 27-28.

49. Christopher Lloyd, 'The Royal Naval Colleges at Portsmouth and Greenwich, *Mariners' Mirror*, 52: 2 (May 1966), 145-156; Alston Kennerley, 'Early State Support of Vocational Education: the Science and Art Navigation Schools, 1853-1863', *Journal of Vocational Education.* 52:2 (2000), 211-224

50. Lewis, *op.cit.*, 172.

51. For a discussion of T.S. *Mount Edgcumbe* see Alston Kennerley, 'Navigation School and Training Ship: Educational Provision in Plymouth for the Mercantile Marine in the Nineteenth Century', in Stephen Fisher (ed), *West Country Maritime and Social History: Some Essays* (Exeter, Universirty of Exeter, 1980), 53-77

52. Lewis, 172-179.

53. Lewis, 179-183. See also Geoffrey Penn, *H.M.S. Thunderer: the Story of the Royal Naval Engineering College at Keyham and Manadon* (Mason,1984).

54. Lewis, 183-186.

55. Lewis, 188.

56. *BPP*, Department of Science and Art (DSA), 4th Report for 1856, appendices E and F. The Chairman was W. Eastlake, Secretary G. Jago (also teacher at the Plymouth School of Art).

57. Lewis, *op.cit.*, 205-6, quoting *PDSH*, 28 April 1955.

58. PRO, DSA reports for 1857-98.

59. 'Technical Education', *The Western Critic* (Saturday, 4 November, 1871), 1.

60. *ibid*, 2.

61. PRO, ED 29/31, application for building grant and statement of building fund; 'The New Technical Schools at Plymouth', *Doidge's Western Counties Illustrated Annual* (Plymouth, Doidge, 1893), 355-361.

62. *ibid.*, Doidge.

63. PWDRO, Acc 1814/13-17, Devonport Borough Council minutes, eg. 9 November 1892, 2 February 1893 12, 23 December 1895, and numerous other minutes.

64. PRO, ED 114/113, Board of Education, *Report of H.M. Inspectors on Plymouth Municipal Technical School, School No. 21233 [evening], for the Period Ending 31st July 1911.*

65. PRO, ED 114/113, Board of Education, *Report of H.M. Inspectors on Plymouth Municipal Technical School, School No. 80800 [day], for the period Ending 31st July 1911.*

NOTES AND REFERENCES CHAPTER 3

1. *Proverbs 10.18.* Following the unification of the Three Towns, the new Borough of Plymouth adopted a modifed coat of arms, which retained the shield, motto and supporters of the old Borough but introduced a new crest. Reproduced by permission of Plymouth City Council.

2. PWDRO, Acc 1644/6/4/1: Borough of Plymouth HESC, 16 April 1915, Minute 2320.

3. Clapp, *op.cit* 48.

4. PWDRO, HESC, 29 May 1916, minute 27: 31 July 1916, minute 27; obituary, *Rep. Trans. Devonshire Assoc,* 66 (1934), 30-1.

5. PWDRO, HESC, 18 October 1916.

6. *ibid.*, 15 June 1917, minute 48, 22 June 1917, minute 25.

7. *ibid.*, 26 November 1917, minute 28.

8. Argles, 65.

9. PWDRO, HESC, 10 January 1917, minute 8.

10. PRO, ED 120/149, Board of Education internal minute, 6 August 1919.

11. Board of Education, *Report of H.M. Inspectors on the Plymouth and Devonport Technical Schools for the Period Ending 31 July 1923* [hereafter HMI Report, 1923] HMSO, 1924).

12. PRO, ED 114/118, Board of Education, *Report of H.M. Inspectors on the Plymouth, Stonehouse Durnford Street Junior Technical School,* (Board of Education, June 1934). see also Michael Sanderson, *The Missing Stratum:, op, cit.*

13. *Plymouth Education Directory, 1916-17*, 94.

14. *ibid.*; UPPLY, Plymouth and Devonport Technical Schools [College] (PDTC) files, Session 1921-22, Principal's Report on Evening Schools.

15. PWDRO, 1644/6/4/1, HESC, Committee minute 31 March 1920;

1644/6/10/4 correspondence with Board of Education, 4 June 1926.

16. PWDRO, Acc. 1657/7, Education Committee minutes, 3682, 22 August 1922.

17. *Western Evening Herald* (Thursday, 30 November 1933); obituary, *Rep. Trans. Devonshire Assoc.*, 66 (1934), 30-31.

18. HMI Report, 1923; Board of Education, *Report of H.M. Inspectors on Plymouth Municipal Technical School, (a) Junior Technical School for Girls, (b) Plymouth, Devonport Ker Street Junior Technical School, (c) Plymouth and Devonport Municipal Technical Schools, Junior School of Domestic Economy, for the Period Ended 31 July 1923* [School Nos. 96052, 96088, 98132] (HMSO., 1923); Board of Education, *Report of H.M. Inspectors on the Plymouth Municipal Technical School, Junior Technical School for Boys, for the Period Ending 31 July 1923* [School No. 96035] (HMSO., 1923); Board of Education, *Report of H.M. Inspectors on the Plymouth, Regent Street Intermediate Council School, for the Period Ending 31 July 1923* [School Nos 29, 90802](HMSO., 1923).

19. Board of Education, *Report of Inspection of Plymouth Municipal School of Art held on 20, 21 and 22 May 1919* [hereafter HMI Report, 1919] (HMSO., 1919).

20. Argles, *op.cit.*, 67-9, citing Board of Education, *Survey of Technical and Further Education in England and Wales* (HMSO., 1926).

21. *ibid.*, citing Eustace Percy, *Education at the Cross Roads* (Evans, 1930).

22. Board of Education Circular 1444 (1936).

23. Bill Bailey, 'The Development of Technical Education, 1934-1939', *History of Education,* 16:1 (1987), 49-65.

24. UPPLY, PDTC files, A report by the Principal comparing expenditure at Plymouth with that at other authorities, nd., but believed to be early in 1923.

25. *Plymouth Education Directory, 1916-17,* 33.

26. *Board of Education, General Report of H.M. Inspectors on the Provision for Technical Education in the County Borough of Plymouth for the Period Ending on the 31st July, 1937* [hereafter HMI Report, 1937] (HMSO., 1938).

27. *ibid.*

28. HMI Report, 1923.

29. UPPLY, PDTC files, Principal's Annual Report, 1923/24.

30. UPPLY, PDTC files, Principal's Annual Report, 1935/6.

31. UPPLY, PDTC files, Principal's Annual Report, 1937/38.

32. PRO, ED83/194, internal minute of 1 July 1930.

33. PRO, ED 93/19, advertised terms of reference.

34. PRO, ED 90/19, internal minutes between Board of Education officials, 24-31

May 1934, and 16-23 August 1934. Board of Education, *Organisation of Art Instruction,* Circular 1432 (Board of Education, 18 October 1933).

35. PWDRO, Acc. 1644/8/4/6-7, HESC, papers relating to the School of Art.

36. PWDRO, Acc. 1644/8/4/3-4, HESC, file on School of Architecture.

37. HMI Report, 1923.

38. HMI Report, 1937.

39. Board of Education, *General Report of H.M. Inspectors on the Central Commercial Institute and Junior Evening Institutes in the County Borough of Plymouth for the Period Ending on the 31st July 1933* [hereafter HMI Report 1933] (HMSO., 1933).

40. HMI Report, 1937.

41. HMI Report, 1937; *Board of Education, Report of H.M. Inspectors on the Plymouth Municipal Art School for the Period Ending 31 July 1938* [hereafter HMI Report, 1938] (HMSO, 1938). The inspections were fully reported in the local press; see, eg., 'Sensational Report on Plymouth Technical Education - Inadequacy of the College...', *Western Independent* (15 May 1938).

42. PWDRO, Acc.1644/8/4/5, HESC, letter dated 8 October 1935 to the Plymouth Education Office.

43. PWDRO, Acc. 1644/8/5/2, HESC, technical education file., 1936-7.

44. HMI Report, 1937.

45. Plymouth and Devonport Technical College Calender, 1939-40.

46. PWDRO, 1574/6, Board of Education Administrative Memorandum, No. 206, 2, December 1939, Training for Members of the Services and of Industrial Workers in technical Schools.

47. PWDRO, Acc. 1644/2/47, Education Committee minute, 27 October 1938.

48. Clapp, *op.cit.*, chapters 1 and 2, *passim.*

49. PWDRO, Acc., 1644/6/4/1, HESC, 26 November 1917, minute 28.

50. A.W. Clayden, 'The Future of Higher Education in Devon', *Rep.Trans.Devonshire Assoc.*, 47 (1915), 62-68.

51. PWDRO, Acc 94/51, HESC, Charles A. Buckmaster, 'Report on Secondary and Technical Education in the Borough of Plymouth' (1915). Buckmaster was a former Chief Inspector and Assistant Secretary at the Board of Education.

52. PWDRO, Acc. 1644/6/4/1, HESC, 26 November 1917, minute 28.

53. Clapp, *op.cit.*, 48-51, 54-56; PWDRO, Acc. 1644/6/4/1, HESC, 28 January 1918, minute 43; 18 October 1920, minute 10; 20 December 1920, minute 8; 21 March 1921, Minute 11; 20 June 1921, minute 28.

54. PRO, ED 90/19, Board of Education internal minute, 17 September, 1925; similar sentiments were expressed at the Board of Education for example in minutes in 1932.

55. UPPLY, PDTC files, H.J.W. Hetherington, Memorandum to Committee of College Council appointed to confer with Plymouth Education Committee (3 March 1924); See also PWDRO, Acc. 1608/2, Plymouth "Higher" Education Development Plan for 1927-32, and council minutes of 31 January 1924 (1154), and 27 March 1924 (1905).

56. PWDRO, Acc. 1608/2, HESC, Programme of proposals for the development of higher education during the five financial years, 1927-1932.

57. UPPLY, PDTC files, Duties of Supervisor, Technical Schools, September 1924.

58. Clapp, *op.cit.*, 67, 70-2, 109.

59. E. Chandler Cook, *Plymouth in Relation to the University Scheme of the South West* (Plymouth, Education Offices, 1927).

60. *Western Morning News*, 16 October 1929. *Plymouth and Devonport Technical College Calendar for the Session, 1939-40* (Plymouth, Education Committee, 1939).

61. J. Paton Watson & Patrick Abercrombie, *A Plan for Plymouth: the Report Prepared for the City Council* (Plymouth, Underhill, 1943); Clapp, *op.cit.*, 112.

62. Clapp, *op.cit*, 116; PWDRO, Acc. 439.

63. Michael Sanderson, *The Universities and British Industry, 1850-1970* (London, Routledge and Kegan Paul, 1972), 360-3.

64. PWDRO, Acc. 439/1, Memorandum as to the Establishment of a University at Plymouth, Plymouth City Council, December 1960.

65. Plymouth Central Library, press cuttings file, eg. *Western Morning News*, 21 January 1961.

66. *Western Morning News*, 22 June 1967.

67. Argles, *op.cit.*, 92-6; Leonard M. Cantor & I. Francis Roberts, *Further Education in England and Wales* (London, Routledge, 1969), 1-6.

68. UPPLY, PDTC, Principal's Annual Reports. See also Brian Chalkley and John Goodridge, 'The 1943 Plan for Plymouth: War-Time Vision, and Post-War Realities', in Brian Chalkley, *et al* (eds), *Plymouth: Maritime City in Transition* (Newton Abbot, David and Charles, 1991), 62-81.

69. PRO, ED 155/100, Ministry of Education internal memorandum, 1950.

70. PRO, ED 155/100, City of Plymouth Education Committee, Development Plan, Further Education (with additions and amendments to May 1959).

71. UPPLY, PDTC, Principal's Annual Report, *1957/8. Technical Education* (London, HMSO, 1956), was followed by Ministry of Education Circular 306/56 on the organisation of technical colleges, which categorised colleges as local, area, regional or advanced technology.

72. Ministry of Education Circular 3/1961.

73. HMI Report, 1963.

74. *ibid.*

75. Amongst those sharing their

recollections is Helen Rowett, lecturer in Biology from 1944.

76. Interview with Helen Rowett, 23 December 1999. Principal Boeree only returned briefly at the end of the war departing in 1947.

77. 'The New College Extension', *Tekel* (Plymouth, 1955) [the magazine of the students' union], 4, quoting a report in the *Western Independent*. Interview with Helen Rowett.

78. UPPLY, Principal's Annual Reports, *passim*.

79. *ibid*.; HMI Report, 1963.

80. John Graymore, 'Message to Tekel', *Tekel* (1954), 4. UPPLY, Principal's Annual reports, *passim*.

81. HMI Report, 1963. This paragraph, and those following on the college departments are largely based on Principal's Annual Reports, 1956/7 to 1968/69, and prospectuses and ephemera for the same period, and will not be given separate references.

82. 'Question and Answer Session with Dr J. Graymore', *The Wanderers* (March 1959), 10. This was a magazine produced by the Overseas Students Association at PDTC.

NOTES AND REFERENCES CHAPTER 4

1. Alston Kennerley, 'Navigation School and Training: Educational Provision in Plymouth for the Mercantile Marine in the Nineteenth Century', in Stephen Fisher (ed), *West Country Maritime and Social History: Some Essays* (Exeter, University of Exeter, 1980), 53-77; Alston Kennerley, 'Education and Welfare of Merchant Seafarers', in Michael Duffy, *et al.* (eds), *The New Maritime History of Devon. Volume II: From the Late Eighteenth Century to the Present Day* (London, Conway Maritime Press/University of Exeter, 1994), 145-154. The author is indebted to Michael Baker, Publisher at Exeter University Press, for permission to draw extensively from the former study, and to Michael Duffy for permission to draw on the latter. Material is also drawn from Alston Kennerley, 'Plymouth School of Navigation', in Alston Kennerley (ed), *Notes on the History of Post-School Education in the 'Three Towns', 1825-1975'* (Plymouth, Plymouth Polytechnic, 1976), 19-24, and Alston Kennerley, 'The Education of the Merchant Seaman in the Nineteenth Century', unpublished M.A. thesis (University of Exeter, 1978).

2. For examples see N. Plumley, 'The Royal Mathematical School Within Christ's Hospital: the Early Years - Its Aims and Achievements, *Vistas in Astronomy*, 20 (1976, 51-59); Donald G. Bovill, The 'Education of Boys for the Mercantile Marine: A Study of Three Nautical Schools, *History of Education Society Bulletin*, 47 (Spring, 1991), 11-22 [South Shields Marine School, Hull Trinity House School, Newcastle Trinity House School].

3. See E.G.R. Taylor, *The Mathematical Practitioners of Tudor and Stuart England*

(Cambridge, 1954); E.G.R. Taylor, *The Mathematical Practitioners of Hanoverian England, 1714-1840* (Cambridge, University Press, 1966).

4. *BPP*, 1836, XVII, VIII (section 31) & IX (section 35), Select Committee on Shipwrecks, Report and Minutes of Evidence; chairman James Silk Buckingham. For a fuller discussion see David M. Williams, 'James Silk Buckingham: Sailor, Explorer and Maritime reformer', in Stephen Fisher (ed), *Studies in British Privateering, Trading Enterprise and Seamen's Welfare, 1775-1900* (Exeter, University of Exeter, 1987), 99-119. Between 1833 and 1835, 1702 vessels were wrecked or went missing with the loss of 2682 lives, and including other losses averaged over 1000 lives lost per year.

5. *BPP*, 1847, LX, 526, 2-5.

6. Mercantile Marine Act, 1850, 13 & 14 Vict., c.93.

7. Jane H. Wilde, 'The Creation of the Marine Department of the Board of Trade', *Journal of Transport History*, 2:4 (November, 1956), 193-206; Clifford Jeans, 'The First Statutory Qualifications for Seafarers', *Transport History*, 3 (November 1973), 248-267. Committee of Enquiry into Shipping, *Report* (Cmnd. 4337, London, HMSO, 1970) [Rochdale Report], 75-6.

8. Kennerley, 'Education and Welfare of Merchant Seafarers', *op.cit*.

9. PRO, BT 1/472/1956, Report by Revd H. Moseley to Rt. Hon. Henry Labouchiere, President of the Board of Trade.

10. Kennerley, 'Navigation School and Training Ship', *op.cit*., 56; W.H.G. Armytage, *Four Hundred Years of English Education* (London, Cambridge University Press, 1964), 114-5.

11. *BPP*, 1854, XXVIII, 269, First Report of the Science and Art Department.

12. *BPP*, 1859, XXI, Report by Capt. Ryder on Navigation Schools, Sixth Report of the Science and Art Department [for 1858], Appendix I, 143-193.

13. *BPP*, 1860, XXIV, 77, Seventh Report of the Science and Art Department, Appendix E; see also Armytage, *op.cit*., 124-5. For the application of the Revised Code ('payment-by-results') in the elementary school system see Armytage, *op.cit*., 124-5. For the introduction of the system in the Science and Art Department generally from 1859 see Argles, *op.cit*., 20-1.

14. Alston Kennerley, 'Early State Support of Vocational Education: the Department of Science and Art Navigation Schools, 1853-1863, *Journal of Vocational Education and Training*, 52:2 (2000), 211-224.

15. PWDRO, W 668 T

16. *ibid*.

17. *BPP*, 1863, XVI, 21, Tenth Report of the Department of Science and Art; *Plymouth*

Directory, 1881; *Plymouth, Devonport and Stonehouse Herald*, 24 March 1849, 8; *BPP*, 1847, LX 526-7.

18. 3 January 1863, 5.

19. *BPP*, 1864, XIX, Eleventh report of the Science and Art Department.

20. *Western Morning News* (17 January 1863), 8 (advertisement)

21. This is based on attendances at South Shields Marine School in the same period: Alston Kennerley, 'The Education of the Merchant Seaman in the Nineteenth Century', *op.cit*., appendix 7e.

22. 'Technical Instruction', *Western Critic*, No. 2 (4 November 1871), 1. From the detail on the Plymouth School of Navigation, it is likely that this article and that under the same title in *Western Critic*, No. 1 (28 October 1871), 2, were written by John Merrifield.

23. For the wider context see Kennerley, 'Early State Support of Vocational Education', *op.cit*. Plymouth Central Library (Local History), Merrifield's teaching certificate; DSA Directories, 1862-9.

24. *Western Critic* (Saturday, 4 November 1871), 1.

25. John Merrifield & Henry Evers, *Navigation and Nautical Astronomy* (London, 1868). Merrifield's other publications include: *The Meteorology and Climate of Plymouth* (Plymouth, Latimer, 1871), *Magnetism and Deviation of the Compass* (London, 1872), *A Treatise on Navigation for the Use of Students* (London, Longmans, 1883), *A Treatise on Navigation and Nautical Astronomy* (London, Sampson Low, 1886)

26. Plymouth Local History Library, Merrifield file; obituaries in *Western Weekly Mercury* (Saturday, 4 July, 1891), Rep. Trans. *Devonshire Assoc.*, 23 (1891), 106-8. The name of the American university was not given in the obituary, and enquiries to date have not substantiated the award. Merrifield was also in demand as a chemical analyst, and was also involved in local politics, popular writing and shipping investment.

27. DSA Reports and Directories 1853-1900.

28. *Western Critic* (4 November 1871), 1.

29. The author is indebted to Helen Doe, great-grand-daughter of Slade, for a copy of the booklet, which is pasted into the copy of Norie which belonged to her great grandfather. It is headed Science and Art Navigation School, Gascoyne Place. Slade's certificate is number 83,310. The first edition of J.W. Norie, *A Complete Epitome of Practical Navigation* was published in 1805, and reached its 21st edition in 1877. Norie's *Nautical Tables* remain in print.

30. E.M. Minhinnick was Merrifield's niece (1881 census). White's copy of *The Elements of Spherical Trigonometry* by James Hann (London, Weale, 1849), is endorsed 'Assist Master, Nautical Schools, Plymouth

1866'; he may be the White who subsequently taught navigation in Bristol. S.S. & R.H. Merrifield have not been identified, but were presumably related to John Merrifield.

31. see Armytage, *op.cit.*, chapter 9.

32. Fifth annual report of the Plymouth Education Committee, 1908.

33. PRO, ED 114/111, TC4089/11, Report of HM Inspectors on Plymouth Navigation School (School No. 90805) for the period ended 31 July 1911. The complete report has been quoted.

34. Plymouth Council minutes, 25 May 1922.

35. Written responses, by Mr R. Stitson of Plymouth, to questions posed by the author in an interview in 1972. Mr. Liddicoat was the author of a textbook on navigation. PRO, ED 98/14, plans of Junior Technical School, Durnford Street, Plymouth, 1928, shows that the Navigation School was allocated a headmaster's study and navigation classroom on the ground floor, and a drawing room, a wireless room and three class rooms on the first floor of the building.

36. PRO, ED 114/122, HMI, 1937.

37. Alston Kennerley, 'Merchant Marine Education in Liverpool and the Nautical College of 1892', *International Journal of Maritime History*', 5:2 (December, 1993), 103-134.

38. Alston Kennerley, 'British Government Intervention in Seamen's Welfare, 1938-1948', *International Journal of Maritime History*, 7:2 (December 1995), 75-113; Alston Kennerley, 'Vocational Education and Training for British Merchant Navy Ratings: the National Sea Training Schools, 1942-1972', *History of Education*, 29:4 (2000),301-327.

39. Correspondence with Capt. Brian Mitchell, a cadet in 1950, and member of staff in the 1960s.

40. 'A History of the Plymouth School of Navigation' (30 March 1962), a centenary commemorative booklet issued by the School. Though signed by the then head, Captain G.R. Hughes, the text was researched and drafted by Captain Warren Hopwood, who was in charge of cadet courses during the 1960s.

41. As a member of School of Navigation staff from 1965, this information and the bulk of what follows is based on interviews with staff and personal involvement in the developments discussed. The author is indebted to the following for their comments on an early draft: Professor D.H. Moreby, Capt. A.R. Lester, Mr. P.F Willerton. Mr P.G. Wright, Capt. B.M. Mitchell.

42. Argles, *op.cit.*, 66-7, chapter 8; Cantor & Roberts, *op.cit.*, 57-59.

43. Despite changes in the name of the Government department responsible for shipping (Board of Trade, Ministry of Shipping, Ministry of War Transport, Ministry ofTransport, Department of of Trade, Department of Transport and Industry),

merchant seafarers long continued to refer to the 'Board of Trade'. The title of the subsection dealing with merchant shipping also changed, latterly to the Marine Safety Agency then Maritime and Coastguard Agency.

44. Notable here was the work of Capt. D.H. Moreby on manning, personnel and the economics of training. His paper to the Honourable Company of Master Mariners in 1968, on Merchant Navy education and training was highly influential. He gave evidence to the Committee of Inquiry into Shipping (Rochdale), which reported in 1970.

45. Kennerley, *op cit*., 'Merchant Marine Education in Liverpool...'

46. Mercantile Marine Act, 1850.

47. Ministry of Transport, *Regulations for the Examination of Masters and Mates* (Exn. 1, London: HMSO, 1962), containing the revised syllabus for Extra Master introduced in 1958.

48. Great Britain, Board of Trade, Committee of Inquiry into Shipping, *Report*, Cmnd. 4337 (London, HMSO, 1970), paragraph 908. [Rochdale Report]

Notes and References Chapter 5

1. The Exeter coat of arms is reproduced with the permission of Exeter City Council.

2. Clapp, *op.cit*, 4. Clapp says it "...opened its doors on New Years' Day 1855...", but as with most establishments several different start dates may be identified, and a school certainly needed a management committee, staff, curriculum, premises and equipment before the first students could commence classes: hence 1854 as the foundation year.

3. *ibid.*, 3.

4. Argles, *op.cit* 18.

5. Stuart Macdonald, *The History and Philosophy of Art Education* (London, University of London Press, 1970), Chapters 4-12; Christopher Frayling, *The Royal College of Art. One Hundred and Fifty Years of Art and Design* (London, Barrie & Jenkins, 1987), Part 1.

6. PRO, ED 28/16, DSA minute of 17 March 1863.

7. UPEXE; *The Guardian*, 12 October, 1971.

8. PRO, ED 28/17, DSA minute of 8 July 1863.

9. Report from the Select Committee on the Schools of Art, *BPP*, 1864, XII, xvii.

10. W.B. Stephens, 'The Victorian Art Schools and Technical Education: a Case Study, 1850-1889', *Journal of Educational Administration and History*, 2:1 (December, 1969), 13-19.

11. K. Holmes, 'Art', in P.F.R. Venables, *Technical Education: Its Aims, Development and Future Organisation* (London, Bell, 1955), 305-331.

12. Macdonald, *op.cit.*, chapter 9, 380-381; PWDRO, 1644/8/4/4, Circular 1432, 19th

October, 1933, *Organisation of Art Instruction;* PWDRO, 1644/8/4/4, Plymouth Higher Education Sub-Committee Minutes, 1936.

13. Holmes, 'Art', *op.cit*, 306.

14. Sam Smiles, Plymouth and Exeter as Centres of Art, 1820-1865 (unpublished PhD thesis, University of Cambridge, 1982), chapter 3.

15. *Exeter Flying Post*, 14 December, 1854, 3d/e; 11 January, 1855, 5e.

16. *ibid.*, 2 August, 1855, 5a; DRO, attendance registers, School of Art, 1856-8; DfEE Library, Department of Science and Art, annual reports, 1855, 1862.

17. Select Committee on Schools of Art, *op.cit.*, return of Exeter School of Art.

18. Smiles, *op.cit.,* chapter 3.

19. WCSL, George T. Dunisthorpe, *An Account of the Origin and Progress of the Devon and Exeter Albert Memorial Museum* (Exeter, Exeter and Plymouth Gazette Office,1868).

20. *ibid.*

21. DfEE Library, DSA Annual reports, 1865, 1867; Dunisthorpe, *op cit.*

22. Macdonald, *op.cit.,*183.

23. *The Dictionary of British Artists,1800-1940* (Woodbridge, Suffolk, Antique Collectors' Club,1976); Christopher Wood, *Victorian Painters* (Woodbridge, Suffolk, Antique Collectors' Club, 1995).

24. Macdonald, *op.cit.,* chapter 11.

25. Clapp, *op.cit.,* 5.

26. Clapp, *op.cit.,* 5.

27. WCSL, Albert Memorial Museum, Schools of Science and Art and Free Library. Reports of the Committees, 1872-84.

28. DRO, Minutes of Schools of Science and Art Sub-Committee, 1870-80.

29. Royal Albert Memorial Museum, *William Widgery, 1826 - 1893; Frederick J. Widgery, 1861-1942* (Exeter, Exeter Museums and Art Gallery, 1972) ; Jane Baker, *A Vision of Dartmoor. Paintings and Drawings by William Widgery (1862-93) and F. J. Widgery (1861-1942)* (Exeter, Royal Albert Memorial Museum, 1998).

30. Youings, Joyce (ed.), *Sir John Bowring, 1792 - 1872. Aspects of His Life and Career* (Plymouth, Devonshire Association, 1993).

31. Dunisthorpe, *op. cit.*

32. DRO, Minutes of School of Art Sub Committee, 1873-89; Clapp, *op.cit.,9.*

33. DRO, Minutes of Sub Committees of Schools of Science and Art, 1888 - 94; Macdonald, *op.cit.,*174 - 176.

34. Clapp, *op.cit.*, chapter 2.

35. DRO, Museum and Technical Education Committee Minutes, 1892-99.

36. Clapp, *op.cit.*, 20; H. Lloyd Parry, *History of the Royal Albert Memorial College,Exeter* (Exeter, University College of the South West of England, 1946), 29; Arthur W. Clayden, *Cloud Studies* (London, John Murray, 1905).

37. DRO, Museum and Technical Education Committee Minutes, 1892-99.

38. *ibid.*

39. PRO, ED 83/170, Royal Albert Memorial School of Art, digest of trusts.

40. This and the following three paragraphs draw extensively on material from: DRO, Governors of the Royal Albert Memorial, minutes and reports, 1900-2, 1903-5, 1906-8.

41. PRO, ED114/105, Board of Education. *General Report of H.M. Inspectors on the Technical Schools, Schools of Art, and Evening Schools in the County Borough of Exeter, July, 1910.*

42. *The Dictionary of British Artists, op.cit*; Grant M. Waters, *Dictionary of British Artists Working 1900-1950 (*Eastbourne, Eastbourne Fine Art, 1975); Christopher Wood, *op.cit.*

43. DRO, Minutes of Sub Committees, *op.cit.*; DRO, Museum and Technical Education, *op.cit.*

44. *Express and Echo,* 22 December, 1939; *The Dictionary of British Artists, op.cit.*

45. Clapp, *op.cit.*, 47.

46. PRO, ED 83/170, Board of Education, *Report of Inspection of Exeter, Royal Albert Memorial College School of Art, held on 25th, 26th and 27th February, 1920.*

47. Parry, *op.cit.*, 29.

48. DRO, Exeter Education Committee Minutes, 1922.

49. Devon & Exeter Institution Library, *Prospectus.* Royal Albert Memorial School of Art, 1923.

50. UPEXE, *Exeter School of Art Magazine,* no. 11, July, 1923.

51. Joyce Dennys, *And Then There Was One* (Padstow, Tabb House, 1983).

52. DRO, Exeter Education Committee Minutes, 1926.

53. DRO, *ibid.*, 1923.

54. UPEXE, *Exeter School of Art Magazine,* 31 July, 1924.

55. DRO, Exeter Education Committee Minutes, 1930, 1933

56. PWDRO, 1644/8/4/4, *op.cit.*

57. *Western Morning News* (9 March, 1940): David Buckman, *Dictionary of Artists in Britain Since 1945* (Bristol, Art Dictionaries, 1998).

58. Interview on 15 July, 1999, with Audrey Parsons, daughter of William Green, and secretary to Clifford Fishwick (Principal

from 1958-84), from 1961 to 1984.

59. UPEXE, posters, advertisements, unidentified local news *ho* (1946).

60. *ibid.*

61. *ibid.*

62 PRO, ED 114/1236, Ministry of Education. General Report by H.M. Inspectors on the Provision of Technical, Commercial and Art Education in the City of Exeter, for the Period Ending 31st December, 1947, 13-15.

63. UPEXE, Exeter School of Art. *Prospectuses,* 1948, 1949.

64. DRO, Exeter Education Committee Minutes, 1944- 1951.

65. Thomas Sharp, *Exeter Phoenix. A Plan for Rebuilding* (London, Architectural Press, 1946).

66. Macdonald, *op.cit.,* 381. I am indebted to research by Professor David Jeremiah on art colleges in the south west at this period.

67. DRO, Exeter Education Committee Minutes, 1946, 1947.

68. UPEXE Exeter School of Art. Prospectus, 1948. E

69. PRO, ED/167/350, 'Historical, Exeter School of Art'.

70. DRO, Exeter Education Committee Minutes, 1955, 1960.

71. UPEXE Exeter College of Art and Design. *Prospectuses,* 1980's.

72. DRO, Exeter Education Committee Minutes, 1952.

73. UPEXE, *Western Morning News,* 14 July, 1953.

74. DRO Exeter Education Committee Minutes, 1958.

75. *ibid.*

76. *The Independent, op.cit.*; *Clifford Fishwick. Fifty years at Exeter* (Exeter, University of Plymouth, 1998)

77. DRO, Exeter Education Committee Minutes, 1958, 1959, 1960; UPEXE Exeter College of Art. *Prospectus,* 1963.

78. Macdonald, *op.cit.,* 355.

79. DRO, Exeter Education Committee Minutes, 1961, 1963.

80. UPEXE Exeter College of Art. *Prospectus,* 1963.

81. *ibid.,* 1963, 1944.

82. William Ruscoe, *A Manual for the Potter* (London, Tirani, 1948)

83. UPEXE, *The Guardian* (18 February, 1965)

84. UPEXE, Exe Gallery.

85. Interview with Alan Richards, 2 December 1999.

86. UPEXE, documents on student

revolution, 1968.

87. Interview with Eric Cleave, 25 November 1999.

88. Interview with Tony Clayden, 3 February 2000; UPEXE, *Express and Echo* (21 November 1983), *Exeter Weekly News* (29 March 1985, 11 October 1985).

89. Interview with John Butler, 2 March 2000; *Arnofini Review* (May/June 1979)

90. I am indebted to Professor David Jeremiah for this section on his period as Principal and Dean.

91. I have been helped with further information on developments in the 1990s by John Butler, Mike Stephenson, John Danvers, and Colin Beardon, all interviewed in March 2000.

NOTES AND REFERENCES CHAPTER 6

1.The motto (Salvation [is] in Heaven) from the badge adopted for Seale-Hayne College, *ca* 1914, deriving from the Seale-Hayne coat of arms. According to Paul J. Presswell, 'The Seale-Hayne Saga' (1983), an unpublished ms. held in the Dean's office, the heraldic device used by the college, which was not regulated by the College of Arms, "...is that of the brother of the present senior titled line distinguished by an esquire's helm in place of the helm of a baronet." In 1991 Ken Tyers and Rosemary Sells completed the draft of 'Seale-Hayne: a History', but failing to find a publisher, presented a copy of the typescript to the Faculty. The last Principal/first Dean of Faculty, Fred Harper, contributed a chapter on recent developments. This document is currently held by Jan Baylis, editor of the *Sealehaynian*, the old students' magazine, who uses extracts as editorial copy. The Tyers/Sells study will be drawn upon in this history for colloboration and augmentation purposes.

2. W.H.B. Court, *A Concise Economic History of Britain: From 1750 to Recent Times* (Cambridge, University Press, 1965), 20.

3. Paul Brassley, 'Agricultural Education', in E.J.T. Collins (ed), *The Agrarian History of England and Wales, Volume VII, 1850-1914* (Cambridge, University Press, 2000), 326-342.

4. A Cheesborough, 'A Short History of Agricultural Education Up to 1939', *Vocational Aspect of Education,* 18:41 (Autumn, 1966), 181-200.

5. Stewart Richards, "Masters of Arts and Bachelors of Barley': The Struggle for Agricultural Education in Mid-Nineteenth-Century Britain', *History of Education,* 12:3 (1983), 161-175.

6. The Report of the Departmental Commission on Agricultural and Dairy Schools (chairman, R.H. Paget); H.M. Jenkins, The Report of the Royal Commission on Technical Instruction, Agriculture, Vol II.

7. Michael Argles, *South Kensington to Robbins, op.cit.,* 35. See also Francis L.C. Floud, *The Ministry of Agriculture and Fisheries* (London: Putnam, 1927), Chapter 6,

The Teaching of Agriculture, and Chapter 7, Agricultural Research.

8. Cheesborough, *op.cit.*, Brassley, *op.cit.*

9. Cheesborough, *op.cit.*

10. Cheesborough, *op.cit.* The investigations were by the Royal Commission on Agriculture (Depressed Condition), 1879, Royal Commission on the Land Law Act, 1881, Royal Commission on Agricultural Depression, 1893.

11. Board of Agriculture, Report of the Departmental Committee on Agricultural Education in England and Wales, 1908, Cd.4206, *BPP*, 1908 XXI [the Reay Committee]. The Seale-Hayne bequest was raised in the evidence of Sir W. Lomas Dyke Ackland (questions 2,658-9), and that of Mr A.E. Brooke Hunt (question 15,587b).

12. *Exeter Gazette,* 29 November 1911; PRO, ED 37/309; MAF 33/47/A12512. The agreement was published as Cd.4886.

13. Cheesborough, *op. cit.*, Brassley, *op.cit.*

14. Harry Tapley-Soper, 'Seale-Hayne, Charles Hayne, 1933-1903', in Sidney Lee (ed), *Dictionary of National Biography, 1901-1911* (Oxford, Oxford University Press, 1920)

15. PRO 33/47/A12512, transcript of Seale-Hayne's will, dated 17 January 1889, and codicil dated 10 August 1897.

16. Newton Abbot Library collection: *Mid Devon and Newton Times,* supplement, 11 October 1902, supplement 20 August 1904; *Mid Devon Advertiser,* 18 February 1977; J.J. MacDonald, *Passmore Edwards Institutions: Founding and Opening Ceremonies* (London, Strand Newspaper Company, 1900); E. Harcourt Burrage, *J. Passmore Edwards, Philanthropist* (London, Partridge,). Passmore Edwards came from Cornwall, and made his money in publishing; he funded over 70 institutions including 23 free libraries.

17. 'Death of Mr. Seale-Hayne, M.P.', *South Hams Chronicle* (27 November 1903): Seale-Hayne had suffered a stroke. 'The late Mr. Seale- Hayne's will', *South Hams Chronicle* (4 December 1903): this unsubstantiated item suggests that Seale-Hayne's solicitors had "quite recently" been instructed to prepare a new will, with variations to bequests, which had not been signed before his death and was, therefore, void; the item also suggests that Seale-Hayne was not pleased with the secondary education provisions in the 1902 Education Act and that he intended that the proposed college should have special provision for agriculture. 'Mr Seale-Hayne's will', *South Hams Chronicle* (11 December 1903): summary of the provisions of the 1989 will and 1897 codicil, without mention of an agricultural dimension.

18. PRO, MAF 33/47/A12512, letter from T.H. Elliot (Board of Agriculture and Fisheries) to George Lambert., M.P., 12 January 1904.

19. PRO, ED37/407, contains a series of minutes receiving Lambert's report of the purchase and internal comments about the nature of the college.

20. PRO, ED 37/407, internal minute, 16 October 1908. A minute of 26 August had previously noted that Seale-Hayne did not intend to found and agricultural college.

21. PRO, 37/407, the case number was 1907 H 2055.

22. PRO 37/407, Copy of scheme and judgement. The annuitant was Madame Ella Bohm de Sauvanne, of Campo San Marcuola, Canal Grande, Venice, Italy. This person is not named in the Seale-Hayne will but must have been able to establish a claim through inheritance from one of the named legatees. The farm had been conveyed on 4 March 1908, from Edward Herbert Bayldon to the trustees Richard Edward Jennings, since deceased and George Lambert, leaving Lambert as the sole trustee.

23. UPNAB.

24. UPNAB, SHGM, 19 November 1909; PRO, MAF 33/47/TE569, Wale's *curriculum vitae.*

25. UPNAB, SHGM, 11 February, 12 March 1910.

26. Geoffrey Shakespeare, 'Lambert, George (1866-1958)', in E.T. Williams & Helen M. Palmer (eds), *Dictionary of National Biography, 1951-60* (Oxford: Oxford University Press, 1971).

27. UPNAB, SHGM, 7 January 1911.

28. UPNAB, SHGM, 26 August 1910, 3 July 1911.

29. UPNAB, SHGM, 4 September, 12 December 1911, 8 July, 3 August, 15 October 1912.

30. UPNAB, SHGM, 16 August 1910

31. PRO, ED 37/407, minutes and correspondence, 6 July 1910, 17 January 1911, 17 June 1911.

32. PRO, MAF 33/47/A12512, Board of Agriculture minutes and correspondence with Seale-Hayne, 1910-1912.

33. PRO, MAF 33/47/TE375, Board of Agriculture minutes and correspondence, 10 December 1912, 28 January 1914.

34. UPNAB, SHGM, 14 March, 1 August 1913, 31 July 1914. "Scheme Regulating the Foundation Called The Seale-Hayne (Agricultural and Technical) College in the County of Devon...as altered by a Scheme of the Board of Education...Sealed by order of the Board this 14th Day of April, 1915" [Order No., 15/193]

35. UPNAB, SHGM, 18 February, 13 May, 1 August, 18 September, 24 October 1913.

36. UPNAB, SHGM, 1 August 1913; PRO, ED 37/409.

37. UPNAB, SHGM, 31 July 1914, 28 January, 12 April, 21 May 1915.

38. UPNAB, SHGM, 2 February 1912.

39. UPNAB, SHGM, 12 December 1913, 13 July 1914.

40. PRO, MAF 33/47/TE375, Correspondence between Bernard Wale and the Board of Agriculture, at the time of his resignation,1919. UPNAB, SHGM, 17 September 1917, 11 January, 23 March 1918. For a short description of experience at Seale-Hayne in 1916, see 'One Countryman to another', *The Countryman* (1994), 127-131.

41. UPNAB, SHGM, 21 April 1917.

42. PRO, MAF 33/47/TE375, minutes and correspondence 17 September 1917 to 15 August 1919. UPNAB, SHGM, 23 March 1918, 11 May 1919.

43. For a general discussion of army medical services in this period see J.A. Hamilton (ed), *A Popular History of the Great War, Volume VI: Armistice and After* (London, Fleetway, nd), chapter 14, Medical Services

44. PRO, MAF 33/47/TE375, Scheme for the Seale-Hayne Neurological Hospital, February 1918.

45. PRO, MAF 33/47/12206 & TE375, internal minutes, 1 January 1917, 15 February 1918, 10 May 1919, 27 July 1919.

46. PRO, MAF 33/47/TE375, internal memorandum, 26 May 1919. The file also contains correspondence between Bernard Wale and the Board of Agriculture, to 18 November 1919, including his cv.

47. MAF 33/47/TE375, Lord Ernle to Lambert, 20 May 1919.

48. Cheesborough, *op cit,* 197. Board of Agriculture and Fisheries, Circular to Local Authorities, No I, 5310/1918 (8 January 1919).

49. Seale-Hayne Agricultural College [prospectus][1919-20], 8.

50. Tyers & Sells,

51. UPNAB, SHGM, 7 February, 10 April, 26 June, 16 October, 15 December 1920.

52. UPNAB, SHGM, 21 February 1921; Tyers and Sells, Chapter 2.

53. K. Fitzgerald, *With O'Leary in the Grave* (Oxford, Oxford University Press, 1988), (quoted in Tyers and Sells, 43). For a fuller description of student life in these early years see Rosemary Sells, *From Seedtime to Harvest: the Life of Frank Horne* (Cambridge, Hobson's Press, 1978), 31-42, 66-84.

54. *Seale-Hayne College Magazine,* 7 (March 1922), 9 (December 1922), 11 (July 1923), 12 (December 1923), 15 (December 1924), (17 July 1925), 24 (December 1927), 34 (March 1931).

55. UPNAB, 30 April 1921, 29 September 1923, 18 December 1925; Tyers and Sells, Chapter 2.

56. UPNAB, SHGM, *passim* (many appointments are noted in the minutes), 17 December 1927, 15 June 1929, 18 June 1932;

Tyers & Sells, Chapter 2. Sells, *Seedtime to Harvest*, 66-84, contains a useful description of Frank Horne's research during his time as Head at Botany at Seale-Hayne. Sells was Horne's daughter.

57. UPNAB, SHGM, 17 June 1922, 10 June 1925, 24 September 1927.

58. UPNAB, SHGM, 18 March 1922, 20 March 1926, 16 March 1933, 9 March 1931.

59. Tyers and Sells, Chapter 9.

60. UPNAB, SHGM, 18, 28 February 1922, 31 July, 13 September 1924, 26 September 1931.

61. PRO, MAF 33/49/TEI 3307, Seale-Hayne Agricultural College: Report of the Committee of Enquiry to the Rt. Honourable George Lambert, M.P., Chairman of the Governors, 17 March 1933, by E.M. Konstam, F.B. Smith, Walter R. Smith, including a financial memorandum.

62. UPNAB, SHGM, 8 April 1933. Edwards-Ker became director of the Exe Fish Production Company and lived in Exmouth. PRO, MAF 33/49/TE13307 notes that relations between the principal and staff had been strained for some years.

63. PRO, MAF 33/48/TE11763: 1926 - 66 students, 1927 - 62, 1928 - 61, 1929 - 78; 1930 - 83. UPNAB, SHGM, 16 December 1933.

64. UPNAB, SHGM, 8 April, 7 October 1933; Tyers and Sells, Chapter 3.

65. UPNAB, SHGM, 10 March 1934, 6 March, 26 June 1937, 12 March 1938.

66. Tyers and Sells, Chapter 3; UPNAB, SHGM, 1933 -1939, *passim*.

67. UPNAB, SHGM, 24 September 1922, 29 September, 10 October 1923, 24 September, 22 October, 17 December 1927, 16 March 1929, 16 June, 24 September 1934, 28 August 1943; Tyers and Sells, Chapter 3.

68. UPNAB, SHGM, 16 December 1939, 24 September 1941, 9 December 1942; Finance and Emergency Committee Minutes SHFECM, 1939-1942, *passim*; Tyers & Sells, Chapter 4.

69. Tyers & Sells, Chapter 4.

70. MAF 33/356, internal minutes, 17 July, 27 July 1943. MAF 33/357, internal minutes, show that replacing the principal was discussed by MAF officials in 1942. UPNAB, SHGM, 28 August 1943, 3 August 1946; SHFECM, 11 August 1943, 16 February 1946; Tyers and Sells, Chapter 4.

71. UPNAB, SHGM, 9 June, 15 December 1945, 21 June 1947, 1 May 1948. SHFEM, 10 November, 15 December 1945. MAF 115/12, copies of minutes of Seale-Hayne sub committee on the future of the Horticulture Department. Tyers and Sells, Chapter 5.

72. UPNAB, SHGM, 17 December 1927, 16 June 1928, 19 October 1929, March 1931, 3 August 1946. SHFEM, 9 June 1945. Tyers and Sells, Chapter 5.

73. PRO, MAF 33/357, internal minutes, 1, 14 April 1948; UPNAB, SHGM, 1 May, 3 July, 23 October 1948. The closeness of the liaison between the college and MAF was demonstrated by the MAF minute of 14 April, the day after the letter of resignation was received by the Governors.

74. PRO, MAF 115/9. Principal Moore to W.R.R. Wall (MAF), 18 June 1949, a lengthy letter setting out the details of the scheme. UPNAB, SHGM, 23 October, 18 December, 1948, 30 April 1949.

75. UPNAB, SHGM, 23 October, 18 December 1948. UPNAB, I.M. Moore, "1948-1971: a Review", Principal Moore's own summary of events during his tenure included in SHGM, 15 May 1971.

76. *The Sealehaynian*, 74 (1956). The painting is in the collection of the National Gallery in London. Quoted in Tyers and Sells, chapter 6.

77. *The Sealehaynian*, 76 (1958), 86 (1967/68).

78. UPNAB, SHGM, 18 December 1948, 30 April, 31 December 1948, 18 March 1950, 13 January 1951, 3 October 1953, 1 July 1954, 16 April 1955, 27 October 1956, 19 January 1957, 24 January, 25 April 1959, 9 February 1963, 10 October 1964, 16 January, 9 October 1965, 14 May, 8 October 1966, 13 May 14 October 1967, 12 October 1968, 17 January 1970; Moore, *passim*. Cantor & Roberts, chapter 8. The reports in this period were: Report of the Committee on Higher Agricultural Education in England and Wales, the second Loveday Report (MAF, 1946); Interim Report on Agricultural and Horticultural Institutes, the third Loveday Report (ME & MAF 1947); Report on Agricultural Education, Carrington Report (MAF, 1953); Report of the Committee on Further Education for Agriculture Provided by Local Education Authorities, De La Warr Report (MAFF & ME, 1958); Advisory Sub-Committee on Further Education for Agriculture, Lampard-Vacuole Report (NACEIC, 1960); Advisory Sub-Committee on Further education for Agriculture, second Lampard-Vacuole Report (NACEIC, 1961); Report of the Advisory Committee on Agricultural Education, Fourth Pilkington Report (NACEIC, 1966).

79. UPNAB, SHGM, 31 December 1949, 6 October 1951, 9 January, 1 July 1954, 16 April, 23 July 1955, 27 October 1965, 19 October 1959, 7 October 1958, 23 January, 2 July 1960, 13 May 1961, 13 January 1962, 9 February 1963., 16 January 1965, 15 January, 2 October 1966, 18 October 1967, 10 October 1970; MOORE, *passim*.

80. UPNAB, SHGM, 4 October 1952, 16 April 1955, 26 June 1957, 26 April 1958, 9 May 1964, ; Moore, *passim*.

81. UPNAB, SHGM, 13 January 1951, 10 May 1969; Moore, *passim*, Tyers and Sells, chapter 6 and appendix 8.

82. UPNAB, SHGM, 15 January 1972.

83. UPNAB, SHGM, 13 May 1972, 19 January 1974, , 31 May, 4 October 1975, 15 January, 4 June 1977, 11 March, 3 June, 30 September 1978, 6 March 1981, 6 March, 4 December 1982, 4 June 1983. For a fuller discussion of the development of environmental education at Seale-Hayne see Haley Randle and Ian Kemp, 'The Role of Agricultural Colleges in Offering Environmental Education: the Seale-Hayne Perspective', in G.M. Harris *et al* (eds), *Monitoring Change in Education,* 2 (1995),

84. UPNAB, SHGM, 15 may 1971, 15 January 1972, 1 June 1974, 18 January 1975, 19 March, 4 June, 1 October 1977, 11 March 1978, 13 January, 6 October 1979, 25 April 1980, 3 October 1981.

85. Tyers and Sells, Chapter 9.

86. UPNAB, SHGM, 9 October 1971, 15 January 1972, 2 October 1976, 15 January 1977, 3 October 1981, 6 March 1982, 5 March, 3 December 1983, 1 June 1985. Tyers and Sells, Chapter 9.

87. UPNAB, SHGM, 6 October 1973, 31 May 1975, 20 March 1976, 1 October 1977, 30 September 1978, 13 January, 6 October 1979, 4 October, 6 December 1980, 5 June 1982, 4 June 1983, 3 March, 2 June, 4 October 1984. Tyers and Sells, Chapter 7.

88. UPNAB, SHGM, 6 October 1984, 1 June 1985, 1 March, 31 May, 29 November 1986, 30 May 1987, 28 May, 17 December 1988, 25 February 1989. Tyers and Sells, Chapter 7.

89. This paragraph is based substantially on Tyers and Sells, chapter 8, by Professor F Harper, augmented with information from Dr Gillett, Deputy Director/Deputy Vice Chancellor, who handled the negotiations with the Charity Commissioners until their conclusion in 1999.

90. F. Harper, 'Seale-Hayne Faculty of Agriculture Food and Land Use: a Description of the Faculty and its Work', University of Plymouth (1993), an unpublished paper; Randle & Kemp, *op.cit.*

91. Harper (1993).

NOTES AND REFERENCES CHAPTER 7

1. Motto from the badge adopted for Exmouth Training College, *ca.* 1949, renamed Rolle College (1951). It was used on the cover of *Exmouth College Magazine* (1949/50). A redrawn version was used on the cover of the prospectus and magazine throughout the 1950s and into the 1960s. The Exmouth Training College *Prospectus* for 1950 bears the Devon County Council shield which has the motto *Auxilio Divino* (by divine aid), and features an Elizabethan ship on sea above a lion rampant. The emergency college magazine, *Etc* (1946), also displays a shield, a bark on a sea having three fish, surrounded by the banner "Exmouth Training College". The 1949 College badge has the motto in the shape of a lozenge surrounding the shield which depicts two medieval ships on a sea, with ramparts above. The shield stands on a ground of two fish and

a banner bearing the Roman numerals MDCDXLVIII (1948). Above the shield, the crest depicts a tower with flagstaff and St George's flag supported by two magnolia flowers. The motto is from Proverbs 3.13, "Blessed is the man who finds wisdom and gets understanding." The crest appears to derive directly from that of the coat of arms of Exmouth Urban District Council granted in 1947. A ship and the sea appear in the Devon County Council coat of arms, while fish and ships are depicted in the Exmouth UDC shield. West Country Studies Library (Exeter), heraldry file.

2. For an overview see H.C. Dent, *The Training of Teachers in England and Wales, 1800-1975* (Hodder & Stoughton, 1977).

3. Annual Reports of the Science and Art Department, 1853-1899, *passim*. Known as the Technical and University Extension College in the 1890s, the Albert Memorial College was to become the University College of the South West of England in 1922.

4. W. Roy Niblett, *et al, The University Connection* (Windsor, NFER, 1975), Chapter 1.

5. A.B. Robertson, 'Vision and Pragmatism in Teacher Education and Training: Richard A.C. Oliver and the Development of the McNair Influence on Teacher Training, 1943-50', *Journal of Educational Administration and History,* 26:2 (July 1994), 164-178.

6. Ministry of Education, *Challenge and Response: an Account of the Emergency Scheme for the Training of Teachers* (London, HMSO, 1950), Ministry of Education Pamphlet No. 17. Public Record Office (PRO), ED 136/152 contains the relevant documents.

7. Board of Education, Emergency Recruitment and Training of Teachers (London, HMSO, 15 May, 1944), Circular 1652; Ministry of Education, Emergency Recruitment and Training of Teachers (London, HMSO, 19 December, 1944), Circular 18.

8. UPEXM Copy of advertisement, dated but unsourced.

9. Interview with Miss Marion Perraton (31 July 1998), who attended Exmouth Emergency Training College from 8 May 1947 to 3 June 1948, in her mid twenties, having been in the services. She was one of eight accommodated in the Vicarage. Most of her teaching career was in Plymouth, her last appointment being as Head of Chaucer Way Infants School. The furniture was familiar from her service experience. Her main subject was needlework.

10. An early mention of the Emergency College occurs in DCC minutes, Education Committee meeting 21 June 1945, when it accepted the transfer of the Southlands site from the War Office. As agent for the Ministry of Education, DCC allocated £38,310 for the first year of operation (14 March 1946). The first staff were: Miss MS Jacques from 1 September 1945 at £507 10s per annum; Mr WF Morris (Principal) from 1 October 1945, at £1000; Miss IM Cooper from 1 September

1945 at £402; Captain CS Short (Bursar) at £400 resident or £500 non-resident; Mrs Brown (Matron) at £250; Secretary Miss DM Graham on CC scale, grade 3. DCC Education Committee minutes 13 December 1945, 14 March 1946.

11. PRO, ED 136/542. ED 78/226 contains the correspondence between the Ministry of Education and Devon County Council on a permanent establishment, from July, 1946.

12. UPEXM, 'Unpublished Pages of Samuel Pepys' Diary', *Etc* [Exmouth Training College student magazine], June/July, 1946, 18-19.

13. *ibid.,* 3. 'House Parade No. 1, Brockhurst'.

14. PRO, ED 78/226, status report from Devon County Council to the Ministry, 20 September 1946.

15. Perraton interview.

16. UPEXM, *Rolle Call* [Exmouth Training College Magazine](Autumn, 1947), 22. The use of 'Rolle' here predates the adoption of 'Rolle' as the name of the college. It may derive simply from the name of the adjacent road; alternatively, it may indicate that ideas about its use as the college name already existed.

17. Perraton interview. Marion Perraton performed in several productions and produced and directed the variety programme 'Magnolia Mirth' in Exmouth Pavilion, to much local acclaim.

18. Correspondence with Mr Phillip Liddicoat, a student in the first entry in 1946.

19. UPEXM, *Etc* (June/July, 1946), 3, reproduces a photograph from the *Western Morning News.*

20. PRO, ED 78/226.

21. UPEXM, draft of obituary.

22. UPEXM, the draft report, draft curriculum, curriculum at Nottingham and a letter from E.C. Mee at the Ministry of Education responding to concerns expressed by Principal Croft.

23. UPEXM, draft prospectus, September, 1948.

24. PRO, ED 115/109, Ministry of Education, Report of H.M. Inspectors on Rolle College, Exmouth, Devon. The decision to abandon the final examination was agreed by the Institute of Education (based at the University of Exeter), when the full system of continuous assessment was introduced.

25. UPEXM, appendix to first annual report of the Principal to the Governors.

26. The Rolle family were wealthy landowners in the area by the latter part of the sixteenth century, having estates at Stevenston and Bicton. Lord Rolle (1756-1842), who was ennobled in 1796, was a very considerable benefactor to Exmouth, funding many of the improvements which were to contribute to the town's development as a seaside resort. He died without issue, and left his estate to the

then Lord Clinton's second son, M.G.K. Trefusis, who assumed the name and arms of Rolle (royal license) in 1852. He was also a benefactor of Exmouth. The Clinton family were active in local government in Devon. T.L. Pridham, *Devonshire Celebrities* (Exeter, Eland, 1869), 207-10; Eric R. Delderfield, *Exmouth Milestones, a History* (Exmouth, Raleigh Press, 1948), 202-3.

27. *Express and Echo,* 4 November 1949, report of comments by Professor Watkins.

28. *Exmouth Journal,* 4 November 1950.

29. *Exmouth Journal,* 19 October 1950, 4 November 1950, 6 February 1954, 19 February 1955; *Express & Echo,* 12 December 1953

30. Principal Croft died only two years after retirement, and it seems likely that she was already unwell in the final stage of her tenure.

31. UPEXM records contain Miss Croft's scrapbook of press cuttings, tickets, invitation cards, programmes, and letters of thanks and appreciation, which reveal the breadth of activity and the wide circle of people who attended college events.

32. Miss Spicer's experience included convent school and technical college teaching followed by a lectureship at Southlands Training College, Wimbledon. She was Deputy Principal at Lady Mabel Training College in Yorkshire before being appointed to Rolle. She died in 1977 having retired to Salisbury. Obituary, *Express & Echo,* 28 April 1977

33. Dent, chapters 20 & 21.

34. Rolle College *Magazine,* 1960, 2.

35. PRO, ED 78/568.

36. Letter dated 1 January 2000, from Francis Cammaerts, sometime Principal at Rolle College, to Robert Hole, a long-serving member of staff.

37. Rolle College *Magazine,* 1961, 1-2.

38. Dent, chapter 23.

39. UPEXM, undated B.Ed definitive document published by the university, possibly 1968.

40. UPEXM, Academic Board minute 156, November 1967.

41. UPEXM, Governors minutes, 18 November 1971.

42. UPEXM, Governors minutes, 30 June 1967, 14 November 1967.

43. UPEXM, Rolle College Student Union Hand Book, 1968/69, 6.

44. DES Circular 18/69, Professional Training for Teachers in Maintained Schools.

45. Dent, chapters 23 & 24. The James report bore the title *Teacher Education and Training* (HMSO, 1972).

46. UPEXM, Rolle Governors' minutes, 12 February, 21 June, 3 July, 25 September, 1973.

47. UPEXM, Governor's minutes, 21

March, 12 November, 1974; 15 March 1975.

48. UPEXM, Statement by the Principal to Rolle staff, 25, January 1977.

49. *Express and Echo,* 3 February 1977.

50. UPEXM, Academic Board minutes, 2, 17 February, 19 April, 1977.

51. Cammaerts' letter.

52. UPEXM, Governors' minutes, 9 February, 10 March, 30 June, 19 December, 1977. Academic Board minutes 27 June, 11 July, 1977

53. UPEXM, Governors' minutes, 17 January, 9 May, 15 June, 16 November, 1978; Academic Board minutes, 5 June1978, 24 April, 8 May, 1979.

54. The following section derived from UPEXM, Academic Board minutes, 1974 to 1979.

55. UPEXM, Governors' minutes, 18 March 1971, 4 June 1976.

56. UPEXM, Governors' minutes, 17 June 1976, Report on Rolle College Club.

57. *Express and Echo,* 9 June 1980; *Western Morning News,* 15 March 1980.

58. UPEXM, Academic board minutes, 6 January 1982; Governors' minutes, 12 February 1982.

59. Department of Education and Science, *Report by HM Inspectors on Rolle College: BA Combined Studies Degree* (DES, 1987).

60. UPEXM, Governors' minutes, 6 July, 18 November 1981, 2 March, 2 April, 17 June 1982, 11 March 1987.

61. The Leverhulme Report; the green paper, Development of Higher Education into the 1990s; the NAB document, A Strategy for Higher Education in the late 1980s and beyond; the Lindop Report, Academic Validation in Public Sector Higher Education.

62. UPEXM, Academic Board paper, 6 February 1986.

63. UPEXM, Academic Board minutes, 4 June 1986.

64. UPEXM, Academic Board minutes, 3 June 1987: letter from Secretary of State, of 14 May 1987, encouraging academic association with the Polytechnic; white paper, Higher Education - Meeting the Challenge.

65. UPEXM, Rolle Faculty Board minutes, 20 June 1990, Faculty Report for 1989/90.

66. *Western Morning News,* 15, 20 October 1992,

67. *Devon Link,* Autumn 1989.

68. UPEXM, Faculty Board minutes, 4 December 1991.

69. Interview with Mrs G.M. Payne, Head of Rolle School of Education. The Rolle name remains important to the educational work at Exmouth, as part of the part of the current identity as well as well as from tradition. It is

in common usage externally as well as within.

NOTES AND REFERENCES CHAPTER 8

1. The 'P' logo, adopted in 1972, was the subject of much ribald comment. In its haste to distance itself from the local authority, it seems that little research was undertaken before abandoning the City of Plymouth coat of arms, and adopting the basic design of two touching lower case letter 'p's. This simple form appeared on publications in 1972/3 and 1973/4. In 1974 the 'lorgnette' version appeared, and remained in use until 1988. The simplicity of this logo was replaced by the complexity of commercially-designed 'elements' logo, in an attempt to reflect the elements of the enlarged Polytechnic South West.

2. Michael Locke, *et al, The Colleges of Higher Education, 1972 to 1982: the Central Management of Organic Change* (London, Critical Press,1985), chapter 1.

3. Paul R. Sharp, *The Creation of the Local Authority Sector of Higher Education* (London, Falmer, 1987), 13-15.

4. *ibid.,* 41-3. *A Plan for Polytechnics and Other Colleges,* Cmnd 3006.

5. *ibid.,* 57-62.

6. UPPLY, Principal's/Director's Annual Reports, 1966/7 to 1969/70. City of Plymouth Education Committee, *Plymouth Polytechnic: Instrument and Articles of Government* (Plymouth, 1969).

7. UPPLY, Governing Body papers, 1971/72.

8. Interview with Mr R.G. Barker, Chief Administrative Officer from 1 September 1970.

9. The title 'Director' was imposed by the government to distinguish Polytechnic chief executives from the principals of other tertiary colleges.

10. UPPLY, Director's Annual Reports,1971-72 to 1975-76; Governing Body discussion papers.

11. Alston Kennerley, 'The Development of User-Education at Plymouth Polytechnic, 1972-1979' (an unpublished paper, 1979), 24 pp. The author was Head of Information Services in the LRC between 1972 and 1979.

12. UPPLY, Governing Body papers, 1971-72. Plymouth Polytechnic, *Plymouth Polytechnic Ten Years On, 1970-1980* (Plymouth, Plymouth Polytechnic, 1980), 24.

13. UPPLY, Annual Report 1973-74. *Plymouth Polytechnic Ten Years On, 1970-1980,* 23.

14. Bridget Rogers, *The Council for National Academic Awards, 1964-1993* (London, CNAA, 1993), 16.

15. Locke, *op.cit,* 9, 65, 105, 154; Rogers, *op.cit.,* 16-17.

16. UPPLY, Governing body papers, 1974-75 J.G. Owen, Development of higher education in the non-university sector, a report

from Devon Education Authority to the DES, 11 October 1974. Several other governors' papers discuss aspects of this topic.

17. UPPLY, Annual Reports, 1971-72 to 1979-80; Plymouth Polytechnic, Quinnennial Review the CNAA (May 1981), chapter 4

18. *Spectrum,* No. 6 (November, 1973), 10.

19. *Spectrum,* No.12 (Nov. 1974), 15; No. 13 (Dec. 1974, 5; No. 14 (Christmas 1974), 10.

20. *Spectrum,* No. 17 (May 1975), 5.

21. *Extension, passim,* The march was featured in 3:18 (26 February 1973).

22. Plymouth Polytechnic, Quinnennial Review to the CNAA (1981), 93-97.

23. The northern relief road appears on several maps in *Spectrum,* and of course in plans placed before the Governors.

24. UPPLY, Governing body paper, site "J" feasibility study, 1975.

25. *Spectrum,* 2:4 (February 1976), 8.

26. UPPLY, Governing body paper discussion papers, 1973, 1975, 1976. Undated press cuttings of articles by Frank Wintle, *ca* 1973, 1974, 'Academic boost for Plymouth', 'Scholarly Revolution', presumably from the *Western Evening Herald.*

27. The following paragraphs are based on UPPLY, papers from the governors meetings, annual reports, prospectuses, etc, for the period 1970 to 1980.

28. The summaries in this section are based on the Annual Reports for the 1970s, *Plymouth Polytechnic Ten Years On 1970-1980,* Plymouth Polytechnic, Quinnennial Review for CNAA, 1981.

29. Sharp, *op.cit.,* chapters 9 & 10, 171-3.

30. M. Kogan & D. Kogan, *The Attack on Higher Education* (London, Kogan Page, 1983), Brian Salter & Ted Tapper, *The State and Higher Education* (Ilford, Woburn Press, 1994), 93-7, 133-40. See also W.A.C. Stewart, *Higher Education in Postwar Britain* (Basingstoke, Macmillan, 1989), chapter 14.

31. Salter & Tapper, *op.cit.,* 132, 207.

32. Department of Education and Science, *The Development of Higher Education into the 1990s* (London, HMSO, 1985, Cmnd 9524); Department of Education and Science, *Higher Education: Meeting the Challenge* (London, HMSO, 1987).

33. Salter & Tapper, *op.cit,* 86-92.

34. UPPLY, Annual Reports, 1979-80 to 1985-86; Plymouth Polytechnic, CNAA Institutional Review (May 1986), four volumes.

35. Salter & Tapper, *op.cit.,* 147-52

36. Department of Education and Science, *Report by H.M. Inspectors on Courses Related to Applied Environmental Science at Plymouth Polytechnic, Devon, Inspected 8-12 March 1982* (London, D.E.S., 1983); Department of Education and Science, *Report of H.M.*

Inspectors on Research in Science at the Polytechnics in Relation to the Undergraduate Experience: an HMI Commentary. Carried Out: Spring and Autumn terms, 1983 (London, D.E.S., 1984); Depratment of Education and Science, *Report by H.M. Inspectors on Aspects of Part-Time Further Education at Plymouth Polytechnic, Inspected 30 April - 3 May 1984* (London, D.E.S., 1985); Department of Education and Science, *Report by H.M. Inspectors on Aspects of Provision at Plymouth Polytechnic, inspected October 1987 - April 1988* (London, D.E.S., 1988).

37. Simon Fairhall (ed), *British Polytechnics Sports Association, 1969-1993: The History of the Association* (Birmingham, BPSA, 1993).

38. The discussion which follows is based mainly on UPPLY, Governors meetings papers, annual reports, prospectuses, etc., for the period 1980 to 1991.

NOTES AND REFERENCES CHAPTER 9

1.The University logo was designed by Lou Jones of Falmouth. It sustains the circular format of the PSW logo. The three bands which make up the stylised south west peninsula, represent the counties of Cornwall, Devon and Somerset, the counties in which the University had at that time established partnerships with local tertiary colleges.

2. Cm. 1541, DES (1991).

3. Section 77 of the Further and Higher Education Act, 1992, made the Privy Council responsible for approving proposed university titles, while section 76 enabled the Privy Council to confer the power to award degrees. Under the Power to Award Degrees, etc, (England and Wales) Order in Council 1992 (4 June 1992), PSW acquired the power to grant awards (including degrees) as specified in Sections 76 (2), (a) & (b), in advance of the change of name.

4. Salter & Tapper, *op.cit.,* 65.

5. John Bull, 'Managing Change or Changing Managers', in Susan Weil (ed), *Introducing Change from the Top in Universities and Colleges: 10 Personal Accounts* (London, Kogan Page, 1994), 81-93.

6. Rogers, *op.cit.,* 27.

7. John Randall, 'A Profession for the New Millennium?', in Peter Scott (ed), *Higher Education Reformed* (London, Falmer, 2000), 154-168.

8. University of Plymouth Annual Review, 1994. The award was presented to the Vice-Chancellor at Buckingham Palace in February, 1995, and comprises a gold medal and illuminated scroll.

9. University of Plymouth, Annual Research Reports, and Annual Reviews, 1991/92 to 1998/99

10. This whole section is based mainly on the University's Annual Reviews and Annual Research Reports during the 1990s.

11. University of Plymouth Research Report, 1995, 43.

NOTES AND REFERENCES CHAPTER 10

1. Sanderson, *The Universities and British Industry, op.cit.,* Chapter 3.

2. Michael Sanderson, *Education and Economic Decline in Britain, 1870 to the 1990s* (Cambridge, Cambridge University Press, 2000), 105.

3. *ibid*, 106.

4. Richard Aldrich, 'From Board of education to Department for Education and Employment', *Journal of Educational Administration and History*, 32:1 (2000), 8-22. A.S. Bishop, *The Rise of a Central Authority for English Education* (Cambridge, Cambridge University Press, 1971), 276.

5. Peter Scott (ed), *Higher Education Reformed* (London, Falmer, 2000), contains eleven papers by different authors which address themes such as future roles, academic environment and structures, virtual universities, individualisation, super complexity, globalisation, new technologies, academic professionalism, and university research .

Bibliography

Primary Sources

University of Plymouth

Plymouth Campus [UPPLY]

Plymouth & Devonport Technical College / Plymouth College of Technology / Plymouth Polytechnic / University of Plymouth: Principal's / Directors' / Vice Chancellor's annual reports; Boards of Governors' minutes and agenda papers; Academic Board minutes and agenda papers; buildings records; research reports; photographic records; prospectuses; *Spectrum* [staff magazine]; ephemera.

Exeter Campus [UPEXE]

Exeter School of Art / Exeter College of Art & Design / Faculty of Arts & Design /Faculty of Arts & Education: prospectuses; *Exeter School of Art Magazine*; photographic collection; ephemera.

Newton Abbot Campus [UPNAB]

Seale-Hayne Agricultural College / Seale Hayne Faculty of Agriculture, Food and Land Use: Governors' minutes, Tyers/Sells, Presswell, unpublished studies; *The Sealehaynian*; prospectuses; photographic collection; Faculty Board minutes and papers; ephemera.

Exmouth Campus [UPEXM]

Exmouth Emergency Training College / Exmouth Training College / Rolle College / Rolle Faculty of Education / Faculty of Arts & Education: Governors' minutes and agenda papers; Faculty Board minutes; photographic collection; ephemera.

Plymouth Central Library

Local History Library: press cuttings files; contemporary publications and ephemera; photographic collection.

Plymouth City Museum

Photographic collection

Plymouth and West Devon Record Office (PWDRO)

Devonport and Plymouth councils, education files: Acc. 94, 186, 439, 850, 957, 1558, 1574, 1608, 1644, 1657,1814. Alderman Mason deposit, Acc. 439. Arthur Clamp deposit, Acc. 1056, 1059. Plymouth School of Navigation deposit.

Newton Abbot Public Library

Seale-Hayne Agricultural College file.

West Country Studies Library, Exeter

Devon County Council minutes; Exeter City Council minutes; press cuttings files; ephemera.

Devon Record Office (DRO)

Files relating to post school education in Exeter: Acc. 150/4; ECA 19, 20, 29; 77/6; 266A/PZ; 1037M/LG3; 1148/MADD4989A/B.

Public Record Office, London (PRO)

Files relating to Seale-Hayne Agricultural College: ED 22/52; ED 37/309, 407-410, 968-9; ED 114/1465; ED 174/60, 158-6, 442; MAF 22/48; MAF 33/47-49, 351-7; MAF 37/969; MAF 39/244, 340; MAF 59/1,41; MAF 115/9-12, 18, 23, 48, 59; NATS 1/172, 174, 201.
Files relating to Plymouth School of Navigation: BT 1/472; DB 3/333-8, 590, 906, 1110, 1308, 1711, 2574-5; ED114/111, 122; ED 168/2014; MT 99/22.
Files relating to post-school education in Plymouth: ED 19/44; ED 29/31; ED 46/99, 113, 214, 383, 955; ED 51/16-18, 159, 161, 318-319; ED 55/18, 100, 166; ED 83/194; ED 90/19-20, 324; ED 93/19; 98/14, 186; ED 114/113,122, 1236, 1531; ED 119/17-18, 92-3; ED120/149; ED 155/100; ED 160/221-2; ED 167/425-427; ED 168/2014-16; ED 172/103.
Files relating to Exmouth Training/Rolle College: ED 78/227-30, 277-9, 658; ED86/207-10, 438-9; ED 115/109; ED 121/404; ED 135/5, 8, 9; ED 136/152, 542; ED143/1-5; ED 159/22-6,117-9.

Files relating to Exeter School of Art: BT 1/473; BT5/62; ED 28/1-4, 16-20; ED 29/30; ED 46/113; ED 51/316-7; ED 83/170; ED 114/104-5, 1236; ED 118/1677-9; ED 155/78; ED 167/348-50; ED 196/8.

Department for Education and Employment Library
Department of Science and Art minutes and reports, 1853-1899.

Newspapers and Annuals
Devon & Exeter Daily Gazette
Doidge's Western Counties Illustrated Annual
Exeter Flying Post
Exeter Gazette
Exeter Weekly News
Exmouth Journal
Express & Echo [Exeter]
The Guardian
The Independent
Mid-Devon Adveriser
Mid-Devon & Newton Times
Plymouth Devonport & Stonehouse Herald (*PDSH*)
Reports & Transactions of the Devonshire Association (*Rep. Trans. Devonshire Assoc.*)
South Hams Chronicle
Three Towns Almanack
Transactions of the Plymouth Institution (*Trans. Plymouth Inst.*)
Western Critic
Western Daily Mercury
Western Evening Herald
Western Figaro
Western Independent
Western Morning News
Western Weekly Mercury

Secondary Sources

Aldrich, Richard, 'From Board of Education to Department for Education and Employment', *Journal of Education Administration and History*, 32:1 (2000), 8-22.

Argles, Michael, *South Kensington to Robbins: an Account of English Technical and Scientific Education Since 1851* (London, Longmans, 1964).

Armytage, W.H.G., 'J.F.D. Donnelly: Pioneer in Vocational Education', *Vocational Aspect of Education*, 2:4 (May 1950), 6-21.

Ashby, Eric, 'Education for an Age of Technology', in Charles Singer, *et al* (eds.), *A History of Technology: Volume 5, the Late Nineteenth Century, 1850-1900* (1959), 776-798.

Bailey, Bill., 'The Development of Technical Education, 1934-1939', *History of Education*, 16:1 (March 1987), 49-65.

Barlow, Fred, (ed.), *Exeter and Its Region* (University of Exeter, 1969), chapter 25.

Bell, Robert, & Tight, Malcolm, *Open Universities: a British Tradition?* (Buckingham, SRHE & Open University, 1993).

Berry, M., *Teacher Training Institutions in England and Wales: a Bibliographical Guide to Their History* (SRHE, 1973).

Bickford, Terry J., Royal Dockyard School, in Kennerley (ed.), *Notes on the History of Post-School Education...*, 27-28.

Birkmeyer, J.B., *Exeter School of Art* (Exeter 1968, Tracts Vol 129).

Bishop, A.S., *The Rise of a Central Authority for English Education* (Cambridge, University Press, 1971).

The Book of Plymouth: Souvenir of the National Union of Teachers Conference, 1910 (London, Jack, 1910).

Bovill, Donald G., 'The Education of Boys for the Mercantile Marine: a Study of Three Nautical Schools', *History of Education Society Bulletin*, 47 (Spring 1991), 11-22.

Bracken, C.W., *A History of Plymouth and Her Neighbours* (Plymouth, Underhill, 1931).

Brassley, Paul, 'Agricultural Education', in E.J.T Collins (ed.), *The Agrarian History of England and Wales, Volume 7, 1850-1914* (Cambridge University Press, 1998), Section C.

Brayshay, Mark, 'Plymouth's Past: So Worthy and Peerless a Western Port', in Chalkley, *et al.* (eds.), *Plymouth Maritime City in Transition*, 38-61.

Buckman, David, *Dictionary of British Artists Since 1945* (Bristol, Art Directories, 1998).

Bull, John, 'Managing Change or Changing Managers?', in Weil, (ed.), *Introducing Change…*

Burrage, E. Harcourt, *J Passmore Edwards, Philanthropist* (London, Partridge, nd.).

Cantor, Leonard M., & Roberts, I. Francis, *Further Education in England and Wales* (London Routledge, 1969).

Carline, Richard, *Draw They Must: a History of Teaching and Examining of Art* (London, Arnold, 1968).

Cattermull, C.C., 'In the Beginning: A Series of Articles Dealing with the Development of Educational and Research Institutes: 18 - Seale-Hayne Agricultural College', *Agricultural Progress*, 26 (1952, part 1), 61-67.

Chalkley, Brian, *et al.* (eds.), *Plymouth: Maritime City in Transition* (Newton Abbot, David & Charles, 1991).

Cheesborough, A., 'A Short History of Agricultural Education to 1939', *Vocational Aspect of Education*, 18 (Autumn 1966), 181-200.

Clapp, B.W., *The University of Exeter: a History* (University of Exeter, 1982).

Clayden, A.W., *Cloud Studies* (London, John Murray, 1905).

Clayden, A.W., 'The Future of Higher Education in Devon', *Rep. Trans. Devonshire Assoc.*, 47 (1915), 62-68.

Clifford Fishwick, Fifty Years at Exeter (Exeter, University of Plymouth, 1998).

Cobban, A.B., *The Medieval Universities: Their Development and Organisation* (London, Methuen, 1975).

Cook, E. Chandler, 'The Growth of Education in Plymouth', in the *Book of Plymouth*, 51-73.

Cook, E. Chandler, *Plymouth in Relation to the University Scheme of the South West* (Plymouth, Plymouth Education Offices, 1927).

Court, W.H.B., *A Concise Economic History of Britain: from 1750 to Recent Times* (Cambridge, University Press, 1965).

Crang, W.H., 'Educational Facilities of Devonport', in the *Book of Plymouth*, 73-78.

Crook, David, 'Universities, Teacher Training and the Legacy of McNair, 1944-1994', *History of Education*, 24:3 (September 1995), 231-245.

Crossing, William, 'A Visit to the Marine Laboratory on Plymouth Hoe', *Doidge's Western Counties Illustrated Annual* (Plymouth, Doidge, 1900, 249-264.

Davies, Peter, *Liverpool Seen: Post-War Artists on Merseyside* (Bristol, Redcliffe Press, 1992).

Delderfield, Eric R., *Exmouth Milestones: a History* (Exmouth, Raleigh Press, 1948).

Dent, H.C., *The Growth in English Education, 1946-1952* (Routledge, Kegan Paul, 1944).

Dent, H.C., *The Training of Teachers in England and Wales, 1800-1975* (London, Hodder & Stoughton, 1975).

Dennys, Joyce, *And Then There Was One* (Padstow, Tabb House, 1983).

The Dictionary of British Artists, 1800-1940 (Woodbridge, Antique Collectors' Club, 1976).

Dixon, Conrad, *Ships of the Victorian Navy* (Southampton, Ashford, 1987).

Dowrick, G.J., 'Meeting the Education needs of the Agricultural Industry', *Agricultural Progress*, 54 (1979) 66-73.

Duffy, Michael, *et al.* (eds.), *The New Maritime History of Devon, Volume II: From the Late Eighteenth Century to the Present Day* (London, Conway Maritime Press/University of Exeter, 1994).

Dunisthorpe, George T., *An Account of the Origin and Progress of the Devon and Exeter Albert Memorial Museum* (Exeter, Exeter & Plymouth Gazette Office, 1868).

Edgerton, D., *Science, Technology and the British 'Decline', 1870-1970* (Cambridge, University Press, 1996).

Edwardes-Ker, D.R., 'Seale-Hayne Agricultural College, Newton Abbot, Devon', *Journal of the Bath and West and Southern Counties Society*, 5 (1931), 59-64.

Elliott, Geoffrey, *Crisis and Change in Vocational Education and Training* (London, Jessica Kingsley, 1996).

Endacott, Andy, *Naval Heritage in the West I* (Plymouth, Endacott, 1986).

Fairhall, Simon (ed.), *The British Polytechnics Sports Association, 1969-1993: the History of the Association* (Birmingham, BPSA, 1993).

Fidler, Geoffrey C., 'The Liverpool Trades Council and Technical Education in the Era of the Technical Instruction Committee', *History of Education*, 6:3 (October 1977), 209-222.

Fieldhouse, Roger, *et al.*, *A History of Modern British Adult Education* (Leicester, National Institute for Adult Continuing Education, 1996).

Fisher, Stephen (ed.), *West Country Maritime and Social History, Some Essays* (Exeter, University of Exeter, 1980).

Fisher, Stephen (ed.), *Studies in British Privateering, Trading Enterprise and Seamen's Welfare, 1775-1900* (Exeter, University of Exeter, 1987).

Floud, Francis L.C., *The Ministry of Agriculture and Fisheries* (London, Pitman, 1927).

Frayling, Christopher, *The Royal College of Art: One Hundred and Fifty Years of Art & Design* (London, Barrie & Jenkins, 1987).

Great Britain, Board of Education, *Survey of Technical and Further Education in England and Wales* (Board of Education, Pamphlet No. 49, HMSO, 1926).

Great Britain, Board of Education, *The Admiralty Method of Training Dockyard Apprentices* (Board of Education Pamphlet, No. 32, HMSO, 1928, revised 1929).

Great Britain, Board of Trade, Committee of Inquiry into Shipping, *Report*, Cmnd. 4337 (London, HMSO, 1970) [Rochdale Report].

Great Britain, Department of Education and Science, *The Development of Higher Education into the 1990s*, Cmnd. 9524, (London, HMSO, 1985).

Great Britain, Department of Education and Science, *Higher Education: Meeting the Challenge*, Cmnd. 9524, (London, HMSO, 1985).

Great Britain, Ministry of Education, *Challenge and Response: an Account of the Emergency Scheme for the Training of Teachers* (Ministry of Education, Pamphlet No. 17, HMSO, 1950).

Great Britain, Ministry of Education, *Education in 1900-1950* (HMSO, 1951).

Great Britain, Ministry of Education, *Challenge and Response: an Account of the Emergency Scheme for the Training of Teachers* (London, HMSO, 1950).

Great Britain, Ministry of Transport, *Regulations for the Examination of Masters and Mates*, Exn. 1 (London HMSO, 1962).

Hamilton, J.A., *A Popular History of the Great War, Volume VI: Armistice and After* (London, Fleetway, nd.).

The Handbook Committee, *Plymouth: a Handbook of the Forty-Second Annual Co-operative Congress* (Manchester, Co-operative Wholesale Society, 1910).

Harte, Negley, *The University of London, 1836-1986: an Illustrated History* (London, Athlone Press, 1986).

Hudson, J.W., *The History of Adult Education...*, (London, Longman, Brown, Green & Longmans, 1851).

Jeans, Clifford, 'The First Statutory Qualifications for Seafarers', *Transport History*, 3 (November 1973), 248-267.

Jenkinson, A.J., 'Choosing the Polytechnics', *Vocational Aspect of Education*, 18 (Autumn 1966), 241-251.

Kelly, Thomas, *A History of Adult Education in Great Britain from the Middle Ages to the Twentieth Century* (Liverpool University Press, 1962).

Kemp, Peter, (ed.), *The Oxford Companion to Ships and the Sea* (London, Oxford Universiy Press, 1976).

Kennerley, Alston, 'Navigation School and Training Ship: Educational Provision in Plymouth for the Mercantile Marine in the Nineteenth Century', in Stephen Fisher (ed.), *West Country Maritime and Social History*, 53-77.

Kennerley, Alston, 'Merchant Marine Education in Liverpool and the Nautical College of 1892', *International Journal of Maritime History,* 5:2 (December 1993),103-134.

Kennerley, Alston, 'Education and Welfare of Merchant Seafarers', in Duffy *et al.* (eds.), *New Maritime History of Devon*, 145-154.

Kennerley, Alston, 'British Government Intervention in Seamen's Welfare, 1938-1948', *International Journal of Maritime History*, 7:2 (December 1995), 75-113.

Kennerley, Alston, 'Early State Support of Vocational Education: the Department of Science and Art Navigation Schools, 1853-63', *Journal of Vocational Education and Training*, 52:2 (2000), 211-224.

Kennerley, Alston, 'Vocational Education and Training for British Merchant Navy Ratings: the National Sea Training Schools, 1942-1972', *History of Education*, 29:4 (2000), 301-327.

Kogan, M., & Kogan, D., *The Attack on Higher Education* (London, Kogan Page, 1983).

Lawson, John, & Silver, Harold, *A Social History of Education in England* (London, Methuen, 1973).

Lloyd, Christopher, 'The Royal Naval Colleges at Portsmouth and Greenwich', *Mariner's Mirror*, 52:2 (May 1966), 145-156

Locke, Michael, *et al., The Colleges of Higher Education, 1972-1982: the Central Management of Organic Change* (Croydon, Critical Press, 1985).

Ludlow, J.M., 'Technical Education', *Contemporary Review* (1868), 23-35.

Macdonald, J.J, *Passmore Edwards Institutions: Founding and Opening Ceremonies* (London, Strand Newspaper Company, 1900).

MacDonald, Stuart, *The History and Philosophy of Art Education* (University of London, 1970).

Merrifield, John, & Ever, Henry, *Navigation and Nautical Astronomy* (London, Longmans, Green, 1868).

Merrifield, John, *The Meteorology and Climate of Plymouth* (Plymouth, Latimer, 1871).

Merrifield, John, *Magnetism and Deviation of the Compass* (London, Longmans, Green,1872).

Merrifield, John, *A Treatise on Navigation for the Use of Students* (London, Longmans, Green, 1883).

Merrifield, John, *A Treatise on Navigation and Nautical Astronomy* (London, Sampson, Low, 1886).

Millis, C.T., *Technical Education: Its Development and Aims* (London, Arnold, 1925).

Montgomery, R.J., *Examinations: an Account of their Evolution as Administrative Devices in England* (London, Longmans, 1965).

Musgrave, P.W., 'The Definition of Technical Education, 1860-1910', *Vocational Aspect of Education*, 16 (Summer 1964), 105-111.

Musgrave, P.W., (ed.), Sociology, *History and Education: a Reader* (London, Methuen, 1970).

'The New Technical Schools at Plymouth', *Doidge's Western Counties Illustrated Annual* (Plymouth, Doidge, 1993), 355-361

Newton, Robert, *Victorian Exeter, 1837-1914* (Leicester UP, 1968).

Niblett, W.R., *et al., The University Connection* (Windsor, NFER, 1975).

'The Opening of the New Museum', *Trans. Plymouth Inst.*, 8 (1883), 270-277.

Parry, H. Lloyd, *History of the Royal Albert Memorial College, Exeter* (Exeter, University College of the South West of England, 1946).

Penn, Geoffrey, *H.M.S. Thunderer: the Story of the Royal Naval Engineering College at Keyham and Manadon* (Mason, 1984).

Phillips, J., 'Technical Education in Devonshire', *Rep. Trans. Devonshire Assoc.*, 23 (1991), 371-75.

Phillips, Rhodri, 'Growth and Diversity: a New Era in Colleges and Universities', in Weil (ed), *Introducing Change…*, 169-182.

Plumley, N., 'The Royal Mathematical School Within Christ's Hospital: the Early Years - its Aims and Achievements', *Vistas in Astronomy*, 20 (1976), 51-59.

Pollard, Sydney, *Britain's Prime and Decline: the British Economy, 1870-1914* (London, Arnold, 1989).

Pridham, T.L., *Devonshire Celebrities* (Exeter, Eland, 1869).

Randall, Haley, & Kemp, Ian, 'The Role of Agricultural Colleges in Offering Environmental Education: the Seale-Hayne Perspective', in Harris, G.M., *et al* (eds.), *Monitoring Change in Education*, 2 (1995).

Randall, John, 'A Profession for the New Millenium', in Scott (ed.), Higher Education Reformed.

Richards, S., 'Masters of Arts and Bachelors of Barley: the Struggle for Agricultural Education in Mid-Nineteenth Century Britain', *History of Education*, 12:3 (September 1983), 161-175.

Robertson, A.B., 'Vision and Pragmatism in Teacher Education and Training: Richard A.C. Oliver and the Development of the McNair Influence on Teacher Training', *Journal of Education Administration and History*, 26:2 (July 1994), 164-178.

Roderick, Gordon W., & Stephens, Michael D., 'National Attitudes Towards Scientific Education in Early Nineteenth Century England', *Vocational Aspect of Education*, 26 (Autumn 1974), 115-120.

Roderick, Gordon W., & Stephens, Michael D., 'The Role of Nineteenth Century Provincial Literary and Philosophical Societies in Fostering Adult Education' [Plymouth Institution], *Journal of Education History and Administration*, 5:1 (January, 1973), 28-33.

Roderick, Gordon W., & Stephens, Michael D., *Scientific and Technical Education in Nineteenth Century England* (Newton Abbot, David & Charles, 1972).

Rogers, Bridget, *The Council for National Academic Awards, 1964-1993* (London, CNAA, 1993).

Ruscoe, William, *A Manual for the Potter* (London, Tirani, 1948).

Russell, J. Scott, 'Technical Education a National Want', *Macmillan's Magazine,* 17: 7 (April,1868), 447-459.

Saddler, Michael E., *Report on Secondary and Higher Education in Exeter* (Exeter, 1905).

Salter, Brian, & Tapper, Ted, *The State and Higher Education* (Ilford, Woburn Press, 1994).

Sanderson, Michael, *The Universities and British Industry, 1850-1970* (London, Routledge Kegan Paul, 1972).

Sanderson, Michael, *The Missing Stream: Technical School Education in England, 1900-1990s* (London, Athlone Press, 1994).

Sanderson, Michael, *Education and Economic Decline in Britain, 1870 to the 1990s* (Cambridge, University Press, 1999).

Scott, Peter (ed.), *Higher Education Reformed* (London, Falmer, 2000).

Sells, Rosemary, *From Seedtime to Harvest: the Life of Frank Horne* (Cambridge, Hobson's Press, 1978).

Shakespeare, Geoffrey, 'Lambert, George (1866-1958)', in Williams and Palmer, *Dictionary of National Biography*, 151-160.

Sharp, Paul R., *The Creation of the Local Authority Section of Higher Education* (Lewis, Falmer 1987).

Sharp, Thomas, *Exeter Phoenix: A Plan for Rebuilding* (London, Architectural Press).

Shattock, Michael (ed.), *The Creation of a University System* (Oxford, Blackwell, 1996).

Silver, Harold, *A Higher Education: the Council for National Academic Awards and British Higher Education, 1964-1989* (London, Falmer 1990).

Sims, Arnold, W., *The Western College, Bristol: an Outline History* (Bristol, Western College, 1952).

Southward, A.J., & Roberts, E.K., 'The Marine Biological Association of the United Kingdom, 1884-1994, One Hundred Years of Research', *Rep. Trans. Devonshire Assoc.*, 116 (1984), 155-199.

Stenning, Gwen, 'One Countryman to Another' [land girl training at Seale-Hayne College in 1916], *The Countryman* (1994), 127-131.

Stephens, W.B., 'Victorian Art Schools and Victorian Education, 1850-1889', *J.Ed.Admin. Hist.*, 2:1 (December 1969), 13-19.

Stephens, W.B., *Education in Britain, 1850-1914* (Basingstoke, Macmillan, 1998).

Stephens, W.B., *Education, Literacy and Society, 1830-1870: the Geography of Diversity in Provincial England* (Manchester, Manchester University Press, 1987).

Stewart, W.A.C., *Higher Education in Post-War Britain* (Basingstoke, Macmillan, 1989).

Tapley-Soper, H., 'Exeter Public Library: an Historical Essay', *Library Association Record* (February 1911, & Aberdeen UP, 1911).

Taylor, E.R.G., *The Mathematical Practitioners of Tudor and Stuart England* (Cambridge, University Press, 1954).

Taylor, E.R.G., *The Mathematical Practitioners of Hanoverian England* (Cambridge, University Press, 1966).

Venables, P.F.R., *et al.*, *Technical Education: Its Aims, Organisation and Future Development* (London, Bell, 1955).

Waters, Grant M., *Dictionary of British Artists Working 1900-1950* (Eastbourne, Eastbourne Fine Art, 1975).

Watson, Paton, & Abercrombie, Patrick, *A Plan for Plymouth: the Report Prepared for the City Council* (Plymouth, Underhill, 1943).

Weil, Susan (ed), *Introducing Change from the Top in Universities and Colleges* (London, Kogan Page, 1994).

Wilde, Jane H., 'The Creation of the Marine Department of the Board of Trade', *Journal of Transport History,* 2:4 (November 1956), 193-206.

Williams, David M., 'James Silk Buckingham: Sailor, Explorer and Maritime Reformer', in Stephen Fisher (ed.), *Studies in British Privateering…*, 99-199.

Williams, E.T., & Palmer, Helen M. (eds.), *Dictionary of National Biography, 1951-1960* (Oxford, Oxford University Press, 1971).

Wood, Christopher, *Victorian Painters* (Woodbridge, Antique Collectors' Club, 1995).

Worth, R.N., *The History of the Town and Borough of Devonport* (Plymouth, W. Brendon, 1870).

Worth, R.N., *The History of Plymouth from the Earliest Period to the Present Time* (Plymouth, Brendon, 2nd ed, 1873),

Youings, Joyce (ed.), *Sir John Bowring, 1792-1872: Aspects of His Life and Career* (Plymouth, Devonshire Association, 1993).

Unpublished Studies

Kennerley, Alston, The Education of the Merchant Seaman in the Nineteenth Century, unpublished MA thesis (University of Exeter, 1978).

Kennerley, Alston, The Development of User Education at Plymouth Polytechnic, 1972-1979, an unpublished study (1979) [Plymouth Polytechnic, Learning Resources Centre].

Lattimore, M.I., The History of Libraries in Plymouth: a Study of Library Development in the Three Towns of Plymouth, Devonport and Stonehouse Amalgamated into Plymouth in 1914, unpublished PhD thesis (University of London, 1982).

Lewis, C.A., The Education of the Adult in Plymouth, 1808-1941, unpublished PhD thesis (University of Exeter, 1982).

Presswell, Paul J., The Seale-Hayne Saga, an unpublished study (1983) [copy deposited at Seale-Hayne College].

Smiles, Sam, Plymouth and Exeter as Centres of Art, 1820-1865, unpublished PhD thesis (University of Cambridge, 1982)

Tyers, Ken, & Sells, Rosemary, Seale-Hayne: a History, an unpublished study (1991) [copy deposited at Seale-Hayne Faculty].

Index

Page numbers of illustrations are in bold type

merger, 113
staff, 120
School of Pharmacy, **98**
schoolmasters' certificate, **107**
schools
art, 132-5, 137
art, Plymouth, Devonport, 73
design, 13, 132
liaison, 251
navigation, 14
science, 15
Three Towns, 24-5
science & art
class enrollments, 49
classes, 45-50
navigation school, 106, **111**
schools, 11
teachers' certificates, 110
science
block, **263**; see also Davy Building
block laboratories, 252
block wall collapse, **258**
lecture, **100**
research, **286**
schools, 14
students, **266**
Science Education Enhancement &
Development, 276
scientific & technical graphics, 251
Scottish Vocational Education Council, 122
Scotland, Andrew, 77
Scott Building, 24, 259; see also Public
Secondary School
sculpture, **149**
Seafarers Education Service, 124
Seale-Hayne Agricultural College, 19, 165-203,
166, **169**, 242, 255
building design, 174
campus, **201**
Chapel, 194
court action 171
development plan, 191, 194
dining room, **178**
Faculty, 199
farm, 189, 191, 194, 197
farm improvement, 184
farm, plan, **172**, 172-4
finances, 185, 198
foundation stone, **168**, 169
Governing Body, **177**, **197**
Hospital, **176**, 177-8
management scheme, **171**, 171

merger, 258
motor club, **184**
old library, **168**
prospectus, **177**
quadrangle, **179**
requisitioning, 177
show stand, **181**
staff, 175, **178**, 191
Union Club, 182
Seale-Hayne, Charles Hayne, **166**, 170
estate, 170-1
Seale-Hayne College Magazine, 182
Seale-Hayne Faculty, 258
Sealife project, 127
seamanship centre, Coxside, 93, 116
secondary education, 5
secondary school, **4**, **12**
secretarial studies, **99**
Select Committee on Arts & Manufactures, 132
Select Committee on Schools of Art, 135
Select Committee on Sea Fisheries, 39
Select Committee on Shipwrecks, 1836, **104**
self-government, Polytechnic, 236
semester structure, 276-7
Shapland, John, 146-7
Shaw, George Bernard, 83
Shell Tankers, 117
Sherwell Centre, 38, 284, **280**
Sherwell Congregational Chapel, **38**, 38
shipping companies, 117
Shortridge, A.D., 51
Shute Park estate, 75
site plan, Exmouth, **211**, 218
site plan, Seale-Hayne, 200
skills development, 241
Slade, Thomas, 111
Smeaton Building, **282**, 283; see also
Engineering Block
Social Policy & Administration degree, 249, 253
Social Science Faculty, 268
social sciences, 238, 253
social work courses, 98
societies, 166
Socrates scheme, 162
Somerset College of Arts & Technology, **277**
South West Art & Design Education, 162
South West Economic Research Centre, 290
South West Regional Advisory Council, 248
South West Regional Council for Further
Education, 88
Southampton Sailors' Home, 174
Southampton School of Navigation, 115

Southlands School, **206-7**
SPACEX complex, 157
SPACEX Gallery, **154**
Spectrum, 245, 248
Spicer Building, **223**
Spicer, D.E.L., **215**, 216, 219, 220
sports fields, 71
sports hall, Seale-Hayne, 196
sports hall, Plymouth, 94
Square, Dr, 36
squash courts, 248, **257**
St Lukes, College, 211
St. James National School, 46
staff
appraisal, 276
induction and training, 276
numbers, 244, 261-3
Plymouth, 76, 90, 99-100
Polytechnic, 237
publications, 282
publications, Human Sciences, 288
Rolle College, 218
salaries, 244
Seale-Hayne Faculty, 202
student ratios, 255, 276, 278
University of Plymouth, 278
Staff Education and Development
Association, 276
statistics, enrolment, 49, 54
statistics, School of Navigation, 109,113
Stitson, R., 114
Stoke Military Hospital, 75, 116
Stonehouse, 22
Stonehouse Mechanics' Institute, 33
Stork Building, **223**
Stork, J.W., 221
Streatham Estate, Exeter, 79
student
access, 280
accommodation, 239-40, 247, 259, **280**, 283
agriculture, 167
art work, **152**
attendance, 71
catering, Rolle College, 226
centred learning, 276
charter, 275
common room, Exmouth, **216**
common room, Rolle College, **212**
common room, Seale-Hayne, **192**
counselling, 240
data, Plymouth, 90
design, cycle, **288**